THE BIG QUESTIONS

THE BIG QUESTIONS
HOW PHILOSOPHY CAN CHANGE YOUR LIFE

LOU MARINOFF, PH.D.

BLOOMSBURY

Grateful acknowledgment is hereby extended to the following for permission to reprint copyrighted material: Charles E. Tuttle Co. Inc., Boston and Tokyo, for the Basho haiku on p. 293, from Yoel Hoffman, ed., *Japanese Death Poems*. The Hokuseido Press, Tokyo, for the Basho haiku on p. 279, from *A History of Haiku*, © 1952 by R. H. Blyth; and for the Basho haiku on p. 314, from *Haiku*, v. 4, © 1952 by R. H. Blyth. Quotations in chapters 7 and 11 from Wilhelm, Hellmut, ed., and Baynes, Cary F., trans., *I Ching or Book of Changes*, copyright © 1960 by the Bollingen Foundation. Reprinted by permission of Princeton University Press.

Martha Nussbaum's case study on p. 209 was first described in her paper "Women's Education: A Global Challenge," delivered at a conference at Washington University, St. Louis, April 12–14, 2002. Anders Holt's case study on p. 160 and Emmy van Deurzen's case study on p. 266 were first described in *Philosophy in Society*, ed. Henning Herrestad, Anders Holt, and Helge Svare (Oslo: Unipub Forlag, 2002).

Published by Bloomsbury, New York and London
Distributed to the trade by Holtzbrinck Publishers

Library of Congress Cataloging-in-Publication Data has been applied for.

ISBN 1-58234-253-9

First U.S. Edition 2003

1 3 5 7 9 10 8 6 4 2

Typeset by Hewer Text Ltd, Edinburgh
Printed in the United States of America by RR Donnelley & Sons, Harrisonburg

To those who dare to question –
and especially who dare to question a philosopher

EIGHT WAYS PHILOSOPHY CAN CHANGE YOUR LIFE

Healing
Vain is the word of a philosopher which does not heal any suffering of man. For just as there is no profit in medicine if it does not expel the diseases of the body, so there is no profit in philosophy either, if it does not expel the suffering of the mind.
— Epicurus

Flourishing
Having understood how human lives are diseased, a philosopher worthy of the name — like a doctor worthy of that name — will proceed to try to cure them. The whole point of medical research is cure. So, too, the whole point of philosophy is human flourishing.
— Martha Nussbaum

Attaining
In the immeasurable expanses of time, you see how life moves onward and upward from infusoria to man, and you cannot deny that infinite possibilities for further perfection still await humankind.
— Thomas Mann

Emancipating
Life is filled with truly unfathomable potential . . . in most cases, our so-called limitations are nothing more than our own decision to limit ourselves.
— Daisaku Ikeda

Awakening
What lies behind us and what lies before us are small matters compared to what lies within us.
— Ralph Waldo Emerson

Managing
Philosophy recovers itself when it ceases to be a device for dealing with the problems of philosophers and becomes a method, cultivated by philosophers, for dealing with the problems of men.

– John Dewey

Purifying
All phenomena of existence have mind as their precursor, mind as their supreme leader, and of mind are they made. If with a pure mind one speaks or acts, happiness follows him like his shadow that never leaves him.

– Gautama Buddha

Being
Be not afraid of life. Believe that life *is* worth living, and your belief will help create the fact.

– William James

CONTENTS

ACKNOWLEDGMENTS

MANY FRIENDS, COLLEAGUES, and associates – as well as a few family members – helped with the conception, gestation, and birth of this book. It is not possible to thank them all by name, but I wish to mention some.

Thanks to my mother, Rosaline Tafler, our family's resident Stoic, for all her advice and encouragement; and to three youthful Marinoffs – Sarah, James, and Julian – for being themselves.

Thanks to several friends who have endured me for more than thirty years, including Bernard de los Cobos, Moshe Denburg, Michael Godfrey, Keith MacLellan, and Mark Seal, for all their advice and encouragement.

Thanks to Tim Duggan, Kristin Ventry, and others at HarperCollins USA, for bringing *Plato, Not Prozac!* to a worldwide readership, and paving the way for this book.

Thanks to many friends and colleagues in the American Philosophical Practitioners Association, including Richard Dance, Wilfried ver Eecke, Vaughana Feary, Pierre Grimes, Michael Grosso, George Hole, Chris Johns, J. Michael Russell, Paul Sharkey, and Michelle Walsh, among others, for their advice, loyalty, and friendship. A special thanks to European friends and colleagues, including Ida Jongsma, Anders Lindseth, Anti Matilla, and Henrik Nyback, for their collaboration abroad.

Thanks to many other friends of philosophical practice, including Julian Baggini, Paul Bennett, Paul del Duca, Jan and Robert Dilenschneider, Jennifer Farrell, David Feldman, Christina Garidis, Thor Henrikson, Merle Hoffman, Sebastiaan Jansen, Robert Kennedy, Tova Krentzman, Katie Layman, Andrew Light, Liv Marinoff, Tan Chin Nam, Len Oakes, Ron Perowne, Christian Perring, Tanis Salant,

Allen Sessoms, Liz Sheean, Jeremy Stangroom, Jennifer Stark, Rose and Arthur Sturcke, and Masao Yokota, among others, who provided all kinds of advice and encouragement.

Thanks to Jeet Khemka for her insight, to Daisaku Ikeda for his appreciation, and to Paulo Coelho and Elie Wiesel for their inspiration.

Thanks to staunch defenders of civil liberties in American higher education, including Steven Hudspeth, David Koepsell, Alan Kors, and David Seidemann, for reminding the forgetful that even philosophers enjoy the protections of the Constitution.

Thanks to the Faculty Fellowship Program at the City College of New York for sabbatical leave from teaching responsibilities this year.

Thanks to Kathleen and Andrew Lawrence for the use of their enchanting abode on Walton Lake, where the bulk of this book was written. Their charming house is still frequented by the spirit of its builder – the late, great George M. Cohan. I reconvey his regards to Broadway.

Thanks to those practitioners whose case studies I have cited: Vaughana Feary, Anders Holt, Alex Howard, Ida Jongsma, Kenneth Kipnis, Christopher McCullough, Martha Nussbaum, and Emmy van Deurzen. Thanks also to those practitioners who submitted case studies we could not include owing to the usual constraints.

Thanks to the many clients of philosophical practice – individuals, groups, and organizations alike – from whom we learn more than they imagine about the applications of philosophy, even as we help them apply it for themselves. Clients' names, occupations, and other details of cases cited herein have been altered to protect their anonymity, but their issues are real, as are the benefits they derived from philosophy.

Last and furthest from least, thanks to those who collaborated most closely with me on this book: Joelle Delbourgo, who (as with *Plato, Not Prozac!*) helped shape its vision; Colleen Kapklein, who (as with *Plato, Not Prozac!*) helped make its message broadly accessible; Jenny Meyer for her facilitation; Santiago del Rey of Ediciones B for his support; and Colin Dickerman, Karen Rinaldi, Alan Wherry, and the entire team at Bloomsbury USA for editing and publishing it.

I assume sole responsibility for the ideas and opinions expressed in this book. My friends, colleagues, and associates do not necessarily share all my views, or necessarily oppose them – and vice versa. To acknowledge another's humanity is to respect their independence of thought.

LOU MARINOFF
Monroe, NY
December 2002

Part I

1

DISEASE OR DIS-EASE?

It is peculiar to the nature of Man, to be inquisitive into the causes of the events they see, some more, some less; but all men so much, as to be curious in the search of the causes of their own good and evil fortune.
– Thomas Hobbes

The important thing is to not stop questioning.
– Albert Einstein

WHAT BIG QUESTIONS did you ask or will you ask today? At every stage of life, we ask important questions concerning ourselves and others, our issues and everybody else's, the wide world and the vaster universe, the meaning and purpose of our existence. We inquire about the past, present, and future. We investigate every conceivable subject. Human beings want and need to make sense of things that happen – or don't happen – in the short run as well as over the long haul. Our ability to inquire is our primary means to that end. People ask even more questions in times of trial and tribulation; the tougher the situation, the bigger the questions. But ironically, the answers we seek most urgently are sometimes the hardest to find.

This is where philosophy can help. And by "philosophy," I don't mean just the study of abstract ideas for their own sakes alone. This is well and good for professional academics, who enjoy and excel at debating theory for theory's sake. But philosophy can also be helpful to ordinary people, through the application of useful ideas to their concrete problems of living. Hearing about philosophical counseling for the first time, an American philosopher working in Asia said, "This sounds like advanced common sense." That's exactly right. Presumably, you already possess elementary common sense, which is why you're reading this. Now you're ready for a slightly more advanced treatment.

Philosophers are relentless inquirers. We question everything under the sun. We take nothing for granted. I always tell my philosophy students that there's no such thing as a foolish question – but naturally, if you ask around, you're bound to get some foolish answers! However, there's a real art to questioning effectively, and getting the right answers frequently depends on asking the right questions. If you need to address or resolve a Big Question in your life, this book will help you draw on great ideas of leading philosophical inquirers, from antiquity to the present. It will show you how philosophy can change your life, by transforming your dis-ease into ease. Not just in theory, but in practice. Each chapter contains cases illustrating how philosophical counselors help clients tackle their Big Questions. And every chapter ends with philosophical exercises that you can do to help yourself as well.

My selection of Big Questions has been informed by important issues that I see people confronting, and confronting people, every day, and about which I frequently counsel clients in my philosophical practice. This chapter introduces the philosophical approach to counseling. In part II, each Big Question has its own chapter: How Do You Know What's Right? Are You Guided by Reason or Passion? If You're Offended, Are You Harmed? Must You Suffer? What Is Love? Can't We All Just Get Along? Can Anybody Win "the War of the Sexes"? Who's in Charge Here: We, or the Machines? Are You a Spiritual Being? How Can You Handle Change? Part III offers advice on building your philosophy of life. Part IV contains additional resources, including a "hit parade" of philosophers and a directory of philosophical counselors.

Before philosophy can help you change your life, you need to ask yourself a basic Big Question: Are you suffering from a disease, or a dis-ease? The purpose of this chapter is to help you discern the difference.

WHAT'S NORMAL?

Formerly, when religion was strong and science weak, men mistook magic for medicine; now, when science is strong and religion weak, men mistake medicine for magic.

– Thomas Szasz

Medical arts and sciences are concerned with maintaining health, healing injury, and curing disease. What is disease? Usually, it is something that affects the body in a way that interferes with or prevents its normal function. Most laypersons can rattle off a list of childhood diseases they have suffered, such as measles, mumps, and chicken pox – not to mention the common cold. Adults can fall prey to a catalog of diseases, and most of us know someone who has battled cancer, or heart disease, or Alzheimer's, among many possibilities. We are all bound to die of something, and more often than not that "something" turns out to be a disease, or complications arising from one.

Even so, we should appreciate that "normal function" is partly defined by social norms as well as biological ones. For example, if you regularly experience hallucinations – that is, if you see and hear things that no one else sees and hears – you might be called "psychotic," and diagnosed with a psychiatric disease. Then again, if you see things that no one else sees and turn them into movies, or hear things that no one else hears and turn them into symphonies, then possibly you're a director or a composer. If you can tame your wild mind enough to bring forth original beauty or clarity, you might win a Nobel Prize, as did John Nash. Then again, if you were hallucinating in a different social setting, you might have been taking a normal psychedelic trip during the 1960s, or you might be functioning normally as the shaman of your tribe.

One moral of this story is: Even democratically elected "illnesses" of the so-called mental kind can be thought of as normal if social circumstances are adjusted accordingly. But this moral is a two-way street. If social circumstances are adjusted accordingly, then many problems that are not diseases at all can be "diagnosed" as if they were. And that can pose big problems for you.

For example: If you had denounced the former Soviet Union from within, you might have been placed in a psychiatric hospital instead of a political prison. Why? Because: the former Soviet Union was declared by the Party to be a "worker's paradise." Anyone who objects to living in paradise is obviously crazy. This is logical enough, but calling hell or purgatory "paradise" every day, en masse, doesn't make it so. It's also clear that medical practice can be abused, as a means of social or political control.

Another example: In the late nineteenth century, all applicants for civil service jobs in New York State (among other places in the United States and the United Kingdom) had to submit to phrenology examinations. Phrenology was ostensibly a "science" that detected people's personality traits by locating various bumps on their skulls. A bump behind your left ear supposedly meant you were courageous; behind your right ear, that you were selfish. Dozens of character traits were similarly "mapped" to bumps all over the skull. But phrenology turned out to be an utterly bogus science, and its ability to exert political and social control was mercifully short-lived.

Take another example: Suppose you had a bad experience in life that left a deep impression on you. Maybe you were robbed or beaten or raped. Maybe you were in a serious car accident, or were attacked by a dangerous animal, or experienced combat or some other life-threatening situation. If you are still bothered by the past, you may be "diagnosed" with PTSD, or post-traumatic stress disorder. Sounds very impressive, doesn't it? What exactly does it mean? It means that you are bothered by the past. That is, you are bothered by your memories of it, your feelings toward it, your questions about it, and your self-preservative desire to make sense of it. Since when did memories become a disease to be diagnosed by doctors and some psychologists? Is that the best explanation they can come up with? Sorry, but philosophers can do as well or better! Everybody has some bad memories along with good ones, but people need better rather than worse explanations concerning their significance.

Is PSTD a real disease? Or is it merely a dis-ease? It's classified as a "disease" by the American Psychiatric Association's DSM (Diagnostic and Statistical Manual). Once any dis-ease is voted into the DSM as a "disease," then psychiatrists and clinical psychologists can "diagnose" it. Yes, DSM "diseases" are democratically elected! Managed health care increasingly demands that talk therapists make "diagnoses," or health insurers will not reimburse them for their services. So they'd better find some "disease" if they want to earn a living. PTSD is a useful one. It covers a lot of ground: your entire past. The older you get, the more will turn out to have been wrong with you.

Everybody has a past, and almost everybody regrets having done or not having done certain things, and almost everybody can remember both pleasant and unpleasant things that happened to them. As a philosophical counselor, I'd say that anyone who's bothered by the past has some dis-ease, but not necessarily a disease. Treating disease as though it were dis-ease is one kind of mistake; treating dis-ease as though it were disease is another. How can you tell the difference? Just like the art of living well, it's not always easy.

The onus is on you to think for yourself, and find the right kind of help for your situation. The best care is appropriate care. Ask around. See a physician, and make sure you're medically okay. See a psychiatrist, psychologist, psychotherapist, social worker, or philosophical counselor, and solicit their professional opinions too. While you're at it, see your grandmother and your local guru. Get your tarot read. But remember one thing: Just as you should be presumed innocent until proven guilty in criminal matters, you should also be presumed stable, functional, and sane until proven unstable, dysfunctional, or insane in civil matters – that is, in the personal and professional conduct of your life. But the presumptions of innocence and of sanity alike have been severely eroded in recent years by political, social, and commercial forces working hard to undermine your fundamental freedoms. This makes it more difficult for you to get an impartial hearing in a court of law, as well as an unbiased opinion about your dis-ease from "mental health" professionals.

For example: Do you have anything whatsoever going on in your life? Do you have to get up and go to work in the morning? Do you

have meetings or presentations or deadlines to make? Are you preparing for a final exam, a job interview, or a big date? Are you going
through a difficult transition, like a divorce or a career change? Are
you parenting a child or adolescent who is going though a difficult
transition? Have you been avoiding a looming confrontation with a
spouse, colleague, or boss? Are you still trying to make sense of
terrorism? If any of these scenarios causes you any concern whatsoever, then you supposedly have a "disease." It's called Generalized
Social Anxiety Disorder (GSAD), and the designer drug of choice for
"treating" it is Paxil. This prescription drug is being widely advertised
on prime-time television as a panacea for the so-called "disease" of
having concerns in life! What does this say about the presumption of
sanity? It says that if you are experiencing any dis-ease whatsoever,
then you have a disease called GSAD. In other words, you are
presumed unstable, dysfunctional, or worse. By whom? By the pharmaceutical companies, who stand to make a lot of money by convincing you that your dis-ease is a disease. This isn't science; it's
business. And in business, let the buyer beware.

As a philosophical counselor, I'd say that having concerns about
important events in life is perfectly natural. Athletes and other
performers routinely experience "butterflies" in their stomachs before
the game or performance begins. And that's a *good* sign: it means they
are engaged with the process, and are preparing to do their best. If they
felt nothing beforehand, it would mean they didn't care. If their
"butterflies" flutter too much, and turn into "performance anxiety"
– another dis-ease that's not a disease – then performers have a range
of options at their disposal. Beta blockers, hypnotherapy, psychotherapy, meditation, yoga, biofeedback, and other relaxation techniques
are all viable options. What's best varies in each case.

And what's best for your particular dis-ease depends on you too. So
if you're content to be "diagnosed" by Dr. TV, then good for you –
and even better for the drug business. But if you really care about your
life, you're bound to experience some dis-ease in anticipation of and
preparation for important events. That's not a disease; it's an opportunity! The entire deception is based on your confusion: If you can tell
the difference between dis-ease and disease, you won't need prescrip-

tion drugs to deal with life's normal challenges. What will you need instead? A philosophy of life! And this book will help you develop one, or articulate the one you've already developed. Life is not a disease. And its trials and tribulations, over which you sometimes experience dis-ease, are not symptoms of diseases either.

Don't get me wrong. Medical research financed by pharmaceutical companies has developed some potent "miracle" drugs for curing or controlling real diseases. Nature, the master biochemist and pharmacist, has also evolved amazing drugs for the same purpose, many of which may remain undiscovered as we turn jungles and forests into parking lots. Some people really do benefit from synthetic formulations like Prozac or Paxil, just as others benefit from a variety of natural herbs. But once your brain chemistry is stable, and you are functional, you still need a philosophy of life to deal with all the dis-eases you are bound to encounter. Fortunately, you can still get philosophical guidance "over the counter."

So please think carefully about the difference between disease and dis-ease. If you really think you suffer from a medical disease, by all means get the appropriate medical help: examination, diagnosis, and treatment. But if you suffer from a dis-ease, which is a discomfort in your consciousness and not a dysfunction of your body, then get appropriate help for that too: Examine your way of thinking and your way of life. Find a way to make sense of your situation, and apply the principles that will best guide you through it. That's called "applied philosophy." Aristotle's name for it was "phronesis," or practical wisdom.

You can't always change your circumstances, but you can always change the way in which you interpret them. The way in which you interpret your circumstances is none other than your philosophy of life! My question to you is this: Does your philosophy of life work for you, against you, or not at all? If it already works for you, good: but you can make it work even better. If it works against you, not so good: but you can get it to start working for you. If it doesn't work at all, that's a waste: but you can get it up and running.

PSYCHIATRY, PSYCHOLOGY, AND PHILOSOPHY

The physician heals, Nature makes well.
                                        – Aristotle

These three disciplines all shed important light on the inner human condition, but do so from very different perspectives. Each has something unique to offer in terms of helping the human being, and – depending on your disease or dis-ease – any of them might be the most appropriate source of help at times. I reiterate that it's up to the help seeker (you) to discover the most appropriate helper. This is sometimes obvious. For example, if you have a toothache, see a dentist. However, life's dis-eases are not always so obvious. If you are experiencing dis-ease, how do you know whether your most appropriate helper is a psychiatrist, a psychologist, or a philosopher – or, for that matter, an astrologer, an aromatherapist, or an astral-travel guide? Sometimes you simply don't know in advance whom exactly to consult about a given issue, so you have to go by trial and error. Philosophically, that makes you an *empiricist:* needing to learn an important lesson from experiment and experience. If you find some discipline whose guiding ideas help you, then you will probably swear by it and recommend it to your friends. Philosophically, that makes you a *pragmatist:* being convinced by something because it works in practice.

Certain kinds of problems are amenable to treatment in a single, contained setting. For example, a dentist and a dental assistant can take care of that toothache while you sit in their comfortable chair – and endure a bit of physical discomfort. Other kinds of problems may require the cooperative intervention of many more professionals. For example, if you are going through a messy divorce that involves a custody battle over children as well as a dispute over assets, you may require guidance from a lawyer, a chartered accountant, a child psychologist, a psychotherapist, a psychiatrist, a mediator, a pastor, and a philosopher – as well as your best friend. And you may have to endure considerable emotional discomfort.

But if you just need to talk to someone about your circumstances in order to make sense of them, or in order to discern their meaning, purpose, and value in your life, then a philosopher may be the right helper for you. Philosophers were available as guides to life's dis-eases in the ancient world, and throughout history; yet in the modern world they made themselves increasingly unavailable, inaccessible, or irrelevant to such concerns. But people missed the kinds of advice that philosophers can give, and the variety of perspectives they can offer. So in the past few decades, philosophical practice has experienced a dramatic resurgence. Philosophers have reemerged as counselors to individual clients, as facilitators to groups, and as consultants to organizations. Some of us are also retraining philosophers to become practitioners, to complement the academic roles they play as professors and scholars. (For more information on finding or becoming a philosophical practitioner, see the resources at the back of this book.)

But we are not trying to replace or supplant psychiatry or psychology. We are simply restoring philosophy to its rightful place, in partnership with other helping professions. Neither are we trying to subvert academic (that is, "theoretical") philosophy: On the contrary, most reputable philosophical practitioners have earned graduate degrees in traditional philosophy programs, in preparation for training as practitioners.

People should get to know themselves medically, so as to be able to preserve their physical health – including the proper functioning of their brain chemistry. Visits to physicians, including psychiatrists, are warranted for this purpose. Similarly, people should get to know themselves psychologically, so as to be able to maintain their emotional well-being. Understanding the forces that condition and influence one's personality, habits, likes, dislikes, ambitions, aversions, and so forth, is necessary for personal growth. Many kinds of psychologists are out there to help with this process. But what do you do when you're medically stable, emotionally contained, yet still experiencing dis-ease over a burning question? This book advises you to address the issue philosophically: It offers you therapy for the sane. Enhancing your point of view can transform your dis-ease into ease. Making philosophical sense of your circumstances is like finding the eye of the storm: you're in a calm and collected state, even though many things may be swirling all around you.

This cuts both ways. A dis-ease, if not eased, can eventually become a disease. It's much easier to treat a dis-ease with good ideas, before it escalates into disease and requires medical attention. A persistent state of dis-ease can taint or mar one's thoughts, words, and deeds – and will negatively affect one's emotional and physical well-being too. An unresolved moral dilemma, an unsettled injustice, or an unfulfilled purpose are all sources of dis-ease; if unexamined philosophically, they can certainly manifest as psychological and even medical problems further down the road.

In a given case, it may become clear that someone needs specific help from a psychiatrist, psychologist, or philosopher. Then again, sometimes more than one profession may be able to lend a helping hand. A given case may fall into a gray area between or among these professions. Then it is also up to the patient or client (you) to discover, empirically and pragmatically, the most appropriate form of help. Each discipline has its own special areas of interest, and each also has overlapping interests with the others. There is also a central area, common to all: What the best psychiatric, psychological and philosophical counselors hold in common is the ability to dialogue effectively with their patients or clients – and one another – about matters of meaning, purpose, and value in life experience.

BELIEF ABOUT BELIEF

> **The greatest discovery of my generation is that human beings can alter their lives by altering their attitudes.**
>
> **– William James**

Philosophers are deeply interested in belief systems. Many philosophers, from Plato to William James, have noted the vital role our beliefs play – for better or worse – in getting us through the day. Hobbes observed that the human world is governed by opinion.

Opinions are only premature beliefs about issues that compel our immediate attention. A philosophical examination of a belief system involves trying to understand not only what people believe, but also how they come to believe as they do, what reasons they have for believing as they do, how their beliefs affect the way they live, and to what extent their beliefs are the source of their ease, dis-ease, or disease alike.

An amazing thing about human belief is that no matter what anyone comes to believe about anything, you can always find someone who believes the opposite, or something incompatible. This can lead to human actions that are also contradictory or incompatible. For example, the pagan Roman emperor Nero cruelly put people to death for believing in Christianity. Some centuries later, the Inquisition cruelly put people to death for not believing in its version of Christianity. Whether Nero and the Inquisitors were insane or merely deluded, we'll never know.

During the American Revolutionary War, the signatories of the Declaration of Independence were considered heroes in the thirteen colonies, but were deemed traitors by the British crown. If apprehended, the American Founding Fathers would have been hanged for treason. Were these signatories suicidal? Absolutely not. They were courageous men, who acted only after much soul-searching and public debate, and who applied deep philosophical principles even as they acted.

To chose a more recent and chilling example: Most Americans, Europeans, and Asians believe that the nineteen Arabs who hijacked the four airplanes on September 11, 2001, were terrorists who committed despicable crimes against humanity and affronts to civilization. Then again, some people in the Islamic world believe that they were martyrs, heroes, and warriors.

Although this book is devoted to helping you effect personal change peacefully, by examining or changing your philosophy, we will see in chapter 4 that even political change can be effected without warfare or violence, again by philosophical means.

Meanwhile, these extreme and violent examples illustrate not only the vital role of beliefs in governing the conduct of people's lives, but also how vitally beliefs about other people's beliefs govern the conduct of people's lives. Understanding all this is a philosophical task. Understanding how beliefs, and beliefs about beliefs, can make human lives better – or worse – is also a philosophical task.

In case this leads you to believe that I am a moral relativist, let me immediately correct your belief about my beliefs. A moral relativist believes that goodness, rightness, and justice are all relative to people's beliefs. In other words, a moral relativist believes not only that the Christians whom Nero fed to the lions were justified in their faith and martyrdom, but also that Nero was justified in martyring them. Moral relativists believe it was a great tragedy that so many innocent civilians died on the hijacked airplanes and in the World Trade Center's destruction, but they also believe that the hijackers were warriors who were justified in waging their jihad according to their rules. The spread of moral relativism, and its unfortunate political sponsorship by American and European centers of higher education, has brought much confusion to the Western world during the latter third of the twentieth century. Deprived of a moral compass, among other philosophical tools necessary for examining and understanding belief systems, millions of people find it difficult or impossible to establish a context for current events, no matter how horrific. This often adds travesty to tragedy.

For the record: I am not a moral relativist. I believe that people should have the freedom to believe in and worship their own god or gods in their own ways, but that such freedom should *never* entail the liberty to harm or kill others who believe differently. I therefore tolerate other people's beliefs, as long as they are not intolerant themselves. So I empathize with the early Christian martyrs – who died for their faith but did not seek to murder others for it – while I deplore Nero, and the Inquisition, and all terrorists as intolerant murderers. My condemnation has nothing to do with paganism, Christianity, or Islam: It has to do with premeditated harm, which always increases and never decreases suffering in the world. By my lights, it is therefore wrong. And that's not relativism.

As a philosopher, I know many ways to defend or attack, reinforce or subvert any belief or system of beliefs. Philosophers can be found who will advocate absolutely any point of view, no matter how sagacious or absurd; and long ago we trained advocates (then called "sophists," now called "lawyers") to do this for a living. As a philosophical practitioner, I am interested in what my clients believe: For if your beliefs cause you to feel dis-ease, and if you lack the philosophical guidance to deal with your dis-ease constructively, then you are liable to suffer unnecessarily yourself and possibly to spread your dis-ease destructively to others, like some virulent contagion of the mind. I firmly believe that some beliefs cause more dis-ease than others; and that some are more harmful than others. This is not moral relativism either. (I'll say more about morality in chapter 2, and about suffering in chapter 5). There are many ways to harm yourself and others, and harm is bad. That's absolute. There are also many ways to help yourself and others, and help is good. That's absolute as well. How you choose to help yourself and others is up to you.

That's relative.

WHAT MAKES YOU THINK?

The happiness of your life depends upon the quality of your thoughts.

– Marcus Aurelius

Now let's get back to you: What makes you think? Like most important questions, this one is deceptively simple. Still, it is a Big Question, and the starting point in our journey. If we're going to think our way into or out of anything at all, we should first know just what thinking is and how it happens to us. Since this question has no single definitive answer, we proceed by exploring different possible answers, and comparing what we learn.

Some contemporary neuroscientists might suppose we're wasting our time on a stupid question, because it is obvious (to them) that it is our brains that make us think. Have you talked to a headless person lately? Or had a fascinating conversation with anyone who has the misfortune to be brain dead? Of course not. From this perspective, brains make us think, and that is that. Once we understand the brain, we will understand thought. Or so they claim.

But pause for a moment and think about thinking, and see just what you understand about thought. What color is a thought? What shape is it? How long is it? What is the mass of a thought? How much does a thought weigh on the moon? How much time does it take to think? Thoughts are not like other things; their properties are very different.

And what about the thoughts known as memories? When you think of childhood episodes, or think of persons you used to know, how are these memories stored? If they are electrochemical states of the brain, how are they maintained? If they are molecular, how are they refreshed? How do you access these data at will and, as you age, why can't you access everything when you want to? And why, toward the end of life, do early memories return with such clarity?

Since no one has the answers to these questions, it is not quite satisfactory to conclude that our brains make us think. That is like saying, "Our legs make us walk," or "The engine makes the car go." While it is clear that people without functional legs don't walk, and cars without functional engines don't go anywhere, just as bodies without functional brains don't think anything, it is quite another matter to explain what engines are (which we can do, since we invented them) or what brains are (which we can't, since we are just beginning to understand how they work).

I am looking at two color photographs of a brain (MRI slides) published in a recent *Newsweek* magazine. One shows a "normally conscious" brain; the other, the brain of a Buddhist in deep meditation (*samadhi*). The two slides show that different areas of one's brain "light up" in ways that correspond to different brain states, which themselves are influenced by different states of mind. This is hardly surprising. If you decide to melt down your credit card on a Fifth Avenue shopping spree, you will doubtless activate certain sets of brain circuits in the process. If, on the other hand, you decide to melt down your attachments to worldly things by practicing meditation, you will doubtless activate other sets of brain circuits. Taking pictures of these brain states is interesting. But, as the philosopher Alfred Korzybski reminded us, "A map is not the territory." The brain states are the effects of causes, and those causes are noetic – that is, they pertain to the mind. Somebody willed to shop, or willed to meditate, and that somebody is different from the shopper or the meditator, and different from the shopper's brain or the meditator's brain. That "somebody" might even turn out to be a fiction! That somebody might be nobody – or a part of everybody.

A picture of the brain is not a picture of the mind, or of consciousness. There is no picture of the mind, because the mind is not a physical thing. We cannot take pictures of volitions, intentions, attitudes, beliefs, attachments, non-attachments, conceptions, meanings, self-conceptions, joys, or sorrows – possibly because these things originate in the mind, and are only mirrored in the brain. Even if minds emerge from brains, minds have properties independent of brains. It is your will – that is, the focusing of your consciousness – that partially determines your brain state. Showing a photograph of a brain lit up in a certain way and claiming that this "explains" *samadhi* is like showing a picture of a tree lit up in a certain way and claiming that this "explains" Christmas.

So, what makes you think is not your brain; rather, it is your consciousness. Minds are local sources of consciousness. Thought is the radiance of the mind. Like physical forms of radiant energy, thought has properties such as amplitude, frequency, intensity. Unlike physical forms of radiant energy, thought also has properties such as attachment, sentiment, judgment.

In sum, your consciousness is the source that allows you to think, and also consumes endless food for thought. It ingests all kinds of nourishments, some more toxic than others: intentions, volitions, revelations, prejudices, reasons, passions. If you want to think clearly, you need to nourish your mind with the healthiest food available. That food is philosophy: great thought, as opposed to junk thought.

Your life is a vehicle. Your brain is the engine of that vehicle. If the engine is performing properly (and if all other systems are okay), the vehicle can move. Next come other Big Questions: Where will it move? How quickly or slowly? By which route? How many stops will it make? Who else will come along for the ride? To make these questions meaningful, we need a driver. That driver is your mind. Without a mind, the driverless vehicle of your life goes nowhere. But with your mind at the wheel, the vehicle can take you on a wondrous journey. Literally and figuratively, it's the journey of a lifetime.

WHAT MAKES YOU THINK SOMETHING'S WRONG?

Nobody, as long as he moves about among the currents of life, is without trouble.
— Carl Jung

There are only two kinds of things that can make you think something's wrong: either disease, or dis-ease. That tiny hyphen makes a huge difference.

If your physical state of health is jeopardized by some disease, say a bacterial infection or a heart condition, you may feel uncomfortable symptoms. That's potentially a good thing: The symptoms are alerting you that something's wrong. If you are able to do something to cure the disease, then in retrospect the symptoms helped you to survive. That kind of discomfort can be a life saver. Would you prefer perpetual comfort? Compare the uncomfortable-symptom scenario to an apparently healthy person who, without warning, suddenly drops dead of a heart attack or a stroke. I'd prefer the warning of discomfort, thanks, and I'd bet you would too. The philosophical moral of this story is that pain and discomfort are not necessarily or always bad things.

And pleasure is not necessarily or always a good thing. Pains are good when they warn us that something is wrong and requires attention, as in a toothache or an attack of appendicitis. Similarly, pleasures are bad when they fail to warn us that something is wrong and requires attention, for instance as in addiction to narcotics. While injecting heroin is supposedly very pleasurable, terrible harms are often perpetrated in getting the money to get the drugs – and the lifestyle of an addict is itself not very enjoyable. Similarly, while sex is definitely pleasurable, one can contract or spread potentially fatal diseases, like HIV, in the process.

In any case, if you have a disease which comes along with a set of symptoms, you will begin to think that something's wrong, because you will feel different from your normal self, however you normally feel. This is an internal situation.

Dis-ease is another matter entirely. For one thing, it is external in origin. The five senses with which we are normally bequeathed can each cause us dis-ease by bringing to the attention of our minds some stimulus or other that we consider disturbing.

Let's take as an example something brought to mind by what you see. For the sighted, vision is the most powerful sense, and accordingly what we see can cause us the greatest dis-ease. Suppose you're walking down the street, and you suddenly see something you're not accustomed to seeing in your neighborhood – perhaps a gay couple holding hands, or a panhandler waiting to ask you for change, or a young blue-haired person whose body is pierced in several dozen places.

These people pose no danger or threat to you personally, yet seeing them possibly causes you dis-ease. Why? Primarily because the images you are taking in jar against some preconceived notions you have about heterosexuality, or prosperity, or fashion. There are really only three ways in which you could deal with your dis-ease. First, you could attempt to remove such people from your neighborhood, and therefore from your line of sight. This will undoubtedly bring you further troubles, not the least of which is violating their rights. Second, you can attempt to convince them to be more like you: heterosexual and employed and unpierced. This might be a big waste of your time. Third, you can ask yourself exactly what beliefs you hold which make these visual inputs cause your dis-ease. As long as these people you behold are not harming you, it will be easiest and best for you to modify your prejudices to accommodate homosexuality and panhandling and body piercing, instead of trying to modify homosexuals, beggars, and body piercers to accommodate your prejudices.

The same applies to all the other senses: hearing, smell, taste, and touch. As long as a stimulus is not harmful, then your dis-ease is mostly a result of your prior judgments about the stimulus. If you want to banish your dis-ease and experience comfort, then banish your prejudices. The philosophical exercises in this book will help you do so. That may be easier said than done, but it is certainly better done than not done.

We encounter myriad pleasures and pains in our journey of a lifetime – ease, disease, and disease. Although most people can almost always find something wrong with their lives, and although everyone will eventually die of some bodily malfunction or other, the norm of life itself is wellness, not illness. Use the signs you receive that something is wrong to correct it. Masking the symptoms without correcting the underlying problem they herald would be a disaster. We should be thankful for those signs, despite the discomfort. Then we will be free to revel in the wellness.

WHAT MAKES YOU THINK SOMETHING'S WRONG WITH YOU?

People are not disturbed by things, but by the views which they take of things.
– Epictetus

Now that we know the only two good reasons to suppose that something's wrong (disease and dis-ease), the next step is knowing when something is wrong with you. Disease and dis-ease can give rise to two kinds of warnings: pain and suffering, respectively.

Not all diseases will immediately cause you pain, so early detection is obviously your best bet. Many people are quite good at "shrugging off" what appear to be minor physical discomforts. Busy and successful people are often most neglectful in this way, partly because success sometimes confers a false sense of invulnerability, and partly because busy schedules do not easily tolerate illness.

If your body is experiencing an unusual pain, there may be something wrong with you – like a disease. That much is clear. But what if you are experiencing suffering? This arises from dis-ease as well as disease. Is there something wrong in your environment, or in a relationship, that is causing your dis-ease? Are you suffering because someone else is making you suffer, or because you are making yourself suffer? Assuming you are not being harmed, this is a false dichotomy. You can blame others for your dis-ease, but your suffering is yours alone. This is good news for you: if it's yours, you can disown it.

We do have to be careful when we talk of suffering as opposed to pain. Sometimes, suffering is a reflection of a physical problem. For example, people who are chronically depressed are clearly suffering from their depression, which may be caused by a problem with their brain chemistry, and so they cannot change it by an act of will alone. In this case, the suffering may be alleviated by a drug. This kind of suffering is the equivalent of a "pain in the brain" – it is really physical in origin. The brain itself feels no pain, so disease in the brain may translate into suffering in the mind. Then again, some apparent pains are really figments of the mind. The classic example of this is so-called "phantom pain," in which amputees claim to have pains in their missing limbs. If your right leg hurts, but it isn't there, then there cannot be anything wrong with your leg.

So our main task is to understand the kinds of sufferings that are brought about by one's own beliefs, prejudices, and habits – and therefore can be alleviated by modifying one's beliefs, disowning one's prejudices, and altering one's habits. This amounts to philosophical practice.

Does all suffering indicate that something's wrong with you mentally? Absolutely not! Suffering, although not necessary or good in itself, can be a great teacher, a means to a better end. (Chapter 5 will reveal some of its lessons.) Please don't get me wrong: I am not claiming that you should seek suffering in order to get beyond it; this is pointless. Californians used to call it the "beat-your-head-against-the-wall-because-it-feels-so-good-when-you-stop" syndrome. But if you are already suffering and seek to understand the true causes of your suffering, then you may discover that you yourself are the true cause. If that is the case, and it is for many, then you choose to suffer, and thus you have the power to reduce or eliminate your suffering by choosing not to suffer.

So here's a Big Question for people who suffer: Are you suffering because something is wrong with you, as in disease? Or are you suffering because you are wronging yourself, as in dis-ease? There is a huge industry out there, backed by shallow thought but deep pockets, whose mission is to convince you that you suffer *only* or *primarily* because something is wrong with you. To counter this, there is a small philosophical industry growing around the world, backed by shallow pockets but deep thought, whose mission is to convince you that you suffer only or primarily because you are wronging yourself.

So if you're ready to tackle some Big Questions philosophically, read on. If you need to get Prozacked or Paxilated first, go right ahead. The Big Questions will remain. If you need a few years of psychother-apy or a few decades of psychoanalysis before getting philosophical for a day, that's fine too. Provided you have the time. The Big Questions will be waiting. Life is always ready to change you. When will you be ready to change your life?

Part II

2

HOW DO YOU
KNOW WHAT'S RIGHT?

**In the world of knowledge, the last thing to be
perceived and only with great difficulty is the
essential Form of Goodness . . . Without having
had a vision of this Form no one can act with
wisdom, either in his own life or in matters of
state.**

– Plato

If you don't like my principles, I've got others.
– Groucho Marx

E VEN THOUGH PEOPLE who seek guidance from philosophy differ
widely in their personal circumstances, careers, and aspirations,
many of them share the same question. What single major concern
could people from many and varied walks of life possibly have in
common? I'll tell you: They want to know what is good, do what is
right, serve what is just. These lofty goals are easy enough to state, but
they can be difficult to attain. So I often find myself sitting across from
someone struggling to do "the right thing." One client asked me, for
example, about *the right way* to deal with noisy neighbors who
disturb his peace. Another wanted to know *the ethical way* to deal
with a messy divorce. Well, it's good that they came to a philosophical
practitioner, as most of them had already entertained a basic misconception: They had assumed there is one single, agreed-upon
conception of right – and, to compound that, that a philosophical
counselor can tell them what it is.

Unfortunately but truly, ethics is not a subject like mathematics.

Simple algebraic equations (like $x + 2 = 3$) have unique solutions. There is one correct answer, which we can easily find, and infinitely many incorrect ones, which we can reject. Ethics more closely resembles two-variable algebra, with equations like $x + y = 3$. Here we find infinitely many correct solutions, with interdependence between x and y. It makes no sense to ask, "What's the correct value of x?" unless you first specify a value for y. Similarly, people who wonder "What's the right thing to do?" need to specify something about their own moral intuitions, or their background ethical theories. Then we have a personalized context – your context – for exploring "rightness."

In theory, there are any number of ways of thinking about goodness, rightness, and justice. In practice, one alternative may be more viable than others, but it has to make sense to you, resonate with your intuitions and experience, and function in your particular case. Since there is no way to adequately address each and every theory in one chapter – or even in a whole book – I'm going to start you with ten ways of deciding what is right. Sometimes you may have to choose between doing the right thing for the wrong reasons and doing the wrong thing for the right reasons. But in the end you have to take your own stand. After we review these ten theories, we'll look at some actual cases and see which ones were utilized.

TEN WAYS OF BEING GOOD, RIGHT, AND JUST

To help you understand how these ways of determining what is "right" operate in practice, I'm going to apply each of them to a case you're presumably familiar with: the legend of Robin Hood. To refresh your memory, when good King Richard Lionheart was away on a crusade, his evil brother, Prince John, usurped the throne and empowered his despotic friends, including the sheriff of Nottingham. The sheriff oppressed and overtaxed the local people. So Robin Hood and his band of merry men hid out in Sherwood Forest, fighting a kind of "guerrilla war" against the sheriff's oppressive regime, stealing from the rich and giving to the poor, as legend has it. And all for the cause of justice.

And so we must ask ourselves: Was Robin right to steal? Here's how to answer that – in ten different ways, according to ten different ethical systems. Please note: This isn't a ranking, just a listing. So don't read anything special into their order.

Deontology. This comes from the Greek word *deon*, related to the notion of duty. In practice, it means following a rule book of morality. The rules themselves are predefined as "good." Following them is therefore "right." If most people followed them, society would appear "just." In religious contexts, one such rule book consists of the Ten Commandments, widely used by Jews and Christians. In both religious and secular contexts, another such rule book is the Eightfold Way, widely used by Buddhists. In secular contexts, some philosophers adhere to a rule of Kant's known as the "categorical imperative."

All these rule books condemn stealing. The Eighth Commandment of Moses is: "Thou shalt not steal." Buddha's fourth factor on the Eightfold Way says (among other things): "Avoid stealing, and abstain from it." Kant tells us to do only those things that we could will everyone to be doing all the time. Since we don't want a population of full-time thieves, we shouldn't steal ourselves. So according to these, among other deontologies, Robin Hood is wrong to steal. Simple enough.

However, like all ethical systems, deontology has its own particular strengths and weaknesses. Its main strength is its clear statement of moral rules. When people are in doubt about what's right or wrong, they have a rule book to consult. Its main weakness, however, is its inability to resolve exceptions to the rules. It doesn't cut Robin any slack, even though he is well intentioned and gives his loot to the poor.

The black-and-white nature of deontologies doesn't easily admit inevitable shades of gray. For instance, most deontologies have a rule along the lines of "Thou shalt not kill." Normally we understand this to mean we should not kill our fellow humans just because they get on our nerves. But there are many possible exceptions to this rule, and no universal agreement over them. Is it right to kill other animals for food? Is it right to kill in self-defense? Is it right to kill convicted murderers? Is it right to kill the enemy in wartime? Is it right to kill fetuses in the womb? Is it right to kill oneself? Not only is there no accord on what constitutes tolerable exceptions, but people even kill each other over arguments about the exceptions. In other words, they do murder for the sake of not killing!

I confess that I have oversimplified how deontology might handle Robin Hood. While declaring the act of stealing to be wrong, some deontologies would also take into account Robin's motives and subsequent actions (giving to the poor). Some criminal-justice systems have rule books that make exactly this kind of moral distinction. In America, if Robin stole and put the money in his Swiss bank account, he'd get a harsher sentence than if he stole and gave the money to charity. Intentions may mitigate punishment, but do not exonerate wrongdoing. Acts of theft or robbery would still be wrong. So while deontology offers very strong moral guidelines, it leaves much scope for debate about exceptions to its rules.

> **Act only on that maxim [i.e. rule] by which you can at the same time will that it should become a universal law.**
>
> **– Immanuel Kant**

Teleology. This also comes from a Greek word, *telos,* meaning "purpose" or "end." Teleology (or consequentialism, as it is often called) asserts that no act is right or wrong in and of itself, but that its rightness or wrongness depends on the goodness or badness of the consequences it brings. In other words, if you get a good outcome, you did the "right" thing. If you get a bad outcome, you did the "wrong" thing.

One of the more prevalent forms of teleology is called "act-utilitarianism." If you had to summarize it in one sentence, it would say, "Act in such a way as to produce the greatest good for the greatest number." On this view, Robin Hood is certainly justified in stealing from the rich to give to the poor. After all, there are so many more poor than rich! Many more people will be benefited than will be inconvenienced by Robin's "redistribution" of wealth.

According to act-utilitarianism, this is a good outcome. So Robin is right to steal.

Teleology's main strength is its open-mindedness. It does not approve or reject any action out of hand, but awaits the outcome before pronouncing judgment. But this is also one of its main weaknesses: almost any action, no matter how heinous, can be justified by an appeal to its consequences. For instance, act-utilitarianism could be used to justify lynching people suspected of crimes, instead of giving them fair trials. After all, the lynch mob is happy with its behavior, even if the one who gets lynched is not. If happiness is good, then lynching is an example of "the greatest good for the greatest number," and therefore justifiable by act-utilitarianism. But using act-utilitarianism this way fails to take into account the greatest suffering of the smallest number, and therefore allows a majority to ignore the rights of a minority. When a group's sentiments overrules an individual's rights, injustice is rarely far behind.

Teleology has other weaknesses too. It presupposes that we know how to measure the "goodness" or "badness" of outcomes, as if they were so much meat or so many vegetables on a scale. In fact, no one has a clue how to measure good or bad. So if there can be no universal agreement as to whether a given outcome is good or bad, there can be no agreement as to whether the act that produced it is right or wrong. There can only be a self-justifying consensus, which could be abused to support even great evil.

So Robin needs to be careful justifying his actions with teleology. Thinking about the consequences of one's deeds is important, but ends are never independent of the means used to attain them.

The ends and means are a seamless web.
– Gloria Steinem

Virtue Ethics. Aristotle, Buddha, and Confucius form the "ABCs" of virtue ethics, so its roots go back a very long way. All three of these wise men preached a kind of moderation, teaching, in distinct ways, that goodness comes simply from practicing virtues and eschewing vices. Virtues and vices (not unlike viruses) are things we acquire from others, and transmit to others. They are like good and bad habits. So if our goal is to see good people acting rightly in a just society, we must create and maintain virtuous settings – at home, at school, at work, in government, and so on.

Virtue ethicists would argue that theft is generally wrong, but would also acknowledge that people do need to take care of themselves. If a government abuses its authority by stealing its citizens' food, over-taxing their wealth, and denying them justice, it may be necessary to redress these wrongs. You might *need* a Robin Hood. Virtue ethics favors people being more self-governing, and not needing to be constantly governed by others, which minimizes the risk of falling prey to anarchy at one extreme and despotism at the other.

In Robin Hood's day, common folk were at the mercy of monarchs, many of whom were corrupt despots. If a prince chose to become a glorified thief and systematically rob his subjects, his subjects had little choice but to indulge in counter-theft themselves, simply in order to survive. It is not ethically desirable, but practically necessary. So Robin Hood could get the virtue ethics seal of approval, owing to exceptional circumstances. In this case, virtue ethics fingers the vicious system as the culprit. Robin Hood would be seen as a victim of his unethical environment. As in: A "good" state is one in which no citizen should need to break the laws, so a person obliged to become an outlaw because of political abuse is not at fault for living outside the law. An outlaw can still be good and right and just.

The main strength of virtue ethics is its emphasis on education and habit formation as guides and channels to good living. It optimistically views the human character as clay, which can be formed in many ways, by family and society, from cradle to grave. Even if it is deformed, it can be reformed. In this system, almost no one is beyond rehabilitation. At the same time, the system also recognizes that different individuals have different abilities. Given equal opportunity in a virtuous setting, people will manifest excellence differently. Given equal opportunity in an indifferent setting, they will manifest apathy differently. Given equal opportunity in a vicious setting, they will manifest vice differently.

Virtue ethics' weaknesses are twofold. At one extreme, in Asia, the

Confucian emphasis on family as the building block of community, society, and polity can lead – and has led – to corruption and favoritism in the form of nepotism and related vices. At another extreme, where the modern Western emphasis on individual liberty has undermined nuclear families, and where political power is a commodity that has to be purchased, there is altogether insignificant attention to virtue. When people are left to their own devices, and are never encouraged – or compelled – to adopt ethical systems, they often choose vices over virtues.

Like the physical world, the moral world is not perfectly efficient. Loss of efficiency or gain of entropy – movement from order toward chaos – is built into the physical world. Every process is less than 100 percent efficient. Similarly, it is easier to acquire bad habits than good ones, and harder to break the bad ones than the good. In the short run, and from an individual perspective, vice seems more fun than virtue. But in the longer run, and from a societal perspective, a vicious society becomes dysfunctional and inimical to the well-being of its members, whereas a virtuous one remains functional and supportive of the well-being of its members. So Robin needs to think about what long-term virtues he is trying to protect through his short-term acts in desperate times.

All persons ought to endeavor to follow what is right, and not what is established.
– Aristotle

Providential Religious Ethics. A number of religions share the view that God created the world, made humans in His or Her or Its own image, and gave us a mission: Be good and do the right things in this world, and you will receive justice as (eternal) reward in the next. Then again, if you are bad and do the wrong things in this world, you will receive justice as (eternal) damnation in the next. "Providence" means care and protection, and providential religions maintain that we are under the care and protection of God. When bad things happen to people – whether these ills are inflicted by nature or by other people – it hardly feels like "care" or "protection"; in fact it's just the opposite: It feels like neglect and insecurity. This is religion's oldest philosophical problem (the problem of evil, or the "theodicy problem") and its standard answer is: You are suffering here and now in order to have your faith tested in this world. If you pass the test, you will be rewarded later – usually in the next world, or next life.

Freud and others have compared the psychology of this claim to the way in which parents care for and protect small children. "Be good in the dentist's chair, and I'll buy you an ice cream afterward." This is also the basis of behaviorism: eliciting desired behaviors by means of rewards or punishments. So Freud concluded that religions were infantile. However, while care and protection of one's children necessarily involves exposing them to some temporary discomforts such as dental or medical procedures, it is less clear that God's "care and protection" of His or Her or Its children (namely us) necessarily involves exposing us to the myriad sufferings of this world. Hence the importance of belief in divine providence: People know full well that far too many ills can never be undone or reversed in this world, yet they can always hope for a better world to come. People think that hope is good for them. Religions offer more hope than many of their adherents can handle.

Religious ethics vary so much from sect to sect that it's impossible to capture them all. However, I will offer brief perspectives from four main religions.

Judaism: Judaism teaches that the Messiah will one day come to right all wrongs. Meanwhile, Jews should not resist evil with evil. (Solomon: "Enter not into the path of the wicked, and walk not in the way of evil men.") Judaism endures because Jews endure suffering. From a Jewish perspective, the sheriff of Nottingham is a minor irritant compared with Egyptian bondage, Roman conquest, Spanish Inquisition, Slavonic pogroms, Nazi genocide, Arab terrorism, and other things. Robin Hood was probably not Jewish: His mother never would have approved of his becoming an outlaw.

Christianity: Here all bets are off. Mainstream Christianity both abhors bloodshed and fights just wars. The Robin Hood scenario is set in Christendom. Jesus himself said, "Render unto Caesar" (i.e. pay your taxes), and taught "Resist not evil" (he was Jewish too). Then again, the thirteen colonies of America were mostly Christian when they fought for independence from England, and from the British crown's taxation without representation. However, American and British Christians were also involved in the slave trade. That wasn't very Christian, so they twisted the rules to justify it. And again, America, England, and their Allies were largely Christian when they resisted the evils of Nazism and Soviet totalitarianism. So Robin Hood is possibly doing a "Christian thing" too, but exactly what that means is highly debatable. Meanwhile, he should probably pray for guidance and forgiveness, and continue his ethical search.

Islam: Islam's mainstream ethical prescription is less ambiguous than Christianity's. To begin with, "good" King Richard was on a crusade somewhere in or en route to Arabia when "evil" Prince John took over. While the spiritual mythology of the Crusades involved a quest after the Holy Grail, materially they were a series of armed incursions, lethal conflicts, with inevitable looting by the victors in any given battle – whether Arab or European. Let us not forget that the destruction of the World Trade Center is perceived by some Islamic peoples as retaliation for the eleventh-, twelfth-, and thirteenth-century European Crusades. Never mind the irony that millions of Americans have never heard of the Knights Templar, and don't even remember the 1991 Gulf War.

Islamic extremists might claim that Prince John's reign was Allah's way of punishing the English "infidels" for sending King Richard to invade the lands of the "faithful." That definitely makes Robin Hood a bad guy for trying to undermine Allah's work. Don't expect support for Robin Hood from any theocratic system in which mass conformity to authority, intolerance of personal liberty, suppression of difference, and suicidal violence against perceived enemies are norms.

Moderate Islamic states and esoteric sects of Islam, such as Sufism, are completely different. These Muslims are warriors for peace, waging their jihad against imperfections within. Khalil Gibran says: "And if it is a despot you would dethrone, see first that his throne erected within you is destroyed." So Robin is exhorted to confront his own demons and defeat them before fighting external battles. If he would confront the sheriff, he must act from deep levels, with pure motives. This is a very advanced teaching, and might lead Robin to contemplate similar teachings from other traditions.

Hinduism: In Hinduism, the soul voyages from life to life, inhabiting and relinquishing body after body in its journey toward unification with the Godhead. This current life is a resultant of the previous lives that one has led. What is "right" in Hinduism is doing one's duty, however this life prescribes it. So the sheriff is doing his duty as an oppressor, and will presumably be reincarnated as the oppressed, to teach him a good lesson. Meanwhile, the serfs are doing their duties as the oppressed, and will probably reincarnate as something better next time – maybe sheriffs. Robin Hood is also doing his duty as an archer and warrior, and he is very close to not having to reincarnate at all. In fact, another great archer and warrior, namely Arjuna, has this very teaching revealed to him by Krishna, his charioteer-God, in the Bhagavad Gita: "It is better to do one's own duty, however defective it may be, than to follow the duty of another, however well one may perform it."

Hinduism can identify strongly with Robin Hood, and would probably advise him to carry on. And also, perhaps, to found an ashram and practice some yoga out there in Sherwood Forest – a perfect location for it.

Existentialism. Existentialism emerged in late-nineteenth-century Europe, based on the idea that the material existence of a thing precedes its immaterial essence. This reverses Plato's position that immaterial essence precedes a thing's material existence. For example, according to Plato, goodness is an eternal idea. What makes a deed "good" is the extent to which it contains the essence of goodness. So to do good, you need to understand goodness, and capture its essence in your deeds. The existentialists, on other hand, reject Platonism. They suppose that you choose to do a given deed according to your personal deliberations and preferences. Once you've done a deed, then we can determine from its existence your essential idea of goodness.

Thus most existentialists reject gods, souls, spirits, and other religious notions – although a few, notably Kierkegaard and Buber, were also quite religious. Humanistic existentialism's guiding insight is that human nature is not necessarily "fixed" by any preconceived ideas about it – whether Augustine's original sin or Freud's Oedipus complex or Nietzsche's superman or anything else. Rather, our essential natures are determined *by* us (not *for* us). Plato would say that what we learn to value in our essential being determines and illustrates what we do and how we exist. Sartre would say that what we choose to do and how we choose to exist determines and illustrates what we learn to value as the essence of our beings.

Existentialism's unrelentingly optimistic view of man unfolds against a cosmic backdrop that is equally and unrelentingly pessimistic. Absent God, the universe is a place without meaning or purpose. It's an immense cosmic accident, which gave birth to a myriad of insignificant sub-accidents, one of which is the human being. If spiritual essences are figments of our imaginations, then so are moral essences. There is no titanic struggle between good and evil unfolding in the cosmos, contrary to what most religions and cultures believe. Rather, there is just a series of events unfolding without particular rhyme or reason. No greater power watches over the world, or cares for or protects its inhabitants.

This is what earns existentialism its reputation for being depressive, despairing, and despondent. This school of thought certainly attracts such personality types, and often makes them worse. I think it has made a lot of people unnecessarily unhappy. I rarely prescribe existential writings to clients, unless they're feeling too much at ease and want to experience some dis-ease for a change (a very rare condition indeed), or unless they are advanced enough in their philosophical journey to touch existentialism's moral bedrock. In fact, French existentialists like Sartre, de Beauvoir, and Camus are quite moral persons. Why? Because they assert the following: We have to try to do the right things in life, even if the universe provides no reliable moral compass that points towards good and away from evil. Precisely because the universe is an amoral place, it is even more incumbent on human beings to behave rightly, not wrongly. This is a courageous and challenging stance.

So what's *right* or *wrong* for existentialists? That is less clear. One key is to assume responsibility for one's actions. Thus, existentialists would say that the sheriff of Nottingham must assume responsibility for being an oppressor (i.e., be accountable for his actions); but that the supposedly hapless serfs must also assume some responsibility for being the oppressed (i.e., be accountable for their *in*actions). It follows that Robin Hood, by his actions, values a world in which there are fewer oppressors and oppressed alike. Unlike the rest, Robin is ready to sacrifice himself for his values. *Himself,* not others! Robin is therefore a good exemplar of the personal authenticity that existentialists prize above all else.

The great strength of existentialism is its insistence that we are free agents, and that we choose our values through actions. But its main weakness is that not everyone is ready to accept the personal responsibility that liberty confers, and the accountability that freedom demands. Another weakness is that many are tempted to wield more power than they can responsibly hold. Following Nietzsche's idea of the *Übermensch* (superman), when man demotes God to imagination, promotes himself to a worldly deity, and then defies moral convention in order to rise above "the herd," he can become a monster. It might be a useful strategy for creative artists (e.g., poets, authors, painters, and composers), but it's a dangerous game for all concerned when religious or political leaders assume this stance.

So Robin has to be careful here to serve justice but not be corrupted by power.

> **It was previously a question of finding out whether or not life had to have a meaning to be lived. It now becomes clear, on the contrary, that it will be lived all the better if it has no meaning.**
>
> **– Albert Camus**

Objectivist Ethics. This philosophy of enlightened self-interest underpins much of the West's success in pioneering democracy, science, technology, economic development, and globalization. It goes something like this: The needs and wants of the individual are granted priority over the needs and wants of the collective, which is better for the group in the longer run as well. Ayn Rand is the most famous champion of this idea. She would maintain that even when we help others, we do so because it is in our self-interest. Her two great novels, *The Fountainhead* and *Atlas Shrugged,* elaborate the theme that the best model for attaining full potential of both the individual and society is one that engenders constructive competition, and asserts the rights of the individual over those of the collective. Without that, she'd say, we are no better than the social insects – ants, wasps, and bees.

The great strengths of objectivism are its recognition of individual merit and promotion of individual excellence. Its main weakness is its romantic assumption that enlightened leaders (or benevolent despots) will triumph over unenlightened leaders (or malevolent despots), and thus that the better interests of the masses will also be served. In Robin Hood's case, this has clearly not happened. The most unenlightened despots – Prince John and his minions – are ruling the roost and wreaking havoc on everyone else. Objectivism opposes dictatorship of all kinds, and condones fighting unfair systems by unfair means.

In *Atlas Shrugged,* one of the world's most talented industrialists becomes a pirate, taking back by acts of piracy what had been looted by despotic individuals acting in the name of "the people." Similarly, other great industrialists perpetrate acts of sabotage on this corrupt system, in which unenlightened despots confiscate the wealth of successful individuals in the name of "the people," while these despots actually wreck the economy and cause the people to lose their jobs and to starve. So Ayn Rand's objectivist ethics would condone the acts of Robin and his Merry Men and condemn the brutal government that forced him into this position.

> **When "the common good" of a society is regarded as something apart from and superior to the individual good of its members, it means that the good of some men takes precedence over the good of others, with those others consigned to the status of sacrificial animals.**
> **– Ayn Rand**

Prima Facie Duties. Prima facie means "at first glance." This system, an outgrowth of virtue ethics, originated in the twentieth century with applied ethicist William Ross. It views each human being as a participant in a social contract, from which we derive certain legal rights and moral benefits, and to which we owe certain legal duties and moral obligations. In civilized countries, citizens enjoy a host of rights and benefits, but at the same time also have duties and obligations – e.g., toward our spouses, children, friends, neighbors, colleagues, associates, employers, employees, and so forth, not to mention jury duty.

Now the question arises: What happens when two or more duties come into conflict, such that honoring one means dishonoring the other, and vice versa? For instance, suppose I have promised to meet an associate for lunch who wants to discuss a business proposal. Now suppose I'm on my way to lunch but am suddenly called to school to collect my child, who has sprained his ankle during gym class. Prima facie duties would support the obvious answer, that my duty toward my child in an emergency takes priority over my duty to my associate at a business meeting. It's too late to "reschedule" the sports injury; but we can surely reschedule the meeting.

It's not always so easy to prioritize one's duties, however. Jean-Paul Sartre wrote about an example involving one of his students, who had to choose between joining the French Resistance to fight the Nazis and staying at home to look after his elderly mother. There is no clear way to prioritize such conflicting duties. And Sartre's humanistic ethics didn't help much either.

Robin Hood's case is similarly complicated. We gather that Robin is an upstanding citizen, who embraces the twin values of individual excellence (in his case, at archery) and social cooperativeness (his men are merry together, not in conflict with one another). We can suppose that his duties to fight against tyranny and for justice take precedence over his duties to be an obedient subject and raise a family with Maid Marion. If he prevails in his fight, he may also be able to enjoy a normal life afterward. But note that prima facie duties do not compel everyone to choose as Robin: some join him in the forest, while others stay at home and honor prior commitments.

Some (duties) rest on the mere fact that there are other beings in the world whose condition we can make better.

– William Ross

Sociobiology. Founded in the 1970s, with E. O. Wilson and Richard Dawkins at the forefront, sociobiology endeavors to explain social behaviors in terms of underlying biological processes. While this makes great sense when studying social insects, and accounts well enough for many social behaviors in animals up to and including monkeys and apes, its application to humans remains hotly contested – especially when we try to reduce moral behaviors to biological concerns. I cannot possibly do justice to this complex debate in passing, but I do want to summarize the key point. In the natural world – apart from humans – we do not encounter anything like morality. Ants, bees, and wasps are not "altruistic" when sacrificing themselves for the good of the nest or hive; they are merely following their biological programming in social contexts. Similarly, sharks, scorpions, cobras, and other dangerous animals are not "bad" because they are dangerous; they are simply made this way and cannot behave otherwise. Not one of these creatures makes a moral choice. Only with apes do we see the true beginnings of deceit, cuckoldry, and other behaviors that herald the human potential for full-blown morality – and immorality alike.

Hard-boiled biological determinists like Jacques Monod would like us to believe that every moral choice is almost entirely determined by one's genes. I find this doubtful, and won't be convinced until sociobiologists can tell a Nazi from a Quaker merely by examining their respective DNA. But in any event, in this view the sheriff of Nottingham and Robin Hood are both "right" in that they are simply doing as their genes dictate. The sheriff has "despotic" genes, the serfs of Nottingham have "oppressed" genes, Robin has "heroic" genes, Robin's Merry Men, of course, have "merry" genes, and none of them could behave otherwise.

If we succeed in reducing moral and immoral behaviors to genetics, it will follow that nobody is responsible for anything. The sheriff is not

a despot because he chooses despotism; his genes made him do it.
Ditto Robin's heroism. So we'll have to close down a lot of correc-
tional facilities and replace them with genetic engineering labs. We'll
have to be replacing genes instead of reforming attitudes, correcting
behaviors, and examining beliefs. We can only hope that Robin's and
Marion's eventual offspring are not a brood of outlaws.

> **. . . the time has come for ethics to be removed
> temporarily from the hands of the
> philosophers and biologized.**
> **– E. O. Wilson**

Other-Centered Ethics. Thank Emmanuel Levinas for the simple
yet compelling idea that the very notion of morality involves a
relationship with others. For Levinas, morality means thinking of
others. Our responsibilities toward others arise from their very existence.

Concerns about oneself are not necessarily moral at all – for
example, feeding myself when I am hungry is simply a matter of
self-preservation. Yet the same concern directed at someone else –
such as feeding a hungry child, or guest, or stranger – means caring for
that person in a moral way. Similarly, "helping myself" to something
can have selfish or greedy connotations, whereas helping others with
something seems always to connote a moral act. For Levinas, the
whole conception of morality therefore involves recognition of *the
other,* outside ourselves, as someone deserving of our consideration
and assistance. Levinas exhorts the human being to realize his or her
full moral potential through understanding that the very *existence* of
other human beings imposes inescapable moral obligations on us. He
provides an existential justification for a universal ethic of caring.
Others exist. They experience dis-ease. We experience their experience
of dis-ease, which causes dis-ease in us. We must help if we can. Our
own happiness cannot be independent of others'. This also the
Mahayana Buddhist position.

Applied to Robin's case, it is clear that Robin Hood has deep
compassion for the suffering of others, such that he even risks his own

life to help alleviate their suffering. Robin, his Merry Men, and Maid Marion are "moral beings" in the noblest sense of the term. The sheriff of Nottingham fails miserably to empathize with others and keeps on inflicting myriad sufferings on others, and is therefore immoral.

The strength of Levinas's system is its emphasis on awareness of others as the key to moral thought and behavior. Its weakness, however, is brought into focus by the very weaknesses of human beings themselves, which commonly include immaturity, vanity, selfishness, egotism, sadism, and all kinds of desires to wield power for its own sake. In far too many human beings, these negative traits override any thought or sentiment for others. Such people have oppressed others throughout human history, and other-centered ethics contains no guidelines for educating or convincing them to recognize the moral being of others. Moreover, if we are considerate of those who are not considerate of us, we may be ethically exploited, or worse.

> **. . . justice remains justice only, in a society where there is no distinction between those close and those far off, but in which there also remains the impossibility of passing by the closest.**
>
> **– Emmanuel Levinas**

Buddhist Ethics. In Buddhist ethics, whatever causes suffering is bad, while whatever relieves it is good. Yet suffering itself is also a kind of teacher, heightening our awareness of the human condition, of its impermanence and illusion, of its fragility, futility, vanity and nobility. Buddha proposed that to be alive and aware is to suffer (his "First Noble Truth"). Suffering is ubiquitous among humans, a fundamental kind of dis-ease that all humans experience, regardless of its particular causes. Rich and poor suffer alike, as do male and female, black and white, old and young, though each one's suffering feels unique to him or her.

Do you know anyone who hasn't suffered at one time or another? Don't you also suffer at times? Some people bear their sufferings more stoically or humorously than others, but all assuredly suffer from something sometimes, even if they express it in a variety of ways. Some suffer in silence; others protest aloud. Some pray for relief; others become cynical. Some blame others; others blame themselves. Some hate or kill others; others hate or kill themselves. Some seek to escape from suffering; others suffer from attempted escapes. Some attain goals to distract them from suffering; others suffer from the very attainment of those goals or from the distraction.

The good news is that Buddha also proposed that sufferings are the effects of identifiable causes (his "Second Noble Truth") and that by removing these causes we can remove the effects (his "Third Noble Truth"). He then taught very simple and practical ways of removing the causes of suffering, and thus of moving one's consciousness beyond a state of dis-ease and into a state of ease (his "Fourth Noble Truth").

This is sometimes called crossing life's sea of suffering. Whoever learns to cross this sea finds the serenity and compassion to help others cross it too. Buddhist practices are like swimming lessons: They teach us how to cross the sea of dis-ease, and reach the shore of ease. One can swim using many kinds of strokes, but the ultimate destination is always the same.

Applying this to Robin Hood: Buddhist ethics would look at everyone's sufferings, and their particular causes, and the best ways to remove them. In Buddhist terms, Robin Hood and his Merry Men suffer less than the others in the scenario because they are less attached to the world, less egoistic and judgmental in their outlook on the world, and less blinded by illusions of the world. Having renounced their own security and become outcasts, they are joyful. Dwelling in the forest, without much material comfort, they are at home in the world. Risking their lives on a daily basis, not for personal gain but in the service of others, they are fulfilled. They are not pleased that others are suffering, but they are not displeased by their own hardships, which they voluntarily accept. Their lives have meaning and purpose. They seek to harm no one, only to balance wrong with right. They alleviate suffering. They afford hope. They inspire good.

The assorted peasants and serfs under the sheriff's heel suffer just because they are alive, and also because the sheriff is making their lives more difficult than they need be. But suppose the sheriff were deposed, and replaced by Robin Hood himself – a good guy. Would the common people stop suffering? No, they wouldn't. If their political oppression ceased, they'd be "liberated" to resume a whole medley of other sufferings. They'd suffer from illness and death, and from the premature deaths of loved ones. They'd suffer from bad marriages, bad harvests, bad weather, bad neighbors, and bad luck – and from unemployment, exploitation, taxation, and all the rest. They'd have good times too, and cherished memories, but they'd be fortunate if their joys exceeded their sorrows in the long run.

The sheriff of Nottingham exercises oppressive power, which causes those whom he oppresses to suffer – and, according to the law of karma, their suffering returns to haunt him too. All oppressors, including the sheriff we're concerned with right now, suffer in this way, more or less. To cease their suffering, they must first cease their oppression. Many make the mistake of increasing their oppression instead, thus increasing their suffering – as well as everyone else's.

> **Because violence can only breed more violence and suffering, our struggle must remain nonviolent and free of hatred. We are trying to end the suffering of our people, not to inflict suffering upon others.**
>
> **– Dalai Lama**

Legal Moralism. This school of thought equates lawfulness with morality. Its motto is: "If it's legal, it's moral." On the bright side, of course we want our laws to reflect our morals. At the same time, we can't allow our laws to dictate our morals. Slavery was once legal in America, though it could hardly be considered moral. Genocide was once legal in Nazi Germany, but no moral human being could possibly justify it. Stalin's purges were legal in the former Soviet Union, as was Mao Tse-tung's Cultural Revolution in China, but they too unfolded beyond the pale of moral sensibility. The problem is that laws and morals are not the same thing. They aren't congruent; that is, they don't cover the same territory.

Obvious examples include abortion and capital punishment. Both are legal in many places, yet many people in those places consider them immoral. On the other hand, look at "victimless crimes" like prostitution and possession of cannabis. Both are illegal in many places, but many people in those places don't consider them immoral.

The question is, then, when laws and morals come into conflict, which one gets priority? This issue, dating back at least as far as Socrates, is one of philosophy's toughest questions. The Athenians, in keeping with their laws, put Socrates to death. But many thought his death sentence was immoral and urged him to escape. Socrates disagreed. He thought the laws were just and so it was therefore morally right to honor them.

Much later, philosophers like Thoreau advocated civil disobedience against unjust laws, an idea Socrates would have approved. That kind of nonviolent resistance was put into powerful political practice by Mahatma Gandhi in India and Martin Luther King Jr. in the United States.

The bottom-line philosophical message is that we have a duty as human beings to uphold just laws and to defy unjust ones. But one key question – what is just? – has never been fully resolved.

As for Robin Hood, legal moralists would say that since the incumbent lawmakers had legalized high taxes and oppression, their actions were legal, and therefore moral. That makes Robin Hood a common criminal, and his Merry Men all accomplices. They should be caught and punished.

If you generally uphold law and order but still don't like this line of argument, you are not alone! Such reasoning has been used to justify many kinds of oppression, injustice, and atrocity. Even in less extreme circumstances this idea can be quite damaging, as when corporate culture dictates, "If it's not illegal, it's ethical." There are many technically legal ways in which businesses and professions can cheat and swindle people, but theft and fraud are never professionally ethical practices.

There's another nasty side to legal moralism, known as "the loyal agent argument." If some lawfully constituted authority orders you to do something, and you do it without question, then you are a "loyal agent." Being a loyal agent is a good thing when it comes to paying your taxes, doing your assigned work, sending your kids to school, and so on. But what if your government orders you to maim, torture, rape, or murder on some political pretext? Or, what if your boss orders you to shred some documents that might be relevant to an auditor? If you later stand accused of wrongdoing, your defense – "I was only following orders" – is morally inadequate (and, for that matter, often legally inadequate as well). Reliance on the loyal agent argument encourages people to become moral zombies, not accepting any responsibility whatsoever for their own actions, however heinous, as long as the actions were ordained from above.

We can also see the weakness of this approach in religious fanaticism, in a related claim: the devout agent argument. If a religious authority issues orders and you obey without question, you are a "devout agent." This may be fine as long as you're in the realm of helping others. However, suppose you start believing that God commands you to explode a bomb in a crowded public place, or to murder a doctor who performs abortions, or to assault a person whose tastes you don't share. Are you following divine orders, and therefore behaving justly? Are callous indifference toward human life, willingness to inflict suffering, and reverence for death good things? Claiming that God has ordained such things is not defensible. So radical religious moralism isn't necessarily conducive to goodness, and can in fact produce and justify evil.

Loyalty can be a very commendable quality, but, like love, it is often blind.

> **We should never forget that everything Adolf Hitler did in Germany was "legal" and everything the Hungarian freedom fighters did in Hungary was "illegal."**
>
> **– Martin Luther King Jr.**

THE BIG PICTURE: META-ETHICAL RELATIVISM

Now that you have learned ten different ways of being good, you face a real paradox: how do you decide which ones are *better,* and which (if any) is *best*? The problem is that we can't decide which theory of *good* is better or best until we know the meaning of *good* itself. And so we're right back where we started, with many competing theories of goodness (of which these are just a sampling). If you were thoroughly indoctrinated early in your life, or if you have settled on a particular ethical theory for some other reason, then you don't have this problem. But if you are a thoughtful person, you may conclude that no single ethical theory can be stretched to cover every moral contingency. The only alternative, then, is to suppose that different ethical systems work better in different situations. This approach is called meta-ethical relativism.

Meta-ethical relativism is not the same as ethical relativism, which supposes, subjectively, that anybody's ethics are as valid as anybody else's and, accordingly, that anything at all is permissible in a given situation. Ethical relativism says that Robin Hood is correct to believe that he is doing right, while the sheriff of Nottingham is also correct to believe that Robin Hood is doing wrong. If you have a problem viewing the very same action as both right and wrong, then you are not an ethical relativist.

But is there an objective perspective that provides a wiser and more trustworthy moral compass? That's where meta-ethical relativism comes in to help us discover which ethical system among those mentioned above – and the unmentioned, and the variations on each – does three vital jobs. First, it must resonate with your moral intuitions. Second, it must mesh with your background experience of ethics. Third, it must help remedy the problem itself. There are no easy answers here, and there's an art (as well as an effort) required to answer the question "Which ethical system do you think is best in your case – and why?" Now we're going to look at three illustrative cases to show you how it's done.

All ethical questions are important, whether they involve matters of life and death or not. An unresolved moral dilemma can cause a lot of dis-ease, and never feels trivial to the person who is experiencing it.

Ed's Case: Noisy Neighbors

Let's start with the client I mentioned at the beginning of the chapter, who asked me about "the right way" to deal with noisy neighbors who were disturbing his peace. The new occupants in the apartment above Ed's had some very noisy children, and no one in the household seemed to know how to walk without stomping or talk without shouting. And they did both at all hours of the day and night. The ceilings were thin, and every footfall sounded like a jackhammer. They also hosted a seemingly endless stream of guests, and blasted the stereo and television at all hours. To make matters worse, Ed had a home office, so he didn't escape the onslaught even to go to work each day. His peace of mind was really disturbed, and his ability to work and relax in his own home was severely compromised. While some people can simply ignore such noises, others are extremely sensitive to them. Ed was the sensitive type.

As Ed and I talked, we explored six possible courses of action: defensive, neighborly, offensive, retaliatory, evasive, and post-emptive. Ultimately, Ed tried almost all of them. Let's briefly characterize the ethics of each one.

Defensively, he could try to block out the noise by soundproofing, listening to music or watching TV through headphones, and so forth. That's a form of benevolent teleology: he'd be getting a good end (peace and quiet), with purely defensive means. No harm done to anyone. Unfortunately, however, the disturbances from above penetrated Ed's technological defenses.

Being neighborly, he tried to sit down with them and make them aware of his distress, see if they would be willing to cooperate, and find ways of diminishing the disturbances. That's Levinas's other-centered ethics at work. However, these were bad neighbors, because they didn't care that they were disturbing Ed. Levinas's system breaks down if the other whom you recognize fails to recognize you as an other, too.

So Ed went on the offensive, and filed a complaint against them with his condominium association. The neighbors were fined for disturbing his peace, but they didn't stop. (In fact, they got worse.) Ethically, this is an instance of legal moralism: we have laws against disturbing the peace and are morally justified in applying those laws to restore peace and quiet. It's also a case of prima facie duties: Parents have duties to their children, which include allowing them sufficient playtime and social time as well. But parents also have duties to teach their children respect and consideration for others, such as neighbors. But, as in this case, some parents do not reflect on or balance their parenting duties.

So Ed thought about retaliating by raising a ruckus himself – giving them a taste of their own medicine. But he refrained from doing this, mostly because of deontology. The Judeo-Christian ethic in Ed's background had taught him that "two wrongs don't make a right." And Kant would also say it's wrong to retaliate, because if everyone retaliated for every wrong (real or imagined), there would be no end to conflict – and ending it was supposedly the whole point of retaliating.

Next, Ed could try to evade the disturbance by trying not to be at home during its peak hours. This was partly a sociobiological issue: Ed believed that he was "high strung" by nature, and was "hardwired" not to tolerate noise very well. He also believed his neighbors were naturally boisterous people. Some are. If that was so, then Ed clearly had to find another place to work. But since he worked at home, logic dictated that he find another place to live.

Finally, and post-emptively, Ed did move to a much quieter place. But his final ethical interpretation of this episode was a Buddhist one. Why? Because: Ed ultimately assumed a measure of responsibility for his own dis-ease. Once he was able to "own" his suffering, he was free to take steps to "disown" it. Before philosophy can change your life, you may have to change your philosophy. It's actually very simple. Rather than trying to compel your environment to change, compel yourself to change your environment. This is mostly an act of will. Visualize the kind of place you need to be in to accomplish your next tasks in life, to do your duty as you conceive it. Now make the visualization as clear as possible, and persist in the willfulness to actualize that vision. Then the pathway to its actualization will gradually materialize. As you will, so shall you become. That is the kernel of Buddha's teaching. It is also possible, desirable, and preferable to attain your goals without harming others.

Do you object? Are you thinking "Why should *he* have to move? Why should he let them chase him away when they are the ones in the wrong?" Your home is supposed to be your castle (from English common law) and your refuge. But bad neighbors had invaded Ed's castle and despoiled his refuge. So it all came down to this: Would he rather wage just war against his neighbors, or live in peace with other neighbors someplace else? That's a rhetorical question: peace is always better. But one needs the will (and courage) to seek it.

The most advanced common sense of all suggests that Ed regard these disturbances as an important lesson from the cosmos (the order of things, the Way), teaching him that it is time to find a better place to live. Once he's settled in, he can send a thank-you note to the noisy neighbors for being the catalysts of positive change. Besides, in terms of karma (in Buddhism that's his will, and the fruits of his will in action, not his fate), Ed's reaction to his neighbors' provocation will determine whether his next home is better or worse than his current one.

On the other end of the scale, Buddhist ethics would rank retaliation as the worst recourse. Why? Because people who knowingly disturb their neighbors on a regular basis, whether thoughtlessly or deliberately, are obviously troubled themselves. If Ed allows his neighbors' trouble to trouble him, all he gains is their trouble. If he tries to relieve his troubled feeling by retaliating, he'll only multiply his own troubles, escalating the conflict, or even committing a crime and going to jail. Should it get that far out of hand, remember that jail is, among many other things, a far less private place than Ed's home ever was, and the very opposite of what he supposedly wanted: peace and quiet. But if he moves away without retaliation, refusing to be troubled by their troubles, and grateful that they are guiding him to a better place, serenity can be his. This solution resonated with Ed, and also resolved the situation.

The world is full of provocation, always. Your philosophical challenge is to respond, or not respond, as wisely as you can. It is, after all, your present response that will determine your future circumstances. This holds true for any kind of provocation in life.

Melissa's Case: A Messy Divorce

I mentioned earlier the client facing the complicated breakup of her marriage. The way Melissa broached the subject with me was to ask, "What is 'the ethical way' to deal with a messy divorce?" Notice that she assumed there is only one way to deal ethically with a given situation. That stems from her intention to do the right thing, but still the first task of our dialogue was to challenge that assumption, to get her thinking about various ways of understanding "right," to see which notions were most compatible with her own (largely unarticulated) ideas about morality, and would also see her through the process.

Melissa was a sincere Christian, and so her religious ethics and personal morality centered on the Bible. She assumed the existence of a correspondingly monolithic system of secular ethics, which is what she wanted to draw on now. For those of you who are wondering why a Christian would bother with secular ethics at all, it may help to know that her husband, John, and her marriage, had been nonreligious. They didn't force any religion on their two kids, either. Living in the United States, Melissa knew that her divorce and its attendant issues of custody, property, alimony, and child support were going to be played out in a secular context: civil court.

Melissa's specific ethical concerns focused on the issue of *fairness*. State divorce laws increasingly prescribe an *equitable* (or fair) division of assets and sharing of parental responsibilities, though not necessarily an *equal* one. Thus the couple (or the court) must determine "What is *fair* in these circumstances?" This is a question right out of meta-ethical relativism, of course.

If Melissa's divorce escalated into a war, she knew very well it would be costly, both emotionally and financially. The court would end up imposing a settlement that would no doubt make her and John both unhappy, would not necessarily be best for the children either – and they would have paid an exorbitant price for it to boot! She wanted them to be able to work out their differences amicably, with mediation along the way, and with independent legal representation at the end to make sure that the state ratified their own terms. It was the only way she thought they could both hope to be satisfied with the outcome – and keep it from becoming emotionally or financially unaffordable. To accomplish this, they needed mutual goodwill, not necessarily an easy thing to maintain through the difficult breakup of a long-standing relationship.

So in sorting through various ethical positions to find the one most suited to her background, intuitions, and situation, Melissa gravitated toward other-centered ethics, combined with Martin Buber's notion of maintaining an I-thou relationship between her and John. For Buber, this amounts to treating the other always as a person (thou), and never as a thing (it). If she sustained a solely self-centered ethic, Melissa might start regarding her (soon to be ex-) husband as a kind of ATM for her and the kids. If he depersonalized her as well, the divorce could become as convoluted and bitter as you can imagine. But if they were thinking of each other, then even though their marriage failed, some mutually respectful and caring relationship would survive, and the inevitable conflicts could be resolved as reasonably, responsibly, calmly – and fairly – as possible.

So ethics are hardly contrary to your better interests: In fact, an ethical framework can help you make the best of a difficult situation.

Gary's Case: The Ethics of Going to Disney World

Another of my clients had a much happier dilemma, but still it stirred up a lot of dis-ease for him. Gary's plan was to take his children to Disney World. You might not see the problem immediately. But Gary, an ardent socialist, felt conflicted about it. How could he spend that much money on his kids' recreation when so many other children in the world desperately need food, clothing, and shelter?

Gary's own childhood had been materially deprived, but he'd become very successful professionally (and financially) in adulthood, earning his living as an aeronautical engineer. That's the American dream for you. But Gary was also experiencing guilt, because so many children were lacking fundamental necessities of life, while he was preparing to squander a small fortune taking his wife and kids to a theme park. Gary's family was certainly excited about the prospect of this vacation, and for them, accustomed to affluence, it did not seem extravagant at all.

This would also be an interesting case for psychotherapists and priests, who tend to get involved when they hear the word "guilt." While there are definitely psychological and perhaps theological dimensions to this case, Gary sought a philosophical resolution to his immediate ethical problem: how to justify taking his family on vacation.

Plato explained how harmful ideas are sometimes implanted in us by others whom we trust, such as our parents, when we are young, vulnerable, and credulous. Although these ideas may later exert unwholesome constricting influences on us – like mental straitjackets – we may defend them nonetheless because we mistakenly believe they are our own. Every human being needs to identify authentic ideas from and for himself – and unmask and reject inimical ideas disguised as old friends. A philosophical counselor can help him do this by means of a Socratic inquiry. The philosopher is like a midwife who helps deliver the client's ideas from the recesses of mind into the light of dialogue, so the client can determine whether they are genuinely his offspring or not.

Thus Gary discovered and confronted a "defining thought" from his early life. His parents had repeated a mantra to him over the years, to the effect that they were good because they were poor. Defining poverty as a virtue therefore made wealth a vice – and all these years later Gary felt guilty because he was affluent. So he resolved to reject the idea that poverty is a virtue (and wealth a vice), and once he did, his guilt abated. It took more time to do this than it takes to explain it, but it can be done.

Like a number of my clients, Gary had actually decided on a course of action before we met, but critically required an ethical justification for it – in this case, for going to Disney World. Aristotle's virtue ethics readily provided him with a new way of thinking to replace his parents' "poverty is good" mantra. Aristotle conceived of every virtue as a mean between two extremes of vice. In Gary's case, one extreme would be having a lot of money and spoiling his children rotten; the other, having a lot of money and spending nothing on his children. The virtuous Aristotelian mean, therefore, was to take his kids to Disney World. Then, to do good for others (and himself, by assuaging his remaining guilt), Gary could give an equal amount to charity. Everybody wins.

A guiding idea of philosophical counseling – whether focused on ethics or another of philosophy's many dimensions – is to work as much as possible in your present, with a view to your future. This can effect positive change. By contrast, spending too much of your present, and scheduling too much of your future, just to work on your past, is a recipe for changing nothing.

PHILOSOPHICAL EXERCISES

1. Elementary-level question: Boy Scouts and Girl Scouts used to be encouraged to do a good deed every day. If you need encouragement too, here it is: Go out and do a good deed today. But before you do, ask yourself, "What exactly makes it good? According to which ethical theories?"
2. Intermediate-level question: Think of something you have a strong moral opinion about, e.g., "Such-and-such is the right (or wrong) thing to do!" What makes it right (or wrong)? If you know someone who disagrees just as strongly with your opinion, what makes it wrong (or right) from their point of view? Is there an ethical system in which you could resolve your differences?
3. Advanced-level question: We have discussed justice only indirectly, but according to Plato, it should flow from an understanding of goodness. Can you give an example of justice having been done? Can you give an example of an injustice? How would you do justice to the injustice? (Be careful not to create more injustice than you alleviate.)
4. Everyday question: Are you experiencing dis-ease because of a personal moral dilemma or a professional ethical issue? If so, which theory in this chapter offers you a resolution, or at least points the way toward one?

3

ARE YOU GUIDED
BY REASON OR PASSION?

**Your soul is oftentimes a battleground, upon
which your reason and judgment wage war
against your passion and your appetite.**
– Khalil Gibran

If passion drives you, let reason hold the reins.
– Benjamin Franklin

H AS ANYONE EVER accused you of being "too rational" – moved
far more by intellect than by sentiment? Or has anyone ever
accused you of being "too emotional" – moved more by feelings than
by principles? Are your reason and passion sometimes or often in
conflict, with your better interests caught in the crossfire? Can these
two forces – the mind and the heart – be brought into more peaceful
coexistence? These are the Big Questions of this chapter.

Nicole and Alex: Two Contrasting Battlegrounds
Nicole and Alex haven't met one another, but they are two clients of
philosophical counseling who had similar problems, yet handled them
quite differently. They were both alcoholics, both very bright and
articulate, both mature adult students, and both wanting to do
graduate studies. As well, their souls were battlegrounds between
passion and reason. Nicole won her battle, while Alex is still fighting
his. Why? It has something to do with their respective willingness to
use philosophy as an agent of change.

Nicole's parents were both alcoholics, so she had a bad beginning in
life as far as parental example is concerned. For these and other

reasons, she had an unhappy childhood and a turbulent adolescence. Nicole had gravitated toward alcohol in order to escape unhappiness, but of course alcoholism is an addictive disease (not a dis-ease) that seems always to cause more unhappiness than it cures. Yet she was also an original and strong-minded thinker, who possessed an inner conviction that she could develop her intellectual resources and enjoy a better life than her parents. So Nicole's initial battle was between her passionate thirst for alcohol and her reasonable aspiration to earn a higher degree – passion versus reason. Note that she, at least, had the "luxury" of fighting a battle. Alcoholics without reasonable hopes might just succumb to drinking. Nicole won the first round of her battle by becoming a recovering alcoholic instead of a practicing one – the usual twelve-step program worked well for her.

Having quit drinking, she was ready for the next round, which pitted her emotional fears and insecurities against her intellectual interests and ambitions – passion versus reason, round two. This is where philosophy helped. In her case, the existentialist idea that she was not condemned by her past circumstances, and could reinvent herself as a graduate student if she made and willed that choice, mobilized her inner confidence and courage. She overcame her anxieties, applied to graduate schools, and was accepted into a program where she is now thriving. Her destructive thirst for alcohol having been transformed into a constructive thirst for learning, Nicole's passion can now be guided by reason, instead of opposing it. This guidance of passion by reason is advised by many philosophers from diverse traditions, for example Khalil Gibran:

> **Therefore let your soul exalt your reason to the height of passion, that it may sing; and let it direct your passion with reason, that your passion may live through its own daily resurrection, and like the phoenix rise above its own ashes.**
>
> **– Khalil Gibran**

In contrast, neither of Alex's parents were alcoholics. Like Nicole, Alex was an original and creative thinker, had also been through a turbulent adolescence, and had turned to alcohol partly as a means of escaping his self-conception as a "misfit." Alex was in fact quite extroverted and popular, and had an active social life, but never felt as though he "belonged" with any group of friends. He preferred to develop his own ways of thinking about things, and aspired to turn those thoughts into an original philosophical system – or at least a graduate degree. So, like Nicole, Alex had a passionate thirst for alcohol and a reasonable aspiration for graduate studies. But unlike Nicole, Alex did not quit drinking. As a result, the time and energy absorbed by Alex's alcoholism detracted from his academic preparation. His grades were good (excellent, considering his drinking habit), but not as good as they could have been. He applied to graduate schools, but was not accepted. As well, Alex's progress in philosophical counseling would be limited unless he quit drinking and gave expression to philosophy as a change in his lifestyle – not just as an interesting distraction between (or during) drinks. Alex did feel helped by philosophical counseling, and probably was to an extent, but he did not win the first crucial battle between his destructive thirst for alcohol and constructive ambition for intellectual development. Alex's passion thus far defeated his reason.

This is not to say that Alex is a "lost cause," or doomed to failure, or anything of the kind. Everyone progresses or regresses on his or her own unique path, and every path has its own particular twists and turns. Every snowflake is unique, as is every wave in the sea. Yet all snowflakes, like all waves, are governed by the same underlying laws of nature. Human beings are like this too. And one of the underlying laws of human nature is that passion and reason compete incessantly in the human soul, like two would-be drivers fighting over the wheel of a car. Another law is that we are usually better off when passion fuels the engine and reason steers the vehicle.

OVERVIEW OF THE BATTLEGROUND

A plethora of great thinkers have addressed this fundamental conflict, and here's a very brief overview. When philosophers use the word "reason," we don't just mean logic. We are referring to the human ability to be rational, which comes from the Greek word *ratio*, meaning balance or equilibrium. This means actively making sense of circumstances, and using understanding to maintain equilibrium, rather than passively being swept away by circumstances and carried away by emotion. When philosophers use the word "passion," we don't just mean passionate love. It's our way of referring to all the emotions and desires that human beings are heir to, and especially our appetites and aversions. That covers a lot of territory.

Ancient Greek philosophers tended to indulge their reason and passions alike, hoping to perfect the former and outgrow the latter. According to Plato, Socrates breathed a sigh of relief once his sex drive had been sufficiently diminished by age, allowing him to exercise reason alone, unsullied by sexual desire. He likened it to becoming sane after a long bout of madness. If you've ever been madly in love, you'll know what he meant.

> **Love is a grave mental disease.**
>
> **– Plato**

In a more modern era, Simone de Beauvoir experienced much the same thing: after menopause, she said, she suddenly saw the world clearly for the first time, as though a dense fog had lifted.

> **Old women take pride in their independence; they begin at last to view the world with their own eyes . . . sane and mistrustful, they often develop a pungent cynicism.**
>
> **– Simone de Beauvoir**

To Buddha and the other Forest Sages of India, who drew many of their fundamental teachings from the Bhagavad Gita and the Upanishads, the most basic human struggle is not the external quest for food, shelter, or a mate – or a trip to Disney World or a larger 401(k) – but rather the attempt to rule our passions – our internal desires and cravings. If they are not contained by meditative practice, or restrained by practical reason, or expressed by wholesome habits, or transcended by conscious awakening, the incessant grasping gives rise to attachments, which are thought to be the source of all our suffering. Unhealthy expression of one's appetites and aversions causes all kinds of dis-ease; but so does their unhealthy repression by misguided societal forces.

The Jewish cabalists, the Christian gnostics, the Islamic Sufis, the Hindu Brahmanas, and the Buddhist awakened ones all teach theories, techniques, and methods for reasonably guiding the self's passions. Whether you practice uniting with the Cosmic Godhead or discovering the Cosmic Void is up to you. The pathways of self-mastery resemble the spokes of a wheel: They all lead, sooner or later, to the center. (Some, however, are more convoluted, and therefore more difficult to follow, than others.) What lies at the center? For some, God; for others, emptiness; for all, equilibrium. That is, in fact, the enlightened meaning of "jihad": a mastery of one's own passions – and not a "holy war" against non-Muslims. Similarly, "nirvana," which most westerners equate with perfection or heaven, means a state of having cooled one's passions – "being cool" with respect to sensuous phenomena, or extinguishing the flame of desire. Being cool *is* being in nirvana: you are fully functional, because you are dis-ease free.

> **Arjuna asked: "My Lord! Tell me, what is it that drives a person to sin, even against his or her will and as if by compulsion?"**
>
> **Lord Sri Krishna said: "It is desire, it is aversion, born of passion. Desire consumes and corrupts everything. It is the human's greatest enemy."**
>
> **– Bhagavad Gita**

Buddhism is reason.

– Nichiren Daishonin

The Chinese sages are essentially agreed, believing that it is reason and not passion that gives rise to virtue (and passion but not reason that gives rise to vice). As Lao-tzu wrote, "He who conquers others is mighty; he who conquers himself is wise."

Despite such abundant and lofty influences from around the globe and across the millennia, most people usually find it difficult to restrain passion by the exercise of reason alone. Passion wins out so often, in fact, that many believe humans are "hardwired" to be that way. Long before the notion of "hardwiring" became current, the essential idea was enshrined in the Roman Catholic doctrine of original sin, invented by Saint Augustine. Yet even he prayed in his *Confessions*, "Lord, make me chaste – but not yet!" He wanted to be rational rather than desirous (passionate) – eventually. And it was, of course, passion that led him to pray for the postponement of its own demise, like a smoker promising to quit . . . after one last cigarette. Or an alcoholic, after one final binge.

So are we somehow born flawed, whether by Genesis or evolution? And if so, is it futile to attempt to conquer passion with reason? If not, how can we go about it? And, are we really supposed to? We are, after all, physical entities, and sustaining life itself requires that we regularly satisfy bodily appetites – primarily thirst, hunger, love, and affection. Even our reason would agree that we must satisfy these in order to be able to exercise reason itself. If you are thirsty, hungry, horny, or simply starved for affection, it might cost you a great effort to perform higher cognitive functions (like developing your philosophy of life) until that appetite is temporarily sated. Highly creative people can transform their passionate energies into great art, which sometimes means leading thoroughly unreasonable lives. Besides, not everyone can do this, or should do this, or can make a living doing it, or can survive making a living doing it.

But with a little guidance, almost everyone can transform their passionate energies into the art of living reasonably. So your goal shouldn't be to eradicate your passions; it should be to use your reason to channel them into beneficial, rather than detrimental, forms of expression.

From this way of thinking, it is clearer why people who do not fear death are powerful – for good or ill. Most parents would sacrifice their lives for their children's. Firefighters risk and lose their lives for strangers. Soldiers give their lives for their country. Such sacrifice is possible when passion for one's own life takes a backseat to principles of duty toward others, or other causes – a victory of reason over passion. It can also be interpreted as the victory of a passion for serving others over a passion for preserving the self. It can even be interpreted as a way of making one's life meaningful, by sacrificing oneself for a "good cause."

Thus courage can be good or bad: The fearlessness of firefighters (for example) is devoted to saving lives, which is a beneficial passion guided by right reason; the fearlessness of terrorist suicide bombers is devoted to taking lives, which is a detrimental passion guided by wrong reason.

In modern times, Freud painted a particularly grim portrait of the struggle between passion and reason, introducing a third element into the conflict: the unconscious. If we are aware of a given desire, we can enlist reason to find the best way to satisfy it. But if we remain unaware, we can't reason our way toward optimal satisfaction, but we still may be driven to try to scratch the itch at all costs. We can become enslaved to our unfulfilled or unfulfillable unconscious desires, and passions lurking in the deeper recesses of our minds may twist our reason into deformed pathways that show up in daily life even if we are unaware of their ultimate source. Entire lives can be ruined or wasted in the process. Better, then, that we get to know our own passions, conscious and unconscious alike, so that reason can help us express them constructively.

Not everything unconscious is bad or devoted to passions either. We can even reason unconsciously, such as when we solve problems in our sleep. The chemist Kekulé, who discovered the shape of the benezene molecule, famously experienced just that. He had been mulling over the possible shape for years, with no apparent success. Instead, his breakthrough came one day while he was dozing on a bus.

He awoke with the precise image of the molecule's ringlike structure in his mind. Many people have learned to work on problems in their sleep, or have accidentally discovered how to give themselves the instructions to do it. Dreams are another way of working on problems, in which the imaginative, intuitive, and integrative aspects of the human mind came into play. Dreams are very rational, but come dressed in fantastic garbs.

While reason and passion both operate at the deepest levels of consciousness, and while both are obvious enough in the flow of daily life, one of humanity's most enduring goals is to be freed from the intrusion of passion into the higher reaches of thought. As we strive, however, it is important to remember that reason, too, can be destructive. To name just one example: the Holocaust taught us many things, among them how abhorrent calculating reason can become in the service of fanatical hatred. Humans are both the most rational and the most emotional of creatures on the face of the earth. Can we balance these forces to attain the best and avoid the worst of humanity? It isn't easy, but we must try.

BALANCING REASON AND PASSION

Of all the capacities our big brains endow us with – language, tools, culture, the ability to shape our environments and structure our lives, and so on – the exercise of reason is our most astonishing power. Still, the more we know, the more we realize we don't know. Even so, reason has gotten us down from the trees, out of the caves, into the sky, under the sea, around the moon, and may yet get us beyond our solar system.

Each person conceives of himself or herself as perfectly rational, yet believes that *other* people act in the most irrational ways. Thomas Hobbes rightly observed that people are prone to envying one another's beauty, wealth, power, influence, accomplishments, and the like, but noted (with relish) that he never met anyone who envied another person's wisdom. That speaks volumes about human conceit – a combination of vanity and arrogance.

Passion is never absent or completely contained. Nor should it be. And what an inhuman world it would be if it were! In the original *Star Trek*, Dr. McCoy is constantly frustrated by Mr. Spock's inability to emote, without which McCoy cannot communicate his human ideals. A world of Mr. Spocks, without any Captain Kirks or Dr. McCoys, would be thoroughly logical but devoid of emotion, and therefore devoid of caring and empathy too. Strong feelings, whether positive (love, kindness, gratitude) or negative (hatred, envy, frustration), impel us to action for their sakes, not for ours. Passion cannot be dispelled by reason alone, and must always be expressed. While the best use of passion is compassion, human passions can be explosive, or smolder underground before suddenly bursting into flame. The key is to shape the direction of the explosion and contain the fire, so that the feeling is expressed while its damage is minimized and its benefit maximized. Even positive passions must have controls in place, as when love allows you (or obliges you) to tolerate some dis-ease, but hopefully not too much. Recent findings in neuropsychology, like those reported by Antonio Damasio in *Descartes's Error*, show us that human beings actually require emotions in order to reason effectively. People are not machines, nor should we behave like machines. (More on this in chapter 9.)

Philosophy can guide us in finding a successful balance in this inherent, incessant struggle between reason and passion, containing the damaging effects of passions, while formulating reasonable principles to live by. Reason can temper passion, loosening the grip of emotion and providing constructive ways to express destructive feelings. Passion conquers reason in the short run, for good or ill. But reason conquers passion in the long run, and more for good than ill. Falling in love makes us behave in (often delightfully) irrational ways, while being angry makes us "lose our heads" and do things we may later regret. Either way, passions tend to flare "in the heat of the moment" – a heat that temporarily melts the power of reason. But our personal, social, civil, professional, and political lives are ultimately governed by principles, and these principles are chosen by reason, and the consorts of reason: including reflection, interpretation, and experiment.

You can save yourself a lot of dis-ease simply by expecting everyone (including yourself) to assert they are rational – but *not* expecting anyone to act rationally in the short run. And, expecting everyone to deny they are governed by passion – but expecting them to behave passionately in the short run. That way, when you run across more evolved beings who have managed to strike some kind of balance, you'll be pleasantly surprised – and you won't waste time and energy expecting what doesn't come naturally from the herd. In chapter 12, we'll look more in depth at the drawbacks of expectation.

This simplistic model runs into trouble, however, because passion and reason are not strictly separable. Unlike sugar and flour, or coffee and tea, they are not so readily contained in separate jars. You might, for example, have a passion for living by those principles you have rationally laid out for yourself. The following cases illustrate the complex interplay between reason and passion in individuals' lives.

Jack's Case: The Existential Tightrope

Jack was a successful physician and author, and a pillar of his community. He had been married to Joanna for twenty-five years, and they had two children in college. Jack and Joanna loved one another, and neither one wished to end their marriage. So why did Jack seek philosophical counseling? It turns out that he was keeping a mistress, a younger woman named Sylvia, with whom he also shared a slice of life. Sylvia was a graduate student, and Jack was paying her rent and helping her make ends meet. They were also passionate lovers. Joanna more or less knew about Jack and Sylvia – it's almost impossible to live with someone in wedlock for twenty-five years and not know more about them than you sometimes care to – but she didn't view Sylvia as a fatal threat to her marriage. On the contrary, she thought that Jack needed a fling (perhaps even a serious one) to maintain his emotional equilibrium, and she thought he'd get over it and return to his "senses" – that is, his "reasonable" life with her. And perhaps Joanna was correct.

But was why did Jack seek philosophical counseling? Wasn't everyone "cool" with the arrangement? Jack himself wasn't. He felt caught in a conflict between the rationality of his marriage to Joanna and the passion of his involvement with Sylvia. A cynic might observe that Jack wanted to have his cake and eat it too, but Jack was not exactly the gluttonous type. He was both a serious intellectual and an observant Jew. And technically, he wasn't committing adultery because Sylvia wasn't married (if you want to split patriarchal religious hairs).

What Jack sought was a reasoned explanation for his passions to maintain his marriage and his mistress alike. That's different from a psychological "diagnosis" or a moral sanction. Jack knew that his present situation was not a psychological response to some childhood trauma. It had nothing to do with Oedipus either. Nor did he see it as a "midlife crisis." Nor did he feel particularly guilty. He wasn't seeking moral absolution. He wanted to understand, in reasoned terms, exactly what kind of creature is a man such as himself, and what kind of social arrangements are sustainable, for him and for those he cares about. These are essentially philosophical questions.

The evolutionary essence of the human male is to be a protector and provider for his family. In turn, he needs their appreciation for his prowess. Jack had done this job very well for Joanna and their children, and she certainly appreciated him, but of course their children didn't. Having grown up with affluence, they took it for granted, along with their college tuition. (Don't expect gratitude from your kids.) But Sylvia didn't grow up affluent, and she really did appreciate Jack's ability to provide. Jack's unfulfilled passion for appreciation as a provider was bound to attract someone like Sylvia, who needed provision and was capable of showing her appreciation for it. All this operates on a sociobiological level, and is independent of the specifics of their relationship: It is a fundamental phenomenon in human relations. It does not manifest in this way with everyone, but it occurs with many people in many cultures. And different societies have found different ways of dealing with it.

Monogamy is workable for some couples, and preferable for most, especially where life is a struggle, or where both parents are heavily invested in their children's success, or where there is a match between soul mates, or where the culture strongly reinforces (or compels) it. But given current divorce rates in the developed world, long-term monogamous marriage has become the exception rather than the rule. At one extreme, the French appear less fastidious than most when it comes to these matters: At President François Mitterrand's funeral, his widow and his mistress openly consoled one another on global television. By contrast, Americans still suffer from a puritanical hangover – as well as from the double standard of supporting the world's biggest pornography industry. Thus President Clinton was impeached for his affair with a White House intern. Once can scarcely imagine a first lady and an American president's mistress consoling one another at his funeral.

There is no general rule for what any affair – whether casual or serious – will do to a marriage. Some wives will want to divorce their husbands merely for looking at other women, whereas other wives maintain lovers on the side while their husbands remain faithful. In my opinion, the ideal arrangement is monogamy wherever it can be sustained. But in my experience as a counselor, I have seen marriages fail yet also survive partly because of affairs. We will revisit this question in chapter 8.

So where does this leave Jack? Philosophically, existentialism is a good place for Jack to begin to reconcile his reason and passion. Nietzsche describes him in the following way: "Man is a rope stretched between the animal and the superman – a rope over an abyss." The animalistic facet of man must express itself at times, yet man's consciousness tells him he is more than an animal. By the same token, man's aspiration to be godlike expresses itself as well, and sometimes arrogantly: the superman flouts common conceptions of right and wrong ("herd morality" for Nietzsche). Yet man's consciousness tells him that if he were truly a god he would not have to flout the rules at all. So he must be less than a god. That strands him on the tightrope: Our self-conceptions as animals and as deities are both connected, and are also both flawed. Jack has spent a lot of time on this tightrope lately, and is looking for a way to get down. He is not afraid to find one.

The way down is into the abyss itself, which some find scary to contemplate, but which is actually a wonderful place. It is there that we discover our true human nature; neither animal nor deity. The abyss is where existential philosophy meets Buddhist psychology, and finds its reasons for passion. Jack must discover who he is independent of Joanna's and Sylvia's appreciation, for only then can he truly appreciate himself, and thus avoid potentially conflicting entanglements with others. Jack's passion for reason may lead him beyond Joanna and Sylvia both, or may bring them all on a group excursion into the abyss.

Barry's Case: Confronting the Unthinkable

Reason and passion vie for supremacy in Barry's case as well. Here again they are not strictly opposed: Reason is harnessed to a sophisticated set of noble passions, including a capacity for unselfish love, an abiding faith in justice, and a burning desire to understand and make sense of painful circumstances.

Barry was completely satisfied with his nineteen-year marriage, and prided himself on being a good husband, father, and provider to Sue and their children. But Sue had been growing increasingly dissatisfied for years, though she hadn't really communicated this to Barry. Ultimately her secret came out in one of the most painful ways imaginable: One day Barry discovered his wife in bed with his best friend, Sam. There is no more brutal confrontation of passion and reason. Making matters worse still, Sam's wife, Patty, was also Sue's friend and neighbor, and the two families' children played together regularly. Both families were being devastated for the price of one affair.

When Barry walked into the bedroom that day, if he had followed his most primitive human passion, he might have grabbed a gun and shot both his wife and best friend – and our justice system would have recognized it as a *crime of passion*, which might ultimately have mitigated his sentence if he were convicted. Had he instead plotted a cold-blooded revenge murder, his crime would have been more severely regarded. Our laws reflect an essential moral distinction between crimes done on the spur of the moment impelled by extreme emotions, and those calculated in advance (even if initiated by the same cause – in this case, the discovery of an affair). We are held less culpable for the former. The implicit assumption is that reason, given time to function, should be able to overrule any passion.

In point of fact, Barry did not respond in any violent way to the awful revelation of his wife and friend's betrayal. His very strong moral convictions enabled him to absorb extreme emotional discomfort without retaliation, and his intellectual commitment to the idea of justice allowed him to seek a nonviolent resolution. That is, his reason commanded him to ride out the storm of his passions. And yet his reason was also grounded in passion – namely, his deep concern for the well-being not only of himself but also of his children, and even his wife, as well as for Sam's wife and children. (Understandably, Barry was less concerned about Sam's well-being. Barry was not pretending to be serene.)

Barry's basic philosophy of life, which saw him through this extended crisis, was essentially Christian. He believed that wrong-doers would be condemned by their very actions ("As ye sow, so shall ye reap"), and that he, as a victim of wrongdoing, must not perpetrate yet more wrong in a vain attempt to right wrongs done to him ("Turn the other cheek"). This kept Barry on an even keel to begin with, and allowed him to focus his passion on justice, instead of retaliation or revenge.

So why did Barry seek philosophical counseling? Because although he had ample faith in God's ultimate judgment, he still sought guidance in applying reason to, and expressing passion about, the here and now. And the "here and now" was becoming more complicated by the minute, for its transpired that Sue announced her intention to divorce Barry, while Sam announced his intention to divorce Patty. It seemed clear to Barry that this was a prelude to Sue and Sam uniting openly. To complicate matters even further, Barry was in the throes of an enforced career change: His employer had just downsized and let him go. So the two things that Barry had held most dear, and that had been rock solid in his life, namely his marriage and his job, evaporated overnight. Barry's life was in turmoil, and yet he remained mostly calm and functional. Nor did he resort to medication. Instead, he developed a constructive interpretation of his circumstances that allowed him to weather this severe emotional storm.

Barry's reason told him that he was shedding his skin, metamorphosing, being transported to a new and as yet unknown stage of his life. That can be exciting, as well as daunting. Barry's willingness to exercise his freedom to interpret events – even hurtful events – in a positive rather than a negative light, encouraged me to introduce an even more daring idea to him: existentialist again, but this time Sartre's brand instead of Nietzsche's. Since Barry had automatically shouldered the responsibility of his freedom to reason, I suggested that he might also consider whether he had any responsibility for his passions too. Jean-Paul Sartre would claim that he did.

If you say, "Sue slept with Sam and made Barry upset," Sartre would reply that while Sue and Sam bear responsibility for what they do, Barry bears responsibility for what he feels. (This is also the Stoic's conclusion, but for different reasons.) One has to be careful here: This idea is both powerful and empowering, but not everyone is ready to accept it. People who feel completely victimized by circumstance will be made worse by it, until they are ready to accept their share of responsibility for what befalls them. If you are struck by lighting, you are surely not responsible for the atmosphere's electrical discharge. But possibly you were responsible for playing golf during a thunderstorm. You see? It's a question of how you play the odds. You might play them well and still be unlucky, but that's no excuse for playing them badly and then blaming bad luck.

It requires wisdom to accept exactly the right measure of responsibility for events that impact your life. If you accept too much, you might become a solipsist – that is, a person who thinks she is the only one in the world, hence responsible for it all. Sartre himself flirted with solipsism at times. But if you accept too little, you might fall prey to the widespread but pernicious doctrine of victimology: that everyone's a complete hostage of their personal past circumstances and collective history, and can do nothing for themselves to improve their lot in life. Their main function is to seek compensation for what was "done" to them. This tragically misguided view cannot accept the wondrous gift of life, except as a great wrong done to oneself that needs somehow to be righted by others.

Since Barry did not embrace either of these damaged and damaging viewpoints, he was ready to contemplate his degree of responsibility in feeling worse – or better – about these sudden changes in his life.

> **. . . I say that man is condemned to be free. Condemned, because he did not create himself, yet he is nevertheless at liberty, and from the moment he is thrown into this world he is responsible for everything he does . . . man is responsible for his passion.**
>
> **– Jean-Paul Sartre**

Once again, this is where existentialist philosophy meets Buddhist psychology. For Sartre glimpsed a deep truth, namely that what we feel in response to events (passion) is at bottom a matter of how we understand the connection between ourselves and those events (reason). Right reason does not eliminate or anesthetize passion – that's what Stoicism (i.e., taking things "philosophically") tries to do. Right reason does even better: It allows the transformation of negative passions into positive ones. Although some existentialists glimpsed this truth in theory, they did not all discover the next step: applying it to their lives in practice. Like existentialism, Buddhist philosophy asserts that a person's psychological attitudes and emotions are changeable via right reasoning. Unlike existentialism, Buddhist philosophy also teaches techniques and practices for making the desired – and desirable – changes come to pass. Barry wanted to read more about these ideas on his own, and then discuss them with me. So I was happy to suggest some readings to him.

In a matter of months, Barry was able to make the best of, and even derive benefit from, what most people would have called a major crisis. He went through the divorce, got custody of his children, and embarked on a new career – in the spirit of undertaking a philosophical journey. There's a lot of talk these days about the Chinese ideogram for "crisis," which combines "danger" and "opportunity." If you can find your opportunity in danger, which might mean getting off that tightrope and exploring the abyss, then you were never in a crisis at all.

MASTERING FEAR

One handy use for your powers of reason is to distinguish between dis-ease and disease, and to sort out your emotional responses (both biological and psychological) and determine the degree to which it is possible to control them with your higher cognitive functions. Fear is among the most powerful emotions we struggle with, so if you can master fear you can master the others as well. Conquering fear does not necessarily mean that you stop feeling afraid, but it does mean that fear stops paralyzing you. Brave people experience fear too – just as they experience hunger, thirst, heat, cold, and pain – but are not debilitated by it. Only rash people are fearless, and that is not especially good for them.

You are biologically programmed with immediate physical responses triggered by any perceived threat – that evolutionarily ancient set of rapid physiological changes known as "fight or flight." Your body doesn't care which it ultimately does, because the preparation for either one is the same physiologically, and either way it is beyond ordinary conscious control. The "fight or flight" response takes place in the oldest part of the brain, the limbic system, which is pre-logical and not amenable to ideas, good or bad. The executive decision on how to act is made in the neocortex of your brain (the "new brain").

Still, you can learn to master fear and anxiety of all kinds, preventing them from escalating into something more debilitating. (Irrational phobias and similar disorders are another matter. Philosophy alone cannot do much to combat them, but hypnotherapy and behavior modification can.) Take my friend Bob as an example. He once jumped out of an airplane in order to impress his girlfriend. Standing out there on the strut, trying to summon the courage to step into thin air – there's an abyss for you – he was simply terrified. His mechanisms of self-preservation were in full panic, imploring him to get back into the plane and find a more mundane girlfriend if necessary. But he jumped anyway. His parachute opened, he floated to earth, and his girlfriend was suitably impressed. Although Bob never jumped again, he proved to his girlfriend and, more importantly, to himself, that he could in fact do it. Similarly, soldiers, martial artists, and others who prepare for combat learn to master elemental fear of death. For that matter, so do millions of ordinary people who fly daily on commercial airlines. If they can control the strongest of emotions, you can control them too, along with a host of weaker ones, using your reason and will. Your higher faculties are ultimately in charge, if you allow them to be, despite your biological programming.

BE MAJESTIC

When we move from biology to the realm of psychology, we encounter a different problem. Facing unpleasant but not life-threatening situations, such as being mocked or taunted, being treated unfairly, or being the victim of a nonviolent crime, causes mild to extreme dis-ease which is strongly (and sometimes detrimentally) recorded in memory. Unknown mechanisms synchronize recollections of the events themselves with recollections of bad feelings associated with them. The problem is that replaying an episode of dis-ease can feel like living through it again, because memories of bad feelings produce equivalently bad feelings. That's quite different from purely biological problems: Remembering having been terribly thirsty on a hot day, for example, doesn't make you thirsty all over again. But remembering a sad episode in your life can make you sad all over again. Even remembering a happy episode can make you sad, because you're not enjoying that happiness now. Then again, remembering a sad episode should also make you happy, because you're not enduring that sadness now. You can benefit from that symmetry. You're in charge of your own storehouse of memories, and you alone dispatch mental messengers to retrieve them. So why not choose to remember happy things instead of sad ones? And why not be happy that sad things have passed?

This loop comes into play when abused children repeat the familiar behavioral pattern and either marry abusers or abuse their own children in turn. But note that this doesn't always or necessarily happen. Some parents are scrupulously good to their children precisely because they themselves were tormented as children. There is no need to repeat mistakes from one generation to another. We are compelled to inherit our parents' genes, but we are not compelled to inherit their moral imperfections.

Being "emotionally scarred" is just a figure of speech. All the parts of your brain lit up by any given emotion, no matter how extreme, would appear normal in a physical exam: no actual scars or lesions. If you need five years of psychotherapy or ten years of psychoanalysis to cope with the figurative "scar," so be it. But you can also use your reason to distinguish between a permanent physical scar and a transient bad memory. You can even replace bad memories with good ones, starting right now, by exercising your will to experience something positive. In this way you can heal even a "wounded" psyche. Those little quotation marks make a big difference: they signify dis-ease, not disease.

There is an emotion beyond happiness and sadness together, and that is majesty. A philosophy student of mine, who had excellent musical instincts but whose musical education had been neglected, began to listen to baroque music at my suggestion. While its harmonic complexity and deep structures appealed strongly to her intelligence, she became immediately overwhelmed by its emotional content as well. "Is it all so sad?" she asked me one day. I replied that it was not merely sad but majestic. Many of the baroque composers were not only great creative artists; they also lived in a culture that afforded them an enriched perspective on life – a window on the world – that precious few artists have been privileged to enjoy since. As a result, their overall view of life became majestic, and they were able to infuse their compositions with that majesty. Their music, like all great music, captures the most profound experiences of joy and sorrow alike – and everything in between, across the entire emotional spectrum. So if that philosophy student had been a happier person herself, she might well have asked "Is it all so joyous?" My reply would have been consistent: "It is not merely joyous; it is majestic."

And this is precisely how you can choose to view your life: as majestic. You may never be able to make yourself happy or sad or indifferent by an act of will, but you can always choose to locate your emotions on a bigger map: the map of the nobility of your existence, even in the face of its impermanence. Every human being can experience the wonder of being alive, and episodes of happiness or sadness only add to the beauty and majesty of it all. Think of yourself as a majestic mountain in the vast human range. Describe yourself as the great environmental philosopher John Muir described the peaks of Yosemite:

> **Some lean back in majestic repose; others, absolutely sheer or nearly so for thousands of feet, advance beyond their companions in thoughtful attitudes, giving welcome to storms and calms alike . . . in stern, immovable majesty, how softly these mountain rocks are adorned and how fine and reassuring the company they keep.**
>
> **– John Muir**

FAITH

Reason alone cannot answer all the questions that human beings are capable of asking. Big questions like "What is life?," "What is consciousness?," and "Is there anything after death?" remain opaque to the light of thought, so faith still has a large role to play in human affairs. Those who cannot live with the inevitable uncertainties that come with a life of reason often turn to religious faith, either seeking comfort from God in the face of the unknown (and unknowable), or in hopes of finding answers to these mysteries in scripture. Faith is very strong passion, for better or worse. Faith in divine justice or simply happy endings helps some people endure the unendurable without making matters worse for others. Yet faith can also impel people to seek violent and premature death for themselves and others, leaving the world a worse place than they found it. So if someone says he possesses great faith, he holds a sword that can cut both ways: for war or for peace. Faith is often inimical to the exercise of reason, which makes it a strong yet also a potentially blinding passion.

By contrast, doubt is an important tool in exercising reason, and is complementary to faith. So people relying entirely on faith will find it difficult to exercise doubt, which will restrict their ability to make philosophical inquiries, leaving them, perhaps, passionately wedded to fairy tales or superstitions. Having faith does not eliminate the experience of doubting, but it may cause you to conceal your doubt, which only leads to unhappiness. But uncertainty and unhappiness, or the commitment to superstitions, especially if shared by large groups, can lead to zealotry, even rabid intolerance – and definitely unreasonable behavior. People of faith suppressing their own doubts often seek to impose their views on everyone, in the vain hope that this will alleviate their doubts. It never does, of course. For me, the acid test of anyone's faith is whether they can simply worship their god in peace, without attempting to embroil or coerce the whole world in their undertaking.

Bertrand Russell observed that people's goodness or badness does not come from their religious faith; their faith magnifies what is already present. Every faith-based religion has the capacity to do this, for better or worse. No faith is reasonable; all faith is passionate. Walker Percy, a great American novelist, philosopher, and social scientist, was agnostic for most of his life. When in later years he sought to profess a faith, his "short list" of religious candidates consisted of Judaism, Roman Catholicism, and Protestantism. After exhausting his reason trying to figure out what choice to make, he finally became a Roman Catholic. When asked why, he said that among the three, Catholicism was the most unbelievable, and therefore the most worthy of his faith!

It is extremely important to emphasize that the good or ill that people do in the world does not depend on whether they have ascended the higher peaks of reason, and likewise does not depend on the depth of their wells of faith. So if you want to improve your life, and also make the world a better place to inhabit, then it's time to consider another perspective on reason and passion, which doesn't view them as direct competitors.

Cruel men believe in a cruel God and use their belief to excuse their cruelty. Only kindly men believe in a kindly God, and they would be kindly in any case.

– Bertrand Russell

REASON AND PASSION TOGETHER: THE TEN WORLDS

As we've seen thus far, much philosophy has been devoted to the question of reason versus passion, and how exercising one often means ignoring the other. Philosophers Eastern and Western have long supposed that the human being is at war with himself, and that the fundamental conflict is between intellect and emotion. However, there's another view of this subject that's well worth considering, and I want to introduce it to you here. It's Buddha's idea of the Ten Worlds, and was applied most effectively to daily life by Nichiren Daishonin in thirteenth century Japan. Nichiren was a kind of Japanese Socrates. A wise and benevolent teacher, also a Buddhist monk and scholar, he got into serious political trouble by exposing the corruptions of his day – especially how Buddhism itself had been corrupted by the ruling classes, and was being abused to control and impoverish the masses, instead of enlighten and uplift them. (Every religion passes through this stage. Some remain there a long time.) As you can imagine, Nichiren made powerful enemies by telling these truths. He also made a few powerful friends. He narrowly escaped execution, and endured harsh exiles. But he survived to become a great exponent of the Lotus Sutra, which embodies, among other things, the teaching of the Ten Worlds.

These Ten Worlds are actually ten different states of mind, which you experience simultaneously. They're all present together, like so many ingredients in a stew. But at any given moment, depending on what you're thinking or doing, or on what's going on around you, you'll experience one of these states on a priority basis. It will leap to the forefront of your consciousness, and overshadow the others, but only for a while. One state changes to another, many times per day (and also when you're sleeping). What are these states? Their names are hell, hunger, instinct, anger, tranquillity, rapture, learning, realization, helping, and awakening. What characterizes them? First I'll summarize each state, and afterward revisit Barry's case showing how they interchange in practice.

Hell: Whenever something terrible or even disagreeable happens, you get upset or distraught. Any anxiety, fear, or other dis-ease can be hellish. Diseases like chronic depression, or the depressed state of bipolarity (manic depression) are also hellish. So is the boss from hell, the job from hell, the date from hell, or the marriage from hell. People consumed by hatred are in hell. Whenever we experience pain or suffering, we are in hell. It's the worst state to inhabit, beyond reason and passion alike.

Hunger: This doesn't refer to physical appetite, but to craving. People who are obsessed have this hunger, as do people who are addicted to alcohol, drugs, or other things. Many obese people have a terrible hunger – whether for meaning, purpose, love, or affection in their lives – which they try but fail to satisfy with food. They eat constantly, yet remain hungry. These kinds of hungers are extreme (or unnatural) passions.

Instinct: These are your animalistic appetites and drives, given to you by bodily nature. Normal needs for air, food, drink, sleep, love, affection, excretion, and sex are all instinctive. They are not learned. No one taught you to feel thirsty, tired, lovesick, or horny. You don't need a clock to know when to eat; your stomach tells you. Our animalistic appetites are normal (or natural) passions.

Anger: This means more than losing your temper. Some people seem constantly enraged; others, intermittently cranky. Others still become irritated by a given stimulus, whether a car alarm on their street or the odor of cheap perfume (or no perfume) on the subway. Still others seem bent on some crusade, and are perpetually and aggressively proselytizing their agenda, whatever it is. Still others are always argumentative or hypercritical. Yet others are arrogant or sadistic. These kinds of angers are unreasonable and exaggerated passions.

Tranquillity: This is a peaceful state in which your mind is unperturbed, like the unrippled surface of a pond on a perfectly calm day. You often attain a tranquil mental state after strenuous physical exertion, or after a heavy meal, or during meditation, or on a long drive, or when daydreaming, or in some phases of sleep. Nothing in particular is disturbing you, nor are you disturbing yourself. Tranquillity is neutrality, and absence of passion and reason alike.

Rapture: This is a state of sudden happiness, or even ecstasy. Perhaps you received a raise or a promotion at work. Maybe you got a personal makeover, or just bought your dream home. Perhaps you proposed and she said yes, or he proposed and you said yes. Maybe your team won a big game. Perhaps you got a pleasant surprise. Maybe the medical test results came back negative and gave you a new lease on life. Nothing feels better than rapture, while it lasts. It is the most joyous passion, but for that very reason it cannot last.

Learning: In this state you are exercising your cognitive skills, flexing your intellectual muscles. You might be learning a new language, a new concept, a new piece of music, a new game. You might be cramming for an exam, researching a term paper, or surfing the Web. You might be catching up on current events or planning a trip. Whatever you're up to, your thinking mind is engaged and in high gear. You are a reasoning being.

Realization: Realization means discovery, creativity, invention, connection. Suppose you are studying geometry and have just learned the relation of the hypotenuse of a right-angled triangle to its other sides. That theorem was originally Pythagoras' realization. Similarly, Shakespeare realized *Macbeth,* Bach realized *The Well-Tempered Clavier,* Einstein realized that $E = mc^2$, and Salk realized the polio vaccine. You have surely realized many things yourself. Plato realized that people can and do realize ideas that others have previously realized. Jung realized that new realizations often take place simultaneously. Realization is reason inspired by creative passion.

Helping: I could not be writing these words, and you could not be reading them, without a lot of help from others. Parents, teachers, coaches, and caregivers are helpers. So are food producers and book producers. Firefighters, and all who risk their lives for others, are helpers. You are surely a helper too, at least sometimes. The helping state of mind is essentially a giving one. In its higher aspects it seeks nothing in return, aiming only to replace others' dis-ease with ease. Helpers of this kind are called "bodhisattvas." Their – and your – ultimate purpose is to help others awaken more fully. They – and you – are lamps that light the Way. Helping is reason motivated by compassion.

Awakening: Many people walk or talk in their sleep. Not many can drive that way, at least not for long. Whatever you can do in your sleep, you can do better awake (except sleep itself). The other nine worlds are partially awakened states of mind; some more so, others less. The world of full awakening is Buddha's state of mind. The Lotus Sutra teaches that you are already a Buddha, but you may not fully realize it. This is the only state in which even pain and suffering are born with ease. It is immune to hell. It is the best state to inhabit. And nothing prevents you from inhabiting it, except your other states of mind.

Now let's briefly revisit Barry's case, to illustrate how all these ten worlds manifested at various stages. For a long time, Barry was in a state of rapture with Sue. And he was a good helper to her and their children. He had tranquillity in his home life and at his job. Through all this, in turn, he was able to satisfy his animal instincts too. When he discovered Sue in bed with Sam, he immediately entered hell. He experienced burning anger at Sam, and hungered to return to a state of rapture with Sue. He learned to contain his negative emotions, learned about Sue's hidden discontents, and learned many things about divorce and custody proceedings. He realized that he was going through a major transformation in his life, realized that he could mobilize inner resources to meet the challenges, and realized too that there were many helpers in the world to lend him support, encouragement, and advice. Through all this, he still had to be a helper and guide to his children. And amazingly, Barry also experienced the serenity to deal with all these other states of mind. Thus Barry continuously inhabited, and moved among, all ten worlds. So do we all.

> **To different minds, the same world is a hell, and a heaven.**
>
> **– Ralph Waldo Emerson**

THE WHOLE TRUTH

Now it's time to let you in on a little secret. I have told you the truth about the Ten Worlds, but not the whole truth. You see, I introduced them from the standpoint of the traditional debate on passion versus reason. As we saw earlier in this chapter, most philosophies, Eastern and Western, have generally sought to conquer passion and extol reason. Passions are portrayed as bad, reason as good. Nichiren's teachings, which are thought to represent an advanced teaching of Buddha, say something quite different. With the exception of the fully awakened state, each and every one of the other nine states of mind can give rise to both helpful and harmful consequences. This is very important to bear in mind – whichever state you're in. Let me give you some examples.

We know that hell is bad. What good can come of it? For one thing, great works of art can emerge from a mind in hell. Van Gogh is one example, Dante another. Closer to our times, Jim Morrison (of the Doors) and Jimi Hendrix are other examples. Beautiful painting, literature, poetry, and music can come from hell. Also, many people who admire and appreciate such works become grateful that their own hells are not so bad compared with these.

We know that hunger (as in craving) is bad. What good can come of it? For one thing, great social or political reforms are often brought about by leaders who hunger or thirst for justice. Nichiren himself was one good example, as was Martin Luther King Jr. One can also crave truth, as scientists sometimes do for years until they experience realization. Kepler and Pasteur are two among many examples. If such hunger is subordinated to a higher cause and remains uncorrupted by anger, it can be a means to a worthy end.

We know that the debate on instinct is still raging. For example, look at the vast variety of attitudes concerning sex, one of our strongest instinctive drives. Some cultures are open and natural about its expression; others are freaked out and repressive. In the Ten Worlds teaching, the instinctive state of mind is neither good nor evil: What really counts is what you decide to do with it. If you express your sexual desire through love with a willing (and not otherwise committed) partner, that's good. If you go out and rape somebody, that's evil.

We know that anger is generally bad. What good can come of it? Sometimes we need the force of conviction to demonstrate our seriousness, or to take a stand. It may be necessary at times to be adamant or even vehement in making a point or serving a cause. Suppose you want to make your child stop playing with matches, but he is too young to understand the reason why. If you convey just enough emotional displeasure when he does it, he will sense your emotion and will stop doing it – either to please you or for fear of your displeasure. You are not angry with him, but you need to protect him from himself. Controlled passion can be helpful, as when used to avert harm, and can therefore be good.

We are habituated to believe that tranquillity is generally good. What ill can come of it? Some people are tranquil to the extent of procrastination, laziness, or sloth. That's too much of a good thing. Others are tranquil to the point of apathy, so that if something actually needs to be done, they won't get involved. Recall the famous case of Catherine Genovese, the unfortunate woman who was assaulted and stabbed to death in New York City in 1964, while thirty-eight of her neighbors heard and watched from their windows, yet none intervened or even called the police. Their tranquillity – in this case apathy – probably cost her her life. So tranquillity can be bad at times.

We believe that rapture is wonderful. What ill can come of it? One always does: rapture ends, and usually ends in hell. The greatest love affairs are inevitably the most tragic, from Antony and Cleopatra in ancient history, to the medieval legend of Tristan and Isolde, to Romeo and Juliet in fiction. Creative genius is also rapturous, and often meets the same hellish end. When Ernest Hemingway could no longer write, he killed himself. After Maurice Ravel suffered a stroke, he could still "hear" his compositions in his mind but was unable to play them or write them down. He lived four years in that hell, until he died. Most people don't experience too much rapture, which is just as well: Most could not afford the steep price of its ending.

We believe that learning is generally good. What harm can come of it? One can learn helpful or harmful things. If you learn medicine, you can heal others and alleviate suffering. If you learn terrorism, you can harm others and engender suffering. Even normally good things, like medicine, can have bad applications. For example, Nazi doctors performed barbaric experiments on human beings. In our times, computers are indispensable tools, but vital facts about people learned through the Internet can result in identity theft. There are many ways in which reason can be applied to bad ends.

We believe that realization is generally good. What harm can come of it? As with learning, realization can backfire. Nuclear energy can be used to generate electricity, which is good unless the reactor core melts down, as almost happened at Three Mile Island and did happen at Chernobyl. The discovery of nuclear energy also allowed nuclear weapons to be built, which is a persistent problem that may yet revisit us. The ancient Chinese discovered gunpowder, and invented fireworks. Early modern Europeans discovered gunpowder, and invented firearms. Sociopaths are calculating beings, using their inventive intelligence to inflict savage harms. Creative reason cuts both ways.

We believe that helping others is generally good. What harm can come of it? A friend of mine gave his daughter a tidy sum of cash as a wedding gift, not knowing (at the time) that she and her husband were addicted to cocaine. Guess what she bought? A road to hell, paved with her father's good intentions. On a large scale, consider the impact of social welfare. While compassionate governments should provide a "safety net" for their citizens, many families in developed socialized nations have been collecting such benefits for generations: They have lost their incentive, initiative, and confidence. This is not good for them. So if we give inappropriate help, it can turn out to be harmful.

Finally, awakening is always good, because it does not take place in the presence of a harmful thought or deed.

So the lessons of the Ten Worlds reform and resolve the ongoing debate about passion and reason. The proper goal for human beings is not to eradicate passion and elevate reason. The proper goal is to cultivate only the beneficial aspects of all your possible states of mind.

That way, whichever states manifest, you will guide yourself toward the best of all possible worlds.

PHILOSOPHICAL EXERCISES

Passion and Reason

1. What's your most constructive passion? What benefits does it bring you and others?
2. What's your most destructive passion? What detriments does it bring you and others?
3. Use your power of reason to imagine ways of transforming your destructive passion into a constructive one. Try some of these ways, and see which ones work best for you.

Stoicism

4. What are you most attached to? Can you sustain this attachment without fear of loss? If so, you are a Stoic. If not, you are in someone else's power. Discover who that is, and strive to become free of their grip by diminishing your attachment. (There's another exercise on attachment following the final chapter.)

Buddhism

5. Which of the Ten Worlds do you spend most time in? If you'd like to *learn* more about transitions from one to the other, *realize* how much say you have in this process, and *help* yourself and others by deriving the best from each world, look at Nichiren Daishonin's Buddhism. Richard Causton's book *The Buddha in Daily Life* is a good introduction.

4

IF YOU'RE OFFENDED, ARE YOU HARMED?

A trifle consoles us because a trifle upsets us.
—Blaise Pascal

What's on trial here today is political
correctness. Now, political correctness is the
idea that assumes that the worst thing we can
do is offend somebody. Well, a lot of people were
offended when Galileo suggested that the earth
was revolving around the sun. A lot of people
were offended by Picasso because in his portraits
the eyes weren't where they were supposed to
be. A lot of people were offended by Rosa Parks
when she wouldn't sit in the back of an Alabama
bus just because of the color of her skin. You see,
everybody's offended by something. A joke, a TV
show, a song, an idea . . . And offending is very
different from hurting . . . Political correctness
tries to protect us from ourselves, but what do
we have to give up for it? We give up our sense of
humor, our sense of romance, our sense of play.
We give up the courage to be different, to think
different.
        – Alfred Molina in the TV series *Ladies Man*

T OO MANY PEOPLE experience needless dis-ease due to a handful of
fundamental confusions. With increasing frequency in recent
times, people have confused privileges with rights, objectivity with

subjectivity, wishing with willing, wanting with needing, price with worth, affluence with fulfillment, reality with appearance, and sameness with equality. Not to mention disease with dis-ease! In this vein, people cause themselves and others a lot of unnecessary suffering by ignoring the distinction between offense and harm. The costs of this ignorance, both personal and societal, have been monumental. Before we get to the troubles this mistaken equivalency causes us, we must first clarify just what "harm" and "offense" are, and thus make clear the difference between them. If you can learn not to confuse the two, and learn how not to take offense, you might just spare yourself a lot of dis-ease, and maybe even harm. I am very serious about this: the confusion of offense with harm is itself a potentially harmful mistake, with dire consequences awaiting those who persist in making the error.

WHAT IS HARM?

Suppose you're riding the subway and somebody big and heavy accidentally steps on your foot. Suppose your foot is actually injured in the process – perhaps some small bones are broken. This is a harm; namely, a physical injury to your person.

Now, further suppose that you need healthy feet to do your work; perhaps you are a letter carrier, or a dancer. With a broken foot, you are temporarily prevented from earning your living. This is a collateral harm; namely, an obstacle to the fulfillment of your normal duties or interests, which disappears only when your injury disappears.

If the person who stepped on your foot says, "I'm sorry," you certainly have the power to accept the apology. However, the apology and your acceptance of it do not reverse the harm to your foot, or the collateral harm to your career.

In America, the person who stepped on your foot might be liable for your medical costs as well as your loss of income, at least in a civil court. If they had planned to step on your foot, or had been hired by someone else to step on your foot, then (although the harms done to you are just the same as if it had been an accident) the perpetrator could be charged with a crime – some kind of assault, most likely.

So there is a difference between intentional versus unintentional harm. Either way, your foot is still injured. But whether it occurred by accident or on purpose makes a moral difference to you, as well as a legal difference to the system. A friend may harm you unintentionally, and you'd probably remain friends. A friend who harms you intentionally – well, that person is not really your friend at all.

Not all harms are caused by other people. Your foot could be injured by a dog, or a shark, or if you are struck by lightning, for example. You can't sue or press charges against a thunderstorm, of course, even though it may have harmed you. Forces of nature act impartially.

In any event, harm is done actively to an unwilling victim who does not have a chance to accept or reject the act, and who does not condone it. That is, victims of harm do not seek to be harmed. If someone tries to harm you, you may or may not be able to defend yourself. If someone apologizes for stepping on your foot, you can forgive them – but your foot will still hurt. The physical harm is done, and apologizing doesn't undo it.

WHAT IS OFFENSE?

Now suppose you're on the subway – with healthy feet – and you notice one of your fellow travelers staring at your toes protruding from your sandals. This seems a bit odd or threatening to you (a stare is a threat among adult primates), or at the very least rude, so you ask "What are you staring at?"

"Your feet," comes the answer. "They are the ugliest feet I've ever seen; I can hardly believe my eyes!" You feel provoked, angry, and upset; you are experiencing dis-ease. You've been offended.

You have not, however, been harmed. Your feet are just fine, and there isn't any collateral harm either. You can still walk or dance, go about your daily life, perform your work unimpeded.

Now I have some news for you: Those who are offended play an active role in being offended. Offense is merely offered to someone, who must then decide whether to accept the insult or not. If someone tries to offend you, you always have the option to refuse to take offense, provided you know how to exercise it. You cannot be offended without your own consent. (But you can be harmed without your consent. See the difference?) Thus, in a civil society, if we say something that unintentionally offends someone, we can always apologize by saying, "No offense intended" – and the other person can answer, "None taken." If someone apologizes for staring at your feet, you can forgive them and feel no insult. And if an offense is offered but not accepted, there is no offense, no harm, and, further-more, no dis-ease.

AND NEVER THE TWAIN SHALL MEET

Then there's the possibility of someone first stepping on your foot and then saying your feet are ugly. We would say they are "adding insult to injury." The very phrase indicates there is a significant difference between the two.

To sum up: harm is a one-way street, while offense runs both ways. You can be harmed against your will, but never offended against your will. That is a powerful distinction. And I urge you to consider the benefits of drawing it as often as necessary. You can maximize your ease by refusing to take offense, or maximize your dis-ease by seeking it at every possible turn. The Roman Stoic emperor Marcus Aurelius knew this very well. He had learned it from his teacher, the freed slave and great philosopher Epictetus: "We are not disturbed by things, but by the views we take of them."

> **Take away your opinion, and there is taken away the complaint "I have been offended." Take away the complaint "I have been offended" and the offense is gone.**
> **– Marcus Aurelius**

THE COSTS OF CONFUSION

As Americans and others have collectively lost sight of the distinction between offense and harm, taking every proffered offense as a definite harm, the costs are mounting. The courts are clogged with frivolous but lucrative lawsuits, rewarding people for perpetuating this confusion. Schoolchildren stage murderous attacks on their classmates and teachers in response to perceived slights. Society has muzzled, and even prosecuted, artists, scholars, political activists, and scientists simply because their work wasn't to everyone's taste, infringing the civil liberties our nation is predicated upon and depriving the culture of everything from scholarly advances to entertainment to insight into our national character.

The rise of "political correctness" in the universities, which has now spread to corporations, governments, the justice system, and the military, has robbed us of our common sense and ability to seek and speak truths for fear of stepping on someone else's metaphorical toes. What may have begun as an exercise in instilling civic virtues such as politeness, which creates ease, has mutated into a totalitarian regime of thought control, which creates dis-ease. We're banning books, inflating grades, censoring scholars, refusing to make vital moral distinctions. Just as with personal issues, social and political dis-eases cannot begin to be eased until they are correctly identified. And they can never be correctly identified if people are afraid to know or speak the truth about their causes.

WHAT'S WRONG WITH KIDS TODAY

Let's look at one extreme example of this phenomenon in more detail: the increase in horrific acts of violence committed by schoolchildren. Typically, the perpetrators – including children of the affluent, from "good" homes – appear to be retaliating for having been taunted or rejected by their peers. Some slight – a word or gesture or casual rejection – is met with lethal force. That is, offense is offered, then it is accepted, next it is confused with harm, and finally the imaginary "harm" leads to drastic retaliation. It's not really any different from the gang-related homicides in American inner cities, where as little as a single act of "dissing" (disrespecting) someone is punishable by violent death.

Thomas Hobbes, who devoted his long philosophical life to the study of human conflict and its resolution, wrote, in 1651, that people will resort to violence "for trifles, as a word, a smile, a different opinion, and any other sign of undervalue, either direct in their persons, or by reflection in their kindred, their friends, their nation, their profession, or their name." In other words, they will kill merely for being "dissed."

Centuries later, in 1914, Sigmund Freud noted the same tendency, and attributed it to the id, the chaotic or infantile domain of unconscious mind. According to Freud, the id is like that ancient tyrant Draco, who sought to eliminate criminals once and for all by punishing every crime by death. (Even these "Draconian" measures didn't work.) Freud thought that the id, hardwired into everybody's unconscious, makes us all wishful Dracos. Thus, if someone accidentally steps on your foot, or says something unkind about your mother, your unconscious Freudian urge is to kill him.

> **In our unconscious impulses we daily and hourly get rid of anyone who stands in our way, of anyone who has offended or injured us . . . Indeed, our unconscious will murder even for trifles; like the ancient Athenian code of Draco, it knows no other punishment for crime than death.**
>
> **– Sigmund Freud**

Notice how Hobbes and Freud used that same word, "trifles," to describe the pettiness of some offenses which, when accepted instead of refused, become pretexts for violent or lethal retaliation. Duels used to be fought for this reason too. Officers sitting together at the same table could hardly get through a meal without offending one another.

To salvage his honor, an officer and gentleman was not allowed to refuse an offense. Instead, he had to "demand satisfaction," which meant dueling – often to the death. The world lost at least one mathematical genius in this way: Galois, the inventor of group theory. The custom of dueling was first abolished by the French army. Gallic peoples can be notoriously thin-skinned, and the French were losing more officers (and mathematical geniuses) in duels than in battles. Contemporary democracies are losing lives as well as productivity over the same trifles. George Santayana famously said, "Those who cannot remember the past are condemned to repeat it." Unfortunately, he was right.

The current epidemic of juvenile violence was anticipated by William Golding in his novel *Lord of the Flies,* in which a group of young English schoolboys, supposedly well brought up and fully civilized, is shipwrecked on a tropical island. Without adult super-vision – and discipline, love, and social structure – they quickly degenerate into a tribe of murderous savages.

Golding reinforces Hobbes's and Freud's points: that civilization is only a thin veneer over animalistic human nature. If you strip away this veneer, or allow it to wear away through neglect, what you expose is a self-centered and rapacious animal that will kill its own kind for no more than looking at it the wrong way – or for failing to share its beliefs.

When *Lord of the Flies* was made into a movie in 1963, director Peter Brook thought he would have a hard time coaxing his schoolboy actors to abandon their civility, forget their table manners, and behave as savages. He needn't have worried: they required very little instruc-tion or encouragement. The director later wrote: "My experience showed me that the only falsification in Golding's fable is the length of time the descent to savagery takes . . . the complete catastrophe could occur within a long weekend."

The failure to make a second vital distinction, between what is thinkable and what is doable, is also causing problems here. If Hobbes, Freud, and Golding are right, then people will always – whether consciously, subconsciously, or unconsciously – think about doing heinous things to others in retaliation for mere insults. In a free society, we don't and shouldn't wish to control people's thoughts or speech. So the imperative becomes to encourage people to *think* freely, including harboring thoughts about what they would like to do to others, while discouraging them from acting on those thoughts. In other words, you should be free to think as you please, and free to speak as you please, but not free to act as you please.

We're missing the larger point if we blame juvenile violence only on vitriolic role models, vile television, vulgar movies, vicious popular music, and so on, without taking into account the confusion of offense with harm. Our children must be taught, early and often, that they will experience all kinds of dis-eases in life, including taunting, rejection, and the many other forms of social cruelty which are daily inflicted on kids by other kids, in the playground and the schoolyard (not to mention by adults on adults in the wider world). Children must also learn the corollary: that no mere insult is a justifiable cause for violent retaliation. We must help them cultivate an internal sense of their own moral worthiness, so that no one can possibly offend them with words. When we do the exact opposite, and try to restrict speech and even thought for fear of offending someone (because we mistakenly think it's harmful), we end up rendering people completely defenseless against any "unsanctioned" thoughts or words. In other words, we cripple their capacity to be autonomous and dignified human beings. That's bad news.

Children must be taught to heed the line between subjectivity and objectivity, so that what somebody else thinks of them, or calls them, is far less important than what they are to themselves, and to those who really count in their lives. If they have a sense of their own intrinsic human worth, which needs to be reinforced when they are young, then nobody can diminish that worth by name-calling or any other kind of offense. They need to know that the only one who can devalue their worth is themselves, by sinking to the level of those who would offend them. This is all part of what I call "moral self-defense" (MSD), and it's the same thing the rest of us grown-ups need to practice to avoid the dis-ease of mistaking offense for harm. I'll go into more detail shortly.

WHEN OFFENSE BECOMES HARM

It is important to note that under certain conditions, offense *can* become harmful. If you take offense on a daily basis, you may not be able to mobilize sufficient moral self-defense, and eventually the repeated offenses can have a cumulative harmful effect. That's especially true to the emotionally vulnerable, such as children. Take, for example, a child whose parents continually call him "stupid." To call a child stupid once is offensive; to repeat that on a daily basis is harmful. Why? The child needs to believe (for a time) that his parents know best, so he will probably behave in accord with their description and expectations of him, at least until he grows up and accepts responsibility for describing himself. (Some people never do, and usually need psychological help.) The child who is repeatedly told he is stupid may then behave as though he *were* stupid. Such deliberate underachievement, caused by the acceptance of repeated offense by one who is unable to defend himself, is obviously harmful to the child's better interests.

Adults can be verbally abused too, and "anger management" programs are not enough to prevent such abuse. Men and women alike could benefit from instruction in moral self-defense, learning how not to provoke, and how not to be provoked in the first place. Then there would be less anger to manage, all around. Both sexes need to understand each other's triggers much better than they do if they wish to prevent offense from escalating into harm. (For more on the sexes, see chapter 8.)

Fortunately, with some philosophical help, adults at least can develop a greater capacity for moral self-defense, and learn how not to take offense even when offense is insistently or forcefully offered. Children need this too. Yet there has hardly been any demand for moral self-defense instruction in schools or corporations. That's a pity; it is desperately needed. An hour of MSD is worth a planeload of grief counselors.

We must be able to tolerate a certain amount of offensiveness in our daily lives, but the emotionally vulnerable need to be able to remove themselves from the offender or the offending stimulus if too frequent or intense, lest it becomes harmful.

CASES OF OFFENSE VERSUS HARM IN HIGHER EDUCATION

You might suppose that the higher education system would be the ideal place for designing curricula to reverse the harms done by confusion of offense with harm, but that's not the case. In fact, it's the opposite. The universities themselves are largely responsible (and morally culpable) for perpetuating this confusion. They have taught and therefore spread this confusion to the whole of society: professionals and laypersons of all kinds, in every stratum. Let me give you a couple of illustrations.

The cases share a common theme, namely the question of race relations in an increasingly diverse cultural mosaic. What holds true in America also holds true in the wider world: For social ease to replace dis-ease, greater emphasis has to be placed on humanity, which unites people, and not ethnicity or other factors that divide them. The lessons here are for the whole global village, not just for America. As populations become more diverse all over the world, it is increasingly vital to personal flourishing and world peace that people perceive and conceive of one another as unique human beings, and not merely as representatives of this or that race or tribe. For ease to replace dis-ease, humanity must take precedence over ethnicity.

Alicia's Case: Grade Inflation and Dehumanization
This case comes from one of my philosophy courses at City College in New York. I had graded a quiz, and one of the students, Alicia, asked to see me after class.

"Did I really earn an A on this quiz," Alicia asked, "or did you just inflate my grade to make me feel better?" Considering the quality of her work, I thought this was an odd question.

"In my courses," I replied, "students get the grades they earn. Your work merited an A, so I gave you an A."

To my surprise, upon hearing this, she actually burst into tears: out of gratitude for having her excellence recognized on its own merits. Then she explained to me that she had transferred from another well-known university in Manhattan, where she had been repeatedly offended (but not yet harmed) by the university's widespread practice of inflating grades for "visible minorities," lately known as "diverse" students. Only then did I understand what she had been driving at with her original question.

I saw before me an intelligent and highly motivated student who wanted to earn good grades on the bases of her ability and effort. That she happened to be a female of color was irrelevant to her understanding of the rudiments of philosophy. Like all teachers, philosophers are supposed to awaken ideas in the mind. Ideas and minds have no race, ethnicity, sex, gender, religion, age, or any other property of physical bodies and collective identities. Alicia was offended by the system's categorization of her as a black female affirmative action statistic, supposedly needing her grades inflated so she would be "competitive" and "feel good" about herself. Accepting an offer of counterfeit grades would have stigmatized her in her own eyes. Alicia needed to be free of the past, and that could happen only if she were free to succeed on her own terms.

So Alicia did the prudent thing, by finding professors who treated her as a human being, not as a statistic or a political project, and who encouraged her to manifest her own excellence. She was able to escape the offending stimulus of grade inflation before it became harmful to her and society alike.

Yes, harmful. Why? For two reasons. First, we are all students in life, and the only way to make genuine progress is to honestly assess what we have learned and what we have yet to learn. If you possess a university degree that says you can read and write at a given level, have mastered a given body of knowledge, and are therefore qualified to pursue a given career, it had better be true. Otherwise, there are no more standards of professional performance. Academic degrees can be faked, but professional performances cannot. Second, it is both offensive and harmful to be treated with bias of any kind, either negative or positive. Depriving people of their entitlements such as civil rights is dehumanizing, therefore offensive and harmful. But providing people with unmerited rewards also dehumanizes them, and is likewise offensive and harmful.

> **No bird soars too high, if she soars with her own wings.**
>
> **– William Blake**

George's Case: Too Much Diversity, Not Enough Humanity

A male student named George attended one of my philosophy forums at a Manhattan bookstore. He was furious. Why? Because of the way he was being treated at his university. George happened to be part African-American, part Latino, and part American Indian. It seemed that just about every club, agency, and organization on campus wanted to "help" George by awarding him this or that special scholarship for "minorities" or "diverse" students. The problem was that no one seemed to care very much about *George*. They cared a great deal that, in their terms, he was a multipurpose statistic: Based on his race or ethnicity or heritage, they could shower him with special awards. But the more they did this, the angrier George became. You see, nobody ever asked him about his academic interests. What had he studied? What did he want study? Isn't it odd that these questions were irrelevant to their concerns? They treated George as a means to their end (i.e., their statistical agenda), and not as an end in himself (i.e., as a good student worthy of assistance). This violated Kant's fundamental criterion of human dignity. No wonder George was angry.

He eventually transferred to another university, into an academic program that actually cared about his academic interests. He also became fulfilled as a student, and his dis-ease abated.

What's the connection with offense and harm? It's this: The system feared that George would be offended (and therefore, it supposed, harmed) if insufficient attention were paid to George's diverse heritage. But the system's way of alleviating its fear of offense actually harmed George's real interests as a student, and therefore also harmed society's larger interests in seeing George succeed as a student.

**Now I say: man and generally any rational
animal exists as an end in himself, not merely
as a means to be arbitrarily used by this or
that will . . .**

– Immanuel Kant

REFUSING TO TAKE OFFENSE

It is one's very sense of dignity and integrity as a human being that is at
risk from perpetual offense, more so than one's ego, image, security,
or identity. At the biological level, where emotions are primal, we are
programmed to react strongly to offense via the ancient and powerful
mechanism of "fight or flight." At the psychological level, where
emotions manifest as feelings and interact with primitive thoughts, it is
the psyche itself that can be metaphorically wounded by offenses to
infantile attachments (insulting your mother), egocentric perspective
(insulting you), group identity (insulting your race or tribe), or deepest
insecurities (insulting your religion or relationship with God). Here
the conditioned response is retaliation or revenge.

At the philosophical level, however, reason and interpretation
combine with will and imagination to rule over both biology and
psychology, and neither genetic programming nor behavioral conditioning need hold sway. The higher powers of the mind encounter
offense – and deflect it, make light of it, or keep it at bay with humor
or principle. This is where you need to be able to discover the good in
the bad and transcend both. Those who have fought their way
through to this domain find little to their distaste. Whatever offends
them never harms them. It is this free and open mind that forms the
foundation of human dignity.

The good news is that, at least once we're past our formative years,
we can refuse most of life's offenses with relative ease. In the civilized
world, if you don't like a book, you can stop reading it. If you don't
like a TV program, you can change the channel. If you don't like your
professor, you can take a different course. In the civilized world, if you
really dislike your spouse, neighbors, job, political party, country, or

religion, you can change them too. We have fought long and hard to gain and preserve that much personal liberty. There's an argument to be made (though not right here) that we may even have too much liberty for our own good – but that's another story. In any event, with so much liberty, there is not really much excuse for taking offense – unless you prefer dis-ease to ease.

LAUGHTER USED TO BE AVAILABLE OVER THE COUNTER

Whether or not they are frequent or intense enough to be harmful, the world is full of provocations. The only part of this scenario you can reliably control is your response. How you respond to proffered offenses depends on your experience of life as well as your attitudes and habits, which in turn depend on your philosophy. If your current modus operandi isn't working for you, the philosophy you are living by may need a tune-up. By changing your philosophy, then, you can also change the way you respond to provocation. You can even diminish the likelihood that others will attempt to provoke you.

Responses to offense vary across a broad spectrum, from culture to culture and from person to person. The worst option is violence, which "pays back" offense with harm. Another option is tit-for-tat: exchanging insult for insult. You can also use humor to defuse the situation. You can be cynical or caustic, retaliating in a way that often goes right over the head of your offender.

Too many people have failed to learn to defend themselves against proffered offense, and they seem to exist in a perpetual state of being offended, or are at least constantly prepared to be offended. A lot of them appear utterly humorless. Many do not love themselves or the world very much. They experience continuous dis-ease. Instead of becoming happy themselves, they want happy people to share their dis-ease. So they invent rules for controlling what people are allowed to say and even think, with a constant eye on not allowing anyone to offend anyone else, thereby protecting (they think) themselves as well. Ultimately this creates a counterproductive system that not only interferes with personal liberty, but also inhibits free-flowing love of life and the healing nature of humor. It's essentially a Soviet-style system, with centrally planned thinking rather than a centrally planned economy. Only one thing is certain about this system: It produces more dis-ease than ease for all concerned.

It is wiser for you to deflect trifles, perhaps subtly turning the tables in the process. My favorite example of this kind involves the conductor Herbert von Karajan. One day Karajan was walking briskly along a downtown city street, and another man was walking just as briskly along an intersecting street. They were on a collision course, but were unable to see one another approaching because a large corner office building obstructed their views. They literally collided at the corner, and both of them bounced back at the shock and surprise of the collision.

"Imbecile!" exclaimed the man to Karajan.

At this, Karajan simply doffed his hat as if in greeting and replied, "Karajan."

This anecdote illustrates an intermediate level of moral self-defense. I call it "social judo" when I teach it in workshops. Instead of taking offense and retaliating by similar name-calling or worse, Karajan did two surprising things. First, he reflected the intended offense back to the offender. As if he were a duck shedding water, it never actually touched him. Second, he transmuted a potential quarrel into a humorous episode – the opposite of offense being not more offense, but laughter. People who can laugh at themselves, and make others laugh, are not only happier in general but are also much more difficult to offend. Now if Karajan were called an "imbecile" on a regular basis, everywhere he went, he would sooner or later tire of doffing his hat, because the continuous stream of offense would wear down even his capacity to defend himself. But as it stood, he struck just the right chord. That's hardly surprising for a great conductor, but you can do it too.

IT TAKES WISDOM TO PLAY SHAKESPEARE'S FOOL

If you have ever wondered why the industry of stand-up comedy is flourishing in America (and worldwide) as never before, consider it in this light. Many if not most stand-up comics bring humor to bear on touchy issues involving sex, gender, race, ethnicity, religion, and politics, while ordinary people feel themselves no longer at liberty to discuss these issues freely in the media, in universities, or in the workplace. So now we have to hire comedians to exercise our freedom of expression for us. And that's no laughing matter.

This was also the role that Shakespeare's fools performed so aptly in his plays, as court jesters have done from time immemorial. Even such "fools" are never completely immune from censure: Offering potentially offensive humor to entrenched powers, and provoking laughter instead of wrath, is an artful but dangerous game, as the tragic careers of pioneering stand-up comics like Lenny Bruce richly illustrate. But as our culture of conformity grows, it also needs ever-wiser fools to balance its stultifying self-righteousness. Thus it sanctions nightly episodes of extreme nonconformity, for the sake of entertainment. Some of the most politically incorrect people on the planet, such as David Letterman and Jay Leno, are staples of late-night TV. Enjoying the temporary immunity of the court jester, their job is to good-naturedly butcher everybody's sacred cows. But you'd better not repeat any of their jokes on the job or in the classroom, in case someone takes "offense" today at something millions of viewers laughed at yesterday. You could be out of a job, as was the poor guy who repeated a *Seinfeld* joke to a secretary at his office. One reporter described it this way:

"Let an employee make sexual jokes at work, and you could lose millions of dollars in a lawsuit. Fire an employee for making sexual jokes at work, and you could lose millions of dollars in a lawsuit. Dinged if you do, and dinged if you don't."

Or we can preempt this whole catch-22 scenario by distinguishing between offense and harm, and teaching moral self-defense to maintain the distinction. That's much less costly, and much more fun, for all concerned.

This fellow's wise enough to play the fool . . .
– William Shakespeare

EVERYBODY OFFENDS SOMEBODY SOMETIME

My apologies to the late Dean Martin and his theme song, "Everybody Loves Somebody Sometime." In life, everybody offends somebody sometime too. That is to say, people may decide to take offense at you. Are you male, female, hermaphroditic, androgynous, heterosexual, gay, lesbian, bisexual, or celibate? Whatever your sex and sexual orientation, you can always find both support for it and opposition to it in the world. Why accept offense at opinions that are opposed to yours? People who cannot accept your sex or sexual orientation clearly cannot accept their own, so perhaps they malign yours. Don't make their problem your own. Is your skin pigmentation black, white, brown, yellow, red, or some other shade? Whatever your skin color, you can always find some people who are biased in your favor because of it, and others who are biased in your disfavor because of it. Why accept offense at remarks that seek to diminish your humanity based on your pigmentation? People who make such remarks diminish their own humanity. Don't make their problem your own. Similarly, others may not share your tastes in art, music, food, fashion, politics, or religion. If they seek to elevate themselves by lowering you, to make themselves feel superior by making you feel inferior, they will succeed only if you sink to the occasion by accepting their offense. Don't make their problem your own.

There is no point in taking offense – as long as prejudices remain verbal, they harm only the interests of the person who harbors them. The best defense lies in refusing to take offense. The worst defense lies in seeking to be offended at every turn. As Eleanor Roosevelt said, "No one can make you feel inferior without your consent."

ADVANCED MORAL SELF-DEFENSE

If the elementary lesson of this chapter is that offense and harm are two different things, and the intermediate lesson is to learn to refuse to accept offense, we've come now to the advanced lessons: accepting harm without being offended, and turning harm into help. Taking to heart the first two lessons will be enough to alleviate much dis-ease in most people's lives, and this last component will not be for everyone. But we can all seek inspiration from it if nothing else, and it just might prove invaluable for you one day.

We'll look at applying this lesson in political, civil, and personal arenas through the examples of Mahatma Gandhi, Martin Luther King Jr. – and Jackie Mason. I want to acknowledge and thank my former student and current friend Joseph Brown for his insight on this theme. Some years ago I was leading a classroom discussion on the philosophy of nonviolent resistance to oppression. Joseph realized that Gandhi and King had gone much further down the road of successfully differentiating offense and harm than we had discussed. Far beyond refusing to confuse the two, or simply refusing to take offense, Joseph observed they had actually accepted harms without taking offense, thereby going so far as to draw progress toward the common good out of harms done personally to them.

Gandhi and King both trace their approaches to Henry David Thoreau, who, in the nineteenth century, endured arrest rather than paying a poll tax that he deemed irrelevant to his labors and an affront to his principles. He spent a night in jail before his friends got him released by paying it for him the next day. Being nothing if not dramatic, Thoreau wrote that in an unjust society, the proper place for a just man was prison. Both Gandhi and King later took this directly to heart, and each spent considerably more time in jail (to great political effect).

> **Under a government which imprisons any unjustly, the true place for a just man is also a prison.**
>
> **– Henry David Thoreau**

Mahatma Gandhi

Gandhi managed to convince the British to give up colonizing India and grant Indians political independence – without holding office, raising an army, or firing a single shot. He deplored violence and went on several hunger strikes in order to quell it in the ranks of his own followers. Gandhi's philosophy of nonviolent resistance is known as *satyagraha*, or "a firm and unflinching adherence to truth." What truth? That people who oppress others are morally wrong to do so, but need to learn (or be taught) that they are wrong. Oppression is both an offense and a harm; it offends one's humanity, and harms a host of human interests.

Gandhi's enlightened form of resistance consisted in turning those who were oppressed into moral mirrors of a sort. By absorbing offense and harm without retaliation or hatred – even, in fact, with love – the oppressed reflected the image of wrongdoing back to their oppressors, teaching them to (eventually) realize the error of their ways and abandon the oppression, of their own free will, out of their own moral conviction. When oppressors are met instead with violent resistance, oppressors inevitably become that much more convinced of the righteousness of their cause and their right to self-defense, which only more deeply entrenches the oppression.

As it was, the British ultimately gave up India, the "Jewel in the Crown" of their vast empire, swayed by nothing more (or less!) than the spiritual fortitude and moral conviction of a man who owned no property, held no office, commanded no army. Gandhi and his followers endured insult and injury alike, without taking offense or returning harm themselves. By the purity of their thoughts and deeds, they attained an unprecedented political victory.

> **This *ahimsa* [non-harm] is the basis of the search for truth . . . It is quite proper to resist and attack a system, but to resist and attack its author is tantamount to resisting and attacking oneself.**
>
> **– Mahatma Gandhi**

Martin Luther King Jr.

In a similar way, adapting Thoreau's philosophy and Gandhi's practices to the American South, Martin Luther King Jr. led the way to the demise of segregation in the United States and helped secure civil rights for African-Americans. By marching peaceably in protest, King and his followers attracted offense in the form of verbal abuse, and harm in the form of beatings, arrests, and other brutality. Still, they remained steadfast in refusing to retaliate against or hate their oppressors. And just as the British gradually learned that their colonial occupation of India was a moral wrong, Americans came to know that their denial of civil rights to people of color was a moral wrong.

> **Just as Socrates felt that it was necessary to create a tension in the mind so that individuals could rise from the bondage of myths and half-truths to the unfettered realm of creative analysis and objective appraisal, so we must see the need for nonviolent gadflies to create the kind of tension in society that will help men rise from the dark depths of prejudice and racism to the majestic heights of understanding and brotherhood.**
>
> **– Martin Luther King Jr.**

It must be noted that this approach will not work in every situation, for it relies on activating the moral sensibilities of the oppressors. Where morality is entirely lacking, resistors find no ground in which to plant the seeds of moral awareness. The British and Americans alike had more than enough Christian morality and Enlightenment philosophy as part of their mainstream cultures to be able eventually to see the moral light.

But think about what might have happened if a Gandhi or King had arisen in Hitler's Germany, Stalin's Russia, Pol Pot's Cambodia, or Hussein's Iraq. No doubt he would have been arrested and murdered in very short order. While the British jailed Gandhi repeatedly, they dared not murder him for fear of violating their own laws and provoking violent rebellion across India. (And each time they jailed and released the popular leader, he gained even more support and strength.) Similarly, authorities in segregated American states feared provoking race riots across the country, and again could only watch as King's following intensified with each new arrest and release. But unlike the British, who had no intention of murdering every Indian in India, or the Americans, who had no intention of murdering every black person in America, the Nazis fully intended to murder every Jew in Europe; Stalin, to murder every "counterrevolutionary" in Russia. If your oppressors intend to murder you, they will not give you much chance to teach them moral lessons. You may need to put them under lock and key to get them into a classroom.

Jackie Mason

I haven't forgotten I promised you Jackie Mason along with more sober-minded role models. His story brings this concept down to a personal level, so I'm sure it will be the one most likely to let you see how this can work in your own life. Mason, a great but definitely politically incorrect comedian, descendant of rabbis, and erstwhile rabbinical student, managed to absorb personal harm without taking offense, and then transmute the harm into humor for the benefit of others.

Mason is a keen observer of humanity and its cultural differences, and it is from there that much of his humor springs. Naturally, this means that some people find him offensive; others, hilarious. (We have already seen that indignation and laughter are opposite sides of the same coin.) Take, for example, Mason's routine about the late, great Frank Sinatra, based on the premise that Sinatra actually couldn't sing very well at all. A great entertainer, yes; a great singer, no. Mason's point was that you don't have to be technically outstanding to be famous. Sinatra won over his fans with popular repertoire, charismatic personality, brilliant orchestration and production, a unique style of delivery – and, famously, with a little help from his Godfather.

One night, after a performance that included the Sinatra bit, Mason was approached in his dressing room by three tough guys warning him to lay off the Sinatra jokes. Frank had heard about them, they said, and he wasn't amused.

Despite Sinatra's backstage reputation for the capacity to be cruel and vicious, Mason ignored the warning. Not too many performances later, Mason was assaulted in the alley behind the theater by three assailants, beaten so badly he had to be hospitalized.

As soon as Mason recovered, he introduced a new routine into his act. Paraphrased, it went something like this:

"I want to tell you about a great friend of mine, a man who saved my life. If it weren't for him, I wouldn't be standing here entertaining you tonight. That man is Frank Sinatra. Here's what he did for me. One night, as I was leaving the theater, three thugs attacked me in the alley. I thought they were going to kill me. They were beating me and beating me, and I thought they were going to beat me to death. But all of a sudden this guy appears from nowhere and saves my life. It was Frank Sinatra! He walked right up and said, 'That's enough, boys.' And they stopped! If not for him, they would have beaten me to death. I owe my life to Frank Sinatra."

This speaks not only of Mason's comic genius, but also his great humanity. He had suffered savage harm, but ultimately transformed it into a hilarious anecdote for others to enjoy. Where Karajan made humor out of offense, Mason managed to create it out of harm. This is moral self-defense of the highest order – proof that you don't have to be in pursuit of major political transformation to stand on higher moral ground.

THE POLITICS OF OFFENSE AND HARM

Credit John Stuart Mill with defining the philosophy behind the enlightened political approach to offense and harm. His essay *On Liberty* lays out the idea that the main purpose of government should be to prevent its citizens from doing harm to one another. This, according to Mill, is the sole justification a state has for restraining any of its citizens. It's known as "the harm principle."

> **. . . the only purpose for which power can be rightfully exercised over any member of a civilized community, against his will, is to prevent harm to others.**
>
> **– John Stuart Mill**

Note that Mill does not include harm to oneself in this category. So if you want to run risks, that's your business, according to him, as long as you don't harm anyone else, and as long as no one else is depending on you. To take this to an extreme: If you're all alone in the world, and want to drink yourself into a stupor every night, and can afford the liquor, then Mill would leave you to it. But if you're behind the wheel, or directing traffic, or performing surgery, or looking after children, or doing any of a host of things that require sobriety, then your inebriation could bring grievous harm to others – in which case Mill would say that you have no right to engage in excess drinking, and, moreover, that the state has an obligation to prevent you from putting others at risk.

Mill is just as clear about offense. While he believes you have a right not to be harmed, you have absolutely *no* right not to be offended. He upholds each person's liberty "of tastes and pursuits, of framing the plan of our life to suit our own character, of doing as we like, without impediment from our fellow creatures, so long as what we do does not harm them, even though they should think our conduct foolish, perverse, or wrong." The initial idea here is to prevent a majority – moral or otherwise – from dictating their tastes to a minority. And that includes *everybody,* because we are all minorities of one.

Adam's Case: Creativity Meets Dictatorship of Taste

Adam's case illustrates how Mill's fundamental idea is being ignored in Western culture, and how creative freedom of artistic expression can be undermined by dictatorship of taste. A composer who studied Western classical music, Adam also studied traditional music of India and Japan, with indigenous teachers. When Adam composed a piece blending Indian percussion, Japanese stringed instruments, and a European chamber ensemble, he was accused by an Indian musicologist of "voice appropriation." The operative notion in this accusation is that only an Indian is "supposed" to use Indian instruments, and so forth. If any non-Indian does, it's somehow "offensive" to Indians. You see where this leads? A female novelist can write only about female characters, or else she's "appropriating the voices" of males. I guess the authors of children's books have to be children, too. We'd better pull *Harry Potter* off the shelves, for double jeopardy! In Adam's case, the commission for the piece was actually withdrawn unless he agreed not to "appropriate" other cultures' instruments. Did the musicologist have a right to dislike Adam's taste in composition and orchestration? Yes. Was the musicologist or anyone else harmed by it? No. Did the system have a right to censor Adam's composition because the musicologist didn't like it? No. Did the system need to take offense at all? No. Did the system confuse offense with harm? Yes.

When Adam learned about Mill's philosophy, his dis-ease abated somewhat. Even though his creative interests had been harmed by political correctness and its dictatorship of taste, and his audience was deprived of the fruits of his creativity, Adam realized that he himself did not have to take offense at the system's confusion of offense with harm, and its subsequent abuse of Mill's harm principle.

AVOIDING OFFENSE AND COURTING HARM

Mill also offers a deeper reason why it's vital for us to tolerate offense but not harm. And that has to do with truth. Why is truth so important? Because if you had to choose between dis-ease and disease, or between feeling offended and being harmed, which choice would you make? Consistently, Mill would say that's also up to you. But as long as you'd rather prevent disease and avert harm, then Mill would also say you're better off knowing "offensive" truths and being safe rather than believing "inoffensive" falsehoods and being at risk. Let me give you a couple of examples.

Europe was ravaged by plagues during the Middle Ages. Most people believed back then that plagues were retributions from God, and so they congregated en masse in places of worship to pray for God's forgiveness. But their gathering together also had the effect of helping to spread whatever contagious disease was going around. Now consider Mill's point. Many religious people would have taken offense at being informed that their prayer gatherings were more likely to facilitate the spread of the plague than its cure. But what's worse:

the dis-ease of challenging one's religious beliefs, or the disease of plague itself? If you know the medical facts about plague, at least you can make an informed choice about your risks. But if truths are suppressed for fear of offense, real harms can ensue with no available choices for minimizing risk. That's Mill's vital point.

If we consider the global AIDS epidemic, the same reasoning applies today. In some places, the spread of HIV is still unchecked because opinion leaders and governments feel dis-ease in speaking openly about unsafe sexual practices that cause HIV to spread, and in addressing the social issues that give rise to unsafe sex itself. To spare themselves dis-ease, they facilitate others contracting the disease. Again, what's worse: reexamining one's beliefs about sexuality and its expression, or contracting a potentially fatal illness?

Surely Mill was right that it's better to ascertain the truth, at least insofar as we can. And we will never know what's true unless we're allowed to think, speak, debate, write, and publish as freely as we can – so that truths can emerge from arenas of freely contending ideas. The alternative is that falsehoods will be dictated to us. And in their train comes untold dis-ease, and sometimes disease and other harms as well.

> **We have now recognized the necessity to the mental well-being of mankind (on which all their other well-being depends) of freedom of opinion, and freedom of the expression of opinion . . . it is only by the collision of adverse opinions that the remainder of the truth has any chance of being supplied.**
>
> **– John Stuart Mill**

Kathi's Case: Back to Square 1 + 1

I've been moderating a monthly Philosopher's Forum in a Manhattan bookstore for several years now, and have facilitated dialogues on any subject the group wants to handle. Over time, we've addressed all the "hot-button" issues you can imagine – as well as the Big Questions in this book – and no one has ever been harmed by our open and frank exchanges of views. In the diverse and eclectic intellectual hothouse of

New York City, nothing makes us more aware of our common humanity than our passionate differences of opinion and taste, and our willingness to respect, tolerate, and even embrace one another on account of those very differences. To really enjoy and appreciate this kind of liberty, you need to distinguish offense from harm in a hurry. So while I'm accustomed to being in the thick of heated debates about politics, religion, race, sex, drugs, tolerance, terrorism, education, and all the rest, I never dreamed that the question "What does one plus one equal?" could cause much of a stir. I was mistaken.

One evening we were debating the perennial question of truth itself when a bright and articulate young woman named Kathi, who held a responsible job in Manhattan, suggested that "all truths are relative." She had been taught this by several professors at her Ivy League university, once a very good one. Nowadays, it too inflates grades systematically (for everybody, since literacy has declined nationwide), and encourages its faculty to teach that all truths are relative.

So I asked Kathi, "How much is one plus one?"

She answered: "It depends." She'd give no other answer, as she was sure it would vary with one's point of view. Moreover, she said she didn't want to express an opinion that might offend somebody else who happened to believe that one plus one equals three (or any other fashionable number). No matter that digital computers, and a lot of other things she needs to do her job, function precisely because $1 + 1 = 2$.

Now, of course, philosophers are supposed to doubt, and we apply doubt as an instrument of inquiry. Socrates made this method famous in antiquity, and it was put to great use by René Descartes in early modern times. But when Descartes declared, "It is certain that nothing is certain," he also left ample room for expressing logical and mathematical truths (e.g., $1 + 1 = 2$), which are the most certain of all knowledge. While Descartes realized that we can be deceived by our senses, he never supposed that all knowledge is just a matter of opinion, or that all truth is relative.

We encountered moral relativism in chapters 1 and 2. Recall, moral relativists refuse to distinguish right from wrong. And their unwillingness to do so causes considerable dis-ease. Now we have encountered a cornerstone of moral relativism itself: the sadly misguided notion that all knowledge is relative, period. Sorry, but it isn't. Life expectancies in the civilized world nearly doubled during the twentieth century because of reliable knowledge. Astronauts got to the moon and back because of reliable knowledge. Computers have changed the way we work and play because of reliable knowledge.

It's also true that the more we learn, the more we realize we don't know. But that doesn't mean we don't know anything! The human world is an increasingly complex place, more and more difficult to understand. Yet people strive unceasingly to make sense of things. How do we do so? Primarily by building on reliable knowledge. Plato had a famous sign posted outside his Academy (the very first university), which said NOBODY DESTITUTE OF GEOMETRY MAY ENTER. Why? Because Plato thought that mathematical truths were the most certain things, and should be learned before approaching more uncertain subjects like ethics and politics. He believed that the bigger questions in life (such as those about rightness and justice) could not even be properly formulated before the smaller ones (such as those about geometry) were answered.

Millions of people like Kathi are grappling with many issues in the global village, issues that concern us all and that can bring us considerable dis-ease: from economy to ecology, from health care to homelessness, from tolerance to terrorism. Plato would say that anyone who cannot make sense of the small questions – such as "What is one plus one?" – stands little chance with the bigger ones. If you can't do arithmetic, which is easy, how can you even begin to tell right from wrong, which can be very difficult at times?

Plato would also say that any system of education that fails to guide its students out of the Cave must either reform itself or face collapse. And one of the first lessons in my reformed curriculum is – you guessed it – how to distinguish offense from harm.

A civilization that can thus succumb to its vanquished enemy must first have become so degenerate that neither its appointed priests and teachers, nor anybody else, has the

capacity, or will take the trouble, to stand up for it.

– John Stuart Mill

PHILOSOPHICAL EXERCISES

First exercise: Draw on your own experience to convince yourself of the soundness of this distinction between offense and harm.

1. Think of an occasion in your life when you were harmed but not offended. (For example: the time you fell off your bicycle and scraped your knee.)
2. Think of an occasion when you were offended but not harmed. (Perhaps you were taunted by your schoolmates, or someone said something unkind to you.)
3. If it is possible for you to be harmed but not offended on the one hand, and offended but not harmed on the other, then offense and harm cannot be the same thing.

Second exercise: Think of something or someone who offended you. Why did you accept the offense? Can you discover a place of moral worth inside you, a place of human dignity that is immune from the shifting winds of external opinions? Remain there, and explore the inviolability of this place, and never allow an offense to intrude.

Third exercise: See if you can practice moral self-defense by refusing to accept an offense the next time it is offered to you. At the elementary level, do not take the offense personally: You are not obliged to. At the intermediate level, see if you can change offense into humor, and deflect it back to the offender. At the advanced level, even harm can be accepted without anger or violent retaliation, provided that you can teach a moral lesson to the one who harms you.

5

MUST YOU SUFFER?

Pain is inevitable. Suffering is optional.

– Anonymous

We derive our grief, as the artist does his inspiration, from the most mysterious point in our being.

– Elie Wiesel

IMAGINE A PRISONER in a cell with heavy bars, in a prison with high walls, with armed guards everywhere. But this is a most unusual prison. The cell door is always unlocked, as is the prison gate, and the guards are there to keep people out, not in.

The prisoner, however, believes this is the usual kind of prison, and so remains in the cell, which is actually quite comfortable. It has decent furnishings, and a lot of distractions to help pass the time. There are books and CDs, cable TV and a personal computer. There's a fully stocked bar, decent food, regular conjugal visits. The prisoner has to do a certain amount of boring work, but can also indulge interests and hobbies.

Pretty good, for a prison. But this prisoner is in fact quite unhappy, simply by virtue of being aware of being imprisoned. He would like to escape, and believes that if he did, then he would be happy. But he also believes that escaping would be dangerous and probably impossible, so he stays put. The prisoner resorts to various other "escapes" within the cell – food, drink, drugs, sex, books, TV. All of them work, but only temporarily. The return to reality is more painful each time, making a greater intensity of diversion necessary to achieve the next temporary escape. These diversions also lead to fantasies of how wonderful life must be beyond the prison walls, and so to regrets about how much one is missing by being imprisoned.

Millions of people are living in a prison just like this. It is the prison of suffering. You suffer when you are wronged, when you confront evil, when you are treated unjustly. You also suffer when you wrong others, when you do evil, and when you perpetrate injustice. So you, like the prisoner, seek to alleviate the discomfort with tangential distractions, thinking all the while that you must stay in the cell. But that's an illusion. In fact you are free to walk out any time you wish, if only you can tear yourself away from familiar diversions and realize the way is open to you.

DOORWAY TO HEAVEN

Every human being suffers, sooner or later, so the operational question is not whether you will suffer, but what you will suffer from. By far a more important question still is how you will seek to alleviate your suffering. The answer you arrive at will determine whether you increase your own suffering (and that of those around you), or diminish it. Unfortunately, there are many ways to increase suffering. Fortunately, there are comparatively few ways to alleviate it. Why "fortunately"? Because limited options make your way much clearer.

Suppose you were in a room with a thousand doors, and you had to choose one, and only one, to go through. If nine hundred and ninety-nine doors led to hell, and only one led to heaven, would that be good or bad? That depends on whether they were marked or not. Because if all the doors looked alike, and you had to choose your door by chance, you'd have pretty poor odds of picking heaven: one in one thousand. Hell would become overpopulated in a hurry – and it is, right here on earth. But if the doors were clearly marked either HEAVEN or HELL, you would be certain of finding heaven sooner or later. That is, provided you could read the signs.

No matter what room of what building you are in, you can always find myriad doorways to hell – and you can always find at least one doorway to heaven. Although everybody says they want to go through the doorway to heaven, a great many walk right through all kinds of doorways to hell. Perhaps we need to learn to recognize the markings on the doors and see that our cells are open, so we can leave suffering behind us.

PAIN VERSUS SUFFERING

Before we get to that, we need to clarify some fundamental things, starting with the difference between pain and suffering. A physical harm, like an injury or a disease, is likely to cause pain. Pain is a physical sensation. So pain is often a warning that something is physically wrong. If you accidentally placed your hand on a hot stove and didn't feel pain, your hand would not last very long. Similarly, if you didn't feel pain from a cavity in your tooth, you'd end up losing the tooth itself. There are exceptions – "phantom pain" in amputated limbs, metastasizing cancer without any painful symptoms – but on the whole, pain is meant to signal you that something is physically wrong and needs attention.

Suffering, on the other hand, is a mental state. As with offense, you must usually be a willing accomplice in order to feel it. Other people can inflict pain on us against our wills, but very rarely can they make us suffer without our tacit consent. Ironically, people who are closest to you and who know you best can often make you suffer most. Why? Because they know what makes you tick, and therefore know exactly how to recruit you and enlist you as a willing accomplice in your own suffering. At the other extreme, those who know you least – that is, total strangers – can also make you suffer most. Why? Because they may choose to disregard your humanity, and impose conditions on you that are intolerable. However, please realize that while pain can be inflicted on you by someone else (or indeed by yourself), suffering cannot be inflicted on you in this way. You can be afflicted by external circumstances that increase or decrease your tendency to inflict suffering on yourself, but that suffering is your own. In one sense, this is good news: If you own your suffering, you can also disown it. You cannot do this with pain.

However, pain and suffering can also be related at times. In cases where disease causes acute or chronic pain, it also causes acute or chronic dis-ease (suffering) on account of that pain. Pain hurts the body to begin with; suffering is pain's echo in the mind. We say that people "suffer" from migraines. We mean that migraines cause blinding pains and other unpleasant symptoms, which in turn cause dis-ease (suffering) because of the pain, unpleasantness, and incapacitation. If your suffering comes from pain alone, then to alleviate the suffering you must alleviate the pain. That is a medical problem, not a philosophical one.

Similarly, people who are chronically depressed because of a brain disorder also suffer chronically from the mental echo of that disorder. They generally feel the suffering and *not* the pain, because the brain itself isn't pained by its disorder. Yet when they take medications that correct the brain's neurochemical dysfunction, their suffering abates. At least, that particular form of suffering ends. They may then need to deal with other forms of suffering, such as moral dilemmas, which are philosophical in origin. In some cases, like bipolarity, they may prefer the disease to the cure: Medication prevents them from sinking too far into the depressive phase, but also "cuts" the exhilarating and creative peaks off the manic phase. Some would rather suffer from the depressive state than suffer because they can no longer attain the summit of their creativity. Such difficult choices fall into Aristotle's celebrated category of the lesser of two evils.

Philosophy is helpful when you are suffering, but most likely not in acute pain. Those who seek philosophical guidance, or any other kind of talk therapy, are usually suffering from something. Nor is their suffering caused by a brain disorder. They are physically and mentally functional people who have created or encountered circumstances that engender or promote their state of suffering. They want not to suffer, and they rightly look upon dialogue as an instrument that both reveals the causes of their suffering and points to a way beyond it. In the ancient world, philosophy was called "medicine for the soul," or "the cure of souls." It did this job admirably well.

To summarize: pain comes from disease; suffering, from dis-ease. Whereas a heart attack produces physical pain, a "broken heart" produces emotional anguish and mental suffering. You may not be able to ease pain at will, but you can surely alleviate anguish and suffering once you know what is causing the dis-ease. If you're having a heart attack, there's little you can do to stop it by yourself. But if you're experiencing a broken heart, that's the result of dis-ease rather than disease, and there are many steps you can take to mend it.

One more thing: While pain itself can be a primary cause of suffering, one's attitude toward pain, or one's ability to tolerate pain, can have a big effect on suffering. If you are in pain because of an untreated disease or the after effects of treatment, then you're probably also suffering. But if you are in pain from intense athletic activity, like running a marathon or climbing a mountain, then I'll bet you're not suffering in the usual sense: You may even find the exertion exhilarating. That's the "runner's high." In general, you may learn to improve your tolerance for pain, but your initial tolerance level seems more a matter of nature than nurture. With suffering, it's the other way around: Just as you can be influenced to suffer greatly but needlessly, you can also learn how to minimize or abolish your suffering altogether.

NEED VERSUS WANT

Before we look at cases, we should also briefly compare need and want. The kind of suffering that comes from needs unmet (as opposed to wants unsatisfied) is probably the worst suffering of all. As humans, we all have definite needs in life, material and otherwise. A list of essentials might include: water, food, shelter, clothing, love, sex, education, health care, family, community, friends, work, and fulfilling a purpose in life.

In the developing world, people tend to suffer because of unmet needs for water, food, clothing, and shelter. In the developed world, people are more likely to suffer from familial strife, insufficient love, unsatisfactory careers, or unfulfilled purpose. Those who suffer from unmet basic needs rarely suffer from lack of purpose. Their purpose is clear: daily survival. If basic human needs are met in a balanced way, then suffering is all about unsatisfied wants rather than unmet needs.

Wanting is a bad thing. If you need something, you will be at least temporarily sated by having that need met. But if you want something, you will never be sated by having that want satisfied. You'll simply want something else, and suffer again because of it. You can't easily suppress your needs, nor should you. You should be able to eat, drink, shelter yourself, and so forth. But at the same time, how you choose to satisfy your needs (whether more foolishly or more wisely) will largely determine the extent to which you suffer. Your wants are another matter entirely. If they are not controlled, you will suffer. But if you try sometime, you just might find you get what you need. There's also an old curse: "May you get exactly what you want." Both getting what you want and not getting what you want lead to suffering. The good news is, you can bring suffering based on want under control, too.

Denise and David, Martha and Alex: Having or Not Having Children

Having or not having children can be a big issue in life. Do people need children or just want them? I believe that children are often more wanted than needed. That would also explain why there are unfortunately so many *unwanted* children in the world. However, many people, especially women but also some men, want children so badly that it begins to look like a need. When motherhood is considered to be an obligatory role, it looks like a need. There's also an interplay between want and need in the case of children, because a woman who *wants* children *needs* to have them while she is biologically able, and also *needs* a man for various purposes, from conception to shared parenting. As well, each parent needs to play a different but vital role, which we'll discuss in chapter 6.

Now let's compare the suffering a couple can feel from either having or not having a child. Denise and David were struggling with the former. Denise's daughter Kathryn, from her first marriage, had been an intermittent misery to both Denise and David in the ten years they'd been together. David tried to be a loving surrogate father to Kathryn, but the girl repeatedly rejected him. Denise was frequently caught in the crossfire between the two. Even though they both love Kathryn, and even though she loves them both (and needs to come to terms with her love for David, and her rivalry with her mother), they are often quite miserable together. During the worst of times, David and Denise quarreled bitterly about Kathryn, and verged on breaking up. Kathryn could hardly wait to go to college, and thus get out of the house. David and Denise could hardly wait for her to go to college for the same reason. This is a classic example of the misery of having – in this case, of having a child. Of course, there are many positive aspects to their life together, but their episodes of strife were undeniable.

Through Martha and Alex we can see the polar opposite. Martha and Alex expected to have children when they got married, but as it turned out their combined fertility issues meant they stood little chance of conceiving. They desperately wanted something they couldn't have, and so were quite miserable. They spent lots of time and money trying alleviate their misery – fertility clinics, surrogate motherhood arrangements, even the "black market" in babies – and each time they tried and failed to acquire a child their suffering only increased. Ironically (but not actually surprisingly) when they eventually got the object of their want – a legally adopted baby girl named Sandra – the misery of not having a child quickly transformed into the misery at not seeing their child often enough. Both were working professionals, and so they hired a full-time nanny for Sandra. This suffering tasted just the same as the previous suffering! And soon they wanted another child, and embarked on the whole process again, enduring identical suffering to what they had felt from not having Sandra. This is a classic example of the suffering of not having, which is not necessarily alleviated by getting what one wants.

Sogyal Rinpoche, a great Tibetan Buddhist teacher, gave some valuable lessons on suffering and its prevention. He taught that there are only two kinds of misery: the misery of having and the misery of not having. Whether you suffer because you have something you don't want or because you don't have something you do want, the experience of the suffering – that is, its taste – is exactly the same. To Denise and David, and to Martha and Alex, their suffering tasted just the same, too. Suffering is suffering, no matter what its particulars. Suffering resides in your mind, and nowhere else. As long as you think that your suffering is caused or cured by external circumstances alone, you will feel like a tennis ball being smacked back and forth by two accomplished players named "Have" and "Have Not." They can rally all day, and never tire. In fact, they can play longer than that: They can play for your entire lifetime if you allow them to do so.

The moral is to learn to be content with what you have – or with what you don't have. True contentment comes from within, and is not dependent on things external to you. The reason why each of these four adults suffers is not really because they have or don't have children, but because they are attached to the idea that by merely exchanging one set of external circumstances for another, they would become happy and remain satisfied. It is people's ideas that most often cause their suffering. Yet people seek to change everything else under the sun in order to become happy. Although they often succeed in making changes, they do not necessarily extricate themselves from misery. Many Americans suffer precisely because they regard happiness as an external goal. Thomas Jefferson enshrined "life, liberty and the pursuit of happiness" as three core values of the American way. I agree that the first two are supremely important: Life should be nurtured and celebrated; liberty should be cherished and preserved. But happiness cannot be "caught" by pursuing it. On the contrary: The more it is pursued, the more elusive it becomes. Personal fulfillment through attaining worthwhile goals is a fine thing; but then inner contentment is possible at every single step on that road.

> **We need to make a very clear distinction between what is in our ego's self-interest and what is in our ultimate interest; it is from mistaking one for the other that all our suffering comes.**
>
> **– Sogyal Rinpoche**

PLENTY OF WAYS TO SUFFER

Simply being human potentiates all kinds of pain and suffering. Every one of us suffers sooner or later, and most people spend too much of their time seeking to avoid, escape, or transform their sufferings without understanding what their true causes are. (Which most often turn out to be the twin miseries of having and not having.)

So if you would rather suffer than be joyous, then the universe will gladly oblige. You can always suffer, and for any number of reasons. You can suffer because of the past, or the future. You can suffer because of yourself, or others. You can suffer because of what you have, or don't have. You can suffer because of your beliefs, or non-beliefs. You can suffer because your God makes you suffer, or because He doesn't make you stop suffering. You can suffer because you're living, or because you're dying. You can suffer for the sake of love, of art, of ambition, or of suffering itself. You can suffer because you suffer too much, or not enough. And you can suffer because you refuse to extinguish your suffering, and instead make others suffer too.

DEALING WITH SUFFERING

There are several ways to deal with suffering: keep it to yourself, escape from it, pass it on to someone else, end it in yourself, or transform it into something helpful. Let's look at each in turn, illustrated with case studies.

Keep It to Yourself. A popular (yet far from ideal) strategy is to keep your suffering to yourself – to "suffer in silence." You may have been taught this is somehow noble, but it's actually needless. It deprives you, unnecessarily, of enjoyment and fulfillment. Or perhaps you believe that your suffering is a necessary preparation for your happiness in the next world. Or perhaps you harbor false beliefs about yourself, implanted by others, which prevent your authentic person from flourishing. Beliefs are not determined by our genes; they are acquired by cultural transmission. A belief that causes you sorrow can be replaced by a belief that causes you joy, but it's up to you to make the change. Alternative beliefs of all kinds are available to you; the world is teeming with them. But it's up to you to find beliefs that are helpful to you, rather than harmful. And while suffering can be a kind of education itself at times (like anything else in life), once you've learned its lessons you're allowed to graduate – and you deserve to.

Ruth: Keeping It to Herself

Ruth suffered needlessly for more than fifty years. She was essentially a very creative person, especially with language, and had aspirations to be a journalist or an author. Her parents were immigrants with a strong work ethic, but they didn't understand literary culture. Ruth and her older sister Alice both had to quit school during the Depression to help the family make ends meet. After the Depression, they married businessmen, raised children, and continued to work at part- or full-time office jobs. Ruth always felt that there was a creative writer "locked up" inside her, yearning to break out. That sense of imprisonment caused her to suffer. But her parents and her elder sister did not appreciate that kind of creativity: They lived in the "real world" of nine-to-five punch clocks, steady paychecks, and traditional aspirations. This was fine for them, but not for Ruth. Yet whenever she expressed her desire to be a writer, they said she was fantasizing or daydreaming. Ruth was once even offered a job as an apprentice journalist but declined it. Why? She lacked the self-confidence, and unfortunately received no encouragement from her family.

So Ruth invented a little a story, to the effect that she would have been a writer if only the Depression hadn't happened. Why didn't she go back to school afterward? Well, by that time she had kids, and couldn't. What about when her kids were grown? Well, by that time she had a lot of responsibility at her office, and couldn't very well leave. She tried to content herself with crossword puzzles, and was really good at them, but all the while that creative writer locked up inside her was serving a life sentence. For decades, she kept repeating the story that she would have been a writer if only circumstances hadn't prevented her. But the story wasn't true, and she suffered from lying to herself about herself. A pleasant personality on the surface, Ruth was creatively unfulfilled and deeply embittered by her life, and those twin toxins caused her much suffering inside.

Eventually that writer got released, but only after Ruth abandoned her false beliefs. With assistance from the Socratic method of philosophical midwifery (which we saw in chapter 3 applied to Gary's case) Ruth finally faced the fact that she had prevented herself from being a writer, and had used her circumstances as an excuse. It took great courage for Ruth to change her beliefs after all these years, but as soon as she did the writer inside her blossomed. By now a very mature student – in her seventies – Ruth began to take courses in creative writing, and within a few years wrote several volumes of poetry and short stories. She even got some of her pieces published. Her life took on new meaning, and she experienced deep contentment. Her long suffering ended.

The moral: Keeping suffering to yourself, however nobly, is not the answer. Rooting out its causes, no matter how long that takes, is the best approach.

Escape from It. This sounds tempting, and also has a heroic ring to it. It is not a coincidence that the theme of escape is perennially popular in Hollywood. Audiences love escape movies, presumably because so many people identify with them. *The Great Escape, Papillon, Birdman of Alcatraz,* and *The Shawshank Redemption,* among many others, share the common theme of a protagonist escaping from suffering by breaking out of a prison. The kind of suffering that we're talking about, however, is not produced by the pain of physical captivity in drastic surroundings but rather by ordinary situations in life, from which people unwittingly, unconsciously, or unerringly fashion their own prisons and then seek to escape. Those who are responsible for their own sufferings cannot escape them except by confronting them, understanding their true causes, and removing them. Attempts to escape from self-induced suffering not only fail, but often worsen the suffering itself. Fight or flight is one of the oldest biological instincts in humans, and since suffering is a kind of threat to one's well-being, there is a natural inclination to fight or flee this threat.

But when the suffering is self-induced, we cannot fight it except by confronting it, and we cannot flee it at all. If you were suffering and someone offered you a free trip anywhere in the world, or the galaxy for that matter, would you take it? You might do so for distraction, or temporary escape, but you know full well that your suffering would accompany you wherever you went, as surely as your shadow. Yet people will naturally attempt to escape – through alcohol, drugs, relationships, cults – whatever medium seems to take them away from themselves, to put time or space or altered states of consciousness between them and their suffering. Yet escape is only temporary. People who wish not to suffer must find a way to face and overcome their suffering. We will look at some traditional ways – both religious and philosophical – and their strengths and weaknesses, later in this chapter.

> **Not in the sky, not in the middle of the ocean, not even in the cave of a mountain, should one seek refuge . . . none of these is a safe refuge, nor is it the supreme refuge. For even after arriving at a refuge, one is not emancipated from all suffering.**
>
> **– Gautama Buddha**

But when suffering is not self-induced, one can neither flee from it nor fight it. Then, I must honestly say, neither medicine nor philosophy can be of much help. Extreme cases of schizophrenia, manic depression, chronic depression, and a host of other dysfunctions of the brain rob the afflicted individual of the capacity to alleviate his or her suffering, because it is not self-induced. It is a question of disease, not dis-ease. Although medications exist that can help stabilize many people so afflicted, many others among them still commit suicide. They find the suffering of their existence too much to bear – even if they are gifted and loved and able to help others greatly. Some try every medication and philosophy known to man, but they live recklessly and die suicidally because there is no other end to their suffering on this earth. For these unfortunate beings, some of whom may be truly beautiful people, life itself is such an unbearable unhappiness that their only way of fighting it or fleeing it is to do both together, and make an end of it. For them, death is the ultimate escape. But for those whom they leave behind, it is only the beginning of new suffering.

Spread It Around. Another very common strategy is to try to pass your suffering on to someone else. In the short run, this looks like the human equivalent of the barnyard pecking order: Your boss yells at you; you yell at your kid; your kid kicks the dog. Unfortunately, suffering is not like a football: You can't just hand it off to someone else and thereby disown it. If you try, you'll find it has a multiplier effect. That is, you can't get rid of suffering it by spreading it around. That just increases its presence in the world. People who seek out others just to implicate them in their suffering are actually suffering twice over: first from whatever's really bothering them at source, and second from the delusion that implicating others will alleviate their own problems.

The most gruesome examples of this are provided by serial killers, terrorists, gangsters, and genocidal mass murderers. Such persons inhabit a hell-world in which they hunger to harm others, and eventually to die themselves. They callously inflict pain and suffering on their victims, and lifelong painful memories on the friends and families of their victims. Some of them appear unable to experience other people as human – perhaps because they do not experience themselves as human either. Daisaku Ikeda attributes to terrorists an "utter and complete numbness to the suffering, sorrow, pain and grief of their fellow humans." The same can be said of anyone who premeditatedly spreads such suffering in the world. There is enough of it already, through natural causes and normal life struggles alone. Why make things more difficult than they are? Spreading your suffering around is by far the worst way of dealing with it, for you and everybody else.

People who follow this harmful path do not endure, and neither do their evil works. Whether they act alone or bend the resources of entire nations to their harmful wills, they find neither refuge nor safe harbor in this world. They are hunted, harried, and reviled, and eventually meet the doom they have decreed for themselves. They can spread their suffering to others for a time, but not for long. They can neither make the whole world suffer nor compel the world to tolerate their hell.

**He who takes delight in the slaughter of men
cannot have his will done in the world.
                                    – Lao-tzu**

End It in Yourself. If you are suffering from a disease, this disease is
in your body, and must be extinguished there. Why should dis-ease be
any different? But it seems to be much more difficult for people to
"own" their dis-ease because they have to accept responsibility for
their mental contents in order to end it in themselves. It is much easier,
at least in the short run, to blame others: "He's making me unhappy,"
or "She's not appreciating me," or "Society is treating me unfairly."
It's much harder to admit that some of your beliefs or expectations are
working against your better interests, and harder still to puzzle out
what to do about it. In the long run, however, the only way to end
your suffering is to disown it. But in order to do that, you have to
admit to owning it in the first place.

Philip's Case: What Goes Around Comes Around
Philip, a handsome but ruthless womanizer, eventually learned that
the suffering he caused others came back to haunt him. He then took
steps to end it in himself. Philip was an aspiring New York actor in his
early thirties – an intelligent, articulate, and very presentable young
man. There are hundreds (for all I know, thousands) like him in
Manhattan, many of them waiting on tables between engagements,
and hoping for that big break. Philip also had many women waiting
on him; he possessed that *je ne sais quoi* – an attractiveness combined
with an apparent indifference that made him irresistible. Many
women of varying ages and statuses fell in love with Philip, and he
had brief but torrid affairs with them, which all ended in one way: He
simply abandoned them one day, and never spoke with them again. So
he left a lot of broken hearts in his wake, and experienced some
sorrow himself – but only for himself. He seemed insatiable, but that
wasn't his problem. Philip suffered from solipsism, which we briefly
encountered in chapter 3.

Solipsists are not to be confused with narcissists. Narcissists pretend
to be in love with themselves – often because they think nobody else is,

or can be. Yet they selectively try to draw others into their world, to "validate" how lovable they are. Narcissists are deeply conflicted beings who mask their conflict with façades of perfection which they need others to acknowledge. Solipsists share a similar intensive self-awareness, or self-absorption, but at the same time they deny that there is anyone else in the world besides themselves. The classic philosophical problem of solipsism is the problem of other minds. You know you have a mind, but how do you know that anyone else does? Whatever data you process about the world, you process in your own mind. You can sense other bodies directly, but not other minds. Most of us, being reasonable and charitable beings, suppose that other humans are very much like ourselves. You have a mind, so you suppose that others have minds too. Solipsists don't. The universe revolves around a solipsist's mind, because he or she can't be sure that there are other minds out there. It's an extremely skeptical position, but skepticism never deters philosophers – it encourages them.

In fact, there's an old insider joke about solipsism that I'll share with you. A woman once approached Bertrand Russell after a lecture, said she was a solipsist, and asked him if he was one too. He thought about it, and said that at the end of the day he just might be. "Oh good," she replied, "but isn't it a pity there aren't more of us?"

If you don't get it, you need to think more philosophically! The point is that each solipsist thinks he or she is alone in the world: If there are no other minds, there are no other solipsists either.

So Philip's problem was that, being solipsistic, he didn't really believe he was hurting the women he dated and dropped. They didn't really exist for him, except physically. Until he met his nemesis, Kathleen. He fell head over heels in love with her. They dated for a while, had an intense romance, and then she suddenly abandoned him. This really got to Philip. His Big Question was "How could she behave so callously toward me? I thought she loved me!"

Suddenly, Philip was not a solipsist anymore: He was supposing that Kathleen had a state of mind in which she loved him. This was a revelation for Philip, who then contemplated the philosophy of karma, or moral cause and effect. Perhaps he was suffering from her sudden rejection because he had caused so many other women to suffer from his sudden rejections. Although cause and effect is rarely this simplistic in human affairs, it still appears true that one's behavior is reflected back to one over time. And Philip's suffering taught him a valuable lesson: that other people suffer too. Moreover, because it dawned on Philip that solipsistic relationships had produced all this suffering, he did not seek to alleviate his own dis-ease through yet another relationship.

Instead, he adopted a different and very courageous stance: He decided to end the suffering in himself. He chose a religious path as his vehicle, and retreated to a monastery for a period of prayer, contemplation, and celibacy. By walking this path of spiritual refinement, Philip was probably going to do himself and others a lot of good, and surely cause a lot less suffering as well.

If you choose to end suffering in yourself, you can too. Your means to that end will be your own to discover or devise, but helpful philosophical ideas abound. There are many paths and many benevolent guides to help you find the way. They are there for you if you are there for yourself.

Transform It into Good. The very best thing you can do with your suffering is to transform it from something hurtful to you to something helpful to others. If all you do is end your suffering within yourself, then that is good for you – as far as it goes. But if you continue to perceive suffering in others and want to help them end it in themselves too, that is good for everyone. And even if you can't fully disown your own suffering, you can help diminish it by helping diminish the sufferings of others. If you can manage this, you will have transformed your own suffering into other people's non-suffering, which is the greatest achievement anyone can aspire to in this life. It is also the explicit goal of Mahayana Buddhism, which we will look at briefly in this chapter.

Ida's Case: Transforming Suffering

Ida, a career woman in her fifties, had borne her share of suffering. Most recently, she had endured a lengthy and painful rehabilitation from injuries sustained in a car accident. Her professional life was undergoing transformation too. An insurance executive, Ida increasingly doubted that her company was doing as much good as it could. Dealing with unsettled or disputed claims, and the added anxieties these caused to the insured, eventually unsettled Ida too. She wanted to change her career. Ida said she had two interrelated goals: first, to do work that was more meaningful to her; and second, to do work that was more helpful to others.

Like most people who seek philosophical guidance, Ida was stable and functional. Less commonly perhaps, she had a fair idea of what she wanted to accomplish. In fact, in Ida's case, she had already thought out many specific details. She wanted to get out of the corporate pressure-cooker of Manhattan and set up an alternative care center in a more rural setting. She wanted her center to offer acupuncture, reflexology, hypnotherapy, homeopathic remedies – and maybe even philosophical counseling!

So why had Ida sought philosophical counseling herself, given that she knew where she was coming from and where she wanted to go? It was during this present fuzzy interval, lying undefined between a past tinged by personal suffering and a future devoted to alleviating suffering in others, that Ida sought shape and definition. She saw philosophy as a bridge between her past and her future. So she sought a philosopher to help her build that bridge, and to encourage or accompany her across it. Among other things, I told Ida what I'm telling you: that I thought her idea was excellent, and her goals worthy. She had found a great way to combine her need for a meaningful career with her desire to help others.

Yet Ida wanted more than a commonsense validation of her mission: A philosophical bridge needs philosophical girders and spans. She wanted to ground her transition in some particular tradition. Why? Because thoughtful people do not simply seek rationalizations for their purposes in life – they can get those from fortune cookies or cereal boxes. Thoughtful people want to develop their philosophical identities, which means they need to find a way of looking at things that resonates with their past experience, accommodates their present circumstances, and justifies their future goals. In other words, people want to craft a philosophy of and for their lives, not just find an aphorism to see them through a bad hair day.

Although Ida was both analytical and intuitive, I sensed she had an affinity for Chinese philosophy, so we reinterpreted her situation from a Taoist perspective. Over time, we explored two main points.

First, from Lao-tzu, was the idea that big things are a sum of little things. What would amount to a major transition for Ida would really be accomplished in small incremental stages. So she didn't have to worry about doing everything at once. She could find some repose in this fuzzy interval of transition, just as the pupa reposes in its transition between larva (caterpillar) and chrysalis (butterfly).

> **All great things in the world start from the small . . . A thousand miles' journey begins from the spot under one's feet.**
>
> **– Lao-tzu**

Second, from the ancient Chinese doctrine of complements that informed Lao-tzu and Confucius alike, we learn the idea that everything contains its opposite. Thus Ida's past suffering contained the seeds of her future non-suffering. Similarly, her present unstructured life contained the seeds of the future structures she envisioned.

Ida soon crossed her philosophical bridge, opened her center, and embarked on her new journey. For me, she is a great example of the magnificent things ordinary people can accomplish, and the tremendous good they can do, if they decide to transform their personal suffering into help for others.

ORGANIZED RELIGION AND SUFFERING

Viewed philosophically, organized religions are truly amazing phenomena. They grant vulnerable, mortal, fallible, and suffering human beings a chance to unite with the immortal and infallible Godhead that quite possibly sustains the universe. Because we inhabit animalistic bodies, we humans are bound to be limited in our presence, knowledge, and power. We are confined to occupy only one place at a time, even though there are infinitely many places we might wish to be. We are constrained to learn only a tiny fraction of the infinite amount that is knowable, and are condemned to forget more than we remember. We are confined to do all these things in an insignificant amount of time, compared to geological and even larger time scales. And finally, we are given relatively little energy to attain our goals, considering how much could and should be done. Unlike our bodies, our minds are unlimited, and so we are free to conceive of a personalized being or a cosmic force that is omnipresent, omniscient, and omnipotent. We often call this "God."

The root of the word "religion" means "to bind." Thus people do more than merely conceive of such a being or force in their minds; they take active steps to join themselves with this being, and so share in all its attributes. Man stands halfway between the atom and the ideal. His animal nature is material, and impels him toward pleasure and suffering alike; his mental capacity is immaterial, and leads him toward spiritual union with the divine. Or so he believes, or possibly imagines.

> **If God did not exist, it would be necessary to invent him.**
>
> **– Voltaire**

Organized religions confront us with paradoxes of many kinds. On the one hand, they grant undeniable solace and comfort to suffering people the world over. On the other hand, they also justify and perpetuate unnecessary suffering themselves. On the one hand, they offer extensive and accessible moral guidance to their followers. On the other hand, they cannot convincingly explain why a benevolent God allows so much evil in the world. On the one hand, all their scriptures preach universal love, peace, and tolerance. On the other hand, all their scriptures have been twisted to justify hatred, violence, and intolerance. On the one hand, every religion has adherents who are wise, benevolent, and saintly. On the other hand, every religion also has adherents who are foolish, malevolent, and profane.

So please pardon us poor philosophers for shaking our heads in *disbelief,* at times. Part of a philosopher's job is to resolve paradoxes, but the paradoxes of religion are so difficult that only God could resolve them – if God exists. Many religions were practiced in ancient Rome during its decline, and Edward Gibbon wrote, "The people found them all equally true; the philosophers, equally false; the magistrates, equally useful." In other words, most people tend to believe whatever authority figures tell them; most philosophers tend to doubt whatever authority figures tell them; and most governments tend to support whatever makes it expedient for them to govern.

Major religions became "major" primarily because of political conquest. It is the combination of religious fanaticism and political ambition that has so often given rise to suffering on a massive scale, throughout world history. Whenever zealots of any faith or of tribal or atheistic cults have acquired political power, they have inflicted needless suffering. In contrast, wherever adherents to faiths (or tribes) are allowed to express their beliefs under the umbrella of secular civil laws or tolerant religious ones, and are prevented from seizing political power and imposing tyranny, people can worship freely but without harming others. One great test of any religious person, or "religious nation," is whether that person or nation can leave others in peace. If not, then it fails this test and increases human suffering.

Bigoted persons only increase suffering, by failing to perceive the humanity of others and by making the grievous mistake of supposing that race or sex or gender or ethnicity makes some people "more" human and others "less" so. Similarly, religious fanatics only increase suffering by failing to perceive the humanity of others who worship different gods in different ways; and by making the equally egregious error of supposing that there are "infidels" in the world, whom they must either convert or destroy. Another great test of any religious person, or any "religious nation," is whether that person or nation needs an enemy, somebody or some group to scapegoat or demonize. If so, then it fails this test and increases human suffering.

Anyone who requires enemies, or infidels, or demons to give their existence meaning and purpose lives in a hellish state of mind. It is best for them, and everyone else, if they change their state of mind; worst for them, and everyone else, if they spread their hell around.

VIA AFFIRMATIVA AND VIA NEGATIVA

Jews suffer. Christians suffer. Muslims suffer. Hindus suffer. Buddhists suffer. So what's the difference? Bhagwan Sri Rajneesh taught one important difference, which I'll share with you. Religions are all on the affirmative path, or *via affirmativa*. They all affirm the existence of a supreme being, or Godhead, who resides outside oneself, with whom the self must join. The joining is attempted by reaching out to the Godhead through prayer, through study of scripture, through observance of ritual, and through leading a good life. These attempts are encouraged, and comfort is offered to sufferers in this world, by the promise of reward in the next. Judaism, Christianity, Islam, Hinduism, some forms of Buddhism, and many other religions are on this path.

One danger of the *via affirmativa*, however, is plain. When you reach out in an effort to extend yourself to God, you are at risk of losing your balance. If you extend yourself but fail to reach the Godhead, you may grasp something lesser while believing that you have grasped God. All too often people reach out and grasp not God, but only corrupt people who claim to be God's representatives, and corrupt doctrines that increase suffering. If anyone teaches you hatred and violence and intolerance, rest assured that you have not reached far enough. If anyone teaches you that some humans are less than human, or demons, or infidels, than you have definitely not reached far enough.

Another danger of the *via affirmativa* is its insistence that salvation lies outside yourself. Just like the "pursuit of happiness" in secular life, which leads more often than not to suffering, so the "pursuit of salvation" in religious life can lead to its opposite: the pursuit of damnation – with plenty of suffering along the way. In its most unfortunate manifestations, the belief that salvation lies outside oneself leads people to embrace fatalism or apathy, in which case they assume no responsibility whatsoever for improving their lot in life. And you know what happens then? Exactly nothing. Your life doesn't get any better all by itself. You have to make it so. The *via affirmativa* is not supposed to be a passive life, but neither is it supposed to be a harmful or destructive one.

> **The path of affirmation means the path of effort, great effort: one is trying to reach God, one has to make all the effort that is possible; one has to do the utmost, one has to put oneself at stake.**
>
> **– Bhagwan Sri Rajneesh**

In contrast, consider the negative path, or *via negativa*. First, I hope you are not unduly biased by the world "negative," which has an undeservedly negative reputation. If you go to a doctor to get tested for some disease, you surely want the results to come back "negative." That's always good news. Similarly, if your fate rested on the verdict of a jury, you'd surely want to hear them say, "Not Guilty." That's negative too, but good news for the defendant. Life itself is "negative entropy" – another "positive" negative, if you happen to love being alive. So negatives are not necessarily bad things; in fact, they can be great.

Instead of reaching outside yourself toward the Godhead, the *via negativa* leads you deep inside yourself, to emptiness, toward your awakened state. Since you grasp at nothing on this path, you latch onto nothing harmful. Since you seek nothing on this path, you find everything. You find it deep within, where (paradoxically) there is nothing. The *via negativa* affirms that you can put an end to your suffering by means internal to yourself. The Tao teaches this implicitly; the Buddha teaches it explicitly. Unlike all the world's religions, which one way or another try to make necessities or virtues out of suffering, Buddha's teaching is a practical philosophy of non-suffering in this life. You can diminish your suffering at this very moment, if you begin to practice Buddha's philosophy. Naturally, such practices (like all practices) have a cumulative effect. The sooner you begin, the sooner you'll begin to acquire immunity to suffering. But this path leads through the abyss, and you must not be afraid to tread it alone at times.

Prayer simply means that whenever you are alone, you are not alone but lonely; you miss the other. On the path of the negative, aloneness is simply the greatest splendor there is.

– Bhagwan Sri Rajneesh

This is why we find Jewish Buddhists, Christian Buddhists, Muslim Buddhists, Hindu Buddhists, and – for those who have made it into a religion – Buddhist Buddhists. One's native religion is bound up with one's formative culture and web of beliefs, and most people do not (and need not) completely abandon their original ways. But many people adopt and practice Buddha's way, because it teaches not only love, peace, and tolerance, but also how not to suffer. As a practical philosopher, the Buddha refused to speculate about whether God exists or not, whether the soul exists or not, whether the next world exists or not. He realized that debating these questions does not necessarily lead to a state of mind beyond suffering. His teachings alleviate and extinguish human suffering by human means, without depending on supernatural beings.

But that comes back to what we said earlier in this chapter: To alleviate your suffering, you must first be willing to assume your fair share of responsibility for it. If you aren't willing, nobody can force you. But by the same token, corrupt or malevolent people can exploit your unwillingness to do so, and mislead you into perpetrating harms that only increase your suffering and that of others. Your unwillingness to assume responsibility for your suffering becomes a potential weapon in the hands of evil people, who can use you and your suffering as an excuse to increase the suffering of others. We should work to alleviate our own suffering and that of those around us, instead of increasing it for ourselves and others.

SECULAR SUFFERING

While religions can provide both suffering and relief from suffering – and sometimes one in the guise of the other – non-religions do exactly the same thing. Sogyal Rinpoche's aphorism applies here too: There is the misery of having gods, and the misery of not having them. In fact, it seems to me that secular people can suffer as much as religious ones. They have all the usual human problems, plus the additional problem of having no God to make everything come out right in the end. I have seen this time and again in my Manhattan philosophy group. Secular intellectuals have come and gone, many of them with a list of grievances to air. Secular political radicals suffer more than most: They have unresolvable *issues*. Many believe that we should be in utopia by now, and they constantly need someone to blame for keeping us out. Creationists, at least, can blame Adam and Eve. Radicals tend to blame the government.

Secularists are certainly not happier than average, and often more cynical. Unable to believe in God, they often fall into a melancholy existentialism or pessimistic fatalism. Prozac or Paxil don't help, because the problem is philosophical. Some turn to Stoicism, which faces suffering bravely but does not directly alleviate it. Others embrace intellectual Buddhism (i.e., the theory without the practice) because it allows them to make some sense of their suffering while perpetuating it. Finally, many secularists practice the Buddha's philosophy, which actually diminishes their suffering.

Michaela's Case: Living with the Unthinkable

Michaela said a very casual good-bye to her husband Ron as he left for work on the morning of September 11, 2001. She never saw him again, alive or dead. Ron worked on one of the upper floors of the Word Trade Center, and he vanished, along with thousands of others, in its collapse. Suddenly widowed with two young children, not by accident but by malevolent intent, Michaela was inconsolable. A year later, she still kept Ron's clothing hanging in his closet, left his personal effects untouched in his den, and wouldn't change the pillowcases, which still bore his scent. She cried herself to sleep every night, hugging the pillow as if it were Ron himself. Michaela kept her body and mind together during the day for the sake of her children, who were too young to understand what was going on, but she felt as though her life were shattered beyond repair. Grief counseling didn't help much, and neither did the support groups she attended. They distracted Michaela mildly from her suffering, but there was a terrible emptiness inside her filled with constant anguish. That emptiness used to be filled with Ron's love, producing abundant joy in her. Now it was a hollow source of sorrow.

Some of Michaela's friends were religious, and she had gone to church a few times to seek consolation and relief through prayer. Reaching out to God on the *via affirmativa*, Michaela discovered only a bottomless well of tears. The more sadness she offered up as a gift to God, the more sadness she experienced in herself. She became angry with God for making her suffer this much. She found it difficult to believe that an all-powerful and benevolent being would cause her so much sorrow. The Book of Job is not a comforting tale, and Michaela knew she personally did not have Job's faith or strength.

Michaela had a neighbor named Maureen, who had been practicing a form of Buddhist meditation for several years. Michaela had never bothered with it much, but now she asked Maureen to explain what it was about. Soon Michaela began to practice too, and very slowly began to get a grip on her suffering, by diminishing it in herself. If you are wondering why the *via negativa* was making Michaela feel better, while the *via affirmativa* had made her feel worse, here are four philosophical reasons.

First and foremost, the key to Michaela's recovery is that she did not hate the terrorists who murdered her husband, nor did she hate God for taking him away from her. Absent hatred, a terrible poison, her hellish state of mind was much more amenable to being changed into something better. Whereas hatred blinds us, sadness can open our eyes.

Second, by facing and owning her sadness through calm meditation and reflection on the attachments that cause suffering, Michaela began to realize and accept that Ron was gone for good. Sleeping with his ghost (e.g., his scented pillowcase), trying to love it, and trying to derive love from it, was actually a way of torturing herself and prolonging her agony. Instead, Michaela could learn to accept that Ron's life had been very beautiful, and that she had been most fortunate to share a few wonderful years with him. Sometimes that's all the time we get with someone, and perhaps we should be grateful for its duration instead of inconsolable at its end. Everything on this earth ends. It's only a matter of time.

Third, by taking this view, Michaela could see Ron's life, metaphorically, as a snowflake – unique and lovely to behold, but fragile and bound to melt eventually. Once melted, it becomes a drop that joins a river, and then evaporates into the sky, and crystallizes into another snowflake, which someone else will find unique and lovely while it briefly endures. These are the cycles of life and death, which are linked. They bring joy and sadness, but not necessarily mental torture. So by deepening her understanding, Michaela could cherish the memory of Ron without needing to be wedded to his ghost. In fact, once she let him go, she could remember their love with joy and sadness but without torment.

Fourth, the *via negativa* also made Michaela a better mother, for now she could see a part of Ron living on in their children, and she could nurture his memory by giving her love to them. Not being ghosts, they could absorb her love and return it.

> **Joys impregnate. Sorrows bring forth.**
> **– William Blake**

James's and Melanie's Case: Living with the Accidental

James and Melanie had three children. The two eldest were already in college, and the youngest, a boy of seventeen named Jordan, showed great academic promise. He was something of a prodigy, and very popular besides. One summer evening, he and some friends went out on the family boat for a leisurely sunset cruise on the lake. But their craft was struck by a speedboat, running at top speed without lights, and being piloted by someone under the influence of alcohol and drugs. Jordan was killed.

After the funeral, James spent much time down at the family dock that summer and autumn, meditating on the sudden death of his beloved son, the waste and senselessness of it all. How and why could such a young and promising life be erased in a careless instant? James did not believe that God or man would ever give him answers to these questions. Indeed, he wanted to know why we had to ask such questions at all. So James's suffering after Jordan's death caused him to ponder the deeper meaning of life. He sat on the dock, recollecting the seventeen summers spent there with Jordan, and the many things they had done together.

Through his meditations on life and death, James came to understood two matters. First, his past times with Jordan would never be undone. Second, his emptiness would be filled by something or someone yet undiscovered. His purpose now was to explore the contours and depths of that emptiness, so he could learn the best way to fill it.

Like Michaela, James did not harbor hatred for the killer of his loved one. And even though Ron's death had been part of a planned terrorist attack, while Jordan's death had been the result of an irresponsible boater, Michaela's suffering and Ron's suffering tasted the same. And by addressing their sufferings within, Michaela and James gradually overcame them.

Most people never realize that all of us here shall one day perish. But those who do realize that truth settle their quarrels peacefully.
– Gautama Buddha

SUFFERINGS OF GROUPS, AND THEIR EXPRESSION

People suffer not only individually but also collectively, because they belong to identifiable groups. They may have communal suffering inflicted on them by external powers. What I said near the beginning of this chapter about the suffering of individuals applies to groups as well. Remember? The operative question for individuals is not whether you will suffer, but what you will suffer from. This also applies to individuals as members of groups. In other words, you may suffer as an individual because you are a man, or a woman, or a child; or because you are heterosexual, homosexual, or bisexual; or because your skin is black, white, red, yellow, or brown; or because you are Jewish, Christian, Muslim, Hindu, or Buddhist.

So the crucial question for groups parallels that for individuals: What will you do with your suffering? Those groups that have won or earned the greatest opportunities for collective emancipation from suffering are also those who have endured the greatest collective suffering without violent retaliation against real or imagined enemies.

The first and most important step toward alleviating one's suffering is to own it, and to stop blaming and killing others for it. Own it, and you can disown it. Otherwise, the cycle of suffering never ends. True, the world is full of people willing to oppress you. But don't join their ranks by oppressing yourself.

AN EXPERIMENT WITH MOORE'S PARADOX

Unlike suffering, this chapter has a definitive end. I'd like to conclude it on an upbeat and experimental note, by asking you to apply one of philosophy's paradoxes to the alleviation of your suffering. G. E. Moore brought the following paradoxical sentence to the attention of philosophers: "I know that such-and-such is true, but I don't believe it." Sentences of this form are called "Moorean sentences," after their inventor. I'll bet you have already experienced some of them in your daily life. Suppose you're on vacation, having a great time. That usually means it passes quickly, too quickly. Suddenly it's time to go home, and back to work. What do people often say? "I know my vacation's over already, but I don't believe it." Similarly, people tend to utter Moorean sentences when something extremely good or extremely bad happens. For example, "I know I just won the lottery, but I don't believe it." Or: "I know my dear friend just died in an accident, but I don't believe it."

Moorean sentences illustrate, among other things, that there's a difference between knowing something to be true in a cold-blooded or matter-of-fact way and believing something to be true, which seems to require an emotional adjustment as part of an overall accommodation to sudden change. (We'll say more about change in chapter 11.)

So how can this help you? Suppose we ponder some variations on a Moorean sentence. First, consider, "I know that such-and-such is true, but I don't feel it." Suppose you have a toothache. Does it make sense to say, "I know I have a toothache, but I don't feel it"? That doesn't make much sense at all, because if you don't feel your toothache, how can you possibly know you have one? Next, consider: "I know that such-and-such is true, but I don't suffer from it." Does it make sense to say, "I know I have a toothache, but I don't suffer from it"? Yes it does, because pain and suffering aren't the same things. While a painful toothache is not fun (unless you're a masochist), it can help you concentrate at times, or make you more alert than usual, or teach you (the hard way) to practice better dental hygiene. Concentrating and learning are not suffering. Similarly, does it make any sense to say, "I know I just lost my job, but I don't suffer from it"? Of course it does. You can mourn a lost job to be sure, but you can also view it as an opportunity to find a new and more suitable one. This applies to many kinds of loss.

Those who have taken steps to immunize themselves against suffering are also able to improve their tolerance for pain, loss, and other phenomena that we are conditioned to regard as inevitable causes of suffering. Recondition yourself, and you will be able to increase your tolerance for normally unpleasant circumstances to the point that they cease to be unpleasant. That's much better than repeating the Moorean sentence that far too many people walk around asserting on a daily basis: "I know there's a way for me to decrease my suffering, but I don't believe it." Instead, try asserting this Moorean sentence on a daily basis: "I know that I am supposed to suffer, but I don't believe it." If you don't believe you have to suffer, your suffering will diminish. Why? Because suffering is not a brute fact in the world. It's a changeable state of your mind.

PHILOSOPHICAL EXERCISES

1. What do you suffer from? What do those around you suffer from?
2. What steps are you taking to alleviate your suffering, and theirs? What steps are they taking to alleviate their suffering, and yours?
3. Are these steps working for you? For them? If so, why? If not, why not?
4. If so, then keep taking them. If not, take new ones.

6

WHAT IS LOVE?

One word frees us of all the weight and pain of life: that word is love.

– Sophocles

All you need is love.

– The Beatles

LOVE IS A VITAL ingredient of human life, and its importance in human affairs cannot be overstated. Most people cannot get through the day without expressing love or being the beneficiary of love's expression. In philosophical counseling sessions, love comes up again and again, owing to its many and varied roles in our experience of ease and dis-ease alike. Many kinds of dis-ease have something to do with absent love, unrequited love, unfulfilled love, love gone wrong, or even love gone right but with strings attached. Beyond even romance and friendship, soul-mating and parenting – the most common contexts for discussing and expressing love – love-related issues arise in individual careers, as well as in complex organizations. Since love plays such a big part in so many people's lives, including yours too without a doubt, it's definitely worth asking some philosophical questions about this powerful yet somewhat mysterious force. What is this thing called "love," which causes everyone so much joy and sorrow alike?

Parents, poets, prophets, preachers, psychologists, and philosophers all have their own ways of understanding love. There are so many kinds of love, or ways of conceiving of love, it would be impossible to do justice to them all in one book, let alone one chapter. So here we'll look briefly some important philosophical conceptions of love, and their applications to daily life. By reexamining your own philosophy of love through these lenses, you'll enhance your experience of life itself, wherever love's winding road may lead you.

The Tao of Freud

We often improve our understanding of something by considering its opposite, or complement. This was Sigmund Freud's approach to the question "What is love?" Freud ultimately answered in three different ways, comparing love to three kinds of opposites: loving versus being loved; loving versus hating; and loving versus indifference (the opposite of both love and hate). Although Freud was innocent of Chinese philosophy in general, and Taoism in particular, he strongly echoed some of its ancient ideas, in that such pairs are not *opposites* but *complements*. Each is necessary for the other to exist.

Freud's first pairing is probably the simplest to grasp. We all understand what it means to love someone or something. You could easily list right now people you love, things you love to do, music you love to listen to, foods you love to eat, and so forth.

In this conception, love requires a subject who loves and an object that is loved. If Dick loves Jane, then he is a love subject and she is his love object. He offers his love, and perhaps she accepts it. If she does accept it, she may well reciprocate: Jane loves Dick. Then Jane is also a love subject, while Dick is also a love object. When people love each other in this reciprocal way, it produces a very powerful bond between them. Such a reciprocating complementary relationship can be illustrated this way:

Dick loves Jane.
Jane is loved by Dick.

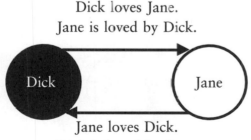

Jane loves Dick.
Dick is loved by Jane.

But it's much more elegant, and also more revealing, to symbolize their relationship this way:

Here, loving someone (offering the gift of one's devotion) and being loved by someone (receiving that same gift) are balanced and joined, as part of a greater whole. When two people both love and are loved by one another, they are in harmony with Tao (the Way). This kind of love is a reciprocal completion of oneself in and with the other. Humans constantly seek this kind of completion. Sometimes they find it, and it lasts a lifetime. If so, then their honeymoon is never over.

We can, however, see two kinds of problems on the horizon. First, what happens when one person's love is received but not reciprocated? Suppose Jane merely tolerates Dick, for her own reasons. He loves her, and she allows herself to be loved by him, but she does not really love him. Then their love picture is obviously unbalanced:

Whatever the short-term pleasures or benefits each one derives from this state of affairs, its inherent imbalance is bound to produce dis-ease in them both.

The same thing would be true if Jane loved Dick but Dick didn't love Jane:

Finally, if neither loves the other at all, we have this picture:

Here we have a physical meeting at the boundaries of their beings, but no gift of love is given or received by either person. This is like sex without emotional content. There is full physical contact at the boundaries, but nothing of one's emotional, intellectual, or spiritual being is established or persists in the other. The sex might still be great, but this is insufficient for fulfillment as a human being.

But things can go wrong with balance, too, if one person invests a lot more love than the other. That leads to a relationship disproportionate in one of these ways:

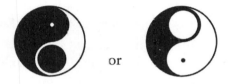

This is exactly what leads a lot of couples to marital counseling; they experience dis-ease at the disproportion and want to try to correct it in order to preserve their relationship. Almost always, the one who loves more and who is loved less feels the greater dis-ease, and seeks to establish or restore a more equitable proportion. Regrettably, this is not always possible. Many conflicts occur in relationships, and many marriages end in divorce, because of an "investment imbalance" of this kind.

Then again, if both people invest too much in each other, the disproportion is such that neither feels like a centered person in and of themselves:

This can happen when two people become "as one," as the saying goes – and are thus reduced to being just half a person each. Each one loves the other at the expense of him- or herself. Each one is therefore hollow, reliant on being loved by the other, with a diminished capacity for self-love, as well as a hampered ability to give and receive gifts of love in a wholesome way. If one were to lose the other on whom so much of oneself depends, it would be tantamount to losing oneself. The "arithmetic" of this kind of love is bizarre: One plus one equals one, if you stay together, but two minus one equals zero, if you split apart.

Stephanie's Case: Two Minus One Equals Zero

Stephanie had a seven-year marriage with Alan, and they had invested a lot in each other – perhaps too much. With Stephanie's strong support, they had weathered many difficulties, and Alan's business had finally begun to prosper. In their late twenties, they now had enough security to think about starting a family. But something was bothering Stephanie. Increasingly, she felt that much of what she had invested in Alan was her own undeveloped potential for a more creative career. She needed to reclaim this potential to move her life forward, to grow into the person her intuition said she really was. She had tried to accomplish this with Alan, but he constantly discouraged her initiatives because he wanted, somewhat childishly and also insecurely, to retain her full attention. But Stephanie felt so stifled that she had to leave him. Part of her really loved him, yet at the same time that part of her was being suffocated by their relationship. Alan needed to grow for his own sake, too, and not be so helplessly dependent on her. When Stephanie finally left Alan, it felt as though a chunk of her being was sheared off, leaving a raw wound that needed to heal. Initially Stephanie took medication for her anxieties and depressive moods, but she actively sought new directions in life. She found them at first through a succession of relationships with older men, whose experience and maturity opened new horizons to her and gave her the metaphysical "air" she needed to breathe. Then she began to discover and value her independence.

Contrary to the stereotype of women in their late twenties, Stephanie did not really need or want a husband or children, at least at this stage of her life. Marriage had agreed with her for a time, but she was now entering a phase of intellectual growth, emotional maturation, and spiritual development that required her to be alone and independent much of the time, for study and reflection. Stephanie gradually regenerated the "missing" part of herself over a period of months, but not through reattachment to another. On the contrary, she emptied herself even more completely, and through emptiness became whole. She was guided by the thousand-year old Indian Buddhist teachings of Shantideva. They helped her through this vital transformation of her life with their no-nonsense approach to taming the tigers (and other wild animals) of the mind. Try dissolving your ego, as Stephanie did. Buddhism is a powerful solvent.

> **All the harm with which this world is rife, all fear and suffering that there is,**
> **Clinging to the "I" has caused it! What am I to do with this great demon?**
>
> **If this "I" is not relinquished wholly, sorrow likewise cannot be avoided . . .**
> **To free myself from harm, and others from their sufferings,**
>
> **Let me give myself away, and cherish others as I love myself.**
>
> **– Shantideva**

LOVE AND HATE

Freud's second pairing of opposites, loving and hating, actually reinvents another ancient philosophical wheel, from both Indian and Chinese traditions: the idea of attachments. Although love and hate are polar opposites, they are bound up in a complementary relationship, just like the positive and negative poles of a magnet. You can't separate the two poles of a bar magnet. If you break it in half, you get two smaller bar magnets, each with a positive and negative pole. As an investment of emotion in someone or something else, also a kind of magnetic alignment, love and hate are like two poles of a magnet called "attachment." In this sense too, they are inseparable. Having a capacity for one means having a capacity for the other.

So once an attachment is formed, it may manifest as love, hate, or a mixture of both – the classic "love/hate" relationship that so many feel toward themselves, or others, or their job, or their country. This is where the magnetic analogy starts to weaken, since love and hate form more of a spectrum than polar magnets, with a continuous mixture of emotions possible. Most romantic love relationships form at the positive end of the spectrum, but some gradually shift toward the negative end. Strong positive feelings can, and do, turn into strong negative ones, and humans are easily and often caught in this trap. Once you make an emotional investment in others, it can turn sour, sometimes for reasons beyond your immediate awareness, but never for reasons beyond your understanding.

When you accept someone else's investment of love in you, and make it part of yourself, you are also – like it or not – wheeling a Trojan horse into the fortress of your being. That gift of love comes with many strings attached. Usually those strings are just the normal human imperfections of the other person, and we are willing to overlook them (if we even see them at all) at the outset. As Shakespeare finely observed, "Love is blind." In the beginning, all is rosy, because your attention is fixed on the good things. As you get accustomed to those things, or start taking them for granted, you begin to fix your attention on the things that get on your nerves and, eventually, that you simply can't stand. That's how love sometimes turns into its polar opposite – a positive attachment changes into a negative one.

This leads to worse news, but also better news. How, you may ask, are people able to hate so vehemently or passionately someone or something they know nothing about? How can people turn into racists or sexists, without ever having known or loved the people they hate? How can fanatics in some faraway county hate America, when they have no understanding of it? That's the worse news. With fanatics, we encounter a different kind of hatred, namely that of one human group being demonized by another group, whose members conceive themselves to be righteous or exemplary humans, but who suffer from many kinds of death-dealing delusions. These are not mental "diseases," only beliefs that prove toxic or lethal to those that carry them – and to those who get too close to them at the wrong moment. We will take up this problem in chapter 7.

But the better news is that this kind of hatred also has its polar opposite in love of humankind. It is certainly possible and desirable to love a group of people whom one does not necessarily know very well on the basis of their humanity, which is always recognizable no matter what language they are speaking or what social conventions they have adopted. Mind you, just as we cannot easily be tolerant of intolerance, we cannot easily love those who hate us. Yet it is far worse to return hatred for hatred. So even when people must be forcibly restrained from doing harm to others, there should be no hatred involved. The guiding idea should be to educate them, and if at all possible to turn their blinding hatred into insightful love.

There are, fortunately, other kinds of love where the positive does not inevitably activate the negative, but we have to get beyond Freud to discover them. As far as Freud was concerned, emotional attachments always potentiate their opposites. To the extent that the basis of attachment in a love relationship is gratification of the ego, then I'd agree that the attachment is potentially unhealthy, and has the capacity to manifest its polar opposite (anger or hatred) in the relationship or cause other dis-eases (like sadness or regret) after the relationship.

Freud's third dimension of love is the recognition of the opposite of both love and hate: indifference. If you are indifferent to someone or something, you make no emotional investment at all. With no emotions invested, you can neither love nor hate. This allows you to exercise impartial reason, which is useful more often than not. It also forms the basis of Stoicism, whose guiding idea is not to overvalue anything that can be taken away from you by others, for by doing so you place yourself in their power. If you become too attached to people or things, you're setting yourself up for trouble. We'll look at attachment itself in chapter 12. Meanwhile, indifference to circumstances can be good, especially when circumstances are bad. This is what people call "taking things philosophically"; they mean "Stoically." This kind of indifference is not callousness or lack of compassion. It is the ability not to take events too personally, even when they seem to be implicating your person. It's more like being cool under fire. It allows you to perform at your best under stress.

So on the beneficial side, indifference prevents you from suffering from negative attachment to something. However, indifference also means you can't experience pleasure from positive attachment to something. If you go through life trying to be indifferent to people and things in order to spare yourself dis-ease, you will be depriving yourself of engagement and enjoyment. You may as well be a rock in a forest: surrounded by all kinds of living beings, and exposed to all kinds of elements and seasons, but unable to relate to any of them organically.

Believe it or not, you can experience happiness without momentary gratification and sadness without lingering sorrow. You can relate to others and engage with life as lovingly as possible, yet at the same time you can also cultivate a detachment that allows you to get off that emotional roller coaster that most others are riding full time, awake or asleep. But to do this, you have to get beyond Freud's "Pleasure Principle" – the idea that the universal fundamental human concern is to seek pleasure and avoid pain – and therefore get beyond the conception of love as merely gratifying attachment.

> **The feeling of happiness derived from the satisfaction of a wild instinctual impulse untamed by the ego is incomparably more intense than that derived from sating an instinct that has been tamed.**
> **– Sigmund Freud**

CLASSICAL GREEK LOVE: EROS, PHILOS, AND AGAPE

The ancient Greeks, whose developments and discoveries in mathematics, logic, ethics, aesthetics, and many other subjects continue to exert primary influence on Western civilization, and therefore also on the global village, were vitally interested in love and its relation to the human soul. In this pre-Christian period, the Greeks were pagans, and their view of the soul was not a religious one involving spirits or ghosts. Plato and others conceived of love as residing in the soul, and the soul itself (and therefore love) as having three parts or dimensions. These dimensions correspond to the gut, the mind, and the heart. The Greeks labeled these three distinct types of love *eros, philos,* and *agape.*

Although today we use the word "erotic" to mean sexual, the Greek conception of eros actually referred to all human physical appetites. The appetite for food and drink were erotic (belonging to the domain of the gut) as much as the appetite for sex. In this view, sex is just another appetite, with no more value judgment connected to it than to food. It is only when religions started controlling human social conduct that we saw sexuality treated as something different from other bodily appetites, which led to the narrowed (and current) meaning of eros. "Erotic love," then, in today's parlance, means sexual love, and carries with it connotations of attraction, allure, mystique, chemistry, and animal magnetism. We cannot deny its importance, but we must also affirm love's higher aspects.

"Philos" means an intellectual attraction to someone or something that develops into a kind of love. Philosophy itself, meaning "love of wisdom," happens to be good example. Philos means loving people, things, or ideas in nonsexual ways. The relationship between a student and a teacher can be philial love, as can the attraction to a friend, poem, landscape, mathematical theorem, moral theory, subject of study, professional practice, or social cause. People who love their work have philial relationships with their careers. Do you love and celebrate life itself? This too is philos. One of the most powerful expressions of philos is friendship.

In friendship the ego is not dissolved in the other; on the contrary, it blossoms. Unlike love, friendship does not declare that one plus one makes one; rather, that one plus one

**makes two. Each of the two is enriched by and
for the other.**

– Elie Wiesel

There is a potential downside to philos, as with any other kind of attachment. If you become philially overattached to something, you can be blinded by the attachment just as you can by romantic love. Or philos can slide into its opposite – phobos, or aversion. Not every phobia comes from a philia gone wrong, but when we speak of familiarity breeding contempt, we mean that attraction can turn to aversion.

We also have to be on guard against infecting philos with eros. Mixing the two usually diminishes both – as we saw in chapter 3, reason and passion are necessarily separate functions at times. It is not uncommon, however, for two people in a close professional or other working relationship to develop erotic feelings for each other, but the erotic relationship can damage the philial one. For every graduate student and professor who transform their intellectual match into a memorable affair or lasting marriage, which neither jeopardizes nor compromises the professor's supervision of the student's progress, many other failed liaisons litter the trail. And that's probably among the most socially acceptable pairings of its kind. It is professionally unacceptable – and for good reason – for philial relations between physicians and patients, or between counselors and counselees, or between lawyers and clients, to turn erotic.

The Greeks' third and highest form of love is agape (pronounced ah-GAH-pay) – love which seeks nothing in return. It is the rarest and most valuable kind of love. Those who manifest agape act beyond purely personal motives: The world is full of beings needing to be loved by a great heart, and agape is love that emanates from such a heart. Agape enables individuals to experience divine love themselves, and to manifest compassion for others. Because agape is unselfish, its expression always helps and never harms another. Where eros makes courtship and family possible and philos makes friendship and society possible, agape makes worship and humanity possible. Agape can also sanction and strengthen eros and philos alike.

What makes agape different from eros and philos is its selflessness. Eros makes people strive to find or lose themselves in another. Philos makes them want to identify themselves with another. Agape manifests without selves and their motives getting in its way. Receiving agape is like feeling the radiant sun shining on you. You do not mind that it shines on others as well; on the contrary, you want others to feel it too. Giving agapean love is like generating the radiant sunlight itself.

There are many ways to experience agape as a beneficiary and then to bestow it on others. Some do so through prayer; some through meditation; others, through hard lessons of life and gradual acquiescence in wisdom; still others, though mystical quests. However it comes into your life, the key is to take the self out of the equation. This was a problem for Freud – and a weakness in his theories on love. Freud had read a bit about "mysticism," and the states of being that can be attained through practices of bringing the appetitive, erotic soul to rest. He had heard accounts by people who experienced oneness with the universe, or unity with things, during which time the ego is temporarily dissolved. People consistently liken this experience to the feeling of a drop returning to the ocean, often accompanied by visual sensations of divine light, or auditory sensations of divine music, or gustatory sensations of divine nectar, or tactile sensations of being bathed in divine love. "I am unable to discover that Oceanic feeling in myself," confessed Freud, with some bitterness. And he was right, for agape does not reside in or emanate from the self, or any "parts" of the self on his psychoanalytic map. Neither the ego nor the superego nor the id can give or receive agape, any more than they can get a suntan.

It is undoubtedly a good thing to experience both eros and philos, for then you will discover their benefits, detriments, and limitations for yourself. And when you are ready for it, agape will be there for you.

Professor Smith's Case: Eros Gone Astray

Appetite should never lose sight of principle, or else its satisfaction will be fraught with wrongdoing and harm. Then again, too much thinking can frustrate eros, and lead to dis-ease. I will never forget a graduate lecture once given by a Professor Smith, who was an expert in decision theory. He started off by telling us that on his way to the lecture hall, he had a sudden appetite for grapes. So he went into a grocery store, and there found two kinds of grapes: an exotic but expensive kind and a domestic but inexpensive kind. He applied decision theory to help him choose which kind to buy but could not resolve the dilemma. So he exited the grocery store without buying any grapes at all!

I tell you this so that you can avoid making the same mistake. If you have an appetite for grapes, then buy some grapes and eat them. (But don't steal them: that's where principle comes in.) You do no wrong by satisfying simple appetites in harmless ways. And if you cannot make the smaller choices in life, how can you possibly make the bigger ones? Just for the record: I later studied decision theory myself, and found it to be an excellent tool for refining complex choices. But I never take it grocery shopping.

Applied to erotic love, one moral of this story should obvious: If you go to a dance, don't use decision theory to decide whom to dance with, or you might end up not dancing with anybody. Another moral: If you decide to pursue a deeper relationship with one of your dancing partners, you should find out whether she or he is the exotic or the domestic type. Relationships also carry "price tags," and not just financial ones: emotional, intellectual, social, and political costs can also be exacted. If at all possible, find out what you can afford before you buy it.

Marina's Case: Appearance and Reality

Marina had a philial infatuation with the image of being a New York author – she was in love with it – and set about cultivating that image, more or less successfully. She really was a promising young writer, who had published pieces in some very well-regarded magazines. She had always been in love with having the "right" background and authentic lifestyle of a "New York author," so she not only acquired the de rigueur academic credentials (putting herself into considerable debt in the process) but also rented an apartment in a chic Manhattan neighborhood with a literary reputation. It was then that she discovered she was not at all in love with her chosen life, and had only been infatuated with the image.

One philosophical idea above all helped Marina to overcome her infatuation: Plato's distinction between appearance and reality. In his Allegory of the Cave, Plato depicts most people leading their lives as though they were chained up facing a cave wall. A campfire burns behind them, and their captors (who represent their own ignorance) hold up objects in front of the fire, which then casts fuzzy shadows on the wall. That's all the captives can see. So they speculate about these fuzzy shadows, which are mere appearances of real things, but which they mistake for ultimate reality. They need to break their chains, turn around, and behold the fire and the objects casting the shadows. But this is not yet reality, because the firelight is artificial, and because these objects did not originate in the cave. So the cave dwellers must exit the cave, explore the sunlit world outside, and discover the true origins of the objects themselves. For Plato, these origins lie in the "ideas" that make all things possible.

Inside the cave is the shadowy world of appearances; outside the cave is the sunlit world of ideas (or "forms," as Plato called them). Here we gain clear vision and profound understanding of reality – including the origins of all the things inside the cave. Seeing the shadow of an apple cast on the cave wall is all the cave dwellers know of apples. That's a far cry from turning around and glimpsing the apple itself, and a farther cry from leaving the cave and tending apple orchards, and producing apples that approximate the ideal apple. Outside the cave we can also conceive and experience the forms of ideals like truth, beauty, and justice, thereby understanding how to make our lives more truthful, beautiful, and just. According to Plato, we can graduate from the world of appearances to the world of ideas via proper education – including philosophical inquiry, of course. Those who fail to graduate will lead their lives in darkness, mistaking appearance for reality, never discovering the nature of reality or their own personal potential.

Marina understood how this allegory captured her infatuation with keeping up appearances as a New York author, which to her seemed like a fuzzy shadow of herself on a cave wall. (Yes, even Manhattan's Upper West Side can be that unreal at times.) Marina left her cave and returned to her roots in the Pacific Northwest, where she both continued her writing career and began to feel more authentic in her person. Instead of servicing someone else's image of an author, Marina discovered her real authorial vocation outside the cave – and inside her understanding. As a result, her writing improved substantially, and so did her view of herself and her life.

Had Marina been less interested in Plato's rationalistic philosophy and more interested in intuitive schools, she could have explored the Hindu concept of "Maya" – the illusoriness of the phenomena we confront, and the associated philosophy that helps pierce the veils of illusion. Either way, philial attachments serve us better when their objects are closer to the ideal, as opposed to being mere images or illusions.

Barry's Case Revisited: Agape Overcomes All

In chapter 3, we saw Barry go through a difficult transformation following his wife, Sue's, affair with his best friend, Sam. Needless to say, Barry's erotic life was not in very good shape at that point. Moreover, his philial devotions, both to his marriage and to his friend, were severely undermined. Clearly, Barry was in the throes of major transition. What helped him though this cathartic time was his experience of agape, which was awakened in him by his general unwillingness to capitulate to circumstances, and in particular by his refusal to allow his erotic and philial attachments to become poisoned by ill feeling toward those who had betrayed him. He maintained his goodwill during the painful process of trying but failing to reconcile with Sue. He sustained no ill will during their unsettling divorce. He even entertained long-term prospects of reconciling with his friend Sam. His thoughts were permeated, and his actions animated, by a transcendent love of God, goodness, and purpose, and by an unwillingness to hate or retaliate against those who had hurt him. This was agape. And thanks to Barry's courage in opening himself to agape and allowing it to flow through his being, his life was not destroyed by these cathartic changes. Instead, he was reborn into a world of new possibilities. Like birth itself, rebirth may entail tribulations, but it also confers opportunities.

ROMANTIC AND UNREQUITED LOVE

The idea of romantic love, as most people currently conceive it, is an ornate tapestry woven from distinct and divergent strands. One strand is Platonic, which gives you notions of your ideal woman or ideal man – the one you sought when you dated, and the one you thought you found when you married. But note the fundamental tension here: A "Platonic" relationship usually refers to a philial, not an erotic one. So is ideal love meant to be consummated sexually or not?

Weighing in against consummation is the (predominantly) Christian cult of the Virgin, which is also a projection of the Platonically pure woman into religious domains. The ideal of the Madonna and child pervades Christian art, while the "virgin birth" is a cornerstone of Christian theology. The emphasis on virginity before marriage remains strong throughout the Islamic world as well, for different reasons. But the ideal of virginity itself is widespread.

In favor of consummation, there is also the significant romantic thread of courtly love informed by medieval literature, notably Thomas Mallory's *Morte d'Arthur*. In these works we find the origins of romantic customs such as giving red roses, defending the honor of a maiden on a field of battle, and rescuing her from a fire-breathing dragon. In such traditions the romance is often consummated, but the endings are not always happy. One way or another, the greatest love stories seem to embody the profoundest personal tragedies. The stories of Tristan and Isolde, Lancelot and Guinevere, Romeo and Juliet, Dr. Zhivago and Lara, *Braveheart,* and *Love Story* itself are epic but uniformly tragic tales of romantic love. Love itself never dies, but the lovers themselves do, heroically but sadly, and usually before their natural time.

In this tradition, romantic love remains a higher ideal than marriage. Romance of the highest order is almost always a prelude to living unhappily ever after, or dying happily together, but not to living happily ever after. True romance is the opposite of a fairy tale. So while courtship often leads to marriage, marriage itself is not always romantic. By contrast, courtly love often leads to romance, which rarely ends in marriage. Do you want to have your cake and eat it too? Then you're a perfectionist! That's a fine aspiration, but enduring romantic marriages are few and far between. If you have ever experienced true romance, you are both lucky and probably somewhat unhappy because it didn't last. If you have ever experienced lasting marriage, you are both lucky and probably somewhat unhappy because it's not always romantic enough for you.

Do you remember the last time you fell in love? It's definitely a serious dis-ease: you probably lost your appetite, neglected your normal routine, wrote poetry, felt yourself in the grip of forces beyond your control. Being "in love" is a form of preoccupation, intoxication – even temporary madness. The only cure seems to be the reciprocation of your feelings by the object of your affection. Dis-ease or not, falling in love is also a wonderful and magical thing – the extreme attraction to another person, the allure of your senses, the aspiration of losing yourself temporarily but completely in the Other, the diminishment of importance of other matters in our lives. Two people *in love* with each other form a closed universe, into which nothing else can intrude (for a while). Nothing feels better than falling in love and having that love reciprocated. Then again, nothing feels worse than falling in love and having that love rejected.

When you fall in love with someone, you offer them a great gift: your being, your time, your energy. If that person reciprocates, you will both experience a romance. But if that person does not reciprocate, then you will probably experience a number of negative emotions: rejection, anger, despair. In the best cases, unrequited love can stimulate great art, like Dante's *Inferno* or Van Gogh's paintings or Nietzsche's philosophy. In the worst cases, it can contribute to depression, madness, or suicide – as it did with Dante and Van Gogh and Nietzsche themselves. Falling in love is therefore uncompromising: It's either requited or not. It's all or nothing. You either reach the heights of emotional bliss or plummet into the depths of emotional despair.

If your romantic love is requited, you may be happy for life – or for no more than a few months, a week, or even an hour. Requited love does not mean perpetual bliss. (Remember the Tibetan view about the potential dis-ease that comes with getting what you want.) It means that you have started at the top. The trick now lies in staying there. I have seen numerous clients who won their hearts' desires very young, and married their high school sweethearts. In the intervening twenty or more years, however, these requited loves have taken some unpredictable turns. Some of the marriages have thrived, but others have broken up. Some are touch and go, while others have endured for the long haul – but under conditions that neither partner would have predicted.

Unrequited love, however, contains more possibilities for both short-term dis-ease (misery from not getting what you want), and long-term adventure. The adventures are made possible by the energy of love stored up inside your heart, which is not released because its intended recipient is unreceptive. Here we're back to the Tao of Freud, in which there are three things that can happen to that loving energy.

First, and best, it can devote itself to a different and possibly higher purpose. If you are in love with someone who does not allow herself or himself to be loved in this way by you, then (instead of pining away or being depressed) you can find another person or pursuit that accepts your feelings – and so allows the investment, development, or expenditure of that energy. Creative pursuits are an excellent outlet: They transmute the energy of unrequited love into something in which others can find beauty, meaning, or inspiration. If arts are not for you, a similar transformation can happen through many other endeavors – athletics, socializing, work, charitable service – that can also turn unrequited love into something beautiful and worthy. In this way, love intended for only one beneficiary transforms into a gift for many. Such love will always be well received.

Second, and worst, you can turn unrequited love into hatred. Unrequited love can easily stir up bitterness, anger, jealousy, and regret, among other negative emotions, any and all of which act as toxins, gradually transforming your proffered love into its opposite: hatred. Unfortunately, hatred is easily requited. This turnabout benefits no one. Everything good can come of love; nothing good can come of hatred.

Third is the middle ground. You can use the potential energy of unrequited love to annihilate the love itself. You can strive for indifference. You can seek escape – common yet destructive routes include drinking or drugs, promiscuity or asceticism, all attempts to anesthetize yourself against your suffering. You may succeed in numbing the dis-ease, but you may also destroy or severely compromise your capacity for love. And that diminishes your very humanity. If you cannot feel love, you may as well not be human.

> **If love is good, then where does my sadness come from? If love is wicked, it seems strange to me that every torment and adversity coming from it is pleasant to me.**
> **– Geoffrey Chaucer**

Isadora's Case: Unrequited Love

Isadora, a sensitive and well-educated professional woman with a successful career in banking, experienced a very bad breakup with someone she loved deeply and romantically. She related to him as a soul mate, but he suddenly abandoned her; she in turn was obliged to abandon all hope that he would ever come back to her. Her sadness was immeasurable, and she was inconsolable. She was very depressed for about seven years, but no therapy or medication helped. Though she remained functional on the job, she derived little satisfaction from it. She became a social recluse, seeking refuge in music, poetry, and literature, but unwilling or unable to seek out personal connections.

Then Isadora met and began to get romantically involved with a brilliant and famous painter. Still, she had many reservations and was wary of establishing an intimate relationship with anyone. Yet she inspired this painter as no one had for a long time: He, like many great artists, was also haunted and tormented by a lost soul mate. Isadora was gratified to be playing this cherished role for him: a muse who inspires with her presence instead of her absence.

Moreover, her association with him gave rise to artistic inspiration of her own. She suddenly began to paint quite wonderfully – she had a gift that had been lying dormant all these years, or perhaps a gift that had to ripen through her trials and tribulations. After much suffering and noble perseverance, Isadora was being reborn into a new life of art, with a new soul mate for mutual inspiration. Yet she feared to embark on this path whole heartedly, lest it terminate as her previous one had, in abandonment and unbearable dis-ease. But she found a guiding light in the philosophy of Emerson, and in the spirit of New England Transcendentalism, which Emerson epitomized. His poem "Give All to Love" reinforced Isadora's courage to embark on her new life:

> **Give all to love; obey thy heart;**
> **Friends, kindred, days,**
> **Estates, good fame,**
> **Plans, credit and the Muse,**
> **Nothing refuse.**
>
> **– Ralph Waldo Emerson**

ARCHETYPAL LOVE

Jung's idea of love stands in stark contrast with Freud's. Jung was for many years Freud's chief student (some might say disciple), but they ultimately went their separate ways over irreconcilable differences. For Jung, all human dis-ease is a manifestation of an unresolved spiritual quest, which can be resolved by embarking on and hopefully completing the quest itself. Where Freud's philosophy anticipated neuroscience (still in its infancy today) and attempted to reduce all human dis-ease to cerebral dysfunction, Jung inclined toward mysticism, embracing the ancient wisdom of Asian philosophies. According to Jung, we are all deeply predisposed to organizing our experiences in similar ways. We share a "collective unconscious" independent of the details of our particular profiles. The contents of the collective unconscious are "archetypes." Joseph Campbell espoused a parallel view, that religious and heroic myths of all cultures are telling essentially the same stories over and over again, just using different characters and settings each time.

Jung's way of thinking about matters of the heart is through archetypes embedded in the collective unconscious, which are possibly reflections of the very nature of the cosmos itself. Archetypal love combines the noblest aspects of romantic love with the deepest aspects of male and female essence, producing a kind of play in which men and women have acted from time immemorial. The action and scenery may vary, but the courtly theme is always the same: the hero rescuing the damsel in distress.

This theme is manifest in myriad ways: the knight rescuing the maiden from the dragon, Prince Charming rescuing Cinderella from her wicked stepsisters, Professor Henry Higgins rescuing Eliza Doolittle from social deprivation, Richard Gere rescuing "pretty woman" Julia Roberts from the streets (and from herself!). Many myths and legends have near-universal appeal precisely because they capture the essence of a particular archetype, and the archetypes of romantic and courtly love are perhaps the most commonly recapitulated.

From a Jungian perspective, what often propels couples into conflict has more to do with conflicting archetypes than irritating habits. As long as a husband is playing Prince Charming to his wife's Cinderella, or she is Guinevere to his Sir Lancelot, all is well. But once wives stop treating their husbands like princes, and husbands stop treating their wives like damsels in distress, then the honeymoon is over. One or both partners may desire a renewal of archetypal love – or feel compelled to seek it outside the marriage. Or they may enact other archetypes, such as the classic pairing of Great Mother and Great Hunter – an especially good match while raising a family – or Matriarch and Patriarch of the clan, more likely once grandchildren arrive. There are archetypes for love at every stage of life. A couple's challenge is to fulfill complementary and not antagonistic roles at each stage.

> **All love stories are the same.**
>
> **– Paulo Coelho**

Karen's Case: The Missing Ideal

My Norwegian colleague Anders Holt counseled a woman named Karen. She appeared to have all the essentials of a fulfilled life, but if you recall Plato's Allegory of the Cave you know that appearance and reality are not the same. Karen was a company director, happily married with two children. Her husband had a good job as well. She loved her husband, and he loved her. They both loved their children. So what was her problem? Karen had never fulfilled her dream of an ideal (and maybe a wild) romance. And now, approaching middle age, she thought she never would. And yet she knew she could. Karen was not pining over an illusion; rather, she was trying to estimate the costs of attaining the vision. For if she allowed herself to be swept away by a romantic adventure, she might well lose her family in the bargain. Her career could be compromised too. She had to wonder whether it was worth the gamble.

So Karen began to understand something about alternatives and regrets. We can lead several different lives within a lifetime, but only one life at a time. Whenever we choose to lead a certain life, we follow its particular path. This also means choosing *not* to lead other possible lives at that time, and *not* following their particular paths through time. There are always parallel paths, forks, and crossroads one can take, but selecting any one of them at a given time also means deselecting the others. There are always potential alternatives, and therefore potential regrets for not having chosen them. Karen had no regrets about her marriage and career but did have regrets about missing the experience of an ideal romance.

Ultimately, Karen decided to remain in her status quo, and to forgo materializing her fantasy. She did not want to risk losing her family and career for the sake of a romantic interlude. There are many ways in which a married couple can attempt to rekindle their romantic flame, or light it brightly for the first time. (Many other books treat that theme.) The philosophical point is this: Ideally, it's best to have no regrets but practically, it's better to have small ones than large ones. One cannot do everything in a lifetime, and anything one does exacts its price. Karen was wise to ascertain the probable costs of a wild romance before buying into one.

When poet Robert Frost encountered a major fork in his life, he famously took the "road less traveled" – not without his own regrets. But there's nothing wrong with taking the road *more* traveled, either.

In fact, your path through life is always unique. Even two people walking hand in hand on the same apparent path are, in reality, each walking their own path alone.

> **Two roads diverged in a yellow wood**
> **And sorry I could not travel both**
> **And be one traveler . . .**
> — **Robert Frost**

PARENTAL LOVE

Children are the greatest treasure any family can possess, yet they must not be possessed at all. Parenting is the most important job any adult can have, yet it is almost impossible to prepare or train for it. Democratic states regulate most endeavors that can prove harmful to others, from driving motor vehicles to practicing professions, yet they have little or nothing to say about the one endeavor that can prove most harmful to children: raising them badly. So here are a few philosophical thoughts about parenting, intended to help make a difficult job easier to understand.

Biologically, human beings are the latest version of God's design, or nature's experiment, in sexual reproduction. Not only are the male and female reproductive roles strongly differentiated; their natural psychological orientations, familial functions, and social behaviors are also differentiated, albeit less strongly. Even though cultural evolution – and with it, political emancipation – has permitted women participation in a range of activities formerly conducted by men only, this has not necessarily made women happier or more fulfilled. Whenever a given cultural arrangement cuts across the grain of one's biological being, it produces mild to severe dis-ease. Modern civilization has done this at many turns to men, women, and children alike, which is why so many people are so full of dis-ease.

Ease of being is restored by allowing human nurture to accord with human nature. But to bring nurture into harmony with nature, we need to understand human nature itself. The twenty-five-hundred-year debate about human nature has been led by philosophers with many diverging views, yet few philosophers have actually addressed what children naturally require from their parents, and what parents are naturally equipped to give them.

I believe that, above all, children need love from their parents. But parental love is of two different kinds: unconditional and conditional. The mother's love is normally unconditional; the father's, normally conditional. To facilitate becoming well-balanced beings, children require both kinds of love. Therefore they also require both kinds of parents, or at least surrogates. While one parent alone, of either sex, may manage well enough to feed, clothe, house and educate his or her children, it is a mistake to suppose that one parent alone, of either sex, is automatically equipped to offer both kinds of love.

MATERNAL LOVE

A mother normally loves her children because they are her children, and for no other reason. She may take pride in their accomplishments, but she loves them whether they accomplish much or little. In fact, she loves them no matter what they do, for better or worse. The mothers of serial killers or mass murderers also love their children unconditionally, even though they do not necessarily approve of their children's deeds. Although mothers love sons somewhat differently than daughters, and may for psychological reasons have more conflicts with their daughters than their sons, motherhood of any kind is a transformative experience for a woman. It changes her identity for a lifetime, and allows her to attain her natural potential as a provider of unconditional love to her children. She is made by nature to nurture a helpless and totally dependent being: her baby. Even when her children grow up and have babies of their own, their mother's eternal maternal aspect will continue to regard them as her "babies."

From the baby's perspective, the mother is the entire universe. Her love is the radiant energy that sustains its world and enables its normal development. Children who receive unconditional love from their mothers will later be able to receive it from the cosmos. As they gradually mature and enlarge their sphere of being by replacing the maternal world with the real one, they will still partly regard the universe as their mother and, circumstances permitting, will expect and find unconditional love in its seemingly impersonal emptiness and vastness. By trusting the world as they trusted their mothers, they attract benevolence and munificence from it. Said another way, if they are made to feel at home in their little newborn sphere of existence outside the womb, a sphere which is so strange and complex and sometimes disturbing, then they will stand a better chance of feeling at home in the gradually bigger spheres of existence – even stranger, more complex, and sometimes more disturbing – they will inhabit as they mature. Feeling that one has a home in this world – in other words, that one belongs here, is valued and loved here – is to be on the receiving end of agape. It is also a prerequisite for giving agape.

Even if you missed out on maternal love, it is always possible to receive agape from the cosmos, by "tuning in" to the frequencies on which it is continually broadcast. You do not need eyes to see divine light, nor ears to hear divine music. And you do not need a mother to feel divine love.

One reason that wives generally demand unconditional love from husbands (whether they get it or not) and require regular emotional support from them is that they usually give these things unstintingly to their children. Just as a well's water needs to be regularly replenished, and a battery's energy regularly recharged, so a woman's capacity for unconditional love needs to be regularly renewed. It is not enough that a man provides for and protects a woman who bears his children, even if he does it well. Although this is necessary, and although husbands usually think that if they are good providers and protectors their wives will realize they love them, it is not sufficient from the woman's point of view. For many women will take a man's provision and protection for granted (which is very vexing for a man), but few women will take his declarations of love for granted. In fact, many women will settle for fewer material benefits if they can get more love. Only in divorce, when the communication of love becomes outdated, difficult, or impossible, will women become more concerned about material things than passionate emotions. So without the unconditional love of a man, a woman may find it more difficult to love her children unconditionally. Hence both parents are necessary, even for one of them to function normally.

It goes without saying that there are always exceptions to "rules" about human behavior. Some women are more like men, in that their primary interests are more focused on careers or material possessions than on children and family. However, even highly successful professional women with no children often exhibit strong residues of maternalism, which they may lavish, for example, on pampered house pets, which they treat like babies and love unconditionally. These days many women juggle careers and motherhood, and this poses other kinds of problems. Often, both their careers and their children will suffer at one time or another, although both can still turn out for the best – it's a matter of organization and timing, plus getting enough sleep at night! Overall, birth rates in affluent societies have been dropping for some time. Women with career aspirations are likely to have fewer children, but are still likely to love them unconditionally.

PATERNAL LOVE

While being valued, loved, and cherished as a human being, at home in the bosom of one's family, would give most babies a very good start in life, it is not enough. Rather, it is too much of a good thing. Why? Because the home is the place wherein we begin and renew our preparations for living life, and living life brings us into contact with all kinds of persons and situations in which we are not necessarily valued, loved, or cherished as human beings. Even at home, in the bosom of our families, we may encounter relatives who devalue, hate, or despise us. And as our children begin to make their way in the world, from the schoolyard to the rat race and beyond, they will almost certainly encounter disagreeable persons and difficult situations. How do we best prepare our children for those encounters? With conditional paternal love.

While unconditional maternal love is a necessary preparation for feeling at home in the world, it is not a sufficient preparation for accepting developmental challenges or facing harsher realities of the world. It is the father's love – conditional paternal love – which offers this kind of preparation. While some fathers are capable of loving their children unconditionally (just as some mothers are capable of loving them conditionally), it is more natural for fathers to manifest their love by establishing conditions. Children need their mothers to love them, but need their fathers to approve of them. They earn their father's approval by satisfying (or trying to satisfy) the conditions that he sets. The world imposes objective conditions on us all: Your ability to further your career, to provide for and to protect your family, are subject to external forces, not all of which are forces of loving kindness. While women have always naturally competed with one another over men, men have always naturally competed with one another over money, power, position, opportunity, influence, and the like. In the developed world, growing numbers of women are now competing in this way too. By testing ourselves against the world, men and women alike discover their strengths and weaknesses, encounter allies and opponents, forge their name and place. None of this can happen in the womb, or in the warm glow of maternal love.

A child needs first to be loved at home, and then to strive in the world. Paternal love, exercised through the setting of conditions, allows the child to strive at first in a friendly environment, with a forgiving guide, while preparing to strive in the wider world, which will be less forgiving, and which contains other friendly guides but also unfriendly imposters disguised as guides. Both parents set and enforce the rules of the household, but the father is primarily responsible for meting out punishments or teaching other lessons if the rules are flouted. The mother usually plays "good cop"; the father, "bad cop." Successful parenting requires both. As all single parents know, it is very difficult for one parent – male or female – to play both roles.

Children need structure and discipline as well as free play and love, and they respond quite well to reasonable rules of conduct. They are glad someone is in charge, but they will also rebel or misbehave in order to test "the system." If the system furnishes loving constraints, e.g., "I approve of you when you finish your homework and do the chores," the child will respond by seeking repeated constructive approval of this kind. If the system does not furnish loving constraints, the children will run wild and seek "the system's" attentions in any way possible, including negative or criminal misbehaviors. To a child, positive conditional attention is better than negative conditional attention, but negative conditional attention is better than no conditional attention. Children without fathers are at serious risk of missing "tough love's" discipline, of finding fewer avenues in which to test themselves constructively in the world, and therefore of failing to find their proper place in life. A mother's love can reassure them when they are faced with some challenge; but it often takes a father's love to set the challenge, to encourage the right effort, to provide guidance in failure, and to approve success.

But spiraling divorce rates and fatherless families deprive children of conditional paternal love, often with catastrophic effects. In America, among other places, the absence of the father can even hasten premature death. The endemic entrenchment of juvenile gangs in American subcultures, the life-and-death grip they exert on their cohorts, the drastically shortened life expectancies of gang members, and the violence that rules their existence are all direct consequences of the absent father. Hobbes warned long ago (1651) that, in the absence of an awe-inspiring authority figure, human society invariably degenerates into "a war of all against all," and the lives of such creatures become "solitary, poor, nasty, brutish, and short." Such is the plight of American and other youths who have never known their fathers, or never found surrogate fathers. When psychologists, sociologists, and politicians speak of "positive role models" for young people, they do not mean movie stars or celebrity athletes who pay lip service to worthy causes; they mean surrogate fathers, who actually spend time with lost youths, giving them the thing they desperately need: conditional paternal love.

While the emancipation of women is clearly vital for their flourishing as human beings, "liberating" a woman does not mean changing her into a man, or removing men from their proper functions in society. A child needs its mother's unconditional love, regardless of whether she is a housewife, an astronaut, or a CEO. And a child needs its father's conditional love, regardless of his occupation too. The male and female essences of human beings are independent of their job descriptions, and it is these two essences that most naturally give rise to the two kinds of love that children need to become balanced adults.

> **Your old grandmother says, "Maybe you**
> **shouldn't go to school. You look a little pale."**
> **Run when you hear that.**
> **A father's stern slaps are better.**
> **Your bodily soul wants comforting.**
> **The severe father wants spiritual clarity.**
> **   – Jelaluddin Rumi**

Magdalena's Case: What Conditions Are Reasonable?

Like many clients of philosophical counseling, Magdalena did not have a problem within herself, but was experiencing dis-ease indirectly, as a result of her family members' issues. Magdalena's fourteen-year-old son Robert told her he thought he was gay. Magdalena didn't harbor any irrational fears or deep-seated prejudices against homosexuality, so this in and of itself was not a problem. She loved her son uncondition-ally, and just wanted him to be happy. Her only immediate concern was that she be able to guide Robert constructively through adolescence – a trying enough time for kids of any sexual orientation.

The problem was that Magdalena's husband, Jim, was strongly opposed to his son's homosexual identity. He simply wouldn't accept it. He wasn't even willing to discuss it. In other words, he did harbor irrational fears and deep-seated prejudices. He loved his son con-ditionally, and imposed a negative rather than a positive condition: namely, that Robert earn his love by *not* being gay.

Magdalena's challenge, then, was to hold the family together in the face of Robert's quest to discover his sexual identity and Jim's resistance to and denial of what Robert's quest was revealing – both in Robert and in himself. In effect, Magdalena would have to learn to become a philosophical counselor for her family. Fortunately, she was emotionally secure enough to offer tremendous love to her family, and open-minded enough to understand and patiently help them work through their respective issues.

Magdalena and her family are engaged in a learning process, not a single problem per se. For Robert, the learning process is adolescence, which often entails, among other things, self-discovery through sexual experimentation. Such growth can bring dis-ease but need not be traumatic. For Jim, the learning process begins with the unhappy consequences of imposing unreasonable standards upon his son. This could lead to disaster if Jim does not open his mind and set more appropriate conditions for offering Robert his approval and love. Finally, Magdalena herself is engaged in a learning process that will involve her practice of education, diplomacy, and perseverance (and that's just for starters). She did not need long-term counseling; she *did* need philosophical reinforcement of three ideas she had already begun to formulate for herself.

The first idea is that homosexuality is not a perversion, sin, or crime. Some homosexuality probably has a biological basis, as the contemporary work of Simon LeVay shows (in his book *The Sexual Brain*). Then again, just how overt such behavior becomes depends largely on social conventions too. And in many cases, homosexuality looks more like a matter of sexual preference, rather than genetic predisposition or social conditioning. As always with human beings, nature and nurture interact, often seamlessly.

Of course people should be free to think and believe as they please, which (if they wish) includes believing in a supposedly all-loving God who at the same time encourages fanatical hatred of homosexuality (or rock music, or philosophy, or other religions, etc.). But people should not be free to stigmatize others for not living up to their beliefs. Homosexuality has always been a fact of human life.

The second idea is that Robert needs to find himself in many ways – his sexual identity being just one. More important than that in the long run, and more worthy of his parents' guidance, is how he will discover his personal excellence, or special talents, or particular interests, and how he will develop them. His intellectual, artistic, or other aptitudes, as well as the formation of his moral and civic character, are far more important than his sexual preferences. He needs his parents to help him find direction, meaning, and purpose in his life, and to support and help set useful limits to his explorations.

The third idea is that Jim needs to open his mind, and examine his own beliefs about homosexuality, parenting, and probably a host of other issues. He is the one who most needs counseling at this stage, for it is his attitudes and behavior that will either build a bridge or open a rift between him and his son. If he does the latter, it will also make things incomparably more difficult for Magdalena. Therefore her most urgent task is to convince her husband to lead what Socrates called "the examined life" in his own case, before passing judgment on his son's sexual orientation.

With her own ideas more fully articulated and supported, Magdalena felt better-prepared and even more strongly resolved to accept and surmount the challenges posed by her family's current dynamics.

LOVE IS MYSTERIOUS

As we have seen, love is many things ("many-splendored"), and much can be made of it philosophically. However, love is also a great mystery – perhaps the greatest – and it bathes perennially in its own wondrous light. In parting, I want to leave you with a remarkable case of undying romantic love, long unrequited, that ended up deservedly and blissfully requited. Some love stories do have truly happy endings, and this is one.

Jill and Tom's Case: The Fifty-Year Courtship

Jill and Tom met during World War II. Tom had been called up to serve, and they had a brief courtship before he went overseas. Tom went into combat, was soon listed as missing in action, and before long was presumed killed. Meanwhile Jill and her family moved away from their hometown to another state, where Jill later got married. Unknown to her, Tom had not been killed. He had been wounded and was hospitalized for quite some time. Eventually he recovered and returned home, where he met and married another girl from his hometown. Jill remained married for fifty-one years, until her husband died. Tom remained married for fifty years, until his wife died. Then Tom began to think of Jill, and made some inquiries through what remained of their hometown grapevine. He soon discovered her whereabouts and phoned her. She was overjoyed to hear from him again (after more than fifty years!), and they arranged to meet. Their reunion took place three months later – how blessed they were for having all the time in the world. They discovered that they were still very much in love, and they resumed their interrupted courtship and got married. And just as in a fairy tale, they lived happily ever after. Each moment together was an eternity of joy to them, and a triumph of the enduring – if not imperishable – spirit of love over the frailty and impermanence of life.

> **The mystery of love is greater than the mystery of death.**
>
> **– Anonymous**

PHILOSOPHICAL EXERCISES

1. Give someone a gift of love today. This can be as little as a good thought, a considerate gesture, an unsolicited kindness.
2. Allow someone to give a gift of love to you today. Again, its magnitude is not important.
3. If there's anything you hate, take immediate steps to reduce your hatred to dislike, your dislike to distaste, and your distaste to indifference.
4. Now you have liberated energy that you used to have tied up in hatred, which was a bad investment. Go back to exercise #1, and reinvest that energy in love.

7

CAN'T WE ALL JUST GET ALONG?

Some kind of philosophy is a necessity to all but the most thoughtless, and in the absence of knowledge it is almost sure to be a silly philosophy. The result of this is that the human race becomes divided into rival groups of fanatics, each group firmly persuaded that its own brand of nonsense is sacred truth, while the other side's is damnable heresy.
– Bertrand Russell

Hell is other people.
– Jean-Paul Sartre

W HEN TWO CHILDREN are fighting over a toy or quarreling about who started the fight, they both believe that the all-consuming issue is the toy itself, or the other child's unwillingness to share it. They are completely caught up in the petty details of their squabble, because their capacity to resolve the situation is limited by their immaturity. When you – the parent, teacher, guardian, or baby-sitter – are alerted by their commotion, your maturity allows you to understand that their fight is not really about this specific toy or that particular playmate. I'm sure you realize that the children are reenacting an age-old human dilemma between competition and cooperation, between monopolizing a resource and sharing it. I'm sure you also realize that their play is not just amusement but a preparation for the adult world, in which they will encounter the same dilemma in more serious – perhaps even life-and-death – situations. So presumably you want to impart to these children the virtues of sharing a resource if possible, or at least of taking turns with it. You do this for their benefit, even though you know that not every resource in adult life can be shared (e.g., a job over which applicants are competing) or taken turns with (e.g., a partner in a monogamous relationship).

In resolving the conflict between these children, and seeing them happily back at play, you have actually behaved philosophically. Why? Because you applied universal principles, such as sharing and taking turns, to a particular circumstance, a fight over this toy with that playmate. To do so, you had to recognize the difference between universals and particulars themselves. And that is something philosophers do all the time – perhaps too much – while most other people don't do it nearly often enough.

Now suppose you're caught up in an adult conflict, whether it's a feud with your neighbor or a war between nations. Philosophers tend to view adult conflicts in the same way as parents or teachers view schoolyard conflicts: They are not really about the specific issues that the conflicting parties are fixated on. Once again, particular details are mere excuses to fight, or to incite others to violence. Adult conflicts must be resolved in the same way as children's conflicts: by the application of universally just principles that emanate from a higher plane.

But many adults are walking around utterly fixated on their own sets of particulars, twenty-four hours per day. And all too often, psychology reinforces this tendency through relentlessly detailed excavations of their past. This only serves to increase their fixations on the minute details of their particular path through life, while blinding them to the universal principles that shape that path itself, along with all other possible paths, and blinding them as well to ways of altering their path for the better. Most human conflicts are perpetuated precisely because people (of all ages) become too fixated on the particulars of their dis-ease, and are unwilling or unable to elevate themselves to a philosophical domain of universals, in which their ease can be found.

In this chapter, as well as the next (on the battle of the sexes), I'm going to assume that you're willing and able to be mature and philosophical about your conflicts, and view your particular circumstances as instances of universal ones. More often than not, the resolution of your specific conflict lies in recognizing the general condition that gives rise to it, and in applying the appropriate universal principles as remedies. You've surely noticed that people get along better in some situations than others. Students learning together in a classroom may disagree, but rarely come to blows. Groups of writers, painters, or musicians may not share the same artistic tastes, but they can cooperate in workshops, mount collective exhibitions, and harmonize in orchestras. Religious devotees praying together in a house of worship may have been sinning with and against one another all week, but not while at prayer. People sitting together in meditative practice are neither armed nor dangerous to one another. So in general, when we perform higher human functions like learning, creating, praying, and meditating, we don't see open conflicts breaking out.

This evidence provides strong clues that the universal sources of human discord lie in our lower animal natures, not in our more elevated human states of mind. So this chapter's voyage explores that natural animalistic source. However, recall (from chapter 3) that the Ten Worlds of the human mind all coexist together, from the most bestial to the most blissful states, and that it is possible to move from any one state of mind to any other, instantaneously. Thus, no matter how refined or noble a life you lead, your animalistic nature is always lurking in the background, ready to pounce on others if you unleash it.

THE DOGS OF WAR

Surely human beings would be better off if they could learn to get along with one another, making their differences the basis of cooperation instead of conflict. But exactly how to turn "peace on earth, goodwill toward men" from a Christmas card sentiment into an ongoing reality remains a big open question. In fact, disagreement over the "best" way to bring about peace and goodwill all too often becomes, ironically enough, a cause of war and ill will.

Each of the world's great religions can be put forth as a compelling force for peace, but every single one of them can be (and has been) corrupted to the point of being used to justify warfare. Various political systems have taken their turn, aiming for greater stability but eventually giving rise to more war. Science and technology have been touted as making wars unnecessary or obsolete, but have also produced weapons of mass destruction alongside life-enhancing advances. Multinational economic interests and the development and modernization of the global village were supposed to usher in an age of worldwide peace and prosperity, but they have also engendered violent protests by those who feel marginalized by the process, or indeed who reject it and favor a return to despotic or theocratic systems of governance.

The Dutch philosopher Desiderius Erasmus described how this eternal cycle of conflict is perpetuated at every level of society in his 1517 book *The Complaint of Peace*.

> **I enter the courts of kings . . . I see every outward sign of the highest offices and humanity . . . It is all paint and varnish. Everything is corrupted by open faction, or by secret grudges and animosities.**
> **– Desiderius Erasmus**

Even philosophy, scholarship, scrupulous devotion to reason, and the search for truth have not succeeded in establishing peace. Erasmus continued: "Here also I find war of another kind, less bloody indeed but not less furious . . . they stab one another with pens dipped in the venom of malice; they tear one another with biting labels, and dart the deadly arrow of their tongues against their opponent's reputation." These words ring as true today as centuries ago: It is also an apt description of small-town gossip, office politics, and political campaigning itself.

None of which has stopped philosophers (along with many others) from trying to express how deeply they've been affected by the human conflicts they have witnessed. Many have been inspired to map out ways of alleviating future conflicts. Plato lived through the destruction of Athenian culture in the Peloponnesian war with Sparta, and in response wrote the *Republic* in an attempt to create a blueprint for utopia. Similarly, after witnessing the sacking of Rome by the Visigoths, Augustine wrote the *City of God*, pointing to utopia in the next world instead of this one. Thomas Hobbes wrote *Leviathan* in exile during the English Civil War, trying to establish a state of lasting civil peace and commonwealth. Immanuel Kant tried his hand at conflict resolution in a little book called *Perpetual Peace*, laying out a plan for settling the European differences of his day nonviolently. He ironically borrowed the title of the book from an innkeeper's sign – at an inn located next to a cemetery. We'll all attain perpetual peace eventually, just too late to do us much good in this world and this life!

Great thinkers of the twentieth century also weighed in, even more heavy-handedly, after witnessing the European carnage of World War I and the global devastation of World War II. Cyril Joad wrote, "Modern Western civilization is the result of endowing with the fruits of a dozen men of genius a population which is emotionally at the level of savages and culturally at the level of schoolboys." And that was before the precipitous decline in Western education and literacy, which has been reducing culture to savagery as well!

Yet, these immortal thoughts aside, mortal conflicts continued apace. At the same time, the literature on conflict became less optimistic, largely gave up the idea of utopia, and waxed more cynical and satirical. Aldous Huxley, George Orwell, Ayn Rand, and Arthur Koestler wrote great but disturbing books about *dystopias* (respectively, *Brave New World, Nineteen Eighty-Four, Atlas Shrugged,* and *Darkness at Noon*), which raised deep philosophical questions about human nature and questioned whether we even have the capacity to live in peace.

Add to this the disheartening fact that many of the greatest peacemakers and advocates of nonviolent resistance to oppression – from Socrates and Jesus to Mahatma Gandhi and Martin Luther King Jr., and even John Lennon – were put to death by governments or assassinated by madmen, and we have to ask whether humanity has any kind of level playing field at all. Perhaps we must conclude, as Freud did, that it permanently tilts in the direction of war and away from peace.

Is it not we who should give in, who should adapt ourselves to war? Should we not confess that in our civilized attitude towards death we are once again living psychologically beyond our means, and should we not rather turn back and recognize the truth?

– Sigmund Freud

Even so, I remain optimistic that reason and wisdom will eventually guide humanity along more peaceful paths. So let's reexamine "the truth" about human beings and their conflicts, as well as a few approaches to finding peace that really do work.

GETTING ALONG WITH YOURSELF

Before we speak of getting along with others, first we must get along with ourselves. It seems to me that all outer conflicts between people are manifestations of inner ones within people. If you suffer from an unresolved inner conflict, then you aren't getting along with yourself as well as you can. And if you aren't getting along with yourself as well as you can, you will not get along with others as well as you can either.

Whenever I witness human beings mistreat, abuse, or injure one another, whether in direct confrontation or in underhanded or back-handed ways, I always notice that the perpetrators do not appear very contented with themselves. People who make war on others have failed to conquer themselves. Walt Kelly's famous comic strip character Pogo summed it up this way: "We have met the enemy, and he is us." The hardest person to get along with in the whole world is, in fact, yourself.

Rachel's Case: How Not to Get Along with Yourself

Rachel was so "successful" at waging war against herself that no one could help her make the peace. As a result, she was also in constant conflict with everyone around her. Rachel was referred to me by her physician for short-term philosophical help. She was seeing him because of anxiety, but instead of taking the medication he prescribed, she was self-medicating with cannabis. While pot may be better than Paxil at times, it only made Rachel's panic attacks worse. What was she anxious about in the first place? Rachel told me that she wanted to make enough money to check into a private psychiatric facility and undergo psychotherapy every day of the week. I asked her why she wasn't taking advantage of public services in New York. She replied that she was suing various branches of social service for denying her treatment. She was also suing her family in a dispute over her late father's will, suing the lawyer who probated the will, suing her former psychotherapist for sexual harassment, suing the phone and electric companies for cutting off her utilities, and suing her landlord over a host of tenant issues. She had an upcoming appointment with a psychiatrist in a hospital outpatient department in six weeks but needed to talk to someone in the meantime – hence the referral from her physician.

Since Rachel's need for psychiatric care seemed quite rational (a variation on catch-22), we explored ways of realizing it. It turned out that Rachel had an opportunity to make some money, as an author. She was very bright, well-educated, and articulate, and knew a lot about the American health-care system and its deficiencies. She had already published some newspaper articles on this subject, and had attracted an editor who wanted her to write a book. So why wasn't she doing that? Because she had to write a detailed outline in order to get a publishing contract, and she needed professional help with it. But she had quarreled with her collaborator and the editor, and had fired the collaborator, so the book project was stalled.

It quickly became clear that Rachel was so conflicted herself that she could not get along with anybody else. Moreover, she was certainly unwilling and presently unable to accept any responsibility for her permanently combative stance against the world. While everyone experiences some form of unfair treatment at the hands of relatives, monopolies, bureaucracies, and even professions at times, we also find friends and allies in the world as well as enemies – that is, provided we can be friends and allies ourselves, and to ourselves. But Rachel was at war with herself, and she made every relationship a casualty of that war. So while Rachel was absolutely right to seek psychiatric help, her way of seeking it was actually preventing her from finding it. When I tried, very gently, to suggest this to her, she became infuriated and "terminated" me as well.

The first moral: Since most people get along with themselves better than Rachel does with herself, they (and you) have the ability and responsibility to ask and answer this Big Question: "What inner conflict is surfacing from my depths when I come into conflict with others?"

The second moral: Not all external conflicts are bilateral. It takes two to tango, but it takes only one to be conflicted. You must assume responsibility for your own combative stance if you hope to get along not only with others, but also with yourself. Your inner conflicts harm your own interests even if they don't wreak havoc on others.

THE CURE IS FORGETTING THE CAUSE

On the other hand, people who treat others with genuine kindness, consideration, and respect – if not love and compassion – almost certainly get along with themselves to begin with. Resolving your own inner conflicts, so that you have fewer storms brewing within yourself, will calm your interactions with others as well. Even those who try to provoke you with their own tempests will be unable to do so. Once you conquer the enemy within, you will have no more enemies without. This is why Gandhi said that in his "dictionary" of non-violent resistance to oppression, "there is no word for enemy."

Of course, all of us experience some temporary internal upsets – whether due to bad hair days, PMS, lack of sleep, a low threshold of frustration, or simply "getting up on the wrong side of the bed" – and may occasionally lash out. But we should be able to get over these foul moods quickly. They are the exception, not the rule, of our habitual conduct. When you are in a bad mood, even for a few minutes or hours, you are not getting along very well with yourself, and you experience dis-ease. If you can forget your dis-ease for even one minute – relying on someone else to cheer you up or take you away from yourself or distract you or make you laugh – then you allow every possible kind of ease to enter into that minute. But if you cling stubbornly to your unhappiness, you prevent every kind of happiness from entering. Even Nietzsche, who was not exactly brimming with the milk of human kindness, realized the importance of forgetting the causes of one's dis-ease.

He who forgets is cured.
– Friedrich Nietzsche

As Nietzsche knew, this applies to groups as well as individuals: "A happy people have no history." By contrast, individuals or groups carrying around too much history are likely to be upset much of the time. Allowing the past to occupy your present and obstruct your future is a sure way not to get along with yourself.

It doesn't work this way with actual disease, of course. You can't recuperate from a trauma or an illness by refusing to dwell on its causes. If your arm is broken, it will not be healed merely by your ignoring how it got broken, just as your migraine won't go away simply because you forgot what triggered it. However, you can dispel dis-ease by letting go of its causes. (Or, prolong it by clinging to its causes.) If you are in a bad mood, it will definitely go away if you are willing to forget what brought it on. We all have the power to do this, although many need to learn to exercise that power and practice exercising it more fully.

LAYERS OF THE COMPETITIVE AND COOPERATIVE ONION

Everywhere we look in the human world, from the family playroom to the local playground, from the university to the penitentiary, from the corporation to the homeless shelter, from the entertainment industry to the military, from the religious community to the government agency, we can see the elaborate interleaving and entwining of two major forces that together ensure the maintenance and sustenance of any given group – and virtually guarantee that we will not all get along with one another on any given day. That is, everywhere you look, you'll see both cooperation and competition.

Both are layered and textured throughout human social endeavor. In fact, each makes the other possible. Virtually every function that human beings perform, from cradle to grave, will have both competitive and cooperative aspects and implications. There has been debate in the social, behavioral, and biological sciences for the past couple of centuries, which has intensified during the last thirty years, between the competitive and the cooperative camps. Each tries to claim that it is primary in importance. But the way I see it, human beings are fundamentally both cooperative *and* competitive. These are two sides of one coin.

To take just one example, suppose you try out for an athletic team. You'll be competing against all the other players who want to make the team. Such competition is good, because it brings out the best in each player. Yet it also gives rise to disappointments, because not everyone's "best" is sufficient for them to make the team. Meanwhile, those who survive the competition and make the team must now cooperate with each other on the team. A great team (whether in marriage, sports, business, professions, or arts) is not made by a collection of individual stars: It is made by cooperative *teamwork*. Your team cooperates, however, in order to compete against other teams. But at the same time, all the teams in the league cooperate administratively and logistically on schedules, rules, and procedures in order to make their competitions possible.

In college and professional sports, each league itself competes against other sporting leagues for a market share of spectators, broadcast rights, and advertising sponsors – while also cooperating among themselves to give the sports industry as big a market share of public patronage and media coverage as it can get, in competition with other entertainment industries, such as music, theater, and film. In life as in sports, competition gives rise to cooperation, from which further competition and cooperation eventually reemerge, in a nested and unending pattern.

One of life's real arts, then, is learning how to compete effectively against others and cooperate effectively with them. In either case, you have to discover and develop your best qualities. You need to experience both to reveal your personal excellence, and to perform at capacity. To do so, however, you need a philosophy of competition that helps you be both a good loser and a gracious winner. And you need a philosophy of cooperation that helps you strive to attain shared goals larger than your own private ends. You're bound to win some competitions and lose others. The important philosophical question is not whether you win or lose, but how you deal with winning or losing. Similarly, you're also bound to encounter both cooperative and uncooperative people. The important philosophical question is not how to cooperate with the cooperative ones, but how to get the uncooperative ones to cooperate with you.

> **Dialogue, trust and collaboration rooted in humanitarian competition, a competition in self-mastery – this is the basis on which a global society can be built, a global civilization for the twenty-first century.**
>
> **– Daisaku Ikeda**

The main thing in competition is to do your best. You cannot control how others are going to perform, but you do exert considerable influence over your own performance. Thus preparation, concentration, and relaxation all play a part in coaxing the best from yourself. Great coaching can help you with these things, but your philosophy of competition can go even deeper. Lao-tzu offers wise advice: When you compete against others, you are not really competing against them, but receiving an opportunity to compete against yourself. Can you perform better today than you did yesterday? How close can you get to being the best that you can be, to realizing your own potential, to refining your own excellence? This is the essence of human competition, its humanistic basis, and its humanitarian purpose.

> **Therefore all the world is pleased to hold him in high esteem and never get tired of him.**

Because he does not compete; therefore no one competes with him.

— **Lao-tzu**

Playing chess or tennis or golf against others is not really about beating them; it's about improving your own chess, tennis, or golf game. Other players are therefore doing you a favor by playing with you: They're giving you an opportunity to better yourself. Win or lose, you should treat your "opponents" with respect and gratitude. Your real opponent is always yourself anyway. By being humble in victory and gracious in defeat, you will learn from and improve your own performance, and will also exercise the much more important and far-reaching human qualities of humility and grace. These will serve you incomparably better in life than any number of trophies in your trophy case.

In terms of group cooperation, the guiding philosophical idea is holistic: The human whole is always greater than the sum of its parts. In other words, a relationship is more than the sum of its two partners; a nuclear family is more than the sum of its parents and children; a team is more than the sum of its coaches and players. Any organization is more than the sum of its constituents. The spirit of cooperation is the glue that binds the group together and allows each member to attain more in conjunction with the others than each one could attain alone. Even creative artists and scientists who appear to be working alone while writing, composing, painting, or discovering universal truths are communing across space and time with the creations of their peer group. Similarly, every philosopher is part of a dialogue that has been going on for centuries, which he or she continues and contributes to, even when in solitude. So the same holistic effect benefits even these individuals, who are not as solitary as they may appear to the casual observer. Each person's best interests are always furthered by co-operation.

Civilization is, above all, the will to live in common.

— **José Ortega y Gasset**

Monica's Case: Cooperation, Competition, and Career Choice

Monica was a feature writer for a popular magazine. She had been assigned to interview a media figure whose political views she personally disagreed with. On the cooperative side, the interview would be great for her career, for the feature team, and for the magazine. On the competitive side, Monica would prefer to represent opposing or alternative views. In fact, during a pre-interview, she found herself arguing with the media figure instead of asking him questions. He was surprised and mildly irritated, because the editor who had assigned the interview told him it would be friendly, not adversarial. So he was prepared to be questioned, but not confronted or contested, by the journalist. Monica's dilemma was a common one: a choice between professional ethics and private morality. Professionally, she wanted to fulfill the cooperative mission she was assigned, but personally, she could not deny her competing political position.

Monica was helped by Ross's theory of prima facie duties (mentioned in chapter 2). If she had been a surgeon operating on a patient, or a mechanic fixing his car, it would be easier for her to do her duty as a professional and not be bothered by politics. So what's the difference in this case? As a journalist, she's helping her subject and magazine espouse views she personally disagrees with. Monica's answer lay in *doing* her job, which meant being entitled to her personal opinions, but not letting them get in the way of her assignment. That places the duty of professionalism above the duty to dispute personal beliefs. It is Monica who must prioritize these duties for herself. If the duty to express her political opinions were more important to her than the duty of professionalism, she could ask to be reassigned, or in the worst case quit her job.

Of course one could also question the editor's motive in assigning this story to her; he must have anticipated a potential clash. And perhaps he did, but knew too that conflict can be fruitful. Monica faces an opportunity here, to learn more about views that are different from hers. Keeping an open mind is vital to both professional and personal growth.

He who knows only his side of the case knows little of that.

– John Stuart Mill

MAKING SENSE OF OTHERS

One of the most basic things that make it difficult for human beings to get along with each other may surprise you. It is the very thing that helped us survive as a species way back when: our eyesight.

We have five (and more) senses that connect our brains with the "outside" world. Of the traditional five – sight, sound, smell, taste, and touch – vision is the most important for humans. Hearing ranks second, touch and taste trail behind, and smell brings up the rear when it comes to how much we rely on them. Of course it is a very tricky business to "rank" the senses. Many composers and musicians would probably prefer hearing to sight, if they had to choose between the two; gourmet chefs would undoubtedly rank taste and smell higher than the rest of us; massage therapists would particularly value touch. And so on. But vision is paramount for most of us.

Sight is the primary way we gather data about ourselves and others, and the main way we establish and reestablish connections to ourselves and others. We observe others far more often by watching them than we do listening to them, sniffing them, touching them, or tasting them. When it comes to getting along with others, the "eyes" have it.

What do we say when greeting people? "Good to see you." And on parting? "See you later." The primary influence of sight is reflected across the spectrum of language. To give just a few examples, the French say, *"au revoir"*; the Germans, *"auf Wiedersehen"*; the Spanish, *"hasta la vista;"* the Israelis, *"lehitraot."* Each of these expressions derives from the same root verb: to *see*.

When meeting people for the first time, or when greeting people you have known for years, the first thing you notice is their appearance. What do you say when you want to compliment someone on greeting them, without risking too much intimacy? "You look great!" When you get up in the morning, one of the first things you do is look in the mirror, to note your own appearance.

We depend on our observations of the appearance (including body language) of family members, friends, business associates, and strangers alike to give us clues as to their moods, intentions, expectations, and the like. We get a strong sense of others by looking at them, long before we talk to them. The visual experience precedes and preconditions the verbal one.

Unfortunately, our sense of others can be very easily distorted by this same sense when we mistake what we see on the surface – race, ethnicity, gender, or garb – for "knowing" something about them. We depend primarily on what we see to form that vital first impression of someone else, but our eyes do not and cannot see the deeply important things about a person – the contents of their heart and mind.

Our higher and nobler visions of humanity are never attained through any of our five external senses. For that we have another, internal sense, which interfaces with reason, emotion, intuition, and memory. It is *mentation*, from the Latin word *mens,* or mind. This is the highest sense of all, because it lets you "make sense" of the myriad streams of information coming to you through your other senses. It would do you no good to see, hear, taste, touch, or smell the world around you if you couldn't then "make sense" of these perceptions. It is by mentating that we screen, edit, refine, and interpret the picture of the world conveyed to us by our other senses.

Your eyes, ears, nose, tongue, and fingertips are basically passive sensors; that is, they convey data to various processing centers in the brain (visual cortex, auditory cortex, olfactory bulb, etc.) without making any judgments about the data. When you see something beautiful or ugly, your eye does not recognize the beauty or ugliness. It merely conveys an image to your brain. It is your *mind* that makes the aesthetic judgment about the image, pronouncing it beautiful or ugly. When we say, "Beauty is in the eye of the beholder," we really mean, "It's in the *mind* of the beholder." The eye itself doesn't know the difference between a Rembrandt and a candy wrapper.

The early modern philosopher George Berkeley explained the importance of the mind in *conceiving* what we are *perceiving*. Without conception, perception would be pointless. Through mentation, we form concepts about our perceptions. As Berkeley said, "The senses make no inferences." In other words, they make no judgments. That is the work of the mind.

Yet human beings too often rush to judgment based on visual input alone, without letting mentation make executive decisions. We take what we see for the whole package. If someone's appearance differs enough from that of the folks we're used to hanging around with, we may actually dehumanize them, or fear them, coming to think of them almost as a different species – alien, or subhuman. This is always a tragic mistake, and usually one with profound social consequences, but it is a mistake our biology helps us make. Noticing visual differences had big survival value in the distant past; it was a primary but oversimplified way of distinguishing friends from foes. But we cannot tell whether people mean us well or ill simply by what they look like. Most Arabs are not suicide bombers. Most Americans are not serial killers. We are certainly entitled to take precautions against would-be murderers from any culture, but it would be a philosophical mistake to do so on the basis of their appearance alone.

The solution, on the other hand, has to do with human culture, or nurture. We'd do better to follow Martin Luther King Jr.'s universal vision about judging people not by their appearance but by the content of their character. Our eyes can perceive someone's skin color, but only our minds can conceive of their character. Character has little or nothing to do with how the person looks (or sounds or feels or smells or tastes), and everything to do with their thoughts and sentiments. Discovering that which our eyes cannot reveal to us is the surest way to form an accurate impression of our fellow humans – and the surest way to get along with them. This is a lesson for the whole global village and needs constant repeating, to people of *every* color.

> **I have a dream that my four children will one day live in a nation where they will not be judged by the color of their skin but by the content of their character.**
>
> **– Martin Luther King Jr.**

Jerome's Case: Crossfires of Prejudice

Jerome's only daughter, Crystal, was engaged to Daniel. Jerome was Jewish and married to Rita, a woman of northern Mediterranean descent; while Daniel was of Afro-Caribbean descent. Race was not an issue for Crystal and Daniel, who had been engaged for several years, were obviously a loving couple, and were ready for marriage. Nor was it an issue for Jerome and Rita as parents of the bride: In fact, they had been looking forward to grandchildren for some time. Jerome had also become prosperous enough in his business to plan to give his daughter and future son-in-law a new house as a wedding present – a house big enough for plenty of grandchildren.

However, Jerome's in-laws were quite intolerant. Rita's family came from a clannish Mediterranean island on which people never married outside their rural village or urban neighborhood, let alone outside their ethnicity or religion. They had barely tolerated Rita's marriage to Jerome, some twenty-five years ago. They had little conception of civil rights or enlightened humanism. Their views may have once helped preserve their clan on their original island home but were now isolating them from realities and progress in contemporary America and the global village. Their perception of Crystal's marriage would be that Jerome had failed to control his daughter. And Daniel's family had issues, too. Their Caribbean island had one of the highest violent crime rates in the Western world, which they blamed on the influences of European colonialism. Similarly, they blamed high crime rates in their adopted Brooklyn neighborhood on poverty and "institutional racism." While Daniel himself was a solid middle-class citizen, well educated and virtuous, many of his relatives were resentful of white people, and accused him of "selling out."

Jerome did not share the prejudices of either group. He just wanted his daughter to be happy, and he wanted to enjoy his grandchildren. He didn't seek to be a poster child – or a whipping boy – for race relations in America. He feared that his grandchildren themselves would be caught in a crossfire of prejudice and identity politics, exposed to intolerance on both sides of the family. How could Jerome ever manage to reconcile these differences? He felt inadequate for this task.

Jerome was aware that the so-called American "melting pot" is hardly uniform in its consistency. Some states, like Hawaii, have such a large proportion of mixed-race marriages that it's the norm rather than the exception. Other states, or neighborhoods within states, are still struggling to learn King's vital lesson, to look beyond skin color and see into human character. New York City is more diverse than most places, but therefore also more unpredictable. People of every origin can be found who exhibit either enlightened humanism or regressive intolerance. Bigotry is no more determined by skin color than is any other character trait. Unfortunately, the triumph of the civil rights movement is not utopian: It is a state in which all are at liberty to get along, but are equally free to harbor prejudice, poison themselves with resentment, or even self-destruct.

Jerome sought a philosophical position that would allow him to make sense of present events in light of his past, and future events in light of his present. Jerome was not religious; in fact, he was an atheist. And neither was he an intuitive sort; he preferred to exercise reason. Given all this, plus his emphasis on the importance of assuming responsibility, Jerome had unwittingly reinvented the main pillars of Jean-Paul Sartre's humanistic existentialism. It was from Sartre, then, that Jerome crafted a philosophical position that allowed him to remain at ease with himself.

Sartre's guiding idea is that our natures are formed by us, not for us. Jerome's nature was therefore not formed by the opinions of Rita's family or of Daniel's family. It was formed by the principles he chose to practice. He had long ago chosen tolerance and respect for humanity, along with a positive work ethic, and he saw these principles as vital for his own success. Perhaps his duty lay in imparting them to his grandchildren. In any case, Jerome realized that he was not responsible for other people's opinions, only his own. He knew he would love his grandchildren, and would not allow that love to be compromised by prejudices from either side of their family.

Man is nothing else but that which he makes of himself.

– Jean-Paul Sartre

THE OPTIMUM NUMBER

While learning to compete and cooperate with others, in all kinds of arenas, we constantly expand the horizons of our identity to embrace larger and larger human groups. You belong to your family, your community, your city, your state, your profession, your nation, your religion, your gender, your ethnicity. You may also consider yourself a citizen of the world. That's a lot of groups to belong to all at the same time. While competition and cooperation within each group ultimately help the individual to survive, prosper, and reproduce, a larger force is necessary to bind the group itself together, across generations, as its individual members come and go and quarrels threaten to tear it apart. One such force is deceptively simple: elbow room.

We evolved from primordial bands of hunter-gatherers, and are hardwired to live in small intimate groups roaming spacious natural landscapes – not to be crushed together in dense hordes of strangers elbowing their way through impenetrable urban jungles. We have the technology to sustain ourselves at population densities that vastly exceed what evolutionary biologists and anthropologists call "the optimum number" for humans, but only at formidable social costs, including daily exposure to indifference, incivility, stress, anxiety, abuse, violence, crime, and deranged behaviors of every kind. This is what happens to humans when our nurture cuts against the grain of our nature. It produces monumental dis-ease.

Various philosophers have recognized this problem, and have attempted to resolve it by retreating into small communes in natural settings. The Forest Sages in India, the Epicureans in Greece, the New England Transcendentalists in America, and a great many hippies in the 1960s discovered tremendous peace, love, and cooperation by living in small, rural bands. Contrary to popular misconception, the original Forest Sages were not ascetic, antisocial hermits. Writes Rabindranath Tagore: "The forest life of the Brahmanas was not antagonistic to the social life of man, but harmonious with it." They sought simplicity in order to cultivate the finer things in life, such as friendship. So Epicurus said, "Happiness and blessedness do not correlate with abundance of riches, exalted positions, or offices or power, but with freedom from pain and gentleness of feeling and a state of mind that sets limits that are in accordance with nature." And Thoreau agreed: "A man is rich in proportion to the number of things which he can afford to let alone."

Nature has devised some ingenious ways to prevent groups from getting too large to sustain themselves, especially when cooperation leads to prosperity and overpopulation. We can learn important lessons from other social animals, including social insects, rodents, ungulates, felines, canines, and primates. Alexander Carr Saunders and Vero Wynne-Edwards found that groups of these creatures imposed limits on their own growth once they had reached an "optimum number" (or population density) in their territory. Its precise value varies from species to species, but in each case it represents a size that won't put the group at risk of extinction by insufficient reproduction, yet also won't put them at risk of starvation by consuming all available food resources. Social behaviors will change in order to keep the group near its optimum number. If the group gets too small, reproduction rates go up or new members are recruited; if it gets too large, it may fission into two groups, or limit breeding, or stop caring for its young, or increase violence toward one another. Whenever the group deviates too far from its optimum number, its normal social behaviors shift so as to bring the group back toward that number.

If you crowd animals together in artificial conditions that make them exceed their optimum numbers, and if they are confined or enclosed, and cannot disperse themselves to reduce their density and return to their optimum number, then their social order will break down. As soon as they regain their optimum number, their normal social behavior resumes. The precise mechanisms that regulate all this are very little understood.

Animals in zoos, even in what look to us like large enclosures, are still often overcrowded way beyond the limits of their optimum number, and it is well documented that their social behaviors become mildly to completely abnormal. Unable to reduce their density by expanding their territory, they resort to diminishing their actual numbers through violence or neglect. A classic study by Solly Zucker-man in the 1920s, of a few dozen baboons living in a five-hundred-square-yard enclosure in the London Zoo, showed that although the animals had plenty of food, they continually fought to death among themselves. Twenty years later, animal scientists (ethologists) discov-ered that baboons in the wild never behaved like this, because they could maintain their optimum number in far saner ways. Even though the London Zoo baboons appeared to have enough "elbow room," they were in fact subjected to a population density one hundred thousand times greater than their optimum number. No wonder they behaved so abnormally.

A large part of human social conflict is rooted in the fact that we are living like so many baboons crowded into a too-small space. Early human hunting and gathering tribes worldwide appear to have had about the same optimum number as wolves – that is, a band of several dozen foraging over a territory of several hundred square miles, or less than one person per square mile. That's a far cry from the post-industrial developed world we inhabit today, where cities sustain population densities of tens of thousands of people per square mile. No wonder cities are showcases for antisocial (and worse) behavior. Even those city dwellers who keep themselves mostly under control experience unprecedented levels of stress and anxiety from the over-crowding alone, even given an abundance of food and entertainment, even if they have what we think of as spacious homes. We're hard-wired to range across woods and fields with lots of elbow room among familiar members of our band, not to live and work in high-rises and ride in elevators and subways crushed among hordes of strangers. Our technological world has changed much faster than biological human evolution can possibly keep pace with, and our innate mismatch with our contemporary environment contributes to monumental levels of dis-ease as well as disease. There are simply too many of us, living too close together, to allow us to get along with each other as well as we might.

. . . sometimes I think that living in a city in the modern world, we are already like the

**tormented beings in the intermediate state
after death, where the consciousness is said to
be agonizingly restless.**

– Sogyal Rinpoche

THE GLUE

Humans are social animals. We stick together in groups – that's part
of our biological inheritance as well. What "glue" binds a social group
of animals together? With social insects, it's purely biochemical: The
queen ant (or bee, or wasp) secretes chemicals called pheromones,
which regulate all kinds of social and sexual functions, a primary one
being to identify all members of that particular colony, nest, or hive.
Every member is smeared with it and is therefore recognized as
belonging to the group. It's the biochemical equivalent of an ID
badge. Rodents use scent in addition to pheromones. The herd
animals like sheep, cattle, and deer are bound together by something
called "herd instinct," which has not really been explained beyond
acknowledging the role of their sense of smell and the demands of the
optimum number. Hunting mammals, like wolves and lions, also use
scent as a primary means of recognizing members of their packs of
prides.

The primates have a diminished sense of smell and lesser phero-
monic detection, and rely primarily on vision – including facial
expressions, gestures, and postures – to identify one another and
communicate their moods and intentions. But life-long studies of
chimpanzee and gorilla bands by pioneering primatologists like Jane
Goodall, Robert Yerkes, and Dian Fossey have made it abundantly
clear that what makes a monkey or ape aware it belongs to a
particular troop comes down to its relationships with the others in
the group. Similarly, a chimp's or gorilla's identity is realized through
its society. A band of apes don't all get along with one another; their
daily social life is fraught with competition, quarrels, and fights as well
as cooperation, affection, and play – just as it is for a clan of humans.

One chimpanzee is no chimpanzee.
                              – Robert Yerkes

Human groups import key behavioral features of all these other animal groups, and more. From our spot at the apex of animal complexity, we mimic behaviors of virtually every other social animal on earth. If you stand on the observation deck of the Empire State Building and watch the streets of Manhattan from this great height, you will see a human ant colony. If you observe the behavior of juvenile gangs, you will see human rat packs. If you watch crowds in shopping malls, you will see human browsing herds. And if you fly economy class, you will see humans herded exactly like sheep or cattle. If you observe sales and marketing teams at work, you will see the human equivalent of a hunting pack. If you watch men trying to pick up women in bars or other settings, or watch women luring men into their seductive webs, you will observe various kinds of solitary social predators. For that matter, we incorporate elements of plants' natures as well: Some people stand on principle as solidly as trees; others blow like grasses in the wind; some people have prickly exteriors, like cacti; others cling like vines.

You can tell what sort a man is by his creature that comes oftenest to the front.
                              – George MacDonald

But what holds human groups together is something entirely human. Once the earliest bands of humans found their optimum number, they still needed something more than biology to maintain their continuity from generation to generation. The real binding force of the human group is its culture – its language, tools, customs, and totems. Humans make their lives meaningful by leaving cultural legacies as well as biological ones. Language, tools, customs, and totems are passed on to the next generation as surely as genes are.

And they are all pressed into the service of one thing: human beliefs. People who share the same philosophy, religion, politics, profession, nationality, ethnicity, and so forth, are not biologically related, do not recognize one another's pheromones or scents, and do not necessarily behave alike or dress alike to make visual identification clear. But shared beliefs allow human groups to bind together – as well as to denigrate other human groups and justify violence against them. Ironically, the same thing that actually permits us to get along in groups much larger than nature intended also explains why we can't all just get along: Every group tends to believe it is the "in-group," and so sees all others as "out-groups," and therefore as potential enemies.

> **Thus it is that no group ever sets itself up as the One without at once setting up the Other against itself.**
> **– Simone de Beauvoir**

INDIVIDUAL VERSUS GROUP IDENTITY

So the core problem of conflict between groups boils down to the abdication of individual identity, thought, and self-expression in favor of identification with the group itself. By losing your humanity through a collective identification, you may fail to recognize the humanity of others not in your particular collection. When you trade individual identity for group identity, you also exchange a measure of your own freedom of thought and action for a measure of submission to the collective's demands for uniformity of belief and conformity of action. Arthur Koestler called this phenomenon "self-transcending identification" and wrote that "the evils of mankind are caused, not by the primary aggressiveness of individuals, but by their self-transcending identification with groups . . . the delusional streak running through history is not due to individual forms of lunacy, but to the collective delusions generated by emotion-based belief systems."

The immediate payoff is security: The group welcomes you, relieves you of the troublesome search for your own self by giving you a comforting identification, and appeals to your instinct to belong. The group makes you feel wanted and needed. Everyone wants to feel needed and needs to feel wanted.

Identification with small groups once favored human survival and furthered cultural evolution, but paradoxically it has always been a recipe for trouble. The bigger the groups supported by cultural evolution, the bigger the trouble. Trading your own identity for identification with any group smaller than the entire human race, you become part of some subgroup of humanity. Sooner or later, you'll think of your subgroup as central to the human cause, and other subgroups as peripheral to it. You will come to view the world as divided between "us" and "them" – ourselves and the others; the saved and the damned; the believers and the infidels; the proletariat and the bourgeoisie; the oppressors and the victims; this tribe and that tribe. And always, the "us" is considered superior to the "them." Any peace will be at best temporary unless we approach each other as individuals equal in our humanity. Dividing ourselves into groups inevitably creates inequalities, or the illusion of them.

If you stopped people randomly on the street and asked them, "*What are you?*" I'll bet that most would answer by producing their identification with some group – "I'm a doctor" or "I'm a Christian" or "I'm a hyphenated American" or "I'm a recovering alcoholic" or "I'm a cop" or "I'm a libertarian" or "I'm a feminist" or "I'm a Pisces." And so forth. Very few would give you a more enlightened answer off the top of their heads, such as "I'm a unique human being."

But if we could all answer that way, with honest feeling, accepting our own uniqueness, and the meaningfulness of our personal identities, we could approach others without conflict. The challenge is for each of us to stand ultimately alone, unafraid, and happy to be just who we are. Then we could identify primarily with humanity as a whole, and as such, live together in harmony. The summit of the human mountain is attained by finding one's identity as a unique being, and not by losing it in self-transcending identification with groups. Be yourself, and part of humanity. Then no one will be able to cajole or coerce you into thinking or doing violence to others because of mere differences in appearances or beliefs. By finding your own humanity independent of a collective identification, you will discover humanity in others wherever you go – and be recognized in return.

TRIBALISM

Tribes are usually bound very tightly together under some totem, such as flag, a book, or an icon – something that symbolizes their unity and mobilizes their sentiment. Tribalism once allowed small human groups to bind as effective social units, and gave individuals strong (and not altruistic) reasons to set aside or resolve their competitive differences for the sake of the group: It is easier for each individual to thrive when he or she has trusted allies and helpers. To be a member in good standing of some tribes, you need to be willing to dehumanize members of other tribes. This is where tribalism ceases to be conducive to human progress. The positive power of tribalism got us down from the trees and into civilizations, to be sure, but at the cost of reinforcing irrational prejudices and fomenting warfare. When tribalism gets out of hand, it can do colossal damage. It's one big reason why we can't all just get along.

Primitive tribes were small in size, and members all knew each other fairly intimately. Technology has made tribes increasingly large, so that they can comprise an entire nation-state, or an international religious nation. As the size of tribes has grown, so has the scope of the damage that can be wrought when they are overzealous in their tribalism. Although members of such large tribes no longer know each other on a first-name basis – or even at all – they can (and will) still be mobilized (thanks to the uniquely human power of language) to hate other large tribes, consisting of even more people they don't know.

Children learn to feel wanted, needed, loved, and welcomed not only by their parents and families, but also by the tribe to which they belong. The emotional attachments that children form to their tribes are as deep and long-lived as those they form to their parents and families. There is one significant difference: Parents and families consist of persons who can be loved or hated in person, whereas tribes consist of shared beliefs, including histories and traditions, which can be loved or hated only impersonally.

In the chapter on love, we established that hatred is a negative attachment to someone – a specific someone, with a name and identity. Now a phenomenon like racism or sexism – clear examples of identifying with your own group to the point that you can't see the humanity in another – is also a negative attachment, but not to someone specific. Rather, it is a negative attachment to a whole group of people you don't even know. If you stop to think about it (which I guess most haters never do), it is rather incredible that you can hate someone you don't even know. But if your tribe holds an idea sacred – e.g., that members of some other tribe are enemies – then to be accepted by your tribe you must share that belief. And most humans feel it is essential to be accepted by their tribes.

So you form a negative attachment to the other tribe, to the point that whenever you so much as hear its name pronounced you are conditioned to react with negative emotions. These prejudices are often reinforced by tribal lore (or propaganda, or the evening news), in which hallowed tales are told about heroic deeds (e.g., violent murders) done by members of our tribe, and heinous atrocities (e.g., violent murders) done by members of other tribes. If you ever actually encounter someone from the other tribe, you will be predisposed to view them as an implacable enemy, and inherently evil.

Of course, you also have the option of loving those whom you do not personally know, by recognizing and respecting the idea of their humanity. But loving them takes much more courage than hating them. Because if you refuse to return harm for harm, as Socrates taught, or if you insist on loving your enemies, as Jesus taught, or if you seek to empower individuals, as Nichiren taught, or if you refuse to have enemies at all, as Gandhi taught, then your own tribe will likely turn on you. For by practicing love of unknown humanity, instead of hatred of imagined tribes, you seem to undermine the force that binds your own tribe.

Plato covered this very subject in his writings about the cave. He warned of the mortal dangers faced by any enlightened human who had escaped the cave and returned voluntarily to liberate others from their blinding captivity to fuzzy, ill-informed opinions and to lead them out of the darkness and into the clear light of goodness, truth, and justice: "If they could set hands on the man who was trying to set them free and lead them up, they would kill him."

Do you have the courage to love humanity anyway? A critical mass of people doing so is the only way we'll ever all get along. We are all interconnected, more than we know. And when more people see themselves as unique human beings, instead of members of this or that tribe, then we'll all get along much better.

> **Since the ultimate enemy is dehumanization, the ultimate solution must be a revitalization and restoration of humanity. The wellspring for this must be a philosophy of humanism.**
>
> **– Daisaku Ikeda**

Jane's Case: A Protestant Family with Jewish and Islamic In-Laws

Jane, a professional Protestant woman, sought philosophical guidance because her son Rick was marrying Abigail, a Jewish woman, while her daughter Kelly was marrying Ibrahim, a Muslim man. Jane feared conflict in the family, and with good reason.

Jane's question, however, was not whether these marriages *should* or *should not* take place. Her question was how to keep the family intact once they *did* take place. Having been raised in a tolerant Protestant tradition that celebrates individual freedom of choice and responsibility for choice, Jane assumed that romantic love takes precedence over inherited beliefs. She also viewed herself and her family as inhabitants of the global village and, as such, she hoped that religious and other cultural differences would become less important as villagers became more unified – or at least more considerate of one another as neighbors. Needless to say, Jane is both an optimist and an idealist.

At the same time, increasing tensions in the Middle East were reflected in her own children's relations, both with each other and with her family. Rick began to absorb Jewish culture and values from Abigail and her family – his future in-laws – which included strong support for Israel's existence and security. Kelly began to absorb Muslim culture and values from Ibrahim's family – her future in-laws – which lately included strong anti-Israeli and anti-American sentiments. This cross-cultural absorption was less natural in Kelly's case, because Ibrahim's family opposed the marriage. Abigail's family was far more accustomed to the phenomenon of Jewish assimilation into Christianity, so they didn't resist. They also wanted love to triumph over religious difference, and sought only an understanding of Judaism from their Protestant in-laws. But Ibrahim's parents were the immigrant generation, and so their son was far more assimilated to American culture than they were. Even though they sent him to a good liberal arts college, they had not anticipated the extent of Ibrahim's self-conception as a liberated Westerner. They didn't want him to marry out of their faith (which was a way of life to them), but, seeing his love for Kelly and his determination to marry her, and fearing to lose him, they decided to woo Kelly as much as possible toward Islamic culture.

Meanwhile, back at Jane's place, family barbecues were getting out of hand. Abigail didn't insist on glatt kosher food, but she wouldn't eat ham or pork; Ibrahim would eat only halal chicken or beef. Neither of them ate hot dogs or shrimp. Rick and Kelly argued incessantly over Middle Eastern politics, while Abigail and Ibrahim exchanged pleasantries but often glared at one another across the table. Jane began to despair at thoughts of wedding parties. She had seen posters of restored Jerusalem hanging in Abigail's apartment, and posters celebrating the Intifada hanging in Ibrahim's apartment.

Jane also wondered about the religious status of her hypothetical grandchildren. According to Jewish law of matrilineal descent, children born to Abigail and Rick would automatically be considered Jewish by Jews, but could be raised in any religion (or none). There would normally be no pressure from liberal Jews to convert the husband, and little pressure to convert the children. Then again, according to Islamic law, children born of Kelly and Ibrahim would have to be raised as Muslims, whether Kelly converted or not. And under Islamic law, which is assumed by Muslims to take precedence over state laws, Kelly would have few rights as a wife, whether she converted or not.

Needless to say, these scenarios were troublesome to Jane, who simply wanted – as most parents do – to see her children happily married, to love her grandchildren a lot, and perhaps to spoil them a little. Jane really had two philosophical questions. First, why had her family become a potential battleground for one of the world's most difficult political quarrels? And second, what should she do about it?

In answer to Jane's first question, I reminded her that since she considered herself a tolerant person, perhaps her tolerance was being tested in order to be strengthened. We live in an age in which the world's most horrific conflicts are being played out on the stages of its most humble citizens. This may yet lead to progress, since simplicity and humility can succeed where complexity and belligerence have failed. Jane didn't ask to raise a "poster family" for the global village, but the global village nonetheless needs such families to point the way. She didn't volunteer explicitly for that job, but she implicitly prepared her family for it by encouraging tolerance, open-mindedness, and individuality in her children. Moreover, sometimes one's duty is foisted on one without one volunteering for it explicitly. Jane was being asked to fight for the peace by holding her kin together. If the village cannot function at Jane's level, it cannot function at all.

> **We must be the change we wish to see in the world.**
>
> **– Mahatma Gandhi**

Jane consulted the *I Ching* (*Book of Changes*), which offered her sagacious advice. (In chapter 11, I'll explain how you can use this ancient Chinese text.) In answer to the question "What should she do?" we obtained hexagram 14: Possession in Great Measure. In this hexagram, one yin or female line, representing Jane, holds together and contains many unruly male or yang lines, representing the conflicting parties. How? "It is done by virtue of unselfish modesty." The text goes on to say, "The sun brings both good and evil into the light of day. Man must combat and curb the evil, and must favor and promote the good." In this case, the good is the continuation and celebration of family life, and the evil is the constellation of political and religious conflicts that threaten to divide the family.

There was also a changing line in the third place. According to the *I*

Ching, it means "A noble person offers it (the possession in great measure) to the Son of Heaven. A petty person cannot do this. A magnanimous, liberal-minded person should not regard what he or she possesses as his or her exclusive personal property, but should place it at the disposal of the ruler or of the people at large. In so doing, he or she takes the right attitude toward this possession, which as private property can never endure."

Applied to Jane's case, the meaning is transparent. The "great possession" is, of course, her family: her husband, her children, and her hypothetical grandchildren. If she treats them as her "exclusive personal property," which means insulating them from conflicts of every kind and protecting them (even against their wills) from life's dis-eases, then they will not endure as a family. But by enlisting her liberalism and magnanimity, she both allows them to follow their own hearts and makes a gift of the whole family to the global village. Through this gift, the universal goodness of humanity may triumph over the particular evils arising from cultural differentiation. And it is Jane's modesty in wanting good relations among her family, not her ambition to solve the world's problems, that makes this possession so great in measure.

PHILOSOPHICAL EXERCISES

Exercise #1: Getting along better with yourself
1. What are some of your life-long dreams?
2. What are you doing to attain them?
3. What aren't you doing to attain them? Why?
4. Can you live without regrets and self-recriminations?
5. Can you live without blaming others for your imperfections?
6. Can you learn to accept yourself in spite of your imperfections? Or maybe even because of them?

If you can answer "yes" to the last three questions, then you probably get along well enough with yourself.

Exercise #2: Getting along better with others
1. Is there anyone with whom you're not on speaking terms because of an unsettled quarrel?
2. Are you willing to make peace, at least to the extent of restoring civil communication?

3. If so, then make an overture of peace. If it's accepted, fine. If not, at least you're willing to be at peace.

4. Try to encounter someone who appears, acts, and speaks very differently from you and your circle of friends, or tribe. Engage this person in conversation. Try to exchange worldviews (that is, your fundamental beliefs about things). What are your differences? What are your similarities?

5. Can you reach a common core of humanity, such that you discover enough commonality to accept your differences?

6. Spend at least one day alone and away from civilization. Go to the country or the seaside. Walk in the woods or hike in the hills. Admire the flora and fauna. Observe and sink into nature, of which you are a part. Don't take your cell phone, CD player, laptop, or any other piece of technology that wires you to the hubbub. When you return to civilization, notice how it has cut people off from the serenity, balance, and flow of nature and has made them frantic, imbalanced, and obstructed. Now ask yourself a philosophical question: "What can I do to make civilization amplify (instead of undermine) the natural human capacity for serenity, balance, and flow?" Tall order, right? Not really. Start with yourself.

7. If at all possible, encounter a tree. It is unique, beautiful, fractal, solid, flexible – and very much alive. It has no prejudices or opinions. It knows no terror. It takes root, and holds down the very soil. It draws water from the earth. It fashions a leafy canopy, sun-drenched above and shady beneath. It breathes. It is wondrous to behold. It harbors and shelters many other life-forms. Its sap flows. It bears fruit in its season. After benefiting its environment, it returns silently to its origins. Can any human aspire to more?

8

CAN ANYONE WIN
"THE WAR OF THE SEXES"?

**By all means marry; if you get a good spouse,
you'll be happy; if you get a bad one, you'll
become a philosopher.**

– Socrates

All's fair in love and war.

– William Shakespeare

H AVE YOU EXPERIENCED any dis-ease lately because of a relationship with a member of the opposite sex? Or maybe because of a non-relationship? Or perhaps you have a great relationship except for just one flaw in your partner, which you (or he or she) can't seem to change. In any of these cases, your dis-ease stems from fighting the never-ending war of the sexes. Nature has made men and women perpetually attractive to one another, yet incessantly at odds with one another too. We are so evenly matched that nobody ever wins the war, although our power struggles can protract almost any battle indefinitely. And that produces dis-ease. In this chapter, we'll see how philosophy can help restore ease to both sexes. But to accomplish this, you must look as honestly as possible into yourself, and into the Other. If you are not used to doing this, your dis-ease might get worse before it gets better. But as Thomas Hobbes said about resolving human conflicts, the first condition of attaining peace is sincerely to desire it. So if you truly seek peace between yourself and your opposite number, you can attain it. But first you should understand why you are at war.

A social scientist once tested the general population to see what most people had on their minds at a given time. The result: Apparently, at any given moment, about 85 percent of people are thinking about sex, or sex-related issues. When he heard this, a friend of mine quipped, "Yeah, and it's always the same 85 percent, 100 percent of the time." No matter how you run the numbers, I'm sure you don't have to be a social scientist to know that sex is a preoccupation of a great many adult humans a great deal of the time. Human beings are sexually active from puberty into old age, and are definitely endowed with more sexual energy than they need just to reproduce. Human sexuality serves all kinds of purposes beyond procreation: It can be used for recreation, domination, exploitation, and inspiration too. It is also a medium of exchange: Sex sells, and so is used to sell everything under the sun. The sexes constantly seek ease from one another, but often end up finding dis-ease instead.

The importance of sex differences in our lives accounts for why the primary conflict in ordinary social and personal life is neither racial nor ethnic – despite the predisposition humans have for those as well, as discussed in the previous chapter – but sexual. Many people, tribes, and nations the world over have learned to get along with their neighbors, but all have struggled with harmonizing males and females. I know plenty of people, of both sexes, who love humanity to a fault. They harbor no racial or ethnic or religious prejudices whatsoever – yet every last one of them has experienced ongoing conflicts of one kind or another with the opposite sex. The primary strands in the social fabric are also the primary antagonists in social conflict: man and woman. This is not so surprising. Unlike the best of friends and the worst of foes, man and woman partake of special intimacies, which can bind them closer together than friends but can also drive them further apart than foes. If mutual intimacy gets transformed into mutual animosity, the ensuing conflict is of the bitterest kind.

Marriage must incessantly contend with a monster that devours everything: familiarity.
– Honoré de Balzac

ENHANCING, CONTRADICTING, AND DISTORTING DIFFERENCES

Sex differences are primal because they are based in our very genes – our biology. Biological sex differences give rise to gender differences, which in turn cause conflicts that need to be transcended on a higher – philosophical – plane.

On the biological level, genes determine sex. And because we reproduce sexually, the human species requires sexual dimorphism – two different physical forms, male and female. But this spectrum is continuous, not discrete. That is, each female also harbors male attributes, as each male harbors female attributes. (As we'll see, this is actually a key to understanding the Other, for those willing to unlock the doors.) Toward the middle of the spectrum, we encounter bisexuals as well as androgynous types, and occasionally even her-maphrodites. Since our bodies are our primary means of interaction with the physical world, our biological differences are foundational. What we make of these differences culturally, however, is largely up to us. So we've invented attitudes that range all over the map, from the celebration of "Vive la difference!" to militant male chauvinism and radical feminism alike.

But our interpretations of biology heavily influence the second, psychosocial dimension of conflict: gender. Being male or female is a biological and sexual matter; being a man or a woman is a cultural and gender matter. The rules of biology and sexual reproduction are fixed by nature; the rules of culture and gender roles are malleable by nurture. As biological beings, male and females have scarcely changed in a hundred thousand years or more; as cultural beings, their roles have changed drastically in less than a hundred years – at least in the developed world. Yet these changes themselves have been, and con-tinue to be, sources of conflict and dis-ease. Gender roles can enhance sex differences, contradict them, distort them, or transcend them. Let's look briefly at some examples of each.

ENHANCING DIFFERENCES

When we see a traditional and functional nuclear family, with the husband and wife providing loving mutual support and each parent providing his or her particular kind of love to their children, then we see an example of the social enhancement of sex difference. This helps human beings to lead meaningful and purposive lives, and to continue their line into the next generation. Enhancement is good for the humanity of all concerned. It produces ease. Notwithstanding its many imperfections, the nuclear family has historically been the best vehicle for the wholesome, long-term enhancement of sex difference. Its increasing disintegration in the developed world is also a source of growing dis-ease.

If the children are a boy and a girl, then both will want to play, yet sex difference will also influence the kinds of toys with which they play. More often than not, boys will want to play with toy soldiers. This does not mean they will grow up to be violent warmongers. It means they are practicing to be adult male primates. As such, they bear the ancient evolutionary responsibility of defending their troop. And more often than not, girls will want to play with dolls. This does not mean they will grow up to be barefoot and pregnant. It means they are practicing to be adult female primates. As such, they bear the ancient evolutionary responsibility of mothering babies. To be sure, some girls are "tomboys," and prefer a bit of rough-and-tumble; and some boys are mild-mannered by nature. But on average, formative human gender roles are natural extensions of sex difference, and should be treated as such. This is also enhancement, and produces ease. At the same time, it is now understood that girls (as well as boys) can benefit greatly from playing competitive sports, and that boys (as well as girls) can benefit greatly from gentler pursuits, such as music lessons. As adults, and thanks to further cultural evolution, boys and girls can also transcend their natural differences: Men or women alike can become conscientious objectors to violence, and women or men alike can join armed defense forces, if they so choose.

CONTRADICTING DIFFERENCES

But at least one mother, Maria, was hoodwinked by the still popular
but misguided idea that all gender roles are "socially constructed,"
and the fantasy that there are no social consequences of biological sex
difference. So Maria forbade her two sons to play with toy soldiers,
and gave them Barbie dolls instead. Then one day she came home and
found them sword-fighting, using the dolls as swords. This convinced
her of the truth: that natural sex difference does have a big say in the
formation of gender roles. Nature cannot be contradicted. Contra-
dictions are bad for those forced to live them; they produce dis-ease.

Similarly, if one's children are a boy and a girl, then they will both
learn to read but may prefer to read different things. Some of their
preferences are sex-based. There is a huge industry of women's
magazines and men's magazines, and their differing social content
is based heavily on sex difference. Most men don't read *Glamour*, but
they do want women to be glamorous. Most women don't read
Playboy, but they probably wouldn't mind looking like centerfolds.
That's sex difference at work in cultural terms. If we forbid women to
read women's magazines and to make fashion statements (as the
Taliban did), or forbid men to admire female beauty in men's
magazines (as some radical feminists would do), we will contradict
their natures and produce dis-ease.

DISTORTING DIFFERENCES

A bigger conflict occurs when sex differences are distorted by culture.
Among baboons, anatomy is destiny. Among humans, it need not be.
But many cultures still reflect this ancient primate tendency, and treat
anatomy as destiny among humans too. The women's liberation
movement had to fight this tendency for a very long time, and began
to win its battles for equal rights in the twentieth century. Even so,
equality is not sameness! We will shortly see cases of women who are
unhappy because they are being treated like men. But at the other

extreme, when sex difference is used as an excuse for oppression, women are prevented from flourishing fully as human beings.

Sita's Case: Excluded from Education

Take the case of Sita, from the fieldwork of philosopher Martha Nussbaum. Sita is a young girl, living in a poor village in Bihar, in northern India. Her daily morning duties include mixing cow dung with hay and bran and forming the mixture into cakes, which she pats onto walls and tree trunks. When dry, these cakes will be used by her mother for cooking and heating fuel. Sita will spend her day performing myriad other manual labors, thus contributing to the subsistence economy that limits their lives. Meanwhile, what is her brother doing? He is studying and getting his books ready for school. In this system, the male child has a chance to develop his mind, and therefore improve his life, whereas the female child is excluded from education. Again, anatomy is destiny among baboons, but should not be among humans.

Martha Nussbaum (among others) works to remedy these and similar cultural distortions of sex difference. Sita's prospects will equal her brother's only through education, and at many levels. First, she needs a primary education too. But in order for Sita to get one, those who govern her life – socially, economically, theologically, and politically – must be reeducated themselves. The design and implementation of such changes are exercises in what Aristotle called *phronesis,* or practical wisdom. Literacy is clearly and universally a passport to a better life.

> **The nature of the world economy is such that illiteracy condemns a woman (or man) to a small number of low-skilled types of employment. With limited employment opportunities, a woman is also limited in her options to leave a bad or abusive marriage. If a woman can get work outside the home, she can stand on her own.**
>
> **– Martha Nussbaum**

However, distortion cuts both ways. In the developed world, women's literacy and liberation have propelled an entire generation of women into the workforce, to the extent that they predominate in some sectors, have parity in others, and are increasingly represented in yet more. Many relatively young women have become, in economic terms, successful big-game huntresses. Yet they are not necessarily fulfilled by this kind of success. My Dutch colleague Ida Jongsma has seen plenty of cases like this in Europe, as I have seen in North America.

Sonya's Case: "Is This All There Is?"

Sonya was a typical career woman: young, intellectual, and self-sufficient. She was a writer living in Holland, earning a good livelihood from her books and articles. So why did she seek philosophical counseling?

Sonya had a Big Question: "Is this all there is?" She had no apparent reason to be dissatisfied with her life, but she wasn't happy. Something was missing. She claimed not to know what it was. She thought something was wrong with her, and had spent time in psychotherapy. She and Ida talked about her ideals in life, about her wishes for the future. Ultimately, Sonya revealed a deep longing for emotional security and a happy family life. She had a new lover, Jan, and wanted to be with him as often as she could. She was even willing to give up her career for him and raise a family with him. But Jan was unwilling, or perhaps afraid, to make such a commitment. Sonya tried to accept this, and allowed Jan to curtail their time together. But this was an unhappy compromise that both interfered with Sonya's work and left her deeper longings unsatisfied.

What's the philosophical moral? This: We do not change women into men by affording them equal opportunities to excel at "the hunt." Thinking that we do distorts many women's natural inclinations toward family, and leaves them with dis-ease, even if they are successful huntresses.

Of course, Sonya's circumstances are only mildly distorted compared to Sita's. Most importantly, Sonya has options while Sita doesn't. We can always find ease by choosing the right option. It's a much more difficult matter to find ease when there is no choice at all.

TRANSCENDING DIFFERENCES

Now we come to a fourth possibility: transcendence. Culture can not only enhance, contradict, or distort sex difference; it can also transcend sex and gender difference alike. Think about it: The noblest, most evolved, and most creative functions of the human being possess neither sex nor gender. If you have a soul, it has no sex or gender. If you compose music, or write poems, or paint canvases, or prove theorems, they have no sex or gender – and neither do your audience's experience of them. If you perform an act of love or compassion, it has no sex or gender. If you formulate and apply a philosophical principle – be it Stoic or Platonic or pragmatic – both formulation and application have neither sex nor gender. If you practice meditation or otherwise heighten your awareness, the consciousness thereby exercised has neither sex nor gender.

It is at this level that you begin to attain your full potential: not as male or female, not as man or woman, but as a human being. As long as human socialization and education do not lead one to this level, then society will consist of a collection of arrested and often tormented beings, with considerable dis-ease. Social conflict is sure to follow. Wars between the sexes will be waged. Peaceful co-existence is always better, and is most surely attained through transcendence.

What does transcendence mean in practical terms? Before I offer some human examples, consider transcendental numbers. Such numbers never end, never repeat, and are never the roots of algebraic equations. Thus they are not limited by any complete definition, and can only be approximated in practice. Take π, a famous member of that family. No matter how many decimal places of π we compute, starting with 3.14159, we can never define π completely. Contrast that with a number like 22/7. Contrary to what's taught in schools, π does not equal 22/7; that's only an approximation. In fact, 22/7 equals 3.142857142857142857 . . . , which never ends but forever repeats itself. It's predictable and definable, therefore not transcendental.

If you begin to think of your life in this way, you will realize that part of it is determined (e.g., your sex and your past) and part is open (e.g., your gender role and your future). The part that can be determined is like your résumé; but that does not define you in your entirety. Your entirety includes your future, which cannot be captured because it has not yet happened. This is wonderful news for you! The numbers that come next in π's sequence are not determined by, or predictable from, the numbers that came earlier. And so it can be in your life. The events that occur next in your life are not necessarily determined by, or predictable from, the events that came earlier. This doesn't mean that π can be equal to anything at all, or that you can do anything at all: Transcendence is not the same as randomness.

You were born male or female; thus you acquired a masculine or feminine experience of life. So initially you see yourself and the Other through the bifocal lenses of your sex and gender. But they convey no image of what you might accomplish as a transcendent human being. So you can capitulate to circumstances and feel limited by them, or you can allow for the possibility that your future doesn't necessarily resemble your past. That allowance is a mental act of transcendence. Your anatomy and psychology are not your destiny: You can will for yourself a future that you envision. Willing brings about real consequences for you. To transcend means to go beyond the limitations of sexual definition and gender predictability. Transcending often combines negating something (the imposed limiting condition), while preserving something else (the will and natural ability to actualize the desired outcome). Here are a few cases that illustrate what I mean.

Jessica's Case: Breaking the Mold

Jessica was a hippie during the 1960s. Part of the Woodstock generation, and guided by Timothy Leary's philosophy, she "tuned in, turned on, and dropped out." She returned to university in the 1970s and became heavily involved in activist politics – civil rights and women's liberation. In the 1980s she founded a nonprofit organization that provided social and other services to all kinds of women in need. A talented fund-raiser and tireless entrepreneur, Jessica's enterprises thrived and diversified during the 1990s. Her successes brought her powerful friends and enemies alike – including men and women in both camps. This is only natural. Some of Jessica's foes were men who didn't want her (or feminism) to succeed for a variety of reasons. As a pillar of the women's movement, she was regularly targeted by its opponents. Her gender wars were fought against a system, not a husband. Yet Jessica was a happy warrior, made joyous by the combat of ideas.

So why did Jessica seek philosophical advice? To further her self-understanding and to articulate her unique identity. Jessica was leading a thoroughly original life. She read voraciously and philosophized courageously. Valuing her independence, she neither married nor had children. To actualize her visions, she wedded and reformed the system itself, and so provided opportunities for many other women. Thus Jessica transcended: By negating the limitations imposed on women, yet preserving her capacity to nurture (in this case, nurture a cause rather than a family), she accomplished much and set a great example for others.

Cynthia's Case: Having Her Cake and Eating It Too

Cynthia managed to juggle a successful marriage with a flourishing career in consulting, and mother two children in the bargain. How? By ignoring the limitations that other people might have imposed on her. Yes, it's hard enough to be good wife, or a good mother, or a good careerist, let alone to do all three well. Many of her friends' marriages were faltering because they didn't have enough time to maintain their basic relationships. Transcending in Cynthia's case meant negating the supposition that she couldn't do all these things superbly, and preserving the fundamental values and duties intrinsic to each of these endeavors. For Cynthia, the guiding idea was not to defeat herself at the outset by believing that she would have to compromise excellence in one area in order to excel in another. She realized her potential as a human being by inhabiting all her dimensions – each in its own constructive way. And her husband was happy to spend less time with a more fulfilled wife rather than more time with a less fulfilled one. So Cynthia "won" her war of the sexes not by fighting it but by transcending it. This takes willpower, hard work, and good organization.

Lenore's Case: Affirming the Unconventional

Lenore's transcendence came about in a different and somewhat unconventional way. She was a philosopher by profession and temperament, and had always valued a contemplative life more than a familial one. Nonetheless, Lenore had tried marriage, but thereby rediscovered what Anton Chekhov and Gloria Steinem both independently asserted: One sure way to experience loneliness is to get married. Lenore preferred to be unattached and at ease with herself, rather than attached and in dis-ease with someone else.

Lenore experienced a moment of transcendence in Amsterdam. She was exploring the Zeedijk, Amsterdam's famous red-light, soft-drug, and bohemian counterculture district. The Zeedijk features legal prostitution, where certified sex workers display themselves in windows and doorways throughout the quarter's maze of streets and alleys. Lenore saw women of every conceivable shape, size, race, and age waiting to cater to the sexual tastes of throngs of circulating men. Lenore wondered why there weren't male sex workers similarly displaying themselves. In her egalitarian mind, men and women should be equal in this way. She thought that women should also have a publicly available choice of men to service them sexually. And because Lenore is not alone in this view, they increasingly do.

Lenore had the capacity to separate sex and love. Thus she preserved her sexuality, but negated the limitations imposed by conventional gender stereotyping, which declares that "normal" women cannot separate sex and love as men "normally" (and sometimes infamously) do. Lenore, and a growing number of women like her, found her own way to transcend the war of the sexes.

Note that transcending sex and gender roles does not mean doing, or refraining from doing, any specific thing. Transcendent beings might be married with children and careers (like Cynthia), or free as the wind (like Lenore), or committed to social and political change (like Jessica). What they have in common is the ease of being and peace with themselves that transcendence so often confers.

THE PRIMARY PARADOX

Before addressing further issues, let's tackle a more basic Big Question: Why is there a war in the first place?

In the natural world, the major theme of animals' lives is the drive to reproduce – to pass their genes on to a new generation, for their own little stab at immortality. That manifests in daily life as quests for food, territory, status, and mates, all of which are minimal requirements for survival and reproduction.

For most beings on this planet, food is by far their biggest daily concern. Getting food, or not becoming food, is number one on most animals' (and plants') agendas, most of the time. Second is generally territory, in large part because occupying or controlling the right territory provides access to food and shelter from predators. Territory also provides a leg up on the third (though in some ways primary) item: mating. The right territory confers the great advantage of reproductive status, as females of many species are attracted to males in proportion to the desirability of the territory the male can defend. In many other species (so-called "tournament species"), females are attracted to males who dominate the competitive and combative male hierarchy. Humans are both a territorial and a tournament species, and more besides.

But most humans in the developed world do not have to worry about food or territory or jobs on a constant basis. So for the civilized human animal, the big and often all-consuming question is not what and when you're going to eat, or where you're going to sleep, but *with whom* are you going to eat and sleep? The biological basis of human sexual behavior is transcended by cultural arrangements. Passing on genes is preserved, but negated as sex's sole purpose. Expressed culturally, sexual behavior ranges from complete abstinence (as in vows of celibacy) to extreme indulgence (as in promiscuity), to homosexuality and bisexuality; from monogamy to polygamy or polygyny; from serial monogamy to lifelong partnerships to "trophy" wives and husbands.

Humans invest tremendous amounts of time, energy, thought, and emotion in embarking on romantic and sexual quests of many kinds, or in inventing cultural restrictions to prevent others from embarking on such quests. But no sooner do men and women encounter one another on such a quest than they also find something to fight about. Why?

Within most species, sexual strategy differs radically for males and females. Generally speaking, the male wants to mate with as many females as possible, so as to leave as many offspring as possible. Biologically, that's his best strategy for his genes to survive into the next generation. He's got a surplus of gametes, and disseminating them as widely as possible is nature's way for him to play the odds. The female, on the other hand, generally wants to mate with the single best male she can attract, so as to give her eggs the finest fertilization available and provide them with the best access to resources (like food and protection) once they are born. Biologically, that's her best strategy for her genes to survive into the next generation: She's got a limited number of eggs, so prudent investment in each and every one is nature's way for her to play the odds.

Thus humans are biologically predisposed to incompatible mating strategies: The male wants as many females as he can get, with as little commitment as possible to each; while the female wants the best male that she can get, with total commitment from him. Culturally, this translates into a contest between profligacy versus monogamy – and if that isn't a recipe for constant conflict, I don't know what is. Mutual dis-ease is an ironic by-product of mutual attraction, nature's little joke on us. This is the primary paradox that gives rise to sexual warfare.

Every woman should marry – and no man.
– Benjamin Disraeli

In the psychosocial dimension, another principal cause of "the war of the sexes" is the expectation that finding or marrying your "soul mate" will make your life complete or perfect. We will explore the thorny problem of expectations themselves in chapter 12, but for now let's just remind ourselves that sharing a real life with someone is not at all the same as the fantasies spun in romantic fairy tales and movies. Even an extremely well-matched couple does not simply live happily ever after, even if both set out to. In fact, the best of intentions can lead to the worst of battles.

True, finding that someone special does resolve one of your pressing problems (namely, finding that someone special), at least temporarily. But the realities and banalities of living inevitably intrude sooner or later, and many issues must be managed for love to endure. Particularly troublesome are learning to be supportive of the other person's view of life, and adopting a shared identity ("the couple") while maintaining your own separate identity as an individual. The boundaries between "his," "hers," and "ours" are somewhat elastic and also permeable, so misunderstandings arise about roles, conflicts arise over duties, and irritations emerge from habits. The battle is joined.

These fundamental conflicts between the sexes are played out regularly at home, in marriages, and in nuclear and extended families. As soon as children are old enough to begin playing the dating game, they begin to engage in this war – which rages for dating adults of every age, whether single, divorced, or widowed, for as long as they maintain an interest in the opposite sex. It also crops up, at least in societies with liberated women, in the business and professional worlds, not to mention schools, religions, community organizations, and just about any other social group you can name. The basic conflict is a fact of life, and your life will be more bitter or sweet depending on how well you recognize the facts and how wisely you adapt to them. If you do both successfully, your dis-ease can be minimized.

THE ENLIGHTENMENT

> . . . either Nature has made a great difference between man and women, or that civilization which has hitherto taken place in the world has been very partial.
>
> – Mary Wollstonecraft

The West has, of late, been through several centuries of hard-won emancipation of the individual human being – man, woman, and child alike. The philosophical turning point in delivering us from the despotic clutches of various kinds of overly authoritarian social, economic, and political structures dates back to the Enlightenment. Enlightenment thinking focused on making reason the primary way to understand our world, including nature. The Enlightenment aimed to dispel subjective superstitions and discern objective laws, and bring human culture – from child-rearing to politics – into better correspondence with natural laws, thereby enabling individuals to reach their full potential as human beings and live according to their transcendent natures. The contemporary combination of Enlightenment politics, economics, and science on the one hand and Asian wisdom traditions embracing profound philosophical practices on the other hand offers the best prospects of emancipation for the greatest number of people in the global village.

This means, for one thing, that humans are best suited to live according to the unique guidelines of *human* biology – not the rules we see in any other animal society. Ant colonies, for example, thrive with government by a monarch, selfless devotion of all other individuals to the monarch and the collective, each individual's life role predetermined at birth by a rigid genetic "caste system," constant deadly warfare with neighboring colonies, and the capture and enslavement of ants from other colonies. If human nature were equivalent to ant nature, then the rules that govern an ant colony could be justifiably applied to human society. Although these rules resemble the very rules of government and engagement that millions of humans have been forced to live by for centuries, and which millions are still forced to live by today, clearly they do not allow us to thrive the way ants do. Colonial and imperial societies lived in this way, but they also produced gross injustices.

As the Enlightenment moved human culture away from living like social insects, it also had to contemplate just what we should be heading toward. The natural hierarchies that define the social and political life of monkeys and apes – our closest animal relatives – are governed by physically dominant males, so perhaps we are meant to follow suit. On the other hand, human cultural development is very new, compared with our biology. The primate style of dominance clearly belongs to the early evolution of humans, and has less and less to do with modern culture and developing technology.

Consider the kind of work done by women in England before and after the World Wars for just one example of cultural evolution in action, on a time scale incomparably shorter than biological evolution. In post-Victorian Britain, women were forbidden to drive buses and trucks, as this was thought to be unladylike. Then, during World War I, someone had to do all the transportation and manufacturing work previously done by the men, now being conscripted and slaughtered in the trenches of Europe; and so women went to work, not only in the factories but also driving buses and trucks. Fast-forward to World War II, and the Battle of Britain, and you see women ferrying fighter aircraft from the factories to the airfields, among many other jobs previously restricted to males. This amounts to a quantum cultural jump in just thirty years' time.

Mercifully, we don't need massive and tragic wars to evolve culturally. More peaceful political, social, and educational action has further accelerated women's liberation in the developed world, and it is by now more than clear that women can fulfill the same cultural roles as men, regardless of biological differences: Culture is capable of transcending biology. The key to avoiding dis-ease, when it comes to the war of the sexes, is to remember that social and political equality does not always mean sameness. Treating women with equality is desirable, but treating them as identical to men isn't – for either sex.

Then again, the Enlightenment has also backfired in certain ways, especially as regards marriage. The more politically independent men and women become, the more self-absorbed, the more self-regarding, and the more affluent, the less they will be concerned for the sacrifices and teamwork required for a lasting marriage and responsible parenting. That's why birthrates in the developed world are plummeting.

Ruth's Case: What Women Still Want

Ruth worked for an investment bank in Manhattan. She was in her late twenties, single, well educated, with a good job that paid quite well. But she was also desperately unhappy. She wanted a husband and children. When Ruth was in college, the educational process was geared to treating women not only as equal to men, but also as identical to men. This came back to haunt Ruth, because she saw clearly, on the job, that she and most of her female co-workers weren't interested only in climbing the career ladder – that is, unless they could balance that climb with marriage and motherhood. Ruth was actually envious of her mother, a housewife, because her mother never had that many choices, yet always seemed content with the life "chosen" for her.

Nowadays Ruth wished she had had fewer choices as well. When she was in college, she was taught to look down on women who were there primarily to earn the degree of "Mrs." Now she wasn't so sure. Moreover, she found herself in a very tough "market" for men: The eligible bachelors in her firm were well outnumbered by the young women hunting them. Facing her thirtieth birthday, she wished for an engagement party rather than another night out with "the girls."

Of course Ruth dated: Plenty of men her age had asked her out. So what was wrong? The problem was that they weren't much better off than she, and so the pair could live very well until one of them (you know which one) would have to quit her job to look after the children. Then they would be faced with a choice confronting many young adults these days: maintaining an affluent, two-income lifestyle while allowing their children to be raised by strangers, or sacrificing affluence and allowing one parent to stay at home while the other worked (a throwback to the 1950s). Ruth's third alternative was to find a man earning essentially twice as much as her, which would preempt the dilemma – she could "have her cake and eat it too." But Ruth's friends were all seeking that elusive guy as well, and most candidates turned out to be either married or gay (or occasionally both).

Is Paxil going to help Ruth? Not likely. What about psychotherapy? She doesn't need it. Neither does she suffer from a medical disease. Is she spoiled? Not really; she works hard for her money. Philosophically, her dis-ease lies in maintaining a certain set of expectations, and then feeling disappointed because they are not being met. More about expectations in chapter 12, but for now consider this: You are always free to maintain any expectation about the world, but the world is never obliged to live up to it. Expecting things to be a certain way is unrealistic and often immature, just like wishful thinking. Whereas *willing* them to be a certain way is quite realistic and effective, provided that you can persist in a state of focused will.

So in the first instance, Ruth was helped by Jean-Paul Sartre's idea: "Man is condemned to be free; because once thrown into the world, he is responsible for everything he does." And believe it or not, this is very close to the Buddha's key insight: "As you think, so shall you become." Ruth may or may not meet the man of her dreams. And even if she did, that dream could turn into a nightmare. But Ruth will certainly meet the man she freely and responsibly wills to meet – whether today, tomorrow, next week, or next year.

The power of the will has become severely underrated in the West, and virtually unexplored in psychological therapies. Yet it is paramount among human assets. Wishing and willing are completely different. Wishing for something almost guarantees you *won't* get it, because wishing passively reinforces the gap between you and the object of your wishes. You need a genie (or deity, or somebody else) to *grant* your wish. But willing something almost guarantees you will get it, in time, because willing actively bridges the gap between you and the object of your will. By willing, you become the genie. Fantasizing is an elaborate kind of wishing in which many indulge to escape from reality. But that's a vicious circle: Escaping then returning never improves reality itself. It just necessitates the next escape. On the other hand, learning to use willpower to improve your reality denecessitates your escape. It breaks the cycle.

Your relationships are selected by your thought forms – just like your wardrobe. By remaining persistently true to her willed image of herself (not a daydream or fantasy), Ruth will actualize that image. She will find her man. But then, as we saw in chapter 5, she will have to be careful about the pitfalls of getting what she asks for: the misery of having as opposed to not having.

All the phenomena of existence have mind as their precursor, mind as their supreme leader, and of mind are they made.

– Gautama Buddha

FIDELITY AND FUTILITY

In attempts to reconcile sexuality and culture, many famous philosophers have experimented with open relationships – with limited
success. In France, Jean-Paul Sartre and Simone de Beauvoir had a
lifelong romance, intense both physically and philosophically, but she
suffered in tolerating his numerous affairs, and was unhappier in her
own. She would have preferred monogamy with him, but she also
preferred an open relationship with him to none at all. This can also
work the other way around, with men hopelessly in love with women
who are not satisfied with them alone.

Nonetheless, a man's or woman's mature power is usually better
harnessed to some social, economic, cultural, artistic, or political
purpose, rather than squandered in sexual escapades (unless, like
Henry Miller or Charles Bukowski, it's their art form). Nietzsche
exemplified the ascetic approach: He actually gave up romance in
favor of philosophy, for he thought it impossible to do both things
well simultaneously. The younger Nietzsche had a very romantic view
of marriage, and wrote: "I'd like to find myself a good wife quite soon,
and then I can look on my life's desires as fulfilled." But he subse-
quently became disenchanted and possibly embittered by at least two
rejections by women to whom he proposed. So the older Nietzsche
changed his tune: "Many short follies – that is called love by you. And
your marriage puts an end to many short follies, with one long
stupidity." Sour grapes? Maybe so. Then again, this was also the
view of at least one leading lady of the nineteenth century, namely the
countess of Blessington: "Love-matches are made by people who are
content, for a month of honey, to condemn themselves to a life of
vinegar." But in this postmodern era, when it's easier to get a divorce
than to fire an employee or cancel a lease on a car, plenty of women
have become as cynical about marriage as Nietzsche.

> **I believe in large families. Every women should
> have at least three husbands.**
> **– Zsa Zsa Gabor**

Sometimes I wonder if men and women really
suit each other. Perhaps they should live next
door and just visit now and then.
                                    – Katherine Hepburn

INFIDELITY, FOR BETTER OR DIFFERENT

While fidelity can be difficult to maintain in a marriage, does infidelity
spell the end of one – or the beginning of the end? Not necessarily. If
either partner wants to wreck a marriage, then infidelity is surely one
way to do it. Then again, infidelity can sometimes bring a married
couple closer together (just as can any other disagreement that gets
resolved). Some people are very possessive of their spouses, others less
so. Sometimes a spouse will see that he or she has driven the other to
become unfaithful through some conspicuous cruelty or neglect. At
other times infidelity may be unprovoked, and used to send a cruel
message to the other.

Ralph's and Lauren's Case: Infidelity Sends a Message
A couple named Ralph and Lauren were not communicating very
well. Lauren tended to come home from work in a kind of frenzy and
dump all her problems on Ralph, without giving him much breathing
room or taking her turn to listen to his inevitable troubles. He tried
communicating his unhappiness with this imbalance to her, but she
wasn't listening. It's difficult to use communication to fix a communication problem! He realized that the stresses of her new job were
taking a toll on them both, but couldn't figure out how to get her
attention long enough to discuss it. He just couldn't get through to her.

Meanwhile, Ralph also needed someone to whom he could un-
burden himself on a regular basis. He wanted that person to be Lauren
– as she had been when she married him. So Ralph had a brief affair
with another woman who was listening to him, and he told Lauren
about it. That certainly got her attention, at which point they sought
philosophical counseling and began to resolve their communication
(and her career) issues. I'm not going into their further particulars

here: I only raise this case to show how one episode of infidelity may have saved a marriage. If you want a philosophical moral, sometimes a bad means can lead to a good end. I wouldn't try it every day, though. Don't push your luck.

WHAT DO MEN AND WOMEN SEE?

> **Men and women "in love" share the mistaken belief that they live in the same world. They come to "love" one another when they acknowledge that they live in different worlds, but are prepared, once in a while, to cross the chasm that separates them.**
>
> **– Thomas Szasz**

Human sex difference is much more than anatomy. The brain itself is sexually differentiated, with the net result that men and women tend to view the world in very different ways. Men and women see the same phenomena with their eyes, but think about them differently. Men tend to be fascinated by things, the properties and parts of things, the way things work with or against other things, and the laws that govern the way things work. Women tend to be fascinated by relationships between and among people and things, and they constantly and minutely observe people's interactions and infer what people are thinking and feeling based on the way they relate to one another. They are both right, of course: Each sex sees approximately half the picture. Together at peace, they can both see the whole. But if they go to war over whose half is "real," then both will miss the whole.

Men tend to conceive of themselves as "stand-alone" objects in the world, governed by their own appetites, aversions, desires, and ambitions, who come into contact with other stand-alone objects, and who then form alliances or enmities with them accordingly. Women tend to conceive of themselves as subjects who relate emotionally to other subjects. A man usually defines himself primarily by what he prints on his business card, and measures himself by what he accomplishes in the world; a woman often defines herself primarily in terms of her relationships with others, and measures herself by the success or failure of these relationships over time. And so, a man sees a woman as a kind of thing (whether playmate, wife, mother, or partner), while a woman sees a man in terms of their potential relationship (whether casual date, serious date, affair, or marriage).

When man and woman forge an alliance, as in marriage, these complementary ways of seeing the world can benefit them both. It is always useful for a man to hear a woman's point of view, and vice versa. However, when a marriage breaks up, these different points of view ordained by nature can wreak havoc, as they become the lines of battle on the field of war.

D-I-V-O-R-C-E

The great philosopher of warfare, Carl von Clausewitz, famously said, "War is the continuation of policy by other means." I would like to paraphrase him, and suggest that divorce is the continuation of marriage by other means.

In my experience with clients, divorce is often more painful for women than for men, owing to their natural difference in outlook. Men see their wives and marriages as things. They also believe if something is damaged beyond repair, or gets lost or stolen, it can be replaced by something else. So a man is predisposed to think, "Even though I love my wife, I can always find another wife if I have to get divorced from this one." He believes he can replace one marriage with another, like a car. Women, on the other hand, view marriage as a unique relationship which can never be replaced. To a woman, a divorce is the death of a relationship, and a part of her dies with it. Women need to preserve their relationships in order to feel whole. A divorce – or any failed significant relationship – is therefore a fragmentation of a woman's being. It is much more traumatic to end a relationship than to lose a thing.

These discrepancies in approaches can show up in the practicalities of divorce, particularly when it comes time for division of property.

There's a nugget of truth in the old joke about the new Divorce Barbie: She comes with all Ken's stuff. Economic needs may mandate that a woman seek alimony or child support from her ex-husband, but beyond that, wrangling over money may actually reflect her emotional needs. Perpetual monetary claims can be a way of preserving some form of the relationship, although since what is really desired is love, not money, it is necessarily an unsatisfying relationship that endures. The courts can compel financial or material commitment, but not, of course, emotional commitment, so this road leads not to happiness but to dis-ease. And even when a divorced couple remains amicable, whether for the sake of the children or simply because they want to get along, being divorced is more like perpetuating a non-relationship than a relationship.

On the other hand, even amicable and reasonable financial arrangements can cause dis-ease for the man, too. They not only hit him where he lives (in the "things"), but also mean he's compelled to provide for (and in that sense protect) a family he is excluded from. He feels that he been turned into a human ATM who has to pay for a thing – the family – that he can no longer see or derive appreciation from. That's a bitter pill for the Great Hunter to swallow. On the whole, however, a man can still derive some satisfaction by providing for his ex-family (a different kind of "thing" than a family), whereas a woman cannot derive much satisfaction from the transmutation of a marriage into a divorce (a relationship into a non-relationship).

In chapter 7, we saw that the human being is capable of mimicking virtually every other animal (and plant) on earth; we can understand by simile what has happened to our social and familial fabric. In the past, humans lived too much like social insects, whose lives are ruthlessly predetermined for them. The Enlightenment project reversed all that, but has now given humans so much individual freedom that they now live too much like ruthless solitary predators. In earlier times, the social fabric was like a straitjacket. Now it is disintegrating altogether. To preserve the institution of marriage, we need to find a happy medium.

WORK

Plenty of my clients come to me with tales of woe emanating from their working lives, and often those issues devolve back to the battle of the sexes. The fundamental problem is that men and women tend to view the workplace quite differently. Men see work as the hunt. Even though hunting has become largely symbolic, involving paychecks instead of big game, male competitiveness, male bonding, and male hierarchies still predominate. Hunting used to be an extremely arduous and often dangerous business, demanding great individual skill, strength, courage, stamina, cunning, and aggression in the solo hunter, as well as organization of space, time, strategy, and tactics among the hunting band. Note that these attributes are *not* universally male: Lionesses, for example, are the primary hunters in that species, and they exhibit all these qualities as well as the nurturing behavior required to mother their young. This is true of many other mammals, both hunting and foraging species, in which the female is the main provider and protector. But in primates that hunt, humans foremost among them, hunting is the male's most natural job.

Males are also the natural defenders of the tribal unit – or family – and a band of males is a defense force as well as a hunting pack. The two roles – provider and protector – are closely related. For one thing, all the attributes necessary for a successful hunt are also necessary for a successful defense. For another, males are predators, who hunt not just to feed themselves and their families, but also to attain property, territory, status, and perhaps more females too. Beyond that, men also hunt to conquer and subjugate others, and to impose their beliefs on the conquered. So man needs to be just as adept at defense as attack, as he'll come into someone else's sights as often as he sets his own sights on others. Human females are top predators as well, but their primary quarry is man himself. Their natural tactic is to disguise themselves as sexual prey, but their strategy is to subjugate their quarry through marriage.

A man's wife has more power over him than the state has.

– Ralph Waldo Emerson

Thanks to the layering of cultural evolution on top of biological evolution, women can also pursue pretty much any career they wish to these days. Yet we have seen that many professionally successful women are nonetheless quite unhappy. They experience dis-ease when their elemental nature as nurturers is unfulfilled. A successful career on its own will satisfy most men – or the elemental hunter in them – but many women on similar tracks actually consider themselves failures if they are not married with children. There are some exceptions, but not as many as early advocates of women's liberation had supposed. Liberated women do not usually turn into men. Then again, liberated women with children often feel overburdened by the juggling of domestic and professional responsibilities, and find it hard to manage both simultaneously. This requires abundant energy, superb organization, and exquisite timing.

So while a great many women want to participate in the contemporary hunt (career path) and do make very fine huntresses (careerists), a great many also find the social and emotional climate of this hunt uncomfortable. When males bond in groups, there is a natural rough-and-tumble aspect to their hierarchy, with threat or challenge to authority, if not outright aggressive confrontation, always lurking in the wings. Boys will be boys, because they must be boys. Women naturally find this male ethos unwelcoming and emotionally unsupportive.

Women experiencing dis-ease in a man's world may want to change men, or else the world, in order to feel more comfortable. The ethos of the workplace has shifted, in many arenas, to reflect the woman's presence in what was previously a man's world. Developed nations are increasingly dependent on equality of men and women's work, and so all kinds of workplaces are trying to adapt accordingly. But you can't just throw a woman into a man's world and expect her to behave like a man. At the same time, attempts to "feminize" the workplace are also causing bitter conflicts. The two sexes need to learn a lot more about one another, and about transcendence, in order to successfully and satisfactorily accommodate each other at work.

For a long time, cultural evolution naturally mirrored human biology in the customs, rituals, and language of hunting and warfare.

But as technology evolved, and these endeavors became more symbolic, biological differences between males and females became less significant. When hunting was primarily about physical strength, stamina, and aggression, involving handheld weapons, then it was mostly a man's job. But now that it's primarily about expertise, communication, and organization, involving computers and allied technologies, women and men are equally adept. Cultural evolution is a great equalizer of the sexes.

Yet still the war of the sexes rages in the workplace itself, when males and females are brought together for the purpose of cooperating in the hunt and in defense of the tribe. Where biology would have separated the sexes, culture has commingled them, and their coexistence is not always peaceful. It's partly because men will be attracted to women, and start competing over them, as nature has hardwired them to do. For their part, women will compete among themselves to attract the most desirable man, as nature has hardwired them to do. Both paths are detours from the work at hand, disrupting the "hunt" (or the defense) as teammates behave instead like rivals.

Many organizations have instituted speech codes, sexual harassment policies, and other measures aimed at smoothing the integration of women into the hunt. But these strategies often exacerbate conflict rather than mitigate it. Now that men and women hunt together, they confront a dilemma. Their natures will always engender eros, and yet the workplace needs to run on philos. Sexual segregation is unworkable, but sexual war in the workplace is unacceptable. Transcendence is preferable.

EQUALITY ISN'T SAMENESS

Assuming that equality means sameness compounds the problems when men and women clash. Even given equal opportunity, some occupations are still going to be more the province of one sex than the other. For example, firefighters need certain physical attributes – such as the strength to carry a heavy adult down a ladder – which most women do not possess, even with training. Firefighting in forests also requires tremendous strength and stamina, for felling trees and building firebreaks. Thus we do not expect to see equal numbers of female and male firefighters – nor would a discrepancy in numbers necessarily indicate systemic discrimination against women. People have been very careless in using "gender imbalance" as an excuse to establish hiring quotas. Equal opportunity does not mean equal outcomes: In fact, truly equal opportunity guarantees unequal outcomes, for it allows natural differences to emerge.

In the professions, more women gravitate toward social and health sciences than to natural sciences. There's no "male conspiracy" to exclude women from physics or engineering (and some women are great physicists and engineers); but, as we've seen, there's a natural tendency for females to be more interested in human relationships than mathematical relations. It would be wrong to exclude women from any field. But it would also be wrong to expect equal interest in every field, and to socially engineer outcomes to reflect mistaken expectations. Such social engineering is itself a major cause of dis-ease.

Women who find the workplace a constant struggle may also be experiencing the time-tested truth that whenever you seek to accomplish something in life, some people will oppose you, often just for the sake of opposition. Moreover, if you set out to do something truly great, or even simply competent, you will bring out the worst in mediocre opposition. Women who encounter opposition in the workplace are not necessarily discovering an "old boys" conspiracy against women, but rather a conspiracy of mediocrity against greatness. Not every battle involving the sexes is between the sexes.

> **Great spirits have always found violent opposition from mediocre minds. The latter cannot understand it when a man does not thoughtlessly submit to hereditary prejudices but honestly and courageously uses his intelligence.**
>
> **– Albert Einstein**

Any woman who does not "thoughtlessly submit to hereditary prejudices" will encounter opposition too: not because she is a woman, but because she wants to accomplish something. Yet opposition can be good, because it teaches us to transcend.

The sexes are not the same, and do not want to be the same, and cannot be coerced into being the same. While equality of opportunity is necessary for human beings to flourish, irrespective of sex and gender, it cannot be used to suppose that they will always do the same things in identical ways, irrespective of sex and gender. To claim that equality is sameness is to create unnecessary conflict. Surely we have enough conflict as it is between the sexes! Why engender more?

PHILOSOPHICAL EXERCISES

What is it like to be the Other? If each one knew this, there might be more ease, and less dis-ease, between the sexes. It is possible to experience life in a wheelchair by confining yourself to one and learning what it's like. It is also possible to experience life as a blind person by bandaging your eyes, and then trying to get through the day without your eyesight. But how can a man experience life as a woman, and a woman experience life as a man? This can be done too, but not simply by cross-dressing! There are many ways for each to experience the Other. I will tell you three.

1. Discover the Other within. This we all do, sooner or later. Many men become less aggressive and more nurturing, and value relationships more, in their later years. They make passionate gardeners and doting grandfathers. Their yang gracefully yields to yin, yet they remain men. Many women become more amenable to abstract principle in their later years. They make strong leaders and wise counselors. Their yin gracefully yields to yang, yet they remain women. The sooner you discover the Other within, the sooner you will complete yourself. Nature will do this work for you in time. Nurture offers you ways to do it for yourself, mostly through wisdom traditions of the East.
2. Live like the Other without. There is increasing opportunity to do this. By playing roles well enough, we learn about the essence of the part. But it takes courage and greatness of spirit to accomplish this. (We'll treat spirit in chapter 10.) John Lennon had such greatness. When Yoko Ono gave birth to their son, John decided to become a "house husband," and so assumed the role of a male housewife. He discovered the Other within. The Williams sisters have such greatness. They have transformed the women's game of tennis, which used to be delicate and frilly, with powder-puff serves, into a robust game more similar to the style of men. They play with power on top of grace. They discovered the Other within. But you don't have to be a world-class pop star, athlete, or

celebrity to accomplish this. Find something you like to do that traditionally is done, or done better, by the Other. Then aspire to do it well yourself. You will soon discover the Other within.

3. Transcend both. To reiterate this chapter's theme: Sex is biological; gender, cultural; consciousness, transcendent. As you ascend a mountain and approach its summit, you can see more and more of the surrounding landscape in all directions. Similarly, as you ascend the mountain of consciousness, you can see more and more of the surrounding human landscapes – both biological and cultural – in all directions. To gain this perspective on them is to transcend them. To transcend them means to perceive the One as clearly as the Other, and thus to rise above their conflicts.

9

WHO'S IN CHARGE HERE: WE, OR THE MACHINES?

Men have become the tools of their tools.
–Henry David Thoreau

"What's one and one and one and one and one and one and one and one and one and one?"
"I don't know," said Alice. "I lost count."
"She can't do Addition," the Red Queen interrupted.

– Lewis Carroll

A T ONE OF MY monthly Philosophy Forums in a Manhattan bookstore, somebody proposed that being overwired to technology has caused people to lose touch with their humanity. Right on cue, one overwired guy got so upset by the suggestion that he stormed out in a huff. It was as though somebody had insulted his religion. If you worship an idol, you don't want to hear that it's interfering with your humanity, especially if it happens to be true. In this case, the idol is a silicon chip, and the god is cybernetic. In fact, machines increasingly dominate our lives, and they really can make us lose touch with our humanity. And that in turn causes serious dis-ease, far more than most people realize. Of course machines can also facilitate human encounters, as we'll see at the very end of this chapter. But let's assess the bad news before we get to the good.

There are two big philosophical issues at stake here. First, are we human beings just glorified machines? If so, then we shouldn't mind having our lives run by other machines. But we do mind, so maybe we're not machines ourselves. Second, like it or not, humans have become cogs in all kinds of machinery. Mostly, we are mere nodes – or error-prone annoyances – in increasingly complex networks of computers and other information technologies. Either way, being treated like a machine or like a cog in a machine causes considerable dis-ease.

In the developed world, we check our e-mail, send faxes, and close deals by cell phone while caught in colossal traffic jams, on our way to a computer workstation where we'll check more e-mail, send more faxes, and close more deals by speakerphone while caught in colossal data jams. Many people have become mere accessories to technocracy – that is, government by technology – and wonder where their humanity went. So they naturally turn to philosophy for help. That's one thing your computer can't do: philosophize with you.

Don't get me wrong. Technology has brought us many wondrous things, eased many of life's burdens, and opened paths to future developments beyond imagination. Technological progress has occurred steadily throughout human history, with the pace in recent years accelerating exponentially. Once we could look upon such benchmarks as the harnessing of fire, the smelting of iron, or the invention of the printing press as unqualified boons to humanity, but of late the great leaps forward come so quickly and furiously that we strain all our resources in vain attempts to just keep up. Once, perhaps, the machines served us. Now, all too often, it seems we serve the machines.

The highways and byways surrounding most major U.S. and other cities are clogged with cars, trucks, vans, and SUVs. People talk on their cell phones while they crawl through traffic, trying to squeeze in a little extra business. Planes, trains, buses, and subways are likewise crammed with people, many of whom are either wired to CD players, riveted to Palm Pilots, or glued to ever-present cell phones. Sometimes we use machines as a line of defense against the jostling hordes, the crush of humanity, unwanted physical contact. Yet the presence of so many machines in our lives interferes with human contact even when that is not our conscious goal. Down this road lie people who behave like accessories to their equipment, not like pensive beings or social animals at all.

More and more people in the developed world are suffering from machine-induced dis-eases like road rage, as well as machine-induced diseases like carpal tunnel syndrome. Burnout is rampant, as people find it increasingly difficult to juggle multiple identities, responsibilities, and interests. Chronic fatigue syndrome abounds. All kinds of anxieties and undiagnosed ailments emerge, and no one really knows what causes them. It seems to me that many of these general malaises and specific problems are a result of the mechanization of humanity and the dehumanization it entails.

Are computers saving us time? Not when they become infected with viruses. Making our jobs easier? Not when they bombard us with ever steeper learning curves required to master incessant software upgrades. Improving our lives? Not when they facilitate identity theft. Eliminating hard labor? Yes, but replacing it with "soft labor" at a workstation which can be ruinous to good posture and other foundations of well-being. We are becoming human cogs in ever more complex machinery, and that can do strange things to our humanity.

Father Gadget's Case: Praise the Lord and Pass the AC Adaptor

On a recent cross-country flight, I sat across the aisle from a priest who, as soon as we reached cruising altitude, removed from his briefcase a laptop computer, a microcassette recorder, and a Palm Pilot. He wired himself up to these various devices, powered them up, and began to move data around from one to the next.

As the plane prepared for arrival, Father Gadget began to power off and pack up all his high-tech gear. He suddenly became distraught because he could not locate an accessory that belonged with one of his devices. He rummaged in his pockets, in his briefcase, and then around and under his seat, but to no avail. He then rummaged around in the overhead luggage compartment above the row of seats I sat in, where he had originally stowed his gear – also to no avail. Convinced that his gizmo was somewhere in the vicinity, he asked if perhaps it had fallen around or under the seat of Mr. Jones, the obviously frail gentleman with a cane sitting next to me.

Wanting to help the priest, Mr. Jones struggled out of his seat with the assistance of Mrs. Jones and a flight attendant – clearly in a lot of pain and discomfort. In conversing with this amiable couple earlier in the flight, I had learned that Mr. Jones was en route to a cancer treatment center. His metastasized tumors made it painful for him even to sit on the airplane. After many medical tests, fatal prognoses, desperate applications to and rejections by clinical trials of new drugs, he had finally been accepted by a study on the East Coast. Mrs. Jones explained that this was their last hope for a cure.

Father Gadget seemed entirely oblivious to Mr. Jones's infirmity and suffering, so intent was he on locating his electronic doodad. When the priest failed to find it, Mr. Jones resumed his seat, again with help, and again in pain and discomfort. When the aircraft stopped at the gate, Father Gadget was one of the first to deplane. Lugging his high-tech load (now short one gizmo) and conversing on his cell phone, he hustled up the jetway without another word to Mr. and Mrs. Jones.

Information technology was operating Father Gadget, and not the other way around. Machines were getting in the way of his humanity; specifically, of his awareness of human suffering unfolding right before him. Gadgetry was also blinding him to ways in which he had caused Mr. Jones additional suffering for the sake of a gizmo. He certainly never troubled to find out why Mr. Jones was in such obvious discomfort from the outset. It seemed strange behavior for a priest. If machines can do this to a man of the cloth, imagine what they can do to those of us who haven't taken vows, or even prayed much lately.

HUMANITY LOST

By networking us with the global village, instantaneously and wherever we are, machines rob us of awareness of the immediate present. Where are you now – on your way to, or from, a computer? In whose company are you when you read e-mail from or send it to a discussion list? Who are these list members to you? Who are you to them? To the extent that machines obscure these very questions, they diminish our humanity.

Consider how the evolution of machines has drastically shrunk the time required to traverse great distances, both in person and by data transfer – and our attitude toward that length of time. It takes weeks to sail from, say, New York to London. It takes days to steam there, hours to fly, minutes to fax, and seconds to e-mail. But a delayed flight causes some people acute dis-ease, as does a busy fax line or a nondeliverable e-mail. Using these technologies creates the expectation that they will work on time, every time. When they don't, people get upset.

Imagine what it used to be like, say in the nineteenth century, to engage in a correspondence between New York and London. First, you'd sit at an exquisite handcrafted writing desk, with beautiful handmade paper and matching envelopes, your favorite hues of ink, your crystal or cut-glass inkwell, your treasured collection of nib pens, and perhaps your personal seal and sealing wax. You'd collect yourself, write a thoughtful letter in a practiced hand, sign it, and seal it. Your letter would sail to London on a ship, and when it arrived it would be the subject of much excitement and speculation, even before it was opened. Then it would be carefully opened with a letter opener, minutely read and reread, and perhaps mulled over for several days before a reply was similarly fashioned. Months might elapse between the time you sent your letter and a reply finally arrived. Yet no one would be fretting or fuming in the interim. There was plenty of time to breathe (and good air to breathe), and many other tasks to accomplish, at a similar methodical pace. Correspondence of this kind was an art, at its best a fine art, and was enabled by the works of a great many artisans. The average correspondents not only had better reading and writing skills than most university graduates of today, but also manifested important virtues like patience.

By contrast, today you dash off an e-mail to London, making sure you do so early enough in the New York morning to account for the time difference, or else it might not be read until the next day. (Who can wait that long?) The message itself is full of typos, and may get reformatted by the receiver's interface, and you bundle little emoticons such as ☺ to convey moods of humor or happiness, or ☹ to convey disapproval or sadness. (Are these pictures worth a thousand words?)

Your e-mail is dispatched to London with a keystroke, and while you're attending to several other e-mails, you're fretting because you haven't heard back from London yet. After all, you sent your message almost an hour ago. (How many years is that for a computer?) If the reply takes a day, it will probably start with an apology: "Sorry it took me *so long* to respond to your e-mail, but I was . . ." You know exactly what he or she was doing: responding to other e-mail.

That is where you've crossed the border, from Humanity into Machineity. Instead of running the machines, the machines are running you. You are no longer in charge of your time. You're fuming because your flight is delayed. And now you have to send a fax. But the fax line is busy, so you try e-mail. But the server is down, so your e-mail is returned. Now what? Reach for your cell phone! And if necessary, disturb the dying man next to you in the process. Don't offer a prayer for his soul; roll him over in case he's lying on your AC adapter. Once we put the machinery in charge, our humanity is imperiled.

Cindy's Case: Technocracy Overdose

Cindy worked for an investment brokerage on Wall Street, and made pretty good money. She and her husband, Frank, wanted to live in a peaceful and quiet neighborhood, so they chose a small town in Connecticut. Cindy rode the train and subway every day, a two-hour commute each way. This has become "normal" for millions of commuters, not only around New York City, but in many metropolises of the global village. At the office, Cindy crunched numbers and networked all day long. She was good at it, but found it increasingly meaningless. On weekends, she was usually too exhausted to pursue her physical hobbies, such as hiking, cycling, and landscape gardening. So she spent her leisure hours watching rented movies with Frank, or even catching up on unfinished work that she had brought home (actually, had e-mailed herself) from the office. This wasn't good for her marriage either, because Frank, a lawyer in a small local practice, loved the great outdoors and wanted to share them with her. They weren't ready for kids yet, but were ready for each other. Only Cindy was usually too burned out.

Cindy felt just like a cog in a machine, and it really bothered her. Even though her paycheck was bigger than Frank's, and contributed to their luxurious upper-middle-class surroundings, they had no time to enjoy them. As well, Cindy had always wanted to "make a difference" in her career, but her experience of number crunching gave her anything but a sense of individuality – just the opposite. Sitting at her computer all day, she often felt as though she could be replaced by one. If she left her job tomorrow, no one would really know or care. They'd just find another number cruncher to sit at her desk.

Cindy needed to make sense of her life, and wanted feel ease instead of dis-ease. And there was some urgency too: Her lifestyle was physically unhealthy. Cindy had gained weight from eating too much junk food at the office, as well as on the couch. She wasn't getting enough exercise for a young woman of her age, which in turn would age her faster. And her posture at the computer was horrendous: She was developing back pain, as well as tension headaches from eye strain.

As I'm sure you've realized by now, philosophical counselors do not simply prescribe wise sayings that instantly cure clients' dis-eases, as taking aspirins might cure a headache. "Take two aphorisms and call me in the morning" is not what we're all about. More often than not, philosophers in the Socratic tradition are "midwives" for their clients' inner wisdom. Cindy already knew implicitly what she had to do; she came to me for help in making her own ideas explicit. Through dialogue, Cindy gradually articulated a solution to her problem. She resolved to disconnect herself from the machinery, which seemed more like "death support" than "life support" in her case. Guided and encouraged to reveal her inner human interests, Cindy decided to open a landscaping and gardening business in her hometown. She could stop commuting, work outdoors, plant shrubs instead of crunch numbers, and use her skills to beautify the world and make a difference. Frank soon left his law practice and joined her in this enterprise. It proved fulfilling for them as human beings and good for their marriage too. To be fulfilled is to love, not loathe, what you are doing.

The reason why the world lacks unity, and lies broken and in heaps, is, because man is disunited with himself.

– Ralph Waldo Emerson

TIME IS EVERYTHING, AT LEAST FOR A WHILE

What is time? Nobody knows precisely. But we do know some things about time. We know, for example, that it seems to accelerate as we age. We also know that things in this world, and the universe that contains it, exist in and somehow define space-time – whose precise geometry and dimensionality are not yet settled issues. Some people believe, as I do, that certain things – perhaps ideas, consciousness, and souls – can somehow exist outside our space-time, but that we, as embodied beings, are partly trapped within it. Life itself, whether created or accidental, is an altogether improbable phenomenon. But here it is anyway, and as long as we are alive we experience much of it via the medium of space-time.

But our experiences of space, and of time, are quite distinct. In chapter 7 we saw how space (or lack of space) affects the social behaviors of animals, including humans. Yet human beings usually find ways to become exceptions to any rules we can postulate about them. In general, people who become overcrowded feel a great deal of stress, while those who have plenty of elbow room are much happier and friendlier. Then again, Alexander the Great and Marin Mersenne both provide glaring exceptions to this "rule." After conquering the known world, from the Mediterranean to the Himalayas, Alexander is said to have wept because he had no other worlds to conquer. He ran out of personal elbow room! By contrast, it is possible to experience liberation in the cramped confines of a cell, as did the philosopher-monk Mersenne. He belonged to the Minim order, devoted to prayer, study, and scholarship. That doesn't take up too much space. Yet so important were Mersenne's studies in mathematics, physics, and philosophy that the greatest French intellects of the day – including Fermat, Pascal, Gassendi, Roberval, and Beaugrand – met regularly in his cell to further the Enlightenment project. They later became the core of the French Academy (and possibly inspired that Marx Brothers scene in the overcrowded stateroom in *A Night at the Opera*). Thus our conception of just "how much space" is adequate for humans is quite elastic. If you "run out" of space, you can always try to acquire more (unless you conquer the world). If you need to occupy less space, you can usually manage to do so, and maybe even thrive.

Time is a completely different matter. Once you run out of time, that's that. You can try to prolong the time you have, but there also seem to be a great many ways of shortening it, whether intentionally, inadvertently, or accidentally. You can use time to make more money, but money will not as reliably buy you more time. Your time or my time might be for hire, but time itself is not. Hence time is our most precious asset – and how we decide to use our time is the most important decision we can make.

In any weather, at any hour of the day or night, I have been anxious to improve the nick of time, and notch it on my stick too; to stand on the meeting of two eternities, the past and the future, which is precisely the present moment.

– Henry David Thoreau

REAL AND VIRTUAL YOU

Machines are supposed to save us time. And they did, for a long time. Steam engines, piston engines, jet engines, and rocket engines saved us increasingly more time. But the logical engines that drive your computer and networks of computers have paradoxically both saved you time and *cost* you time.

This happens mostly because computers give you a virtual identity to complement your real one. I don't have to tell you that being your flesh-and-blood self already takes up plenty of time, without having to deal with a new appendage. The real you is born, grows up, and experiences all the joys and discomforts of living. There are uncountable lessons to learn and to teach, endless affairs to manage, and even more business that remains unfinished. You may have a career, a family, a hobby, dreams, goals, aspirations, friends, and foes – not to mention in-laws, lawyers, doctors, and accountants – and all your interactions with them take up time. Outside of fulfilling the numerous roles you play, and taking care of all your obligations, what time is left for you to discover who you really are? "Real" life can be so unreal at times that we feel as though we are not really living it. So who's the "real" you? Is it the one who goes through life wishing you had more time to discover the "real" you"? Is it the one who makes time for that journey of discovery? Is it the one you discover along the way? Is it the one who awaits you at the end? One thing is for sure: The demands of real life can become so pressing and time-consuming that many people can't even find the time to ask these questions, let alone to try to answer them.

Our "real" lives are vastly more complicated than those of our parents, whose lives were vastly more complicated than those of their parents, and so forth. Most of these complications are driven by increasingly complex machines and technologies. In theory, there is no end in sight to this ever-evolving complexity. The further we delve into complexity, the more complex it becomes. So it is with reality. Life is organization that emerges from disorganization, and its patterns are infinitely deep as well. The longer you live, the deeper your life becomes. The deeper your life becomes, the harder it may seem to touch bottom.

Rapidly evolving machines have played a trick on us. Many of the time-saving gains they offer are illusory. Physical engines move us faster and faster from place to place, saving us time on old journeys but making so many new journeys possible that there's no time to take them all. In that sense, physical engines can make us lose more time than they help us gain. On top of that, while physical engines are busy moving the real you around – or making the real you wait because they're behind schedule – logical engines (computers and their networks) have been busy creating a "virtual" you. As if the real you weren't busy enough, now your virtual self receives and responds to e-mail, maintains Web pages, and surfs the waves of cyberspace to search, to research, to shop, to date – all of which takes up increasing amounts of your time. But looking after your virtual self takes *real* time, and your real time is already scarce enough.

Even as you sit in front of your computer, doing things you know how to do, a huge industry is busy inventing new learning curves for you to ascend. The ongoing and rapid evolution of information technology means that the hardware and software you are currently using are already obsolete. Faster computers and bigger software suites are already available, or in production, or on the drawing board, and short of buying new ones there will still be increasing pressure on you and your computer to manage the latest updates and downloads, bells and whistles. Whatever you are using could stand to be replaced within a year or two or three, even if it's just for your modest home purposes. If you're telecommuting or involved with e-commerce of any kind, you'll need expert technical help on an ongoing basis just to keep your virtual head above virtual water, and remain competitive with everybody else.

The two big questions all this raises are: Why are machines running our lives? And how can we make them serve us, instead of us serving them? The first question pertains to what has happened already, and while the past can't be changed, it needs to be understood. The second question pertains to what you can do about the present state of affairs, which will lead to future states. The future is open, but will be shaped by the present.

CAN COMPUTERS SET US FREE?

You may wish for a simpler life, but the fact remains that billions of people cannot live reasonably (or even unreasonably) together on this planet without electricity, potable water, production of goods and services, sustainable markets for them, higher education of many kinds, communication and transportation infrastructures, and other fruits of globalized civilization – including fair measures of secular human rights and religious freedoms. And as much as all these things enhance our lives, and even though many millions of people in the developed world take them for granted, still they are not easily accepted by all cultures.

Many indigenous peoples around the globe have found it difficult or impossible to adjust to our technocratic ways and bridge the "digital divide." When people derive their livings and beings from nature, or very close to nature, they are animated by an experience of nature that is all-encompassing. They become holists. They see the connectedness of all things. They live at a pace that is nature's own. But when their naturalistic and organic ways of life encounter our scientific and mechanistic ones, they can neither withstand nor resist our cultural onslaught. This has been true from Arctic Canada to the South Pacific, from the Inuit to the Polynesians. A chief of the Digger Indians summed up the loss of his culture in this poetic way: "Our cup is broken." On a brighter note, it has proved possible for many such cultures to recover their ways under the umbrella of ours, and to mend their broken cups with our superglues. That seems a workable compromise for all concerned.

In any case, it's still hard for many to relate to the accelerated, manmade pace of life, which includes the commute, the rat race to the computer, the mouse race at the computer, the eight-minute workout, and the instant message. These are among the seemingly efficient but increasingly discomforting facets of our technocracy that microman-age more and more of our time. ATMs, automated telephone systems, and all kinds of other interfaces make you wait as they offer you all the options you don't want, while so often reserving the option you do want for last. Once a machine presents you with a list of options, it has predetermined all possible modes of interaction with you and all possible futures involving you. You become part of a predetermined process, and your role is merely to provide sufficient input to satisfy the process. Your humanity is irrelevant. You have become an ex-tension of the machine.

But the machines that were designed to automate the functions of human beings can never replace us, since one of our most important functions is *being human*. When you encounter actual human beings, even in a bureaucratic context, there is always the opportunity to transcend the mechanisms in place. Even if the process itself is predetermined, a human-to-human encounter leaves modes of inter- action open and enables possible futures outside the process itself. Humans function best in the realm of possibility.

Technocracy, like fatalist religious culture, robs its human consti- tuents of the sense of possibility, even in cultures that are otherwise non-fatalistic. One's daily life is mechanized to the point that it is reduced to a set of predetermined "encounters" with machines. Mechanisms always impose limitations. Human beings are by nature organisms, not mechanisms. To be fulfilled as human beings, we need to celebrate our organic qualities.

Do you recall that when computers began to infiltrate office systems, people actually feared being replaced by them? As it turns out, of course, computers mostly replaced typewriters with much more interesting machines – and ended up creating endless work. What people should have been more anxious about was not being replaced by but becoming accessories to the networks of new ma- chines. The computer is the most important invention since the printing press, and no one can avoid networking and being net- worked. The big question is, Will computers and technocracy make us freer, or will they enslave us?

The following "Zen error messages," haikus written for and about our computing generation, humorously illustrate some frustrations that computers have induced in us:

> **A file that big?**
> **It might be very useful.**
> **But now it is gone.**

> **The Web site you seek**
> **cannot be located but**
> **countless more exist.**

> **Yesterday it worked**
> **Today it is not working**
> **Windows is like that.**

Lal's Case: Burnout

Lal was an American who had emigrated from India as a young man. Now turning fifty, he had maintained traditional Hindu precepts – including beliefs in reincarnation and in leading life as a dutiful service – and yet had grafted onto them distinctively American dreams, including desires for material security and leisure to pursue his own interests. This may sound like a problem of so-called "double consciousness," which occurs when dual identities do not mesh and moreover come into conflict, but Lal was adept at juggling his Indian and American identities. However, his situations at home and at work had changed in ways that posed new difficulties for him.

First, he was happily married to an American woman, Lucy, who used to help provide for their home and also provided some financial support for her mature children (from a prior marriage). But Lucy had become ill, and could no longer earn an income, so these burdens now fell upon Lal. And he had shouldered them willingly enough, even though Lucy began to resent his capacity to do so, owing to her sudden incapacity.

His situation at work, at a large Manhattan bank, was such that he had reached his top rung on the corporate ladder. There were no more promotions in store. Moreover, he suspected that he was going to be pushed into early retirement in a few short years. So just when he needed to earn more, his income had leveled off. But that wasn't all. Like so many middle-class careerists who work in Manhattan but reside well beyond it in order to afford more living space, Lal faced a two-hour commute in each direction, five days per week. He returned home increasingly exhausted, uninspired, spread too thin, and unable to pursue his other interests (reading and yoga).

Lal's dis-ease was not about the circumstances of his life, but its meaning. He felt tired and unhappy all the time. "Is all I'm doing working and paying bills?" he asked aloud. In a word, or rather in two words, Lal was burned out. Lightbulbs burn out when, after many repeated cycles of heating up and cooling down, their filaments become brittle and snap. Human beings burn out when, after many repeated cycles of working and paying bills, their capacities for finding meaning in life become brittle and snap. When a bulb burns out, it is finished. But when a human being burns out, he or she can be revitalized.

The Indian part of Lal could easily accept working as doing service, without being particularly attached to his paycheck, just as the Bhagavad Gita prescribes.

But thou hast only the right to work; but none to the fruit thereof . . . In this world people are fettered by action, unless it is performed as a sacrifice . . . Having abandoned the fruit of action, he wins eternal peace.

– Bhagavad Gita

But the American part of Lal was too dispirited to work at all, even as a sacrifice. He felt like an overworked and underappreciated machine. His humanity appeared nowhere in the equation; hence life had correspondingly little meaning for him. So Lal contemplated doing something he'd never seriously entertained: retiring to India, where his extended family would receive him as a long-lost relative, a human being, and not as a walking ATM. At the same time, Lal knew that India was changing too, because of globalization, and that the culture he had left behind decades ago was becoming increasingly materialistic.

Meanwhile, he had to recover some short-term energy, just to charge his batteries: enough to continue working toward an early retirement, whether in America or India. Lal discovered a transformative idea in Aristotle: the notion that happiness is the highest virtue, which comes from the habitual exercise of excellence. Was there some personal potential that Lal was neglecting to exercise? There was: Lal had always wanted to do creative writing, but had never found the time. Now the time found him. So he joined a Saturday writers' workshop, led by an experienced and inspiring poet. Nothing like writing poetry to restore your humanity! Creative writing returned meaning to Lal's life, enough to change the burned-out machine into a motivated human being.

I could cite numerous other cases of burnout here, but they all share a common theme: Men and women all too frequently acquire the technocratic habits of behaving like the machines they serve, which robs them of their humanity and of meaning in their lives. We can restore our humanity only by doing uniquely human things. Philosophy is one of them! It is also a guide to others.

> **We are what we repeatedly do. Excellence, then, is not an act, but a habit . . . By human virtue or excellence we mean not that of the body, but that of the mind, and by happiness we mean an activity of the mind.**
>
> **– Aristotle**

WHOLESALE BURNOUT

I must also tell you that these cases of individual burnout are starting to add up in organizations, where they translate into big costs in terms of lost productivity and lack of continuity. Organizations are reporting unprecedented levels of employee absenteeism, sick leave, chronic fatigue syndrome, and other undiagnosed malaises. These are the diseases, and diseases alike, of overmechanized human beings. Philosophical practitioners have many approaches to this problem, from Socratic dialogues with groups and teams in the affected organizations, to philosophical counseling with the afflicted individuals. Overall, corporate cultures have been too short-sighted to utilize philosophy to anything like its full advantage. They would apparently rather take growing losses in productivity and health-care costs than make small investments in preventive measures – such as treating their employees as thoughtful, meaning-seeking human beings instead of cogs in the corporate machine. Too many executives think that allowing their employees an hour per week to participate in a Socratic dialogue or to have a one-on-one session with a CPO (Chief Philosophy Officer) would be a "waste of time." Instead, the same burned-out or unmotivated employees are squandering days per month in lost productivity!

What gets in the way of a solution here is partly a corporate hangover from the "Protestant work ethic" binge, which made science, technology, and technocracy possible in the first place. So we'd better take a brief look at that.

ENLIGHTENMENT REVISITED

Science and technology evolved most powerfully in the West, as a continuation of the quest for rational knowledge that flowered in ancient Greece. It was the sixteenth-century English philosopher Francis Bacon who first wrote that "knowledge is power." He reasoned that by better understanding nature, we could better understand ourselves as extensions of nature, thereby making our personal, social, and political lives that much more meaningful and purposive, and becoming better able to serve God's intended purpose for us (even if we had to reject some religious dogma along the way).

This, in a nutshell, was the philosophy of the early modern period that gave rise to the Enlightenment. The early modern philosophers, including Bacon, Hobbes, Boyle, and Harvey in England, Mersenne and his friends in France, and Galileo in Italy, made contemporary science and technology possible. Yet they also believed in God. They thought that science and technology would be used to liberate humanity for more important tasks – such as educational, artistic, and contemplative ones – and would also yield improved methods for governing people, societies, and polities. If we could learn the laws that govern physical, chemical, and biological processes, they reasoned, perhaps we could also learn the laws that govern psychological, social, and political ones. Then utopia would lie within reach. Or so they surmised.

The Industrial Revolution itself was conceived in a Christian feudal system. The mechanization of society meant, for the peasant classes, a shift from agricultural to industrial serfdom. Instead of being politically chained to parcels of land, on which they worked for their feudal lords, they became economically chained to mines and factories, in which they worked for their capitalist bosses. Yet the middle classes emerged from this system, and "bourgeois" life offered novel comforts to increasing multitudes. Trade unionism also gradually emerged, though not without a struggle, and allowed "labor" to win securities and benefits from "management."

This mechanization of society is ongoing. It currently unfolds in the developing world much as it once unfolded in the now-developed world. Yet it continues in the developed world too, with the replacement of people chained to machines producing goods with people networked to computers producing services. Though the technology has changed beyond imagination, very little has changed in the perception and reality of humans caught in the grip of machines. We may use computers instead of cotton gins, but the automating principle is the same. The human being stranded in this process gradually becomes an automation: an unthinking extension of the mechanism. The Band-Aid solution is "casual Friday," where employees can feel "free" for a day by dressing in the uniform of casual clothes, instead of the uniform of business attire.

THE PURITAN MANTRA: "KEEP BUSY, BUT DON'T ENJOY YOURSELF"

The real issue, of course, is not what you wear to the office. More to the point is the underlying philosophy of the place. Yet most people seem not to realize exactly what that philosophy is (even in a nutshell), nor how it came to exert such decisive influence on their working lives – and not always for the better. In essence, the Protestant Reformation got wedded to the Industrial Revolution and produced a secular offspring called the "Protestant work ethic." This is still the reigning corporate philosophy, and its Puritan mantra is probably running your office: "Keep busy, but don't enjoy yourself." Let me briefly explain how this came to pass. By understanding its origins you can circumvent the outcome, change the mantra, and make the machines serve you. So here are the relevant historical snippets.

The Roman Catholic Church adopted Saint Augustine's theology, written in the fifth century C.E., which holds that humans are born sinful. According to Augustine, our main task is to attain salvation, and avoid damnation, in the next world. By confessing sins and being absolved by a priest, who is God's representative, one's soul can be kept pure enough to be redeemed. One social consequence of this is that many Catholics enjoy life a great deal, and sin as often as they wish, because they can always confess and be absolved later.

The Protestant Reformation of Martin Luther and John Calvin, on the other hand, removed the priest as the intermediary between God and man. Protestantism generally allows each individual to interpret scripture pretty much as he or she pleases, and to pray personally to God for forgiveness and redemption. But in the absence of confession, it is much more difficult for a Protestant to expiate sin. Thus Protestants generally seek to avoid sin, because they cannot get immediate absolution.

Calvin went even further than Luther, and supposed we are all born saved or damned. (Yes, he was a Christian fatalist.) This is a tricky doctrine: How can you get people to behave themselves if they're already "prejudged" at birth? If you're born saved, why not have a good time? After all, you can't be damned. And if you're born damned, you may as well have a good time. After all, you can't be saved. So either way, it looks like Calvinists are bound to throw the wildest parties. But in fact the reverse is true; they are among the most austere of Christian ascetics. Why? Because of Calvin's catch. He argued that although we can't know for sure whether we're born saved or damned (and won't find out until we die), we can still get some pretty strong clues from our behavior. He concluded that people who "behave themselves" (i.e., practice austerities like self-denial) are more likely to be among the saved, while those who run hog wild (i.e., indulge themselves at every whim) are more likely to be among the damned. Although philosophers are strongly divided on the credibility of Calvin's argument (it's a kind of paradox called a "Newcomb problem"), a lot of people bought it – including Puritans, Quakers, and other sects of British and American Protestants.

Thus, in their more puritanical aspects, Protestants try to avoid all possible pleasures. Catholics don't, because they can always indulge now and confess later. In other words, Puritans can do pretty much as they please, within limits, as long as they don't enjoy themselves. If something feels good, it must be bad. But as long as it's not fun, it's probably not sinful. So the idea is to avoid sin by avoiding fun. This is the Puritan attitude toward sex, food, and other appetites: Pleasure is fun, therefore sinful. Non-pleasure isn't fun; therefore permissible. Is this convoluted logic? You bet. But it's good for self-discipline, hard work, long hours, low pay, and postponement of gratification. Austerities became virtues for the working classes during the Industrial Revolution and for the middle classes later. This also explains why the French developed savoir-faire and joie de vivre while the English kept stiff upper lips and took cold showers. This is reflected in the "New World" too: The formerly French places (such as New Orleans and Quebec) were always more fun-oriented, but also more corrupt than their formerly English counterparts (such as New England and Ontario).

Max Weber, a pioneer of sociology, first pointed out that this same logic directly informs the Protestant work ethic. The idea is that sleeping in, taking a day off, or doing absolutely nothing feels pretty good sometimes. Ergo, it must be pretty sinful. But as long as you keep busy and don't enjoy yourself, you'll avoid sin. And there you have the governing philosophy of the Western workplace in a nutshell. According to Weber, it made capitalism hugely successful, but at a price: Nobody loved their work.

> **. . . the essential elements of the attitude . . . called the spirit of capitalism are the same as what we have shown to be the content of the Puritan worldly asceticism, only without the religious basis.**
>
> **– Max Weber**

If you are overloaded but unfulfilled at work, your workplace is probably governed by the mantra "Keep busy, but don't enjoy yourself." Take a walk anywhere around midtown Manhattan (or any metropolis) during the working day, and you'll see thousands of people as busy as busy can be, but not enjoying themselves in the least.

In theory, they have more liberty and opportunity than any mainstream society has ever had; yet in practice, many of them are utterly miserable. Why? Because they feel like machines, not like people. Machines work unquestioningly until they break down or become obsolete. Machines also lack the capacity for enjoyment and fulfillment.

And their obsolescence is planned. Just as with actual machines, which are often purposely engineered to last less time than they could so new units can be marketed sooner, workers are frequently cast aside by a system that continues to lower the retirement age even as average life spans increase. Ageism is another sour fruit of the Protestant work ethic. People who hate their jobs look forward to early retirement, but that's because they bought into the Puritan game plan of keeping busy without enjoying themselves. For them, the mantra of retirement then becomes "Enjoy yourself (you've earned it), but become useless."

The most fulfilled people are those who always keep busy at work and leisure, who love both, and who celebrate life according to their own game plan. And cultures which typically revere elders are potentially more humane than cultures which treat their elders like so much outdated machinery. The quality of one's contribution to immediate family, and the human family at large, usually increases with age (at least for a while), so it is both foolish and inhumane to waste the potential of those who have attained wisdom through a lifetime of experience.

ALL'S RIGHT WITH THE WORLD

Extremes of dehumanization through mechanization include the nineteenth-century factories of the English industrial north. There, small children were often forced to work twelve or more hours per day if they or their families hoped to eat, yet they received only starvation wages. This was the grim scenario that moved and inspired not only Marx and Dickens, but also Robert Browning. In his poetic portrait "Pippa Passes," Browning reasserted the triumph of the human spirit by presenting one little girl's indomitable love of life and irrepressible humanity. Pippa goes to the country on her annual day off (yes, her single day off for the year), to commune with and celebrate nature. She sings:

> The year's at the spring,
> And day's at the morn;
> Morning's at seven;
> The hillside's dew-pearl'd;
> The lark's on the wing;
> The snail's on the thorn;
> God's in His heaven –
> All's right with the world!

You can interpret this verse as extreme irony, but the optimist in me reads that anyone can find and appreciate nature's organic luster, even when immersed daily in mechanistic drabness. Pippa reaffirms the divine ease and joyous unfolding of the cosmos in the face of the manmade dis-ease and futility of mechanization. She is a ray of hope piercing what the great humanist and pacifist Lewis Mumford called the "mechanically engineered coma" that the Industrial Revolution induced in so many for so long. And now that the Industrial Revolution has given way to the computer revolution, we have replaced mechanically engineered coma in the factory with cybernetically engineered trance at the office. The more time you spend in cyberspace, the less real your life will seem.

A CYBERNETIC GOD

In 1956, about thirty years before the personal computer became so pervasive in our lives, Lewis Mumford wrote: "In creating the thinking machine, man has made the last step in submission to mechanization; and his final abdication before this product of his own ingenuity has given him a new object of worship: a cybernetic god."

Machines are extensions of our limbs, organs, and senses. Bicycles and cars extend our legs; power tools extend our arms; telescopes and microscopes extend our eyes; telephones and fax machines extend our voices. These machines are all passive, awaiting our command and control. We certainly don't suppose that they have brains or minds.

Full-blown computers are another matter. Although they are only logical engines equipped with various devices for receiving, reading, writing, storing, displaying, rearranging and processing data, many people hope that they will eventually become more "intelligent" than humans, and answer all our unanswerable questions for us. Some envision a future world in which computers will settle for us, once and for all, Big Questions about the meaning of life and the existence of God, and will explain death, consciousness, and the purpose of the universe. Philosophers, logicians, and computer scientists are divided over whether such a world will ever come to be. No one knows whether a computer can think, and the arguments rage on both sides.

Proponents of "thinking machines" cheered when the computer program called Deep Blue defeated world chess champion Gary Kasparov, but that feat should not have been surprising. In terms of game theory, chess is exactly like tic-tac-toe, only with vastly more possible complications. If you find your best move in either of these games, you cannot lose. If both you and your opponent find your best moves, the game will end in a draw. It's easy to find your best move in tic-tac-toe, which is why even small children get bored with it pretty quickly. Chess is much more intricate, yet the top masters know how to find their best moves much of the time. That's why they draw so many games. But to a logical engine, tic-tac-toe and chess are just the same – at least in theory: Compute your best move and you cannot lose. Gary Kasparov was visibly upset after he lost to Deep Blue. Somehow he had hoped that human ingenuity, or creativity, or inspiration would defeat computational power. He was mistaken. In games like chess, advanced logical engines are superior to expert human brains.

Or are they? After all, Deep Blue is an extension of a team of expert human brains. Humans programmed it to find more best moves than the best human player. So weren't those computer scientists who conceived, developed, and perfected the program really playing chess themselves, using the computer as an extension of their brains? And if so, then aren't we chasing our tails by supposing that the machine is in some way superior to us? Racing cars are designed to move much faster than humans can run, but driving a racing car to victory is a task that only a human can accomplish. Cranes are designed to lift objects heavier and higher than humans can lift them, but operating a crane on a construction site is a task that only a human can accomplish. And computers are designed to accept input, manipulate data, and display output in much faster and more complex ways than humans alone can manage, but programming a computer to do so is a task that only a human can accomplish.

The deeper question that concerns both philosophers and computer scientists is whether composing symphonies, writing poems, and improvising dialogues are simply other kinds of "games" that computers will one day play better than humans do. Computer programs will surely simulate human creativity and spontaneity. But is a simulation equivalent to the real thing? Or are the creative powers of the human mind forever greater than any computer simulation?

FORMALISM VERSUS HOLISM

Formalists adhere to an essentially outdated Newtonian view, that the universe itself is one gigantic machine. They believe that any process can be mechanized. To them, human brains are merely biological computers running biological programs, and sooner or later we will program logical computers to compose better symphonies, write better poems, and improvise better dialogues than we do ourselves.

In contrast, holists look at the universe as a gigantic organism. They believe that some processes cannot be mechanized. Holists see computers as extensions of minds, not as copies of brains. To a holist, even if we could simulate creativity and intuition and such with computers, computers would still be simply extensions of our brains and – more significantly – our minds. Holists believe that the creative powers of the human mind are not fully explained by brain "hardware" and linguistic "software" – there must be something else in there that allows Bach to find some of the best notes, Milton to find some of the best words, Rembrandt to find some of the best hues, Socrates to find some of the best ideas – and you and I to appreciate these and other works of immortal art.

According to the holistic view of the world, machines are merely the sum of their parts, and the parts are preconceived by the designers. Organisms have properties not explicable by their mere parts, properties which emerge unpredictably from the parts' interactions. Great works of art register more deeply in human consciousness and emotion than paintings by number, because they possess qualities not reducible to numbers. Quantity is mechanistic; quality, organic.

In terms of complexity theory, the single-celled amoeba is vastly more complicated than any machine yet designed, from the Vax supercomputer to the space shuttle. And you, like every other human being, are vastly more complicated than an amoeba. So to begin to reach your full potential as human being, you need to appreciate the difference between mechanism and organism, and to conceive of a society in which people are cells of a larger organism, instead of cogs in a machine or nodes in a cyber-network.

Teams of people are more than machines. The players are more than parts; they are individuals whose particular qualities redefine the form and function of the whole. The team's positions may be predetermined, but its players are not. No team is assembled from parts, like a machine. To feel like a player, you need to work in an organization with an organic philosophy, as opposed to a mechanistic one. Here's an organic philosophy of management from possibly the greatest football coach of all time, Vince Lombardi:

> **Individual commitment to a group effort – that is what makes a team work, a company work, a society work, a civilization work.**
> **– Vince Lombardi**

Lombardi's players never felt like cogs. The legendary inspiration he provided, and the commitment he demanded, gave them meaning and purpose enough to last a lifetime. His teams worked harder, played harder, enjoyed themselves more, and also won more often than the rest.

Raphael's Case: Eloping Through Cyberspace

Raphael's story reminds us that machines are neither good nor bad in and of themselves – it all depends on how they're used. Computers can rehumanize as well as dehumanize us, as Raphael's experience shows. He was a retired teacher, slightly hard of hearing and also short of breath due to asthma. Having been educated in the "old-school" style, Raphael was very well read and loved the art of correspondence. He didn't have much use for computers; that is, until his second wife lost her battle with cancer and died. They had only been married for six years, but they had shared a deep rapport. Raphael not only missed her but despaired that he would never be able to find someone else. Being hard of hearing and asthmatic, and well read to boot, Raphael was not a good candidate for the smoky, noisy, and often lowbrow bar scene. Then again, although public libraries were quiet, smoke-free, and full of good books, they were hardly ideal venues for meeting women.

Raphael had often been guided by the Book of Ecclesiastes, but suddenly found some of its advice ironic: "Enjoy life with the wife whom thou lovest . . . for that is thy portion in life." It seemed to Raphael that his portion had been too small, and he wondered what he could do about it. One of his grown children (from his first marriage, which had ended in divorce) suggested that he get a computer and meet women by networking, but Raphael had initially scoffed at the idea.

So he returned to Ecclesiastes. But suddenly this passage spoke to him in a brand-new way: "Cast your bread upon the waters, for thou shalt find it after many days . . . In the morning sow thy seed, and in the evening withhold not thy hand." It dawned on Raphael that this could also be interpreted as a suggestion to start networking. So he bought a computer and learned how to use it. He began networking through dating clubs, and developed e-mail correspondences with women from around the country. His hearing impairment and his asthma were no barrier to e-mail, and his love of fine literature and letter-writing skills won him many female pen pals and a lot of virtual romance.

One woman in particular, named Evelyn, appealed to him enough for the real thing. She was also a retired teacher, widowed, and shared Raphael's taste in books. They had exchanged photographs and even sound bytes. They finally made a date. Since they lived in different states not that far apart, they each drove for a day and met halfway.

Their virtual attraction blossomed in reality. To Raphael, it felt just like eloping. They eventually began living together. Their fulfilled romance was made possible in the first place by Raphael's philosophy of life. He was neither a cog in anyone's machine nor a node in anyone's network. Rather, he was an organic being who used computing machines and cyberspace as media for extending his consciousness, his mind, and his heart. Raphael and Evelyn had understood that the global village is the ultimate meeting place, and that the better uses of machines enhance human relations.

Raphael took a final piece of advice from Ecclesiastes: "To everything there is a season, and a time to every purpose under the heaven." To Raphael, that meant there was a time to use computers and a time to stop using them as well. So when he and Evelyn set up their new home, he packed his computer in mothballs.

A time to seek, and a time to lose; a time to keep, and a time to cast away.

– Ecclesiastes

REALITY, VIRTUALITY, AND SPIRITUALITY

The younger generation, born into a world already made over by computers, may face tougher challenges in experiencing their humanity. Confronted by *The Matrix,* it is more difficult for them to distinguish the real from the virtual. The confusion of reality with virtuality takes place in stages, which always depend on machines.

Consider, for example, the way in which machines have impacted both music and music's effect on social life. In the eighteenth and nineteenth centuries, people played instruments together, at home, on a regular basis. Their shared experience of chamber music was a cultural enrichment and a social enhancement. In the twentieth century, the inventions of the phonograph, the radio, and the TV brought music into the home from afar, but changed the family from active producers to passive consumers of music. The marketing of different genres of music to different generations, plus the availability of music-playing machines with private earphones, have divided the family into a collection of individuals with distinct tastes. While this is the kind of individualism the Enlightenment project stands for, something less than enlightening is also happening here. When family members are gathered in the same room, but each is wired to a personal CD player, then they inhabit their own separate universes. Mechanized music is dividing them rather than bringing them together. From a marketing standpoint, the Imperial Roman slogan "Divide and conquer" works pretty well. But from a social standpoint, they are passive and alienated beings, and would be better off making music together at times, as an active and connected family.

What mechanized music does to social experience, computers do to social consciousness. Each family member now sits at his or her own personal computer. Each one is experiencing a separate awareness, stimulated by a machine. They are only dimly aware of one another. Virtuality gradually supplants reality. Summed over the hours and years each child spends in front of TVs, computer monitors, and video-game screens, hours and years passively displaced from real human contact and active social engagement, virtuality ends up replacing reality. Some young people can scarcely tell the difference any longer.

One way to reexperience humanity, at (or in) any age, is to ask another Big Question: What's the difference between mechanisms and organisms? One possible answer, namely that there is something spiritual about organic life, is the topic of our next chapter.

PHILOSOPHICAL EXERCISES

First Exercise: Demechanize yourself
1. Try disconnecting from your machines for a day or more. After a few hours, you'll quiet down and they'll stop running you. Unplug the phones, the TVs, the VCRs, the DVDs, the computers, the stereos, the electric and digital clocks. Take the batteries out of your quartz clocks. A real

pendulum clock is okay; it's a low-frequency antique that runs on springs and gravity. It won't disturb you. Turn off the cell phones. Put away your Palm Pilot and Walkman. If you can't refrain from picking up a remote, hide them in a drawer. Now you should be able to sail around your home without a machine as the next port of call.

2. What in heaven's name are you going to do now? That's right: Go ahead and panic.

3. Now find something to produce from your own organic energy, instead of consuming a machine's energy and products. Draw. Paint. Sculpt. Read. Write. Play. Sit. Think. Talk. Walk. Experience your humanity. If you can resist machines, you can also resist machinations. This is also good for you.

Second Exercise: Rehumanize yourself.
This takes one step: Spend some time with nature, in the country. The more, the better.

10

ARE YOU A SPIRITUAL BEING?

There is a soul at the center of nature, and over the will of every man . . . place yourself in the middle of the stream of power and wisdom which animates all whom it floats, and you are without effort impelled to truth, to right, and a perfect contentment.

– Ralph Waldo Emerson

The finest emotion of which we are capable is the mystic emotion. Herein lies the germ of all art and all true science . . . the core of the true religious sentiment. In this sense, and in this sense alone, I rank myself among profoundly religious men.

– Albert Einstein

IF YOU NEGLECT, IGNORE, or deny the spiritual aspects of your being, you will fail to live life as fully as possible. And that can produce dis-ease and disease alike. Even in America, possibly the most acquisitive and materialistic society the world has yet seen, many people are also incredibly spiritual beings. The satisfaction of material, emotional, and intellectual needs are not enough to sustain people meaningfully. Thus most people sooner or later seek spiritual pathways through life, whether via traditional organized religions, nontraditional belief systems, perennial wisdom of the East, New Age approaches, or even secular philosophy. Spirit can be manifested on many different paths, yet itself is still one thing; just as ice cream comes in many different flavors, yet itself is still one thing.

And what is spirit? Simply stated, it's a kind of nonmaterial force or energy. Even hard-boiled materialists are bound to acknowledge the existence and influence of nonmaterial things. Gravitational and magnetic fields, for example, are nonmaterial things that exert forces and store energies. Light, too, is composed of nonmaterial bundles of energy. Without gravity there would be no atmosphere; without magnetism, no biochemical ions; without light, no way for plants to photosynthesize. Thus life itself depends on forces and energies of nonmaterial kinds. If this is true for plants, how much truer is it for conscious beings like humans? Life and consciousness have undeniable spiritual (that is, nonmaterial) aspects. Your thoughts themselves are nonmaterial, yet they ultimately determine which of the Ten Worlds you inhabit right now. If you deny spirit, it may also be at your own peril, for if the root cause of a dis-ease is indeed spiritual, then denying that domain's existence will make it impossible to alleviate the dis-ease itself.

Take a concrete example: obesity. America and the developed world are witnessing an obesity epidemic. Too many American adults and children, from diverse cultures and many ethnic backgrounds, are grotesquely overweight. This is partly because they lack good dietary habits. So they consume fast food and junk food, as well as bovine growth hormones (thanks to the dairy industry), all of which contribute to obesity. They also watch too much TV and get too little exercise. But there's something else going on here: I believe that many such people are starving spiritually, and are trying to satisfy their spiritual appetites with food. Of course it doesn't work; in fact, it backfires. People who are fulfilled in life eat less and better food on average, not more and worse; whereas people with unexamined diseases are trying to fill a spiritual void with cheeseburgers and fries. John Lennon once sang, "Now they know how many holes it takes to fill the Albert Hall" – meaning an infinite number. You can say the same about obesity, in an opposite way: It takes an infinite number of Big Macs to fill a spiritual void.

Take another concrete example: cigarette smoking. People smoke cigarettes for many possible reasons. The standard ones include addiction to nicotine, enjoyment of the addiction, habituation, diversion for the hands and mouth, oral gratification, amusement with the smoke, and peer pressure. Additionally, people used to smoke because of direct and indirect advertising: The Marlboro man was "cool," and everyone's favorite movie stars used to chain-smoke their way through feature films. Even though smokers can kick the nicotine addiction (which disappears after a few days), find other enjoyments, acquire better habits, redivert their hands and mouths, discover alternative gratifications and amusements, and resist peer pressure, many still can't quit smoking. Why not?

Maybe there's another reason why people smoke, which is not on the above list so isn't being overtly addressed. At bottom, it's a spiritual reason. People smoke cigarettes in order to sense their breath. When you inhale through a cigarette, you really feel the smoke (and therefore the breath) entering your airways and lungs; when you exhale, you can both feel and see the smoke (and therefore the breath) exiting your lungs and airways. Breathing is the basic fact of your life: It's the first thing you started doing when you were born, and drawing your last breath will be your final act in this life. The breath and the spirit are intimately related. By learning to breathe correctly, you bring your body and mind under control. Then, and only then, can your spiritual energy manifest fully. So people are right to want to feel their breathing, but need to learn helpful rather than harmful ways of doing so. You can't fill a spiritual void with smoke any more than with cheeseburgers.

Obesity and smoking are just two examples of pervasive and serious problems that prove quite resistant to conventional treatments. Perhaps that's because they – among many other issues – are rooted in nonmaterial domains. If so, then they need spiritual remedies. Needless to say, even if you're already eating healthfully and breathing properly, there's always room for spiritual progress.

FREUD VERSUS JUNG

Spirit is the thing that parted Freud and Jung, and so parts Freudians and Jungians. Jung thought that most dis-eases in adults were caused by unresolved spiritual crises. Freud supposed that all dis-eases in life were symptoms of diseases, and considered psychoanalysis an indirect way of managing disease until brain science could give us direct answers. Freud wrote, "Let the biologists go as far as they can and let us go as far as we can. Some day the two will meet." A materialistic scientist, Freud denied the very existence of spirit in the human being, while Jung, an intuitive mystic, proclaimed its primacy in all of human affairs.

While Freud's basic premise is right at home with our runaway diagnose-and-drug approach to dis-ease, Jung's insights support a more holistic interpretation of life's challenges. Jung saw each of us as a pilgrim on a personalized spiritual quest. In his view, life is a miraculous journey filled with surprises and challenges, brimming with joys and sorrows, teeming with thoughts, feelings, and experiences that bring both ease and dis-ease alike. But we are mistaken to treat life's intermittent dis-eases as symptoms of dis-ease. When we are doing the thing we are made to do – when we are pursuing our quest – we endeavor to attain unity and harmony among the competing forces of mythos (mythology), logos (reason), cosmos (order), and chaos (disorder), forces which otherwise push and pull the human being in many different directions. The unifier and harmonizer of this quartet – in other words, its conductor – is spirit.

> **Modern man does not understand how much his "rationalism" . . . has put him at the mercy of the psychic "underworld." He has freed himself from "superstition" (or so he believes), but in the process he has lost his spiritual values to a positively dangerous degree. His moral and spiritual tradition has disintegrated, and he is now paying the price for this break-up in worldwide disorientation and dissociation.**
>
> **– Carl Jung**

Kevin's Case: A Rocky Road

Kevin was a rock star who sought philosophical counseling from my British colleague Emmy van Deurzen. Kevin had done what many young people probably dream or fantasize about: He had recorded albums, traveled worldwide on tours, thrown wild parties in hotels, and indulged in excesses of sex and drugs that rock musicians' lifestyles are famous (or infamous) for. After several albums, multiple tours, innumerable parties, and seemingly limitless extremes, the band had finally broken up. Kevin now faced a sudden and drastic change of lifestyle. He confronted a new and possibly hopeful future, accompanied by old and certainly despairing habits: cocaine addiction, alcohol abuse, and cigarette consumption. Kevin had the good sense to want to kick all these habits, and in his case the cocaine addiction was easier to cure than the alcohol and tobacco abuse.

Kevin's first philosophical lesson, however, was to understand the pitfalls of hedonism, which was the philosophy he had lived by for some time without being aware that he was doing so. A hedonist is essentially a pleasure seeker who values the attainment of pleasure above all else. Hedonists face at least three big problems. First, they choose immediate pleasures of the senses over deferred pleasures of longer-term (and longer-lasting) goals attained by discipline, effort, and patience. Why is that a problem? Because instantaneous gratification is always short-lived; thus hedonists are constantly hungry for more. This leads to the second problem: Not only are their appetites insatiable, but they also need increasing amounts of gratification just to maintain their customary levels of dissatisfaction. Initially Kevin wanted one drink, one fix, and one girl; soon he wanted two of each; eventually, three or more. Hedonism's appetite is never satisfied, but its cumulative effects on the body, mind, and spirit are truly debilitating and destructive. And that's the third problem: A hedonist's craving for immediate gratification may gradually kill him. This is ironic but true.

So as Kevin got rid of his bad habits and the philosophy of life that had sustained them, he also confronted a void: the gap between his past existence as a rock star and his future existence as something else, whose precise identity was currently unknown to him. This is

Nietzsche's abyss again, and the temporary despair it brings is actually a passport to spiritual growth and enduring satisfaction. Note that this is the opposite of hedonism's temporary gratification, which was Kevin's passport to spiritual decay and enduring dissatisfaction. So Kevin could see the merits of this viewpoint, even though he still felt despair. Existentialism became a more wholesome substitute for his hedonism, and helped Kevin get through the period of withdrawal and transition.

Kevin described his recovery process as akin to climbing an uncharted mountain. Sometimes the route was easy, at other times arduous, at the worst times impassible. Then he had to retrace his steps and find a better way. But he had a philosophical counselor as a climbing companion, and she helped him discover something else as well. In effect, Kevin was undergoing a spiritual journey, from one kind of life to another. Drastic changes like this are not deaths, rather rebirths. They represent the progress of the human spirit as it discards older and more destructive habits of living and thinking and replaces them with newer and more constructive ones.

> **Finish each day and be done with it. You have done what you could. Some blunders and absurdities no doubt crept in; forget them as soon as you can. Tomorrow is a new day; begin it well and serenely and with too high a spirit to be encumbered with your old nonsense.**
> **– Ralph Waldo Emerson**

SPIRITUALITY AND RELIGION

Spirit plays a major part in organized religions – as it should. But it is also possible (and sometimes desirable) to grow spiritually without belonging to a particular religious group. That is the preferred method for some, for if religion becomes too dogmatic, which is a risk inherent in all doctrinal teaching, followers may lose their capacity to exercise doubt, and may find their spiritual growth actually stifled. You can be religiously observant without being spiritual, and following rituals as mere rote behavior may even impoverish your spirit. On the other hand, spiritual practice enriches life, whether or not you are religious.

Each of the world's great religions has an esoteric (or inner and often guarded) set of teachings that involve practices beyond communal rules, rituals, liturgy, and prayer, and that are intended for spiritual growth. Such teachings are often labeled "mysticism." The teachers themselves – be they Taoist sages, Hindu Brahmanas, Jewish cabalists, Christian gnostics, Moslem Sufis, Buddhist bodhisattvas, or eclectic gurus – are committed to the individual's spiritual awakening as opposed to the group's conformist worship. The spiritual path always develops one's inner capacity to explore and exalt the mysteries of the universe, in the name of love and beneficence. The spiritual path never leads to destroying oneself and others in violent, futile, and harmful conflagrations of hatred and suicidal ill will. Dis-ease is one of the basic ingredients in every esoteric stew, which when properly cooked renders it into ease. Dis-ease is a friend, not an enemy, for it opens our minds, hearts, and souls to experiences of spiritual life, obliging us to refine our animalistic aspects and humanize our mechanistic ones. I will very briefly summarize some mystical traditions for you. I will also suggest some further readings you can pursue if you are interested. Reading great books can change your life for the better: This is "bibliotherapy."

> **There are a thousand and one gates leading into the orchard of mystical truth. Every human being has his own gate. We must never make the mistake of wanting to enter the orchard by any gate but our own.**
> **– Elie Wiesel**

The Taoist sages are sublime, but hard to find. The Tao itself is a path that cannot be defined, except by the rational contradiction that every definition of it is (by definition) incorrect. Don't let that deter you! This pathless path leads beyond dis-ease to ease, but you can't download "driving directions" from the World Wide Web. The sage

Chuang-tzu counsels: "Practice having no thoughts and no reflections and you will come to know the Tao. Only when you have no place and can see no way forward will you find rest in Tao. Have no path and no plans and you will obtain the Tao." A student of the Tao complained that "it is like drinking medicine that makes me feel worse than before." That's because following Tao means emptying yourself of non-Tao. You are bound to notice some discomfort. Not to worry. You will then be able to begin to draw on what Chuang-tzu calls "the generosity of life." But to do this, you must first empty yourself of the stinginess of life. That's unpleasant, like draining an abscess: But it's necessary to get rid of the infection. The *Tao Te Ching* can teach you how.

The greatest encapsulation of Hindu spiritual philosophy, and inducement to its practice, namely the Bhagavad Gita, begins with the utter despondency of the student Arjuna, who is also a mighty warrior. Yet Arjuna's martial prowess is like a straw in the wind compared with the cosmic spiritual forces he must now begin to understand, as patiently and methodically revealed by Krishna. Arjuna's dis-ease makes him question the meaning of life and death, which unlocks a gate to the spiritual practices of the Forest Sages. His despondency was the key to his salvation. Your despondency might be the key to yours, too. To find out, read the Bhagavad Gita.

Many practices of Jewish mysticism (cabala) are premised squarely on something even worse than despondency: namely, disaster. Forces beyond our control may at any instant wreak havoc on our lives, dealing death and destruction in their wake. Look at the Book of Job. Look at September 11, 2001. It follows that every moment in which disaster does *not* occur is actually a precious gift, which should be celebrated by maximizing one's love of life itself. This celebration, the heart of cabala, is a spiritual practice. As Rabbi David Cooper says, we are swimming in "an unrealized sea of miracles." Your mission is one of realization. You fulfill it spiritually. If you like to accomplish missions, why not investigate the cabala? You can start with Cooper's *God Is a Verb*.

Christian mysticism evolved both within the Roman church and outside it – the latter thanks to the church's ancient ban on gnosticism.

Interestingly, religious orders within the church are currently import-ing other traditions to reinspire their own faith, exemplified by Roshi Robert Kennedy, SJ, and his gift of Zen Buddhism to Roman Catholic monastic and lay communities. The gnostics, however, emulated esoteric teachings of other religions from the outset. They see this world as imperfect at best, and a hell at worst. Their way beyond dis-ease lies in the evolution of human consciousness: a progression from materialism and enslavement of the senses to ethical awareness, to the spiritual liberation of gnosis. The gnostic scholar G. Quispel writes: "The world-spirit in exile must go through the Inferno of matter and the Purgatory of morals to arrive at the spiritual Paradise." If you feel like a spirit in exile, why not study some gnostic texts? An early and anonymous pre-gnostic wrote one of my favorite works of Christian mysticism: *The Cloud of Unknowing*.

Islamic mysticism, or Sufism, is congruent with Taoist, Hindu, Jewish, and Christian spiritual ideals and practices. The most recently evolved of major mystical traditions, Sufism incorporates elements from all its predecessors. Like the Taoists, Sufis value emptiness. Like the Hindu Forest Sages, Sufis dwell apart from the herd. Like the cabalists, Sufis exultantly celebrate life. Like the gnostics, Sufis reject official dogmas and seek higher truths. And like all of them, Sufis acknowledge the transformative potential of dis-ease. Here, for ex-ample, is Rumi's advice on the matter: "These pains that you feel are messengers. Listen to them. Turn them to sweetness." How? By making sweet music with them. Dis-ease can sometimes feel like emptiness. But, as all mystics know, emptiness is supremely useful and beautiful: "We are lutes, no more, no less. If the sound-box is stuffed full of anything, no music." Only by emptying yourself of the mundane can you be filled with the divine, and become its instrument. To find out more, read Rumi and other Sufis.

BUDDHISM

Buddhist traditions are originally both nonmystical and nondenomi-national in their origins, which is why they attract seekers from every religion. The generic goal of Buddhism is the attainment of an awareness unfettered by cravings, attachments, desires and other intoxicants of consciousness. Some Buddhists believe there is a soul that gets reincarnated; others believe in no soul at all. Either way, their practices are spiritual because they tap dormant human resources, elevate awareness of the true causes of suffering, and awaken compassion toward other sentient beings. All that is required is an exercise of one's humanity in its simplest yet most powerful and benevolent manifestation: sitting still for a while. That is enough to reveal the human spirit. "Buddha-nature," the noblest and most egoless essence of one's humanity, is neither an emotion nor an idea, neither a soul nor a non-soul. Its realization, for lack of a better word, is spiritual. And just as with the mystical schools reviewed above, dis-ease facilitates one's introduction to Buddhist theory and practice. Suffering can be a guide to a better destination.

> **Most of the evils of life arise from man's being unable to sit still in a room.**
> **– Blaise Pascal**

THEOSOPHY

These deeper mysteries of being and consciousness – spiritual matters – have been explored by Western thinkers in contact with the East in every century since Pythagoras, if not earlier. Closer to our time, British and European theosophists blended mystical theology and spiritual philosophy in secular practices. Influenced by the eighteenth-century theology of Emanuel Swedenborg and the eclectic wisdom traditions of the East, theosophy was pioneered by Helena Petrovna Blavatsky in the nineteenth century. Blending the allegory of Plato's cave with its Hindu counterpart, the doctrine of the illusoriness of ordinary perceptions (Maya), Madame Blavatsky wrote:

"As we rise in the scale of development we perceive that during the stages through which we have passed we mistook shadows for realities, and the upward progress of the Ego is a series of progressive awakenings, each advance bringing with it the idea that now, at last, we have reached 'reality,' but only when we shall have reached the absolute Consciousness, and blended our own with it, shall we be free from the delusions produced by Maya."

George Gurdjieff and Peter Ouspensky explored our spiritual dimension in a similar vein, and wrote eloquently about their discoveries. They mapped out a dimension of consciousness removed from emotional and intellectual dis-ease, in which one bathes in a radiance of ease. But again we encounter the same theme: Spiritual progress always requires external pressures, as does the transformation of coal into diamond. If you gravitate toward integrative, eclectic, or individualistic approaches to spiritual quests, then follow the paths of Blavatsky, Gurdjieff, and Ouspensky. Their writings are also guides.

Remember, I am telling you all this for an important reason. To reiterate: Most clients who come to philosophers, or any other kind of counselor, are caught up or bogged down in the particulars of their situations. This is only natural. But if you and your counselor focus on your particulars alone, your net may only tighten, or your bog may only deepen. If you think you are in some kind of spiritual crisis, then the best overall help comes not only from examining your own circumstances, but also from investigating the journeys of others who found themselves in similar or parallel situations to yours. Gurdjieff, for one, had a remarkable life, and wrote about it in a very accessible way. He may not be exactly your cup of tea, but if you survey the "mystical" literature you will eventually find someone whose situation resembles your own, and whose path you might like to ponder for a while. The world is full of guides, and nowadays full of guide books too. This wasn't so a century ago, as we'll see in the case of R. M. Bucke.

Richard Bucke's Case: Cosmic Consciousness

Around the turn of the twentieth century, when he was thirty-six, Canadian physician Richard Bucke had a sudden and unexpected spiritual awakening. One day, when he was engaged in nothing of any particular note, minding his own business, he was bathed in pure white light, radiant awareness, and experienced a dramatic transformation of consciousness. With no teachers available in the West at that time to offer him a plausible context for these remarkable yet baffling experiences, he embarked on a quest to discover an explanation. He ended up investigating the lives and similar experiences of many prominent mystics, prophets, poets, and philosophers – as well as some very "ordinary" people – all of whom had been similarly transformed (and some of whom are mentioned in this chapter). Bucke eventually understood that he and these others had experienced a breakthrough of awareness to a higher plane, and he wrote a wonderful book about it called *Cosmic Consciousness*. He recounted his spiritual awakening as meaningfully as possible, revealed key signs of awakenings among those who had preceded him on this path, and held out hope that all of humanity would one day so evolve. Bucke's gift to us was to link many such experiences by showing their commonalities, and raise human consciousness about human consciousness and its untapped potential.

> **The world peopled by those possessing cosmic consciousness will be as far removed from the world of today as this is from the world as it was before the advent of self-consciousness.**
> **– Richard Bucke**

NEW ENGLAND TRANSCENDENTALISM

There are no greater guides to modern spiritual life than the New England transcendentalists. They created a remarkable philosophical community in and around Concord, Massachusetts, around the same time the theosophists were emerging in Europe. A nucleus of exceptionally open-minded, reflective, intuitive, and benevolent philosophical beings, including Ralph Waldo Emerson, Henry David Thoreau, Louisa May Alcott, and Nathaniel Hawthorne, began a movement in American idealistic philosophy whose potential has not yet been fully realized, though their individual and collective influence continues to be felt. The common threads of their work include an egalitarian love of humanity, an assertion of the basic rights and dignity of human beings, a reverence for nature, a celebration of life, a profound gratitude for the gifts of life, a belief in the purpose of being alive, and a childlike sense of enchantment with the world. Shortly before Thoreau died, his aunt Louisa asked him if he had made his peace with God. He answered, "I did not know we had ever quarreled, Aunt."

The best guides to life's complexities are the simplest. The spiritual life conducts the music of the soul as it is truly meant to be heard. Being grounded purely in the intellect or solely in the emotions, or focused on materialism or hedonism, or blinded by dogmatic prejudices, stifles or distorts the soul's music and makes it sound harsh, jarring, and discordant. But by appreciating the finer aspects of nature and by living in accord with them, we also learn to appreciate the finer aspects of our humanity, and learn to live in accord with them as well.

Nay, be a Columbus to whole new continents and worlds within you, opening new channels, not of trade, but of thought.
– Henry David Thoreau

Ben's Case: Beyond the American Dream

Ben's case comes from my colleague Christopher McCullough. Ben's was a common experience during the 1990s economic boom in America: His financial payoffs often exceeded his efforts. Everything he tried seemed to work out in his software business, and he felt ecstatic despite the complaints from his wife and children about his long hours at the office. When the dot-com bubble burst, creating a sharp downturn in his profits, Ben at first enjoyed spending more time with his family but soon started feeling the dis-ease of emptiness. The business that was now failing was the only kind of work he knew, and at forty-five years of age he couldn't imagine starting another career. Ben had already been to a psychological counselor, and had explored issues involving his self-esteem, his permissive father, his anger, his resentment – the usual emotional baggage. But Ben now sought a philosophical path through his current difficulties and into a promising future, as opposed to an inventory of his past.

Ben mentioned that a few of his colleagues were having some moderate success by really "digging and scratching," as he called it. He admitted that he could do that himself but didn't really want to: "Damn it, I worked too hard to get where I am to go back down to that level."

Ben was suffering at the hands of "hope," which is sometimes a temptation from Pandora's box – left there to trick us into believing in a future we cannot always control. Ben was passively hoping things would get better, instead of mustering his spiritual fortitude in the face of difficult challenge. In *Wandering in Eden*, Michael Adams wrote: "Bent by the years so that he knows he must soon die, he bends further to plant acorns and apple seeds." When we cannot resist or alter a given situation, we need to discover what can be done not merely to acquiesce in it, but to transform ourselves to make the best of it.

So perhaps Ben was facing a golden opportunity to affirm himself in the face of this negation, as philosopher Paul Tillich would phrase it. Ben may never have a better chance to experience the depth and capacity of his spirit. He was being asked to transcend his circumstances; that is, to negate his apathy and preserve his determination to succeed.

> **He who risks and fails can be forgiven. He who never risks and never fails is a failure in his whole being.**
>
> **– Paul Tillich**

Alternatively, to transcend can mean to look for deeper truths and higher consequences. One deeper truth Ben found was this: All markets ebb and flow, under the influence of forces nobody fully understands or controls. Thus he was not a failure. Another deeper truth: Ben had resources that he wasn't marshaling, because he had allowed himself to become apathetic and almost self-pitying. And Ben found higher consequences too: for one, a finer appreciation of the importance of balancing his work and his family life.

Several weeks later, Ben came back and reported that he had been planting some "acorns and apple seeds" of his own. In order to increase sales in his software business, he had decided to give free seminars and to write an information technology column for a local newspaper. Although he did not yet have oaks and apples, he felt very good about his efforts and was once again enjoying his family. Ben had discovered that courage was not dependent on anything outside himself, and that his courageous acts constituted values on which no price could be placed.

In essence, Ben had become a New England transcendentalist. He was reinventing himself by mobilizing his inner resources, in the spirit of Thoreau. And he was helping himself by helping others through public educational service, in the spirit of Emerson.

> **Whatever you do, you need courage. Whatever course you decide upon, there is always someone to tell you that you are wrong. There are always difficulties arising that tempt you to believe your critics are right. To map out a course of action and follow it to an end requires some of the same courage that a soldier needs. Peace has its victories, but it takes brave men and women to win them.**
> **– Ralph Waldo Emerson**

PLAYING WITH SPIRIT

If you're still skeptical of or exasperated by all this abstract discussion of "spirit," let's take a more concrete approach. A venerable Chinese master taught that to practice any art effectively, you must understand it at three different levels: the technical (or physical), the ideational (or mental), and finally the integral (spiritual). Even though they overlap, these levels of understanding are usually consecutive; that is, you must first make substantial progress at one level to start making headway at the next.

Let's take music as an example. To make music on your instrument, you first need to learn some techniques: how to hold the instrument, then how to play notes and scales on it, and so forth. These techniques are necessary, but hardly sufficient, to make music.

Once you have acquired some basic techniques, you can go to the second step, which is to learn some of the many ideas behind the techniques. You hold your instrument (and your body) in a certain way so as to able to breathe properly, and thus to execute techniques on the instrument itself (and eventually, to release music from your soul). Basic ideas behind the scale include development of attack, tone, coordination, and other playing tools. Compositional ideas include the expression of a melody, a harmony, a cadence. Dynamic ideas behind the scale include possibilities like crescendo or decrescendo, and many subtler nuances. All these ideas are necessary, but still not sufficient, to make music.

What lies beyond technique and ideas? The spirit of the musical idiom itself. It doesn't matter whether you play bluegrass, country, folk, blues, rock, soul, gospel, jazz, classical, or any other idiom of music. Each idiom has its particular spirit, which is more than the notes and the ideas. The spirit of the music must be captured and reflected by the musician, or the music won't sound right. It is the player's spirit that allows him or her to integrate the idiom's spirit – to make the piece his own – and the player's talent that allows him or her to reflect that spirit in performance. Audiences possess musical spirit too: They are receivers of the gift, without whom there could be no performance at all.

For the would-be musician, this whole process takes, on average, fifteen years of practice: five years to start mastering the techniques, then five more years to start mastering the ideas, then five more years to start integrating the spirit of the idiom.

This is also true of other arts, and sports. A tennis coach realized this same truth in the context of his chosen sport. He said that it takes fifteen years to build a player: five years to learn the strokes (technical level), five years to learn how to use the strokes in the game (ideational level), and five years to learn how to win (integral level). You need to feel the spirit of the game so that you can make it your own: that is, find your way to construct a point under pressure, or your way to break your opponent's serve, or your way to serve out the match itself. Once in a while, you will strike a ball as cleanly, and place it as perfectly, as any tennis legend – without thinking about it consciously. Then you have captured the spirit of the game.

IN A ZONE

Athletes call this being "in a zone." When you are in a zone, everything unfolds naturally and easily. Time slows down in a zone, and you have no sense of anxiety or urgency. Your technique is effortless, your ideas exactly right, your execution flawless, all without any conscious thought. Your spirit merges with the spirit of the game. You *become* the game. You will definitely make the highlight reel that night!

But when a zone seems entirely out of reach, you struggle. Technique breaks down, execution fails, plays don't work, players become dispirited – they've literally lost the spirit of the game. In his delightful classic *Zen in the Art of Archery*, Eugen Herrigel describes a zone as follows:

"This state, in which nothing definite is thought, planned, striven for, desired or expected, which aims in no particular direction and yet knows itself capable alike of the possible and the impossible, so unswerving is its power – this state, which is at bottom purposeless and ego-less, was called by the Master truly *spiritual*."

THE ULTIMATE ZONE

The path of spiritual development is pretty much the same as the path of musical, or athletic, or any other kind of development – aside from being the path that contains all these other paths! Musicians and athletes both engage in spiritual exercises, using different kinds of instruments. If you set aside the external instruments and develop your internal ones instead – primarily breathing and mentation – then you will be on a spiritual path that contains all other paths, and which leads to the ultimate zone that contains all other zones. Not everyone is musical or athletic, but everyone breathes and thinks. Therefore everyone can, in theory, experience the ultimate zone.

Some assert that the zone is empty, and the only way to inhabit it is to leave your self behind. This is the teaching of Zen, as well as some other schools of Buddhism, epitomized by the legendary master Basho:

> Along this road
> Goes no one
> This autumn evening.

Others say that the zone is full – full of cosmic love, radiant light, divine music – and the only way to enter it is to merge your drop of spirituality in the sea of the Divine Spirit that creates, sustains, destroys and renews the cosmos. Thus says Krishna, an incarnation of Vishnu, to Arjuna, the fearless but despondent warrior: "Whenever spirituality decays and materialism is rampant, then, O Arjuna, I reincarnate Myself . . . Howsoever men try to worship Me, so do I welcome them. By whatever path they travel, it leads to Me at last."

If you are on a spiritual path, then you will encounter guides at important times in your life. Sometimes these guides will appear in the guise of benevolent or even malevolent persons; at other times they will manifest as triumphant or tragic events; at yet other times they will appear as fleeting sensations or intangible dreams. Your guides will show you what you are ready to see, when you are ready to see it. The ancient Chinese knew this well: "When the student is ready, the teacher will appear."

Yitzhak Perlman's Case: No Strings Attached

Musicians, athletes, and other performers who have truly attained mastery over their art forms are able to do extraordinary (and often unrehearsed) things in performance. Why? Because their bodies and minds no longer impede their expressions of the spirit of their art itself. On the contrary, they experience unity of being with their art, with their audience, and with the cabalistic miracle of each instant.

The ordinarily brilliant violinist Yitzhak Perlman exemplified the extraordinary in an unforgettable recital at New York's Lincoln Center. At the very beginning of an orchestral work in which he was the featured soloist, he broke a string. Everyone heard it snap, and the orchestra stopped playing. Normally, a musician would replace the string. There would be an understandable delay. In Perlman's case, such an occurrence would also be more arduous. A victim of childhood polio, he walks slowly and painfully – yet majestically – with leg braces and crutches. He lays down the crutches and removes the braces before he starts playing. Now he would have to put them on again, and make his way offstage and eventually back onstage, in order to effect the replacement.

Instead, he did something unthinkable. He stayed where he was, with the imperfect instrument, and nodded to the conductor to restart the piece. Jack Reimer, a reporter for the *Houston Chronicle* who was in the audience, later wrote: "And he played with such passion and such power and such purity as they had never heard before. Of course, anyone knows that it is impossible to play a symphonic work with just three strings. I know that, and you know that, but that night Yitzhak Perlman refused to know that . . . When he finished, there was an awesome silence in the room. And then people rose and cheered. There was an extraordinary outburst of applause from every corner of the auditorium. We were all on our feet, screaming and cheering, doing everything we could to show how much we appreciated what he had done."

Then Perlman said something profoundly philosophical to the audience, and as unforgettable as his performance: "You know, sometimes it is the artist's task to find out how much music you can still make with what you have left."

And even if you are like the majority of us, who are not world-class musicians or athletes, Perlman's moral still applies. To what? To our very lives. Living well is an art form too, and requires all the mastery of music or sports – and then some. This is the great lesson that Jack Reimer and many others took away from that recital. In Reimer's words: "So, perhaps our task in this shaky, fast-changing, bewildering world in which we live is to make music, at first with all that we have, and then, when that is no longer possible, to make music with what we have left."

Yes! And this is the function of your spirit: to make that music, even with no strings attached.

DENIALS OF THE ZONE

Many people, including some noteworthy scientists and philosophers, sustain purely materialistic views of the world. They believe that material existence came out of nonexistence by an accidental "quantum fluctuation" of the void. Given the Big Bang, we can explain a lot of things. But nothing explains the Big Bang itself, or how so much comes out of nothing. Materialists also believe that life is an arrangement of "self-reproducing molecules" that accidentally evolved from nonliving matter. Again, given a primordial life-form, Darwin's theory explains how it could have proliferated. But nothing explains how that primordial life-form came out of non-life.

Then, too, materialists believe that consciousness – as well as thought, memory, and understanding – is just an electrochemical state of the brain. Given consciousness, we can consciously assert that thought is just elaborate biology. But no one has explained the biological basis of being conscious, or thinking thoughts. Materialists also believe that spirit is a figment of the imagination (the brain again), and that spiritualism arises from a forlorn hope that there is more to the world, life, and consciousness than mere matter in motion.

Yet other experts know that these materialistic views are beliefs, not explanations. How does something come from nothing? How do living organisms arise from dead matter? How is consciousness produced from brains? How are experiences of pure light, divine music, perfect love, boundless grace, and cosmic consciousness dismissed as wishful thinking, hallucinations, or figments of the imagination? It is equally possible that materialistic denials of the special significance of existence, life, mind, and spirit are themselves wishful thinking, hallucinations, or figments of the imagination.

If you believe only in the birth and death of the body, and in the waxing and waning of the mind, then you're missing the opportunity of a lifetime: the fulfillment of your spiritual quest. To those who persistently deny the spirit, I offer Shakespeare's reminder that many things surpass our understanding – but we should embrace them nonetheless.

> *Horatio*: **O day and night, but this is wondrous strange!**
> *Hamlet*: **And therefore as a stranger give it welcome.**
> **There are more things in heaven and earth, Horatio,**
> **Than are dreamt of in your philosophy.**
> **– William Shakespeare**

SPIRIT OF AN AGE

In Europe, the 1720s marked the twilight of the baroque period – one of the greatest ages of music (and my undisputed favorite). That so-called "twilight" blazed as brightly as high noon with the light of the composers who defined it, including Handel, Telemann, Bach, Vivaldi, Scarlatti, and Weiss. Each one individually was a prodigious talent and a great musical spirit. Taken together, the assembly of such spirits defined the age itself. Although three centuries have elapsed since the baroque period, and have seen the emergence of classical, Romantic, and modern periods, replete with composition in many new idioms, hardly any classical solo or ensemble recital is given anywhere in the world today, on any instruments, without including late-baroque pieces in the program. Such is the enduring musical spirit of that age.

For me, growing up in the 1960s, the musical spirit of that momentous decade was defined by the Beatles, the Rolling Stones, Bob Dylan, Paul Simon, the Doors, Jimi Hendrix, the Mamas and the Papas, and many other kindred spirits. Collectively, they characterized and preserved the Woodstock generation just as the baroque composers characterized and preserved their musical age. There is something very special and enduring about the popular music of the 1960s, which is why so many young people still appreciate it today. They understand that while every adolescent generation loves its own music, they don't usually to relate to the popular music of other generations. The 1960s was an exception, partly because its music reflected and enhanced expansions of consciousness that still endure and inspire. When one of my students, born in the 1980s, returned from her very first trip to Paris, I asked her what she had seen. Neither the Louvre nor the Eiffel Tower topped her list of attractions; Jim Morrison's grave did. It remains to be seen whether the musical spirit of the 1960s will endure as long as that of the 1720s. But the spirit of the 1960s has withstood forty years of accelerated technocratic time, and counting.

In any case, and for reasons no one can truly fathom, it sometimes happens that a constellation of great talents is assembled during a given period, to memorialize its spirit and to inspire future generations. This happens not only with music, but with painting, sculpture, film, dance, architecture, literature, philosophy, mathematics, science – and even politics. When greatness of the human spirit is concentrated in this way, we call it a renaissance: a rebirth of spiritual power, manifested in art.

If you can contribute something to the spirit of your age, or perpetuate it by appreciating the contributions of others, then you will have understood something very special about the transcendent power of assembled great spirits. Either way, you will have experienced something beyond space and time. You will have caught a glimpse of immortality.

ORDINARY MAGIC

Matter and spirit are not opposites, but complements. The spirit of nature is manifest in the unparalleled beauty of her material arrangements. From flora to fauna, from marshes to mountains, from planets to pulsars, there is ordinary magic that all children and poets and artists can plainly see. Sadly, many adults become blind to ordinary magic in the process of so-called "growing up." I am reluctant to call this "growth." Arranging matter so as to evoke spiritual harmony is what creative people constantly strive to accomplish, whether they are orchestrating symphonies, designing buildings, planting gardens, or redecorating homes. This idea has lately become popularized through the Chinese art of Feng Shui, but it has been known throughout the East for a very long time. The Japanese, for instance, have celebrated it through flower arrangement, the tea ceremony, and the Zen garden.

The Tibetans use the word *"drala,"* which literally means "beyond the enemy," but which really signifies the ordinary magic constantly accessible in everyday life. Accessible, that is, to those who know how to invoke it by arranging matter so as to harmonize spirit. "The enemy" in this case is any arrangement of matter that represents aggressive spiritual discord, which in turn drives away *drala*. Forests are full of *drala,* whereas landfills are not. If you attract *drala,* you will derive profound delight from the simplest things, as children do. If you repel *drala,* you will derive profound misery from endless complications, as far too many adults do.

If you want to attract *drala,* then keep a clean and orderly house. When you have *drala* as a houseguest, good things will happen. If you want to repel *drala,* keep a filthy and squalid house. When *drala* moves out, bad things will happen. Don't believe me or the Tibetans? Think this is a fairy tale to induce children to tidy their rooms and make their beds? (Of course it works for that as well.) Then conduct the experiment and find out for yourself. This is independent of the kind of home you inhabit – whether it's a mansion in Beverly Hills, a walk-up in the Bronx, a trailer in an RV park, a cabin in the woods, a tent in the desert, or Mersenne's cell in Paris. What matters is the orderliness and harmoniousness of your environment. This idea also appears in Judeo-Christian cultures, where most people have at least heard the homily "Cleanliness is next to Godliness."

If entire neighborhoods are maintained like garbage dumps, with no regard for cleanliness and order, *drala* departs and social behaviors become unsavory and disorderly. New York City, famous for excesses of every kind, cleaned up its worst subway crime and street crime rates in decades by repairing broken windows, eradicating graffiti, and removing garbage without delay. New York City didn't expel its criminals; it attracted *drala* instead. I'll wager City Hall didn't know it had unwittingly applied a precept of Tibetan criminology. A philosophical practitioner might have suggested it to them, of course, and a lot sooner.

If you want to learn more about ordinary magic and *drala*, read Chogyam Trungpa's *Shambhala*. This late, great Tibetan teacher explains these things with clarity and in depth.

> **When you express gentleness and precision in your environment, then real brilliance and power can descend onto that situation. If you try to manufacture that presence out of your own ego, it will never happen. You cannot own the power and magic of this world. It is always available, but it does not belong to anyone.**
>
> **– Chogyam Trungpa**

VITALISM

Vitalism takes its name from what Henri Bergson called the "élan vital" (vital spirit) – the life force that inhabits certain arrangements of matter, making living and nonliving beings fundamentally different. To vitalists, it's clear that to be alive means to incorporate a vital spirit with the body; to die means to disincorporate the vital spirit from the body. This spiritual view appealed to many scientists and other observers of life who were not, a century ago, automatically materialists. I am telling you this because the last three cases in this chapter touch on the idea of vital spirit – and why you shouldn't lose yours.

> **The time will inevitably come when mechanistic and atomic thinking will be put out of the minds of all people of wisdom . . . When that happens, the divinity of living Nature will unfold before our eyes all the more clearly.**
>
> **– Johann von Goethe**

CAUGHT ON CAMERA

The public eye is constantly fixed on those who have most conspicu-
ously realized the American Dream: for the most part, celebrities of the
entertainment world – film, stage, and sport. Have you ever wondered
why some of the most beloved stars sometimes lead quite tragic lives,
and often die well before their time? I believe that in such cases, fame
has a way of eroding the spirit. When people's names become very
much larger than life, their own vital force can become correspondingly weakened and dissipated, so that their very existence becomes
hollow and precarious.

    Believe it or not, photography abets this process like nothing else.
Think of how many so-called "primitive" (that is, nontechnological)
peoples refuse to allow themselves to be photographed, because they
believe that a process that captures their images would also steal their
souls. Westerners tend to scoff at such superstition, but in fact we've
all seen it happen, at least in a metaphorical way. I will illustrate this in
three cases of very famous people. Of course I don't mean you should
avoid all snapshots. Some can even reinforce spirit, like wedding
photographs that capture the bonding of two souls.

Marilyn's Case

Marilyn Monroe was probably the greatest pin-up girl and screen idol
of all time. Millions of her posters hung on admiring men's lockers,
walls, and heaven knows where else. Yet as the adulation of the
masses grew, her loneliness increased. Worshipped as a goddess by
millions, she was utterly alone and despondent the night she committed suicide. With all her fame and fortune, why couldn't she get
through the night by herself? Why did she experience such fatal
dis-ease? I believe this is neither a psychiatric, nor a psychological,
nor even a philosophical issue. I believe it is spiritual. Marilyn Monroe
had lost her soul to adulation. In her case, every pin-up photograph
siphoned a bit of her vital force. One or two, or even hundreds, would
have made no difference. But multiplied millions of times over, these
little siphons eventually drained her completely. Having no soul force

left to sustain her, she was empty inside. Yet she desired communion with those who "owned" her soul, which is natural but in her case was impossible. If you have one soul mate (or one at a time!) you can commune with that person. But if your soul has been parceled out to millions of worshippers worldwide, you become powerless to commune with any of them. Her dis-ease was extreme, and she succumbed to it.

Elvis's Case

I need not tell Elvis Presley's story, for it is parallel to Marilyn's. Except that Elvis's audience may have been even larger than hers, and his dis-ease was possibly even greater. He had hundreds of millions of fans and at his peak was probably the most recognized – and photographed – person on the planet. And probably the unhappiest. Emptied of soul force, he tried to fill his void with drugs. That void was so great that he took enough drugs to kill himself.

Diana's Case

As a third example, look at Princess Diana of Great Britain. She was royalty and a huge celebrity – and if the Brits don't mind me saying so, a sex symbol too. She bore an even bigger burden than Marilyn. She was also intensely miserable in her private life (take note, you young women who yearn for Cinderella's glass slippers). The night she died in that horrific car crash in Paris, the paparazzi were chasing her as usual, at least one of them on a motorcycle, like some camera-carrying motorized hound from hell. This unfortunate young woman was almost literally worshipped to death.

I realize that there are many other possible explanations for these three untimely deaths. Some conspiracy theorists believe that Marilyn was murdered by the CIA because of her alleged affair with JFK and the state secrets he divulged. (Who would refuse to tell her anything?) Other people believe that Elvis was abducted by aliens – after all, he is still being sighted in shopping malls whenever they let him visit earth. Yet other people may believe that Princess Diana is alive and well and hiding in Argentina with her lover. My belief is that they lost their soul force through their inability to handle celebrity of such great magnitude.

Now for some good news: Fame of this magnitude does not necessarily drain one's soul force irreplaceably. Strong spiritual leaders endure it because, unlike celebrities, they actually commune personally and regularly with throngs of their vast flocks. In so doing, they offer love, strength, encouragement, compassion, and hope to their masses, through real contact with them. And thus they recover as many measures of such fortifying qualities themselves. In other words, they replenish and restore their souls.

And contact with great souls will help you restore your own spiritual vitality, if you are open to receiving such gifts. Everyone who teaches you something is great in some way, and everyone from whom you can learn something is great in some way too. Moreover, as Lao-tzu says, even bad men are good men's instructors. We can – and we must – learn from evil too (principally, learn not to do it ourselves, and educate others to refrain from it as well). Learning in the presence of greatness makes you improve no matter what the subject – arts, sciences, sports, anything. Through this kind of exposure, your soul becomes more aware of its own greatness. Then you can help to restore the spiritual vitality of others.

PHILOSOPHICAL EXERCISES

1. Have you practiced anything in particular for fifteen years or more, whether as a profession or a hobby? If so, how would you explain its main techniques to a beginner? How would you illustrate its guiding ideas to an intermediate student? How would you demonstrate its spirit to an advanced student?
2. If you answered "No" to the first question, then practice something for fifteen years or so, and then return to the first question.
3. Which of the esoteric teachings in this chapter appeals to you most? Your mission is to find a teacher in that tradition, and learn something from him or her.
4. Abraham Lincoln said: "I have often been driven to my knees by the conviction that I had no place else to go." What exactly was he looking for down there?

11

HOW CAN YOU
HANDLE CHANGE?

**The universe is change; our life is what our
thoughts make it.**

> **– Marcus Aurelius**

**Change is always powerful. Let your hook be
always cast. In the pool where you least expect
it will be a fish.**

> **– Ovid**

I N ONE WAY OR another, most Big Questions for which people seek
philosophical advice involve change. Life's situations are constantly
in flux, and so people are perpetually on the lookout for ways of
understanding and dealing constructively with change.

Change happens whether we wish for it or not. It also happens in
contrast with its complement, constancy – that which does not change
– for if all things changed all the time, the universe as we know it could
not exist, and we would be unable to make sense of the world around
us. We need constancy of physical, chemical, and other natural laws to
provide a backdrop to change. We also need regular, cyclical changes
in nature – like the seasons – to provide a context for irregular,
acyclical changes in the human world.

As embodied beings, we change whether we will it or not. We are
born, grow, mature, age, and die. We can participate in the shape of
our change by eating better or worse foods, by learning better or
worse lessons, by making better or worse of our circumstances, by
adopting better or worse principles to govern the conduct our lives.
But we cannot change the direction of change itself, which progresses

as inexorably as time, and cannot be canceled or reversed – even if it can sometimes be diverted, accelerated, or slowed. The things that remain unchanging and impervious to time exist in a dimension outside of time: your inner spirit, your intrinsic beauty, your great ideas, your true love, your legacy to others, and, outside yourself, the forces that sustain these things and the dimension of eternity that preserves them.

People seek philosophical guidance when they are experiencing dis-ease derived from change: Either circumstances are changing from better to worse, or they have already worsened and are not getting better. Perhaps a relationship or career is in crisis; a friend or family member is ill; a natural or manmade disaster has struck. Or perhaps there's injury, divorce, bankruptcy, a shattered dream, or some other unpleasant situation confronting them. And at the end of every life, no matter how smoothly or turbulently lived, there comes an inevitable change called death.

When devastating change occurs, or when change brings about a devastating state that does not seem to change, those caught up in such circumstances may need many kinds of assistance: medical, psycho-logical, theological, social, legal, and so on, not to mention emotional support from loved ones. Ultimately, however, what is often required at bedrock is to make sense of changing (or unchanging) situations in order to regain the inner harmony or balance that change so often upsets. Philosophy can help a lot with that. While ideas alone cannot change change itself, they can vitally change the way you respond to change. Good ideas can help you to interpret present changes in their most favorable light. By doing that, you not only improve your present prospects, you also enhance your future ones.

Jim's Case: Confronting a Fatal Prognosis

My dear friend and colleague Vaughana Feary has pioneered the offering of philosophical counseling to two very different and very troubled populations: incarcerated juvenile offenders, many of whom need critical thinking skills just to understand how they ended up behind bars; and cancer patients, many of whom seek philosophical guidance in fighting their medical and ethical battles, win or lose. A courageous cancer survivor herself, Vaughana is able to guide others from her own experience and conviction.

Vaughana said that the dogwood trees were in bloom outside her office window the day Jim came for his first session with her. At age fifty-three, he had a wife and three teenage children, and was vice president of a large insurance company. He had also been diagnosed with inoperable lung cancer. Jim's assessment of his situation went like this:

"First, I felt numb. Now I feel crazy. So many thoughts running through my head, I can't think. A friend of my wife's was in one of your programs. Linda thought you could tune me in to a philosophy that might give a reason not to jump off a bridge. Just don't want to prolong this hell for my family or myself. I'm responsible for this mess, but I still have a right to end things my way, don't I? Why suffer and make my family suffer when there's no hope? The specialist agreed I had, at most, a 15 percent chance of beating this, and that I'd probably never see another spring."

Jim's assessment was similar both to those Vaughana had heard from other cancer patients and to her own analysis of her issues at the time of her diagnosis. And it was philosophically suspect, for several reasons. First, there were unresolved philosophical tensions between Jim's desire to find some meaning in suffering and some basis for hope, versus his desire to be reassured that he had a right to die "his way." Second, what did he mean by "a right to die"? By "suffering"? By "hope"? By "responsibility"? How should these concepts be understood? Third, Jim had made several questionable assumptions at a time when he conceded he couldn't think straight. Would it be better for him, and for his family, for Jim to die? Was his death from cancer inevitable? Was the cancer his fault? Was the specialists' prognosis correct? Fourth, as Jim recognized, his present philosophical outlook was not conducive to fighting for his life.

Vaughana reassured Jim that she respected his right to make autonomous decisions about life and death, and agreed that in some cases suicide was a rational option. However, she pointed out that decisions made in the heat of emotion were rarely rational ones. She suggested that he meet with an oncology social worker at the hospital and join a support group to work through understandable feelings of despair. However, she expressed a willingness to discuss end-of-life choices with him at a later date and, like the friends of Socrates, to be present at his end if need be. After these reassurances, he said that he no longer felt helpless. Jim was now ready to focus on fighting for his life as opposed to ending it. His reason and passion were working together.

Vaughana then examined Jim's critical thinking, and through dialogue they agreed on three points. First, it was possible that his conclusion about being inoperable might be mistaken. She suggested that other tests be done and other specialists consulted. As it turned out, other specialists Jim consulted split evenly over the issue of whether he was a candidate for surgery. After examining the pros and cons in terms of a value system in which he accorded "quality time with family" first place, he opted for aggressive treatment because it offered a better chance to retard the course of the disease.

Second, they looked at "hope" as a disposition to assume that happiness is possible even in the face of terrible adversity. They agreed that hope, through reducing stress, may promote healing; that healing has emotional, mental, and spiritual dimensions; that those who hope will either heal or die a better death.

Third, they examined different senses of "responsibility" in order to diminish the burden of guilt, which could only weaken Jim's confidence in himself. They agreed that while he was partly accountable for all his years of smoking, in health issues the personal is often bound up with the political. The politics of the tobacco industry and health-care providers, motivated by economic interest, accounts for much of the campaign to hold patients wholly responsible for their own health. They also agreed that as a responsible moral agent, he did have an obligation, which he had neglected, to overcome the nicotine addiction that had ruined his health.

Following aggressive treatment, Jim enjoyed life to the hilt while his cancer was in remission. He and Vaughana had further dialogues on Asian philosophy, which Jim credited for his ability to live in the moment and accept the impermanence of his life. He eventually died in hospice care, only a week after learning his cancer had recurred. But since their very first meeting, Jim had seen the dogwoods blossom twice.

> **No sign**
> **in the cicada's song**
> **it will soon be gone.**
>
> **– Basho**

Lisa's Case: Winning a Lottery and Losing an Identity

A psychologist whom I know had a client, Lisa, who faced an unusual change: She won the lottery. You might think this is a strange issue to seek help with, but sometimes good things come with bad strings attached. Dreams of sudden wealth making your life perfect or buying you happiness rarely come true. As Lisa found out, instant riches can pull a train of undesirable consequences.

In Lisa's tightly knit small town, every change in someone's situation – a freshly painted fence, a new car in the driveway, a new addition to the family – can have an impact on many. Lisa's sudden windfall – more money than anyone else in the community was likely to see in a lifetime – created huge strains in the social fabric. Lisa knew that if she offered monetary gifts to her friends and neighbors they would be too proud to accept them – it might seem like charity. And how would she calculate the amounts, anyway? If she didn't offer gifts, she would appear selfish. And if she refused the lottery prize itself, she would surely appear not in her right mind. Lisa felt a lot of negative energy (envy, malice, and the like) circulating around the village, directed at her, and unkind gossip flew. She'd lost the comfortable status quo of her place in the community.

So she sought counseling. Lisa knew she needed to adjust to her new wealth, and in particular to the unpleasant effects it was having on her social identity. There were no philosophical counselors nearby, so Lisa saw a psychologist, who later asked me how a philosopher might handle such a case.

Had Lisa come to my office, I might have discussed Rudyard Kipling's fable "The King's Ankus" with her. Mowgli, the wolf-boy, finds a gem-encrusted elephant goad, part of a long-forgotten royal treasure, in the jungle. He carries it for a while because it sparkles but soon discards it, because it is useless to him. Next day, Mowgli finds human tracks leading from that spot, and the ankus gone. He follows the tracks, which lead to a corpse of a man, murdered for the ankus. So Mowgli follows the trail of the murderer, only to find his corpse too, and the ankus taken again. So he follows the new trail. He brilliantly reconstructs each crime from clues at the scene, using his jungle lore. He eventually finds the ankus again, at a place where two people have killed each other over its possession. So Mowgli buries it deep in the jungle, saying:

"If it be left here, it will assuredly continue to kill men one after another as fast as nuts fall in a high wind . . . I would not have them die six in a night."

While money is not a root of evil, love of money surely is. Greed or sudden wealth can stir extremes of bad behavior in people. At bottom, Kipling's parable is also about the worthlessness of money compared with family, community, love, and friendship.

I might also have prescribed a little "TV therapy." Why not? Television has done so much damage to culture – to attention span, reading, thinking, philosophizing, and socializing – that we may as well put it to some positive use too! If Lisa could spend some time in a television archive watching episodes of that classic *The Millionaire*, she might obtain some valuable clues about how others managed sudden wealth. In each episode of the fictional show, an eccentric billionaire gives away a million dollars to an average citizen, who is able to solve some pressing problems with the money, but who also discovers that gains of one kind usually bring losses of another.

The Cathy Munson episode was especially relevant to Lisa. Cathy and her identical twin sister, Carrie, lived together in a small midwestern town and jointly operated a school of beauty. But whereas Carrie was extroverted, alluring, vivacious, and had an ardent suitor, Cathy was introverted, unappealing, lackluster, and had no boyfriend in sight. When Cathy received the million dollars, she used it to gain her independence from Carrie, in whose shadow she had subsisted. Cathy moved to Chicago, built her own institute of beauty, became more glamorous than Carrie, and attracted a marriage proposal from Alan, the handsome architect who had designed her building.

Cathy had always felt that Carrie was somehow leading life *instead* of her; now the million dollars enabled her to lead her own life for the first time. Yet something was wrong. Cathy grew increasingly unhappy. She wanted to accept Alan's marriage proposal, but couldn't. She became too dispirited to work. Money could not buy Cathy what she really needed: her sister Carrie's blessing to lead her own life. So the sisters reunited in Chicago, where (after a few twists and turns, including Carrie dating Alan while pretending to be Cathy) that blessing was conferred. Cathy gave her institute of beauty to Carrie, married Alan, and moved to New York with him. One moral of the story is that while money can facilitate personal transformations, it does not resolve tensions in human relationships. That always requires humanity itself.

The Tao provides another moral to Cathy's and Lisa's stories alike: Gain and loss are also inseparable (though nonidentical) twins. The Tao offers specific advice for Lisa as well: ". . . the Sage does not hoard. The more she helps others, the more she benefits herself; the more she gives to others, the more she gets herself." This suggests that Lisa should find ways of funneling money back into her community, through local charities, trust funds, or foundations. She could also give her town a beautiful gift – a park, a library, a community center. There are many ways to transform the loss that accompanies one's gain into gain for others.

WHY IS CHANGE AN ISSUE?

We are creatures of habit. We cultivate particular preferences which, although changeable over time, tend to stay fixed for long periods of time. We assemble the same outfits over and over again, frequent favorite restaurants, and follow the same route each day on our evening stroll. Spontaneity is wonderful – but by definition impossible to practice! Habits insulate us from change; they allow us to maintain a safe harbor in a sea of flux, affording us the comforting notion (or illusion!) of permanent scenery in an otherwise shifting lifescape.

Bad habits are easy to establish but hard to break; good habits are harder to establish but easier to break. The personal and social habits people cultivate are usually underpinned by their habits of thought (or lack of thought). So your habits are actually a reflection of your thinking, because they make very strong statements about the things that you want to keep constant. What you wish to preserve must be significant to you. So habits are a key to understanding not only one's personality, but also one's philosophy of life.

Then again, sometimes we crave change and avidly seek it. People periodically need personal makeovers, interior redecorations, new relationships, different careers. We are like animals that need to shed their skins or shells in order to accommodate growth. Paradoxically, though we often wish to dictate the changes in our lives, we often must admit we don't really know exactly what we're supposed to do. Circumstances are sometimes wiser than those caught up in them. So we end up in a struggle between resistance to and acceptance of change. We seek change, then resist it when it isn't precisely what we imagined we'd get. Or we seek to avoid changes, including potentially beneficial ones.

> **Habit may lead us to belief and expectation but not to the knowledge, and still less to the understanding, of lawful relations.**
>
> **– David Hume**

Mr. Park's Case: Quality Care and the Wounds of Diversity

This case illustrates the importance of learning to handle change – and the pitfalls of not learning to handle it. My colleague Kenneth Kipnis is a philosopher at the University of Hawaii, and is also on call, as a medical ethicist, at a large hospital in Manoa. One day he was called in to see an elderly Korean patient, Mr. Park. This gentleman had perplexed the medical staff, because on the one hand he had refused treatment for a treatable illness with a decent prognosis, while on the other hand he had signed an order asking to be resuscitated in case of cardiac failure or other life-threatening emergency. So it looked like he wanted to die but wanted to live – a contradiction to be sure. He was examined psychiatrically and found to be sane. So, when all else failed, they sent for their "secret weapon": a philosopher.

Ken got to the bottom of it. He patiently questioned Mr. Park about the apparent contradiction for forty minutes, but initially couldn't make sense of it. The elderly man was definitely concealing a vital piece of information. Finally, perhaps caving in to persistent questioning, Mr. Park asked quietly asked if could say something embarrassing. In the most timorous of voices, he asked if anyone had noticed that all of his doctors were Japanese.

This was a lightning bolt to Ken, who immediately grasped the significance of what was going on. For most of the first half of the twentieth century, Imperial Japan had occupied and oppressed Korea, much as Nazi Germany had occupied and oppressed Poland during World War II. Exploited as inferiors, many elderly Koreans still retain powerful anti-Japanese sentiments today. The unfortunate Mr. Park perceived himself as exquisitely vulnerable, surrounded by his too-familiar oppressors of long ago.

No one else had noticed that Mr. Park's doctors were all Japanese, because the contemporary global village (for those who wish to inhabit it) is an increasingly ethnically diverse place, in which almost anyone might be found doing almost anything. Hawaii is an especially diverse state, containing many Caucasians and almost as many Japanese-Americans. There is also a cosmopolitan blend of Chinese, Filipinos, Hawaiians, Samoans, Koreans, Puerto Ricans, Native Americans, African-Americans, and other groups. About 40 percent of its current marriages are interracial.

However, anyone who recalls enough Korean–Japanese history can appreciate Mr. Park's concerns. He "knew" why he kept getting worse: The Japanese doctors were not trying to make him better (so he imagined, based on his wartime experience). What the doctors had seen as failures to improve, he saw as successful attempts to worsen his condition. To complicate matters, Mr. Park was familiar enough with Western ideals of tolerance, equality, and individualism to know that, in Hawaii, it was politically incorrect to express his candid opinion of Japanese physicians.

There was, however, a cryptic note in his chart: He had once asked a nurse if he could have a doctor in a three-piece suit. Mr. Park had noticed, Ken later learned, that all the Japanese doctors wore white coats but many of the other doctors wore three-piece suits. When this ploy failed, he had then tried to evade the "deadly ministrations" of his Japanese physicians by refusing their offers of treatment. Paradoxically, he was refusing lifesaving treatment in order to save his life.

Ethical and other philosophical considerations aside, Mr. Park's quandary was resolved by assigning non-Japanese doctors to his case. He then accepted treatment. But to me, there is one overriding moral here, which perhaps Mr. Park was too elderly or too habitual a thinker to appreciate. In a nutshell, it's this: Thanks to change, the future does not necessarily resemble the past. Countries once at war are now at peace. Mr. Park was neither paranoid nor delusional (even the shrinks thought he was okay). He had acquired a habit of imagining the worst about certain aspects of the world, but those aspects had not corresponded with reality for more than half a century. He had been aversively conditioned by unfortunate experiences long ago, but the aversion had prevented him from being reconditioned by good experiences in the ensuing years.

Both Thomas Hobbes's and David Hume's philosophies of causation and change show very convincingly that just because something happened a certain way in the past, even many times over, that still doesn't prove it will continue to happen the same way in the future. In other words, the fact that the past is closed doesn't mean the future isn't open. The leopard cannot change its spots, but the political and military behavior of a given set of people should not be used to stigmatize their descendants. Japanese-American physicians of today cannot be held responsible for the actions of the former Japanese Imperial Army, nor can they be assumed to be following anything like those footsteps.

. . . for though a man has always seen the day and night to follow one another hitherto; yet

**he cannot thence conclude they shall do so, or
that they have done so eternally: experience
concludes nothing universally.**

– Thomas Hobbes

THE BOOK OF CHANGES

Chinese philosophy provides an exceptionally wise set of answers to
the perennial question of when to resist change, when to acquiesce,
and how to tell whether a given change is for better or worse. These
answers are contained in a book called *I Ching*. Literally, the title
means "The Book of Changes." This great anonymous work, practical
and sublime, heavily influenced both classical schools of Chinese
thought, Taoism and Confucianism alike.

The basic philosophy of the *I Ching* is simplicity itself: In every life
situation, you can choose either a better or a worse move. But as we
saw in chapter 9, life does not resemble chess, in which there's always
a best move. Rather, life is a sequence of much fuzzier and more
complex situations, about which you have partial but never perfect
knowledge. There may not always be a single "best" move – or if there
is, there may be no surefire way of finding it. So the *I Ching* makes a
simpler (but in this context more useful) distinction: In each life
situation, you can make a better or a worse choice. If you're wise,
you'll choose the better way; if foolish, the worse one.

Your present situation is influenced, but not completely determined,
by past ones. Your future situation is partly determined by your
present situation, inherited from the past, and partly determined by
what you decide to do with the present – your future legacy to
yourself. While you may be affected by circumstances beyond your
control, you still make vital decisions, independent of circumstance.
You are free to choose actions in light of the principles you live by, and
in anticipation of the ends you seek. The *I Ching* helps you identify
better and worse actions, principles, and outcomes, and leaves the
choice to you.

MAGIC OR MIRROR?

Some people view the *I Ching* as an oracle, and consult it for prophecy about the future, but I prefer to think of it as a mirror that reveals what is in one's heart and mind at a given time, affording us a perspective on our innermost sentiments and thoughts. There are undeniably strange things in this world that await explanation, but I see no need to consider the *I Ching* part of the parapsychological realm. Anyone can reap its clear and sage advice about the better and worse consequences that flow from better and worse choices, its deep insights about social and political relations, and its wisdom about the cyclical nature of change. To attain the best possible outcome in a time of crisis, you must act with insight, integrity, and authenticity. The *I Ching* is an unerring revealer of one's own principles, purposes, and aspirations. It is more or less a philosophical Rorschach test, a conceptual ink blot in which you visualize your virtues and vices alike.

I have drawn both applause and criticism for recommending the *I Ching*. The most common complaints I get are from the rationalists, who don't trust the *I Ching*'s intuitive approach. (In case you missed Philosophy 101, rationalism holds that we can make sense of things, including ourselves and our place in the world, by means of reason alone.) What they object to is the method by which we access the *I Ching*'s wisdom: typically by tossing coins to construct a "hexagram" – a sort of code that points you to a particular reading, out of sixty-four possible ones. Because the text you end up consulting appears to have been arrived at by chance, rationalists think the method is irrational, and so some look down their noses at its use.

Throwing coins is actually more rational than, say, opening the book at random. If you did that, you'd be more likely to encounter the middle hexagrams more often, and the earlier and later ones less often, just as when you cut a deck of cards. The coins ensure you have an equal chance of finding any given passage – all passages are equally accessible to you.

Beyond that, it is important to remember that many rationalists also suppose that worthwhile things *can* happen by chance – including the creation of the universe, according to many cosmologists, and the origin of life, according to many biologists. Come to that, we are each a product of very long odds indeed, in that our conception depended on a sperm fertilizing an egg. The odds of any given sperm reaching that egg first, and becoming you, were one in hundreds of millions. Does this mean that your life isn't meaningful, just because its conception depended partly on chance? Of course it's meaningful in any case! And aren't the secrets of the universe and the mysteries of life interesting and worthy of our understanding whether they came about by chance or by design? Of course they are! And shouldn't good advice be sought for the sake of goodness, even if we sometimes find it by tossing coins? Of course it should!

It is also possible there's no such thing as chance, in the sense of "random accident." Even things that appear random may have been produced by the opposite of chance, as when a computer generates sequences of "pseudo-random" numbers that in fact are produced by deterministic instructions. In a holistic or Gestalt interpretation of events, each instant is a unique manifestation of an assembly of interconnected processes. In this view, throwing a set of coins to obtain a certain result is interdependent with your situation and state of mind at the time. Jung called this "synchronicity."

> **Synchronicity takes the coincidence of events in space and time as meaning something more than mere chance, namely, a peculiar interdependence of objective events among themselves as well as with subjective (psychic) states of the observer or observers.**
>
> **– Carl Jung**

And one of the greatest skeptics of all time, David Hume, who disbelieved in every kind of mysticism and religion, also disbelieved in chance itself, which he called a synonym for our ignorance.

> **Though there be no such thing as *chance* in the world, our ignorance of the real cause of any**

**event has the same influence on the
understanding and begets a like species of
belief or opinion.**

– David Hume

All the great rationalists, including Plato, Descartes, Leibniz, and Kant, admitted that our reason does have its limitations, and that reason alone cannot and does not answer all our Big Questions. These great thinkers recognized, if reluctantly, that understanding, revelation, insight, and intuition can also be legitimate ways of furthering our knowledge and attaining wisdom. They would have approved of the *I Ching* if they were familiar with it (as Leibniz was and did). It is obvious to anyone who reads the book that it is full of wise advice. No rational person could deny the merits of a system that helps us reliably identify our "better" moves.

BUILDING THE HEXAGRAM

It is easy to use coins to arrive at a particular passage in the *I Ching*. (Skip this section if you already know how.) Toss three pennies onto a flat surface. Count each head as 2, and each tail as 3, and add them up. The total (which will always be 6, 7, 8, or 9) will tell you whether you have a "yin line" or a "yang line," and whether it is "changing" or "unchanging." This table summarizes all four possible outcomes of your coin toss:

Coin configuration	Value of outcome	Type and name of line
3 heads	$2 + 2 + 2 = 6$	–– yin (or broken) line, changing
2 heads and 1 tail	$2 + 2 + 3 = 7$	—— yang (or unbroken) line, unchanging
1 head and 2 tails	$2 + 3 + 3 = 8$	–– yin (or broken) line, unchanging
3 tails	$3 + 3 + 3 = 9$	—— yang (or unbroken) line, changing

Repeat this process six times, placing the results one on top of the other, from the bottom up. That is, the first number you attain – the first line – goes on the bottom; the sixth is the top line. This is your hexagram. The corresponding passage in the book refers to your current situation. If you obtained all unchanging lines, the advice pertains indefinitely. But if you obtained any 6's or 9's, further advice awaits you. This being Chinese philosophy, the changing lines change into their complements: yin to yang, yang to yin, changing to un-changing. Special commentary in the text addresses each hexagram with changing lines. After you read your hexagram and the special commentary, then change the changing lines to get a new hexagram. The wisdom therein is meant to pertain to your next situation, offering advice about the future.

Martha's Case: Progress Through Conflict

Martha, a forty-year-old lawyer who was both highly rational and deeply intuitive, consulted the *I Ching* when her reason alone was unequal to resolving her issues with changing circumstances in her marriage and career.

Martha had moved to the East Coast when she married a successful businessman and took a position with a prestigious Boston corporate law firm in order to be with him and also pursue her career. But now, a couple of years later, there were tensions in both her marriage and her career. Her husband, Sam, wanted her to use her legal expertise to further his own business. And so she had – a favor for the man she loved – but he was pressing her to spend more and more of her energy that way. At the same time, her firm was placing increasing amounts of pressure on her, and her case load was as large as she could possibly manage.

An overachiever by nature, Martha took on each case as it came up, without a second thought. But now she was saddled with so much work she felt she had no life outside her career. Martha was over-committed and sleep-deprived. Her asthma was acting up, she'd put on weight, and she suffered from mild depression. But she was also strong-willed, determined both to make her marriage succeed and to make partner in the firm.

Then her life was really thrown out of kilter when Sam suddenly announced he wanted a divorce. (Turns out he was having an affair.)

Moving on with her life without Sam resolved half of the quandary she felt she was in, but a burning question still remained: Should she keep her pressure-cooker of a job? If she stuck it out even for another couple of years, her professional reputation would be made, and her contacts could really begin to pay off. And she'd never been a quitter. On the other hand, the job was stressing her so much that she began to hate it. As well, her parents and married siblings lived on the West Coast, and were having various problems she could help with if she didn't live so far away.

When Martha threw the coins, she obtained hexagram number 6, Conflict, with changing lines in the second and fifth places. It advised, among other things: "If a person is involved in a conflict, her only salvation lies in being so clear-headed and inwardly strong that she is always ready to come to terms by meeting the opponent halfway . . . In times of strife, crossing the great water is to be avoided, that is, dangerous enterprises are not to be begun, because in order to be successful they require concerted unity of forces." Another passage stated: "If rights and duties are exactly defined, or if, in a group, the spiritual trends of the individuals harmonize, the cause of conflict is removed in advance."

The changing line in the second place added this commentary: "One cannot engage in conflict. One returns home, gives way . . . Timely withdrawal prevents bad consequences. If, out of a false sense of honor, a woman allowed herself to be tempted into an unequal conflict, she would be drawing down disaster upon herself. In such a case a wise and conciliatory attitude benefits the whole community."

To Martha, the hexagram was clearly saying that she should not continue her quest for partnership in the firm because her personal life was too strife-ridden at this time for her to concentrate her efforts. Just as importantly, her bosses had deluged her with duties to the firm, but had never properly defined her rights, and her overwork there had partially blinded her to her own troubled marriage. Her better choice, she felt, was moving to her family's area, helping them out, and accepting a standing job offer with a less prestigious but more convivial law firm in the vicinity.

When Martha changed both of her changing lines to their complements, the hexagram became #35, Progress, which presents very
optimistic circumstances. That's exactly what anyone making their
better choices should encounter.

Jonathan's Case: An End that Endures

Jonathan, too, found worthy guidance in the *I Ching*. A successful
physician in his late forties, he had been faithful to his wife,
Yvonne, for the first twelve years of their marriage. But during
the past few years, their relationship had soured as Yvonne gradually withdrew from him, and their mutual interests, until it
seemed they led essentially separate existences. Yvonne came home
late from work every evening, had her own circle of friends,
assumed no household responsibilities, and simply wasn't there
for him or their marital partnership. So Jonathan strayed into
an affair with Megan.

Megan was a medical resident in her early thirties, and she admired
and looked up to Jonathan. Eventually Jonathan and Yvonne legally
separated, but as these things sometimes go, Jonathan and Megan
soon ran into trouble. Though they'd been together through the last
year of his marriage, Megan broke up with him within a few months
of his separation from Yvonne. She confessed to have been seeing
other people in spite of their mutual attraction. In the midst of that
drama, Yvonne sought to reconcile with Jonathan, having realized
with time apart how her apathy and neglect had doomed the relationship.

Confused by his pleasurable but stormy interlude with Megan and
perplexed by Yvonne's desire to make amends, Jonathan looked to the
I Ching for guidance in making sense of it all. He couldn't have
obtained a more illuminating hexagram if he had somehow rigged the
coin toss. Number 54, The Marrying Maiden, said, in part, "Undertaking brings misfortune. Nothing that would further. A girl who is
taken into the family, but not as the chief wife, must behave with
special caution and reserve. She must not take it upon herself to
supplant the mistress of the house, for that would mean disorder and
lead to untenable relationships."

In ancient China, a husband had but one official wife. These marriages were often arranged for political rather than romantic reasons, so it became part of the wife's "gracious duty" to help her husband satisfy his personal inclinations by bringing a young girl into the household. The marital relationship could become "beautiful and open," although the I Ching cautions that "it is a most difficult and delicate matter, requiring tact on the part of all concerned." (This too is from hexagram number 54.)

Megan had indeed behaved tactlessly, and made every effort to "supplant the mistress of the house," and this had led swiftly to disorder between her and Jonathan, and to an untenable relationship between them. Of course Jonathan had also invited this disorder, perhaps to facilitate his separation from Yvonne, and certainly in response to his sense of homelessness with her.

Another portion of the hexagram offered, "Thus the superior man understands the transitory in the light of the eternity of the end . . . every relationship between individuals bears within it the danger that wrong turns may be taken, leading to endless misunderstandings and disagreements . . . If on the other hand a man fixes his mind on an end that endures, he will succeed in avoiding the reefs that confront the closer relationships of people."

But just what is "an end that endures" in the flux of constant change? This is an enduring philosophical question that Jonathan had to consider, just as countless thinkers (and lovers) had before him. What is an end that endures? If he could answer that, Jonathan would know how and where to invest his capacity for love. This is a question not just for Jonathan, but for everyone.

WHAT ENDURES?

Death is one thing that apparently endures for eternity. All relationships – even lifelong marriages – are transitory in the face of death. But undying love, even if professed by a transitory being, somehow endures forever. To say to someone, "I will love you forever" is to fix one's mind on "an end that endures" because even though the "I" and the "you" must change, the love itself remains. The spirit of love cannot be depleted by time, and the light of love cannot be extinguished by death.

As illustrations, here are two short Celtic poems full of deep insight into the eternity of love in the face of change. One is by the Scottish poet Robert Burns; the other, by the Irish poet and mystic W. B. Yeats. Burns speaks with the voice of a wife professing eternal love for her husband, even though change has aged them. Yeats speaks with a loving but posthumous voice to his true love, now grown old with change.

John Anderson

John Anderson my jo, John,
When we were first accquent,
Your locks were like the raven,
Your bonnie brow was brent;
But now your brow is beld, John,
Your locks are like the snow;
But blessings on your frosty pow,
John Anderson my jo.

John Anderson my jo, John,
We clamb the hill thegither,
And mony a canty day, John,
We've had wi' ane anither:
Now we maun totter down, John,
But hand in hand we'll go,
And sleep thegither at the foot,
John Anderson, my jo.

Now her spirit and John's are long departed, and their earthly remains lie together in their grave at the foot of the hill they climbed in the flush of youth. So what else endures? This poem, infused with her eternal love. If you read it and it moved your heart, then you have felt her love of him, which has indeed survived their deaths.

When You Are Old

When you are old and grey and full of sleep,
And nodding by the fire, take down this book,
And slowly read, and dream of the soft look,
Your eyes once had, and of their shadows deep.

How many loved your moments of glad grace,
And loved your beauty with love false or true,
But one man loved the pilgrim soul in you,
And loved the sorrows of your changing face.

And bending down beside the glowing bars,
Murmur, a little sadly, how Love fled
And paced among the mountains overhead
And hid his face amid a crowd of stars.

His love of her did not die with his death: It "fled" back to the cosmos, from which it originated, and into which it dissipated. But if your heart is touched by this poem, then his love of her has also survived their deaths.

It is love, not reason, that is stronger than death.

– Thomas Mann

UNCHANGING FORMS

Ideas also endure. Philosophers trade in ideas, of course, so this is a popular way to look at the eternal. Plato was an amazing fount of enduring ideas, and I want to give you just one example here, because it provides a useful way of looking at change.

When Plato addressed change, he had plenty of personal experience to draw on. He lived through many difficult changes in his beloved Athens, which undoubtedly caused him much dis-ease. His highly cultured city-state fought a war with Sparta and never regained its former greatness. He saw his mentor, Socrates, put to death for bringing philosophical inquiry into public and political arenas. His own Academy became corrupted and turned out tyrants instead of philosopher-kings.

Plato's personal response to these changes was to invent a political system immune to change: his legendary *Republic*. No matter that it didn't work in practice; the odds of establishing a permanent utopia on earth are surely slim to none. Plato embedded something truly eternal in his visionary (if often brutal) idea of the Greatest Society: his idea about ideas themselves.

Unlike things, perfect ideas stand outside space and time, and are therefore not subject to change. For instance, the idea of the perfect sphere is changeless. Anyone can imagine a perfect sphere. And if you remember high school math, you can even write down its equation ($x^2 + y^2 + z^2 = r^2$). But Plato made the point that we can never construct a perfect sphere. Planets, moons, beach balls, pumpkins, oranges, and ball bearings are all better or worse copies of the perfect sphere, but all copies have irregularities or imperfections. Moreover, all copies change in space and time – and usually they accumulate more irregularities and imperfections, or get changed completely into something else (like orange juice, or pumpkin pie). Only the perfect sphere is without flaws, and remains without flaws, but that's because it's an ideal, not a material thing. In Plato's system, it's a pure form. It cannot be improved, and all spheres that we discover or make are merely better or worse copies of that ideal.

There are Platonic ideals for everything: the ideal cloud, the ideal mountain, the ideal lover, the ideal spouse, the ideal child, the ideal novel, the ideal symphony, the ideal movie, the ideal citizen, the ideal state, the ideal economy, the ideal life, even the ideal death. Greatness lies in emulating the ideal as closely as possible. Plato would say that the love poem that moved you has captured some of the essence of love, by virtue of the poet of having glimpsed or experienced the pure form or ideal of love. And in order to be moved, you must have glimpsed or experienced it too – having spent enough time outside the cave yourself.

So the purpose of change, for Plato, is improvement. That starts with improving our understanding, for it is only through the lens of the mind, and its ability to understand, that pure forms can be observed. This includes the ideals of truth, beauty, and justice. As we improve our understanding, we will improve the copies we make of our ideals. This improvement is accomplished largely through education. Neither political indoctrination nor regurgitation of book learning will prepare the mind to apprehend the forms. The ideal education not only teaches you facts about the world – although there is essential information you need to know – but awakens your philosophical understanding, so that you can enlist your love of wisdom to perceive pure forms.

So Plato is an enemy of change that proceeds from blindness or ignorance of the forms, because such change will always make things worse instead of better. And he is a friend of change that proceeds from awareness or understanding of the forms, because such change will always make things better instead of worse.

> **They must lift up the eye of the soul onto that which sheds light on all things; and when they have seen the Good itself, take it as a pattern for the right ordering of the state and of the individual, themselves included.**
>
> **– Plato**

ZENO, CHANGE, AND HAPPINESS

Many philosophers have regarded our world as a shifting veil that masks an absolute reality which does not change. When we mistake the appearance for the reality, or the veil for the thing veiled, we experience dis-ease. Western philosophers have often tried to pierce that veil with their minds alone – Plato's attempt being one of the noblest. Eastern philosophers have relied on being, rather than thinking, to pierce the veil. The Western way often ends in paradox. That can be good, in the sense that a paradox is like the final veil that stands between our minds and our understanding of some enduring idea. If we successfully resolve a paradox, we understand a truth we never understood before. That's progress.

The ancient philosopher Zeno of Elea, in the fifth century B.C.E., sought to demonstrate that motion is actually impossible. If motion is impossible, then so is change. And if change is impossible, then there is an absolute or enduring reality.

To make his point, Zeno invented four paradoxes meant to show, in slightly different ways, that ordinary motion cannot take place. Although these paradoxes contradict our experience of everyday life, they were technically impossible to resolve until the late nineteenth century, when mathematical tools equal to the task were developed. That's what made them paradoxical for twenty-three hundred years. And they can still teach us something about change.

One paradox will suffice to make the point: Achilles and the Tortoise. Achilles is of course extremely fleet of foot, while the tortoise is exceedingly slow. Yet Zeno contends that if the tortoise is given a head start in a race, Achilles can never overtake it. His argument goes like this: Imagine the tortoise travels a certain distance before Achilles starts running. By the time Achilles covers that distance, the tortoise will have moved a bit further ahead. And by the time Achilles covers that additional smaller distance, the tortoise will have moved ahead again. And so forth, with the tortoise always ahead, by increasingly smaller amounts. The distance between them continues to shrink, but never disappears. Achilles can never quite catch up, even though he runs faster.

I'll spare you the mathematics, and resolve the paradox in words. Of course Achilles *can* overtake the tortoise – just as any faster-moving thing can overtake a slower-moving one – but he does it on one curious condition. There is a single moment in space and time at which Achilles draws exactly level with the tortoise. Before that moment, he was behind the tortoise; after that moment, he will be ahead of it. But there is no such final moment located *just before* Achilles overtakes the tortoise. To say it another way, there is a definitive first place and first time at which Achilles draws level with the tortoise. But prior to that, there is no definitive last place and last time at which Achilles fails to draw level with the tortoise.

That's what Zeno found so paradoxical. If there is no finite end to Achilles' failure to draw level with the tortoise, how can there be a finite beginning to his success in overtaking it? This is actually a brilliant question, and the one that proved mathematically unanswerable for twenty-three centuries. Before the mathematicians caught up to Zeno, no one could properly explain why Zeno was wrong to conclude that Achilles could not catch up to the tortoise.

What does all this have to do with change in your life? Everything! When you are caught up in unpleasant change, you probably experience dis-ease. That's partly because you are thinking that the changes will never change – things will be unpleasant forever. But since you also believe that motion and change are taking place, shouldn't you consider that things may change for the better? Why not focus on the possibility that pleasant situations can result from unpleasant ones? Why not believe that change is taking you to a better place? None of this may change your situation, but changing your attitude toward your situation is often all you need to alleviate the dis-ease arising from it.

A similar phenomenon occurs when you are caught up in *pleasant* change – and still experiencing dis-ease. Now you're stuck thinking that the change *is* subject to change; you believe the pleasantness is bound to slide into unpleasantness sooner or later. The moral is that the experience of change itself is likely to cause dis-ease, whether the change is for better or for worse.

Now take a page from Zeno to help you alter your unhelpful view of change. Imagine you're like Achilles, trying to overtake the tortoise. Think of this race as "the pursuit of happiness." Applying the lesson Zeno taught us, there is no final moment in space or time at which you will fail to be unhappy (just as there is no final moment at which Achilles fails to overtake the tortoise). There is, however, a first moment in space and time at which you will succeed in being happy (just as there is a first moment at which Achilles succeeds in overtaking the tortoise). In other words, although there may be no definite place and time at which your unhappiness ends, there can be a definite place and time at which your happiness begins. This is not a paradox: It is a good reason to embrace motion, and therefore change. People who can't see the end of their unhappiness may become blinded to the beginning of their happiness.

Andre's Case: A Dying Minister

For humans, the most drastic change is death. And although television and movies increasingly glorify violent death, people need help managing death in reality. Philosophy can provide it. My British colleague Alex Howard counseled a minister named Andre, who knew he had only a few months to live. Unlike the case of Jim presented earlier in this chapter, Andre really was beyond a possible cure (barring miracles), or even a probable prolongation of his life by means of aggressive therapy. He had medication to palliate his pain; now he sought philosophy to accommodate his dying.

Andre had many unanswered philosophical questions about life (who doesn't?), and wanted to use his remaining time to ponder some of them. It was Andre's "last chance" to be a philosopher, and he didn't want to miss it. That rings true to me. I've met many fulfilled people – in business, politics, and the arts – who say they want to be philosophers in their next lives. I always tell them they can start right now!

Andre had so many questions, and so little time. "Why are we born? Why do we die? Why do some of us die young? What will happen next? What does my life amount to? What has been, and will be, important? Why do we ask these questions? Why are our answers not always satisfactory? What would have to happen for them to be satisfactory? What questions am I avoiding? What have I left undone? What do I feel most proud of? What do I most regret? What do I really know of God?"

Regularly and for weeks, Alex and Andre engaged in dialogue on these questions. Andre's questions were personal, pressing, and urgent. Yet Alex knew they are also everyone's questions, regardless of how much or how little time one is given to ponder them. They did not, of course, sort out all the answers before Andre died. Yet there were moments of tremendous peace.

Alex once said to him: "You could, perhaps, be calm without knowing why, or finding reasons. As you speak right now, it's like listening to a canary singing in a cage. It's a beautiful sound, ringing out into vast space."

This image transported Andre out of his turmoil. He could see himself from afar; his human song quietly absorbed into the riddle all around. This image resonated with him in a powerful way. Andre didn't have to pin down every answer. Canaries sing. Humans philosophize. That's what we do. It's a wonderful mystery. Andre relaxed, and smiled. And sometimes they just sat together in silence.

> **The sea darkens;**
> **the voices of the wild ducks**
> **are faintly white.**
>
> **– Basho**

CHANGE AND PURPOSE IN THE WORST CASES

You may be able to make more sense of unpleasant change if you can discern a purpose in it. That's why parents who have lost a child may wrest some comfort from their terrible dis-ease by seeking ways to prevent a similar fate befalling other families (as is the case with Mothers Against Drunk Driving). Alternatively, they might consider organ donation, to salvage precious gifts of life from the very jaws of death. To transform one's personal grief into benefit for others is one of the most noble, courageous, and charitable acts possible, and ordinary people do it every day. It is a testament to the wonders of the human spirit.

As we saw in chapter 5, the worst thing you can do with your dis-ease is to spread it around (as though it were a contagious disease). Making others miserable because of your own misery will only make you more miserable still. This is what terrorism does: It multiplies dis-ease instead of assuaging it. It perpetuates suffering instead of alleviating it.

Looking for meaning and purpose within the changes you are experiencing will steer you toward the better path, and guide you toward ease. The art lies in using change to discover what is unchanging – and in using what is unchanging to accommodate change.

PHILOSOPHICAL EXERCISES

1. What are the best changes you ever experienced? What did you do to make them even better? Or worse?
2. What are the worst changes you ever experienced? What did you do to make them better? Or worse?
3. What is the best change you can imagine? What are you doing to enhance its occurrence?
4. What is the worst change you can imagine? What are you doing to prevent its occurrence?
5. If you could change something about yourself, what would it be?

Part III

12

BUILDING YOUR PHILOSOPHICAL HOUSE

Again, the work of man is achieved only in accordance with practical wisdom as well as with moral virtue; for virtue makes us aim at the right mark, and practical wisdom makes us take the right means.

– Aristotle

Nothing can bring you peace but the triumph of principles.

– Ralph Waldo Emerson

YOU BEHAVE AS you do for a complicated set of reasons, including biologically fixed personality traits, acquired habits, imposed conditioning, and strong emotion. But you also act according to your reason, experience, belief, principle, and duty – in other words, according to your philosophy of life. Everybody has a philosophy of life, although in many cases their guiding ideas may be implicit, as opposed to explicit. Not everyone is able to articulate their philosophy precisely. The important question is whether your philosophy of life is working for you, or against you, or not at all.

When Socrates proclaimed "the unexamined life is not worth living," he was of course prescribing a philosophical examination. Just as a physician examines your body, a psychologist examines your psyche, an accountant examines your finances, or a mechanic examines your car, a philosopher can examine your life. However, while you wouldn't rely on yourself for your annual physical or a complicated audit, examining your own life philosophically is not only possible but also recommended.

Once you've made your implicit ideas explicit, it will be a lot easier to lead the examined life. Then you can articulate your philosophy of living and see how well (or poorly) you are measuring up to it. You can compare your approach to others, and perhaps modify or improve your own in some way. You can adjust your philosophy according to lessons learned from new life experiences. You can, in short, make sure your philosophy works for you, not against you.

The MEANS method in this chapter will help you examine your own life philosophically. Think of it as inspecting the philosophical house that you inhabit, making some worthwhile home improvements, and refurbishing or refurnishing a room or two along the way. If you want to start from the ground up, fashioning your philosophy of life is analogous to building your own house. You have the land on which to build it (your lifetime itself), the raw building materials (your power of reason and your life experiences), and the tools to do it (the accumulated philosophical wisdom of the ages). Now what you need is a blueprint or design to follow, plus some practical knowledge about the sequence, content and coordination of construction steps to assist in actualizing the design. That's where this chapter comes in handy.

The MEANS I'm suggesting is an acronym. I will walk you through Moments of truth, Expectations, Attachments, Negative emotions, and Sagacious choices, all of which are explored in detail below. Don't get the idea, however, that this is a one-day project. Unlike pitching a tent, building a house takes much time and effort. It can't be done all at once. The directions are (perhaps deceptively) simple and straightforward, but implementing them will take different amounts of time depending on the individual and the situation – where you are starting from, where you are headed, how much time you want to devote to the project, and so on. And even once your house is built, maintenance and repairs will always be required.

MOMENTS OF TRUTH

Fire is the test of gold; adversity, of strong persons.

– Seneca

We all experience moments of truth in our lives; that is, times when we are severely tested by circumstances. Such moments can arise through accident, injury, illness, the loss of a loved one, the breakup of a marriage, a sudden career change, or any similarly cathartic situation to which there is no immediate resolution, and from which there is no apparent refuge. Though the insight offers precious little solace in the moment itself, these moments of most trying dis-ease (which can stretch into weeks or months or even years) are also the greatest opportunities for making quantum jumps in personal growth.

These moments are even more significant for the truth they reveal than for the suffering they entail. They strip away your normal ease of living, exposing how well or poorly you are equipped to cope. The equipment is none other than your philosophy of life.

When things are going well, people rarely question circumstances or seek guidance. They feel they personally merit a good life, and will probably not spend much time giving thanks for it all, or expressing gratitude to their numerous helpers, or helping those less fortunate than themselves. But when things are going badly, people are suddenly full of questions about their circumstances: Who did this to me? Why is this happening? What is its meaning? What is its purpose? What should I do about it? What shouldn't I do? And so forth.

In good times, everybody wants to take credit themselves; in bad times, everybody wants to blame somebody else. Nobody questions good times; in bad times suddenly everybody's a philosopher. Since some bad times are inevitable, you'll be better off if you have a philosophy of life ready and waiting to serve you when they arrive. Like a life jacket or a lifeboat, your philosophy can keep you afloat if you're shipwrecked. It will serve you in good times, too, helping you to make the best of them.

It isn't until we encounter difficult circumstances that our inner strengths and weaknesses, and the ideas we hold dearest, are most strenuously tested. Thus spending some time in dire straits is the truest test of character. It provides the quickest way to shed your skin and grow, and illuminates most brightly your innermost guiding principles. This is the proverbial silver lining inside every cloud: the opportunity for good results to emerge from bad situations. Of course, it is up to you whether or not you answer when opportunity knocks.

To open that door, the first thing you need is to recognize a defining moment of truth. What calamitous event or events have been watersheds in your life, when you have been obliged to do some serious philosophical stock-taking? Your childhood should have been a vista of delight, but perhaps it contained some traumatic scenes. Those scenes were moments of truth. Your marriage should have been a celebration of joyous union, but if it ended in divorce, your divorce was a moment of truth. The birth of your child should have been a blessed event, forever etched in wondrous memory. But if that child was born with a severe illness or disability, or later had a serious or fatal accident, that was a moment of truth. To fall in love with someone, or to love someone, is magnificent beyond words. To lose one's beloved is a moment of truth. To encounter a soul mate is enchanting beyond imagination; to lose a soul mate is a moment of truth. To build a house or make a home is to find a place in this world; to see the house destroyed by forces beyond one's control, or the home shattered by behaviors beyond one's control, is a moment of truth. To attain success in one's career is an emblem of distinction; to fall prey to others' malevolent machinations is a moment of truth. To dream a wish-fulfilling dream is to weave a cocoon of fantasy; to awaken from a nightmare, terrified that it is real, is a moment of truth. To live life insulated from all risks is to avoid vitality; to confront stark naked death is a moment of truth. To befriend and embrace the devil you know is to resign yourself to a familiar falsehood; not to shrink from encountering the devil you don't know is a moment of truth. To follow the pathways that others have marked for you is to neglect yourself; to blaze your own trail is a moment of truth. To mouth the words on the printed page is to hide behind an illusory veil of comfort; to fill the blank page yourself, or to acquiesce in its emptiness, is a moment of truth. To remain willfully blind is to squander the precious gift of sight; to open the gift and behold what is, is a moment of truth.

Exercise 1. Make a short list of your moments of truth thus far. If you want or need to, choose the most important one from your list and elaborate it. Write your story down, whether it's a paragraph or a page or a book in length. Now answer this question: When you arrived at your moment of truth, what was the guiding idea that saw you through? If you are able, write down the guiding ideas that saw you through each moment of truth on your list. These guiding ideas are the blueprint of your philosophical house.

What philosopher or school of philosophy do your guiding ideas most closely resemble? You can think back to the cases in this book, or look at the "Hit Parade" of philosophers at the back of this book, to find a thinker or system of thought that resonates with you. Identifying the philosophy of life that guided you through your moment(s) of truth is the quickest route to understanding it. And understanding your own philosophy is the first step toward examining your life.

EXPECTATIONS

> **So look out that you do not set your hopes . . .
> too high, and thereby have an experience like
> people who see things under water. They
> expect them to be as large as they looked
> through the water, from above, when the
> image was magnified under the light; and when
> they fish them up, they are annoyed to find
> them a great deal smaller . . . you will have
> yourselves to blame for your expectations.**
>
> **– Lucian**

We all harbor certain expectations. Expectations of ourselves, of others, of things in particular, of the world in general. My advice is to get rid of every single one of them! The more expectations you have, the more they will interfere with a constructive philosophy of life.

If you've ever had a vacation ruined by bad weather, you've experienced just what I mean. Your vacation could only have been ruined by your unfulfilled expectations of good weather – not by the weather itself. Or perhaps your parents were disappointed in you because you didn't choose the career they had in mind for you. In fact, they could only be disappointed by their own unfulfilled expectations of you, not by the choices you made. Maybe your spouse upsets you by not always behaving or reacting as you'd like; you could only be upset by your own unfulfilled expectations of your spouse's behavior, and not by your spouse himself or herself.

Every expectation sets you up for an episode of dis-ease. Get rid of the expectations, and you'll be rid of the dis-eases too. Virtually every dis-ease is caused by some unfulfilled expectation. The most horrible example usually involves the sudden death of a loved one. We all know perfectly well that no one is immortal, yet somehow we fully expect death to deal only with other people, not our own families or friends.

The world watched a most poignant illustration of unrealistic expectations when the space shuttle *Challenger* exploded shortly after liftoff. The catastrophe was broadcast live on national television, and so were interviews with stunned students and shocked colleagues of the civilian astronaut and teacher, Christa McAuliffe, who had been aboard. There'd been a huge party at her school to celebrate the launch, and now partygoers faced the cameras, tears streaming down their faces, still wearing their party hats and holding their streamers, their jubilation turned instantaneously into devastation.

The true cause of their devastation was not the *Challenger*'s explosion. It was their unexamined and unquestioned expectation that their beloved teacher would return from the mission safe and sound, a heroine and history maker. But space travel is a very risky business. If there is any realistic expectation about high-risk jobs, it's surely that something can go dreadfully wrong at virtually any moment. If something doesn't go wrong, then one should be thankful, grateful, or pleasantly surprised. But being astonished when something goes wrong in a high-risk enterprise is very unrealistic: It is completely at odds with the nature of things.

When men went down to the sea in ships, their wives did not throw beach parties to see them off. Rather, they prayed solemnly for their husbands' safe return. Their expectation was, rightly, that many ships and their crews would never come home. A realistic expectation like this is better than an unrealistic one, because it prepares you for the worst. If the worst does occur, at least it is not a shock. And if the worst doesn't come to pass, then there is cause for celebration.

Having no expectations is better still, because nothing can happen that is contrary to expectations you don't have. Having no expectations allows you to make the best of every circumstance, and not just those circumstances that conform to your own (perhaps arbitrary) notions of what "should" happen. If you reduce your expectation of what *should* happen, you will rarely be disappointed by what *could* happen, and you may exert more influence, overall, on what *does* happen. Reducing your expectations doesn't mean abandoning your attentiveness or efforts; on the contrary, it means not taking anything for granted.

This applies on a much smaller scale, too. Having no expectations about the end of the day when you leave for work in the morning, for example, will allow you to live most fully in the present moment.

If you think about the dis-eases you have experienced in your life, I'm sure you'll find you can trace many of them back to expectations you held. If you are unhappy in your current career, you probably expected to be doing something else. If your expectation was unrealistic, why did you maintain it? If it was realistic, why aren't you fulfilling it? If you had no expectation of having any career at all, you might be very glad to have the one you've got. To take another example, suppose you are angry at being stood up on a date. You must have had an expectation that your date would show up. While this is a reasonable expectation, the reality is that any number of things could have happened to waylay that person. With no expectations, you'll simply be happy when your date shows up – and won't be upset if they don't. Instead of fuming at someone who isn't there, try engaging with someone who is.

Exercise 2. 1. Make a short list of your unfulfilled expectations, and beside each one describe what kind of dis-ease it brought you.
2. Next, make a list of your current expectations, and beside each one describe the kind of dis-ease you're setting yourself up for.

Aren't you better off without the expectations? Getting rid of them clears the ground for your philosophical house.

ATTACHMENTS

> **From attachment arises sorrow . . . To him who is free from attachment there is no sorrow.**
>
> **– Gautama Buddha**

We all form attachments, both beneficial and detrimental. Either way, attachments generally fall into two different types: appetites and aversions. Each of these can be normal, such as an appetite for food and an aversion to a particular dish because of allergy or taste, or an appetite for friendship and an aversion to a particular person who rubs us the wrong way. We need both appetites and aversions to function biologically and socially, but if carried too far they impair our philosophical functioning. Appetites can turn into obsessions; aversions can become prejudices. Having fixed attachments diminishes our possibilities for being at ease and joyful in the world, and increases our odds of experiencing dis-ease and unhappiness when the world fails to conform to our idea of it.

Part of the reason children are so delightful – and so easily delighted – is that they have not developed deep attachments to too many people or events, but are instead imbued with the joy of living. So if one toy is unavailable, they will happily play with another. If one friend is busy, they will happily make another.

Expectations are actually a type of attachment. If you expect your brother to meet you for lunch, and become angry if he doesn't show up, it's because you were attached to your idea of him being there. If you had instead been prepared to improvise, you would have been content whether or not you met for lunch because you would not be attached to an idea about one particular set of events, and would therefore remain open to other possible events. This allows you to make the most of any situation, instead of making the least of it.

Unlike expectations, attachments can become much more spread out in space and time. For example, consider your attachment to other people, which generally stretches over long periods of time. If allowed to go to the extreme, attachment to another person can become a feeling of possession. If the person whose love you think you possess offers that love to another, the dis-ease you suffer is a result of your attachment to their love as your possession. Whereas, if you can receive what is offered when it is offered (whether love or anything else) without becoming excessively attached to it, then you can also let go of it without regret when it ceases to be offered.

Non-attachment is not meant to be non-enjoyment. The idea is to enjoy what is there when it is there, but not lament when is not, and not to crave its presence when it is absent. At a university lecture, I heard Chief Abbot Fukushima Keido of Tofukuji Monastery talk about how he greatly enjoyed flying business class from Tokyo to New York for his annual visit. He said he particularly relished the gourmet food service, and most especially the Godiva chocolates that were on offer. But he made it clear that the meaning and purpose of his life would not be changed if he never flew business class again, or if a Godiva chocolate never again passed his lips. In other words, he had enjoyed these things fully without forming any attachment whatsoever to them.

That's not necessarily easy to do, as even the abbot admitted, and it is certainly difficult not to form any attachments at all. Your best bet, then, is to form only positive attachments and to avoid forming negative ones. Telling the difference is your first task.

Lest you think that's simple, consider a problem often brought up by clients who are convinced their attachments are primary causes of their dis-ease: How can they possibly avoid becoming attached to their children? The simplest answer is: As with any other attachment, you can be attached to your children in positive or negative ways. Loving them for their own sakes is positive; for your sake, negative. Being their custodian and guide in life is positive; treating them like your property is negative. Helping them fulfill their excellence is positive; making them into extensions of yourself (living vicariously through them) is negative. Subjecting them to a measure of structure and discipline in their better interests is positive; spoiling or punishing them for your convenience is negative.

Here are two cases that illustrate this point. Daniel suffered from negative parental attachment, while Justine benefited from positive parental attachment.

Daniel's Case: Negative Parental Attachment

By his early teens, Daniel had a clear talent for playing the violin and composing music, but his parents were saving for medical school. Daniel's father ran a successful business, but had no artistic inclinations and no appreciation for classical music. His mother wanted to provide her son with the material things she never had as a child, and wanted him to be financially secure as an adult.

Daniel wanted to honor his parents' wishes, but he also wanted to pursue a career in music. He couldn't prepare for both medical school and the conservatory, as they are both highly competitive. Either preparation required a full commitment. Daniel eventually succumbed to his parents' pressures and got accepted to medical school.

But Daniel hated medicine (a negative attachment) and still loved music (a positive attachment), though he had no time to play. His parents were so busy living vicariously through "Dr. Daniel" (negative attachment) that they failed to perceive the signs of his growing inner conflict. One day Daniel simply snapped, just like a violin string stretched too tightly. He had what used to be called a "nervous breakdown," dropped out of school, and, enraged, refused to speak to his parents. He also became temporarily incapable of playing the violin. He was hospitalized and given massive doses of antidepressants. He eventually recovered and, though he never went back to medical school, soon began playing the violin again. Today he earns a modest living as a musician. And loves every minute of it.

The philosophical moral of this story is that Daniel's parents were overly attached to a future for Daniel that Daniel didn't want or need for himself, and they missed the opportunity to guide him positively in the development of *his* idea. That derailed not only Daniel's capacity to fulfill himself, but also his capacity to relate to them.

**Do not confine your children to your own
learning, for they were born in another time.**
– The Talmud

Justine's Case: Positive Parental Attachment

Justine, a devoted divorced mother of two in Manhattan, had a difficult time making ends meet on her dental hygienist's salary, so she moonlighted on weekends as an exotic dancer. Some people who knew about her "second shift" morally condemned her, and she endured self-doubt about the rightness of her second job as well.

Justine's daughter Kirsten, as it turned out, had both a passion and a talent for ballet and modern dance. Justine encouraged the development of this gift, and eventually her daughter gained admission to one of Manhattan's finest dance schools – paid for with proceeds from Justine's exotic dancing. Whether or not Kirsten eventually finds a career dancing on more artistically renowned stages than those her mother frequented, Justine will have been pivotal in helping Kirsten develop her excellence, if not fulfill her dreams. Justine has a positive attachment to her child, which helped Kirsten to become self-realized.

Many important philosophical schools have cautioned against the pitfalls of attachment. In ancient India, the Bhagavad Gita described one who is spiritually awakened this way: "Expecting nothing, his mind and personality controlled, without greed, doing bodily actions only; though he acts, yet he remains untainted . . . He who is without attachment, free, his mind centered in wisdom, his actions, being done as a sacrifice, leave no trace behind."

That is, no trace of dis-ease. Similarly, without a karmic doctrine but as a means to the best earthly life possible, the Stoics advised against all unwholesome attachments to things that others can take from us – up to and including our lives.

One should count each day a separate life.
– Seneca

ATTACHMENTS TO MEMORIES

Just as dis-ease is brought about by expectations, which are attachments to future events, it can also be caused by attachment to past
events – your memories.

In a way, your identity is the sum total of your memories. Most
people store all kinds of memories – the good, the bad, and the ugly –
and together they give you a pretty good idea of what kind of life
you've led. A significant part of your memory storage area may be in
the unconscious mind. If Freud is right, that's where we'd find
unpleasant memories we've repressed in order to defend our egos.
But Socrates' dictum "know thyself" implies that conscious knowledge of one's unconscious memory is vital to self-understanding.

Philosophically speaking, you have more power over the dis-ease
caused by unpleasant memories than many psychological and psychoanalytic theories concede. What's going on in your memory is
just another set of circumstances. We are all powerless to change the
events of the past, and we must confront the past as honestly as
possible in order to understand these events and ourselves. But past
events and our roles in them are merely sets of circumstances
presented to the active mind, and (with philosophy as a helpful
guide) you have considerable latitude in choosing your view or
interpretation of the past. As Epictetus reminds us, it is not the
circumstances themselves that cause ease or dis-ease, but the views
we take of them.

You also choose how you are involved in present events – and so,
how you are forming your soon-to-be past. If you want to have better
memories, start working in the present! Good things you do today will
become good memories tomorrow.

You should work on dissolving your attachments to bad memories.
If you can manage that, you'll spare yourself a lot of dis-ease. Of
course you need to know how to effect that dissolution. You do not
need to obliterate your brain cells, or eradicate your recollections. One
of the worst ways is to attempt to escape from the past. People who try
to avoid remembering unpleasant things, or who try to anesthetize

themselves from the suffering produced by their recollection of un-pleasant things (by alcohol, drugs, or other means), usually end up reinforcing their attachment to these memories.

It's much better to ask yourself, "Whose memories are these, anyway?" Although "you" have an "identity" based largely on your particular memories and on other people's memories of "you," your deepest human essence – the real you – is independent of those memories themselves. Discover who that "you" is – standing alone without the memories – and you will dissolve your attachments to the memories your "identity" possesses. Without the memory-identity, you are a vessel filled with ideas, judgments, appetites, aversions, desires, and attachments of all kinds. But originally, the vessel was empty. Return to that original state, and your memories will be like so many leaves on the trees, leaves that are beautiful to behold, but that change their attributes with the seasons. Appreciating the beauty of changing leaves is like remembering things without attachment. The new growth of spring or the colors of autumn do not cause dis-ease to anyone who admires the forest. On the contrary! Neither should delicate memories, or colorful ones, cause dis-ease to anyone who admires life. On the contrary!

In sum, everything that you are accustomed to doing can be done better without attachment. Moreover, dissolving your attachments enhances goodness in the things that you do, and diminishes badness and ugliness alike.

Exercise 3. Make a list of your greatest appetites and aversions, and then try to distinguish which ones are most helpful to you (i.e., which ones promote your ease of living) and which one are most unhelpful to you (i.e., which ones promote your dis-ease of living). Next, take this a step further and make a list of the ideas for which you have the greatest appetites and aversions, and see which ones are most helpful to you. These most helpful ideas are the foundations of your philo-sophical house.

NEGATIVE EMOTIONS

> **While our pulse beats and we feel emotion, let us put off the business. Things will truly seem different to us when we have quieted and cooled down. It is passion that is in command at first, it is passion that speaks, it is not we ourselves.**
>
> **– Michel de Montaigne**

Emotions are part of our biology and, together with their translation into feelings we identify in our psyches, are vitally important for normal human function. Without love, empathy, or compassion, we could have neither nurturing families nor progressive societies. However, negative emotions and feelings like hatred, hostility, or resentment can be just as powerful. Negative emotions impel us to do ill instead of good, and to experience (and cause) dis-ease.

Take anger as an example. Everyone becomes angry sooner or later, and in the short run (as we saw in chapter 3) passion is definitely stronger than reason. Even if you meditate regularly, or take "happy pills," or work on diminishing your expectations and attachments, there are bound to be times when prevention fails and provocation succeeds. Moreover, some people are by nature more placid and slower to anger while others are more hair-triggered and hot-tempered. For all of us, the question is what we will do with our anger when it surfaces.

I'm sure you've witnessed or experienced many inappropriate and ineffective ways of expressing anger: lashing out, absorbing hurt, spreading dis-ease, plotting revenge. Retaliating is a purely emotional response, and although it produces a discharge of angry energy, that energy is uncontrolled and so more likely to do more harm than good. Absorbing it also causes dis-ease (and maybe even disease), unless you can neutralize what you're absorbing. Poisoning others with your anger – via emotional toxic waste like malicious gossip, insidious propaganda, political indoctrination, and the like – poisons you as well. Plotting revenge may postpone and control the expression of anger, but can't transform its negative energy into positive energy.

Amid a family replete with short-tempered people, the resident philosopher otherwise known as Mom used to say: "No matter how often you lose your temper, you can never get rid of it." If you prefer wisdom more ancient than my mother's, consider Philemon: "We are all crazy when we are angry." To avoid dis-ease (and preserve your sanity), spend as little time as possible in the grip of such negative feelings. In the short term, the best way to deal with anger is not to feel it at all. If you can manage not to take things too personally – that is, minimize your ego's involvement in your life – you will be a happier and much less angry person.

To the degree that you can achieve this in the short term, you will not require longer-term strategies. But just in case you have your moments, like the rest of us, and want appropriate ways of managing your anger when it flares up, I have a suggestion: transformation. Energies of all kinds – physical, chemical, biological, and more – can be transformed from one into another. Just as stars transform the energy of atomic fusion into heat and light, and plants transform the energy of sunlight into sugars, humans can transform emotional, mental, and spiritual energies in a variety of ways, from using lethal force to creating art, from oppressing others to uplifting themselves, from spreading the toxin of hatred to applying the balm of love.

You can transform your anger and other negative emotions in two basic ways: by converting the negative energy into neutral energy or into positive energy. By "neutral energy" I mean an activity or diversion that allows you to dissipate your anger without harming anyone. Physical exercise – like chopping wood, hitting golf balls, or pedaling a bicycle – is great for this. You can also make the conversion through mental exertion: Chess, cards, board games, and similar activities will not harm anyone, and yet will serve as sinks for sources of anger.

Better still, transform negative energy into positive. Rather than simply avoiding harming others, exuding positive energy can actually help others. Either way you help yourself, so why not aim for the higher path? Art is the primary channel here, be it writing a diary, poetry, short stories, or novels; playing, performing, or composing on a musical instrument; engaging in fine arts or crafts such as painting, sculpting, photography, or pottery; or participating in dynamic arts such as debating, acting, dancing, or cinematography. If you can learn to be a crucible for this kind of transformation, it will do you and others a world of good, and will put your negative emotions to the best possible use.

Finally, take note that many if not most of our negative feelings are aroused by our old familiar enemies, expectations and attachments. By diminishing our expectations and attachments – but not our achievements and enjoyments – we can decrease the frequency and intensity of negative feelings in the first place.

Exercise 4. Draw up a list of things that make you angry or occasions on which you became angry. Next to each, write the expectation or attachment that made your anger possible. What steps can you take to reduce your habitual expectations and attachments, and thus to maintain your equanimity? What steps can you take toward converting negative emotional energy into neutral or positive energy? Taking these steps builds the remaining stories of your philosophical house.

SAGACIOUS CHOICES

> **Chief among our gains must be reckoned this possibility of choice, the recognition of many possible ways of life, where other civilizations have recognized only one.**
> **– Margaret Mead**

We all make choices in life, on matters ranging from crucial to trivial, on a regular basis. A philosophy of life should give guidance when most required; that is, it should help us make the most difficult decisions.

If we think of life as a game, then we'd like to make our best move in each situation. However, as we have seen, in the game of life we are never guaranteed that a "best move" exists in any situation; nor are we sure that we could find it if it did. So we usually have to content ourselves with an imperfect or relative choice, namely choosing between a superior and an inferior move, or a wise decision and a foolish one. Even that can be difficult at times. This, however, is our greatest challenge: to make better choices as opposed to worse ones.

By now, I hope you have found some ideas and resources that help you formulate or elaborate your personal philosophy of life. If so, then you should now be in an improved position to assess what is better and worse for you, and to select and abide by those principles that increase your ease and reduce your dis-ease. Life itself is not a disease: It is an opportunity to experience all kinds of things. What you experience in life may not be entirely up to you – after all, with so many billions of people on earth, you are bound to get in the way of others' experiences (for better or worse) while having your own. Nonetheless, how you choose to make sense of your experiences is largely up to you. Be wise or foolish as you wish, and transform yourself accordingly. I hope that your philosophy of life inclines you toward positive transformations, in which case you will be joyous in the best of times and never far from ease even in the worst of times.

Exercise 5. Make a list of your life's most difficult decisions, and beside each one note the idea you used to guide your decision. These ideas are the furnishings of your philosophical house. Once you will have employed these MEANS to build and furnish your philosophical house, it will have become your philosophical home.

Part IV
Additional Resources

Appendix I

HIT PARADE OF IDEAS: NINETY-NINE USEFUL THINKERS IN PHILOSOPHICAL COUNSELING

Aristotle (384–322 B.C.E.)
Greek philosopher, scientist, and naturalist
Themes: logic, metaphysics, ethics
Refrain: the golden mean (avoiding extremes in ideals and behavior)
Greatest Hits: *Metaphysics, Nicomachean Ethics*
A student at Plato's Academy, Aristotle's main concern was knowledge, gathered through observing natural phenomena. He loved to categorize things (he even wrote a book called *Categories*). He virtually invented logic, and pioneered several sciences. He also tutored Alexander the Great. For almost two millennia, Aristotle was known as "The Philosopher."

Augustine (354–430 C.E.)
North African philosopher and theologian
Theme: original sin
Refrain: Redemption is not in this world.
Greatest Hits: *Confessions, City of God*
Augustine, Bishop of Hippo and a Platonist, happened to be in Rome when it was sacked by Alaric in 410. But Rome had already converted to Christianity, so was supposedly under God's protection. Augustine reconciled this problem by inventing the doctrine of original sin. He is also famous for a prayer in his *Confessions*: "Make me chaste – but not yet."

Marcus Aurelius (121–180 C.E.)
Roman emperor and stoic philosopher
Theme: Stoicism
Refrain: Do not overvalue what others can take from you.
Greatest Hit: *Meditations*
"Even in a palace it is possible to live well." Marcus Aurelius was not an entirely happy emperor, but consoled himself with Stoic philosophy. When people talk about "taking things philosophically," they usually

mean "Stoically" – that is, with indifference to worldly pains and pleasures.

Francis Bacon (1561–1626)
British philosopher and politician
Theme: empiricism
Refrain: Knowledge is power.
Greatest Hits: *Novum Organum, The Advancement of Learning*
The godfather of the scientific revolution, Bacon advocated generalizing from specific instances of observed phenomena into scientific laws or theories that could be tested by experiment. He died as a casualty of one of his own experiments, having developed pneumonia after trying to freeze chickens on Hampstead Heath.

Basho (Matsuo Munefusa) (1644–94)
Japanese haiku master
Theme: understanding beyond intellectualizing
Refrain: Truth abides in simplicity; ease of mind, in following natural laws.
Greatest Hit: *Narrow Road to the Interior*
Basho is perhaps the greatest haiku poet, using his mastery of this form to convey profound truths through deceptively simple yet powerful images. Influenced by the fourth-century B.C.E. philosopher Tchouang-tseu, Basho teaches that following nature's way is the best path for humans to tread.

Simone de Beauvoir (1908–86)
French philosopher and feminist
Theme: existentialism, feminism
Refrain: Moral responsibility, natural differences between the sexes
Greatest Hits: *The Second Sex, The Ethics of Ambiguity*
Simone de Beauvoir was a stalwart supporter of Jean-Paul Sartre's brand of existentialism, as well as his soul mate. She also wrote eloquently and philosophically about human sex difference and its social consequences.

Jeremy Bentham (1748–1832)
British philosopher
Theme: utilitarianism
Refrain: the greatest happiness of the greatest number
Greatest Hit: *Introduction to the Principles of Morals and Legislation*
The founder of utilitarianism, Bentham's primary argument was that actions are moral if they maximize pleasure and minimize pain for those affected by the actions. This is called the "hedonistic calculus." Bentham's waxed bones are clothed and on display in the cloisters of University College, London, which he founded. According to his will, his remains are carried into the senate each year, where he is recorded as "present but not voting."

Henri Bergson (1859–1941)
French philosopher and humanist; 1927 Nobel Prize for literature
Theme: vitalism, dynamism
Refrain: *élan vital* ("life force" not explainable by science)
Greatest Hit: *Creative Evolution*
Bergson criticized mechanistic and materialistic ways of looking at the
world, arguing for a more spiritual (but not necessarily religious)
approach to life.

George Berkeley (1685–1753)
Irish philosopher and bishop
Theme: idealism
Refrain: To be is to be perceived.
Greatest Hits: *A Treatise Concerning the Principles of Human
Knowledge, Three Dialogues Between Hylas and Philonous*
Berkeley denied the independent existence of material things, arguing that
reality is made up of minds and their ideas. "Things" exist only in so far
as they are perceived. Thus Berkeley came close to the Buddha's tenet
that phenomena are a creation of mind.

Bhagavad Gita, author anonymous (attributed to mythical sage Vyasa)
(250 B.C.E.–250 C.E.)
Ancient Indian epic poem, sixth book of the Mahabharata
Theme: spiritual consciousness, extinction of unwholesome craving, duty,
karma
Refrain: Atman equals Brahma: Your "personal" soul is part of the
divine Oversoul.
The Bhagavad Gita is full of useful teachings on human suffering, its
causes, and its cures. It espouses the classical doctrine of reincarnation
and progress on a spiritual path toward cosmic consciousness.

Helena Blavatsky (1831–91)
Russian theosophist
Theme: No religion higher than truth
Refrain: The esoteric teachings of all wisdom traditions share a common
root.
Greatest Hit: *Secret Doctrine*
"Madame Blavatsky," as she is best known, recombined theology with
philosophy to found the movement of theosophy. Her essential teaching
is that all mystical traditions – from East to West – contain transcendent
paths to higher truths which humans can discover and experience for
themselves. The universe is holographic; each part contains information
about the whole.

Anicius Boethius (circa 480–524 C.E.)
Roman philosopher, theologian, and consul
Themes: Platonism, Christianity, paganism
Refrain: the use of philosophy to gain perspective on all things
Greatest Hit: *The Consolation of Philosophy*
Boethius, a Roman aristocrat, rose to considerable power before falling
from favor and being sentenced to death. He wrote his masterpiece
awaiting execution in prison, and it remains an enduring and inspiring
work.

Martin Buber (1878–1965)
German-Jewish philosopher and theologian
Theme: human relations and human–divine relations
Refrain: I–It versus I–Thou
Greatest Hit: *I and Thou*
To Buber, relationships are either reciprocal and mutual connections
between equals, or a subject–object relationship involving a degree of
control of one over another. Relationships between humans, or between a
person and God, should be of the first order ("I–Thou," versus "I–It.")

Buddha (Siddhartha Gautama) (563–483 B.C.E.)
Indian sage and teacher
Theme: Buddhism
Refrain: how to get beyond sorrow
Greatest Hits: *The Four Noble Truths, Dhammapada,* and many Sutras
(teachings) recorded by his students and followers.
"Buddha" is a title meaning "the enlightened one" or "one who has
awakened to the truth."
Siddhartha Gautama is the founder of Buddhism. His teachings and
practices, which comprise an unorthodox branch of Indian theology/
philosophy, show the clearest way to lead a meaningful, useful,
compassionate, and pain-free life without invoking religious superstition.
Then again, some people practice Buddhism as a religion. Either way, its
heart is pure.

Albert Camus (1913–60)
French novelist and philosopher; 1957 Nobel Prize for literature
Theme: existentialism
Refrain: Do the right thing even if the universe is cruel or meaningless.
Greatest Hits: *The Stranger, The Plague*
Camus's novels and essays explored the experience of believing in
nothing beyond a person's individual freedom and actions, and the moral
implications of that way of thinking.

Thomas Carlyle (1795–1881)
Scottish man of letters, historian, and social critic
Theme: individualism, Romanticism
Refrain: Accomplishment is individual.
Greatest Hit: *On Heroes, Hero-Worship and the Heroic in History*
A lapsed Calvinist, Carlyle rejected both mechanistic and utilitarian ways
of looking at the world for a dynamic outlook. He believed in the
individual morality of a "strong just man" as opposed to the will of the
masses and the influence of ordinary events. Interestingly, he also believed
that no deceiver could ever found a great religion.

Chuang-tzu (369–286 B.C.E.)
Chinese philosopher-sage, second only to Lao-tzu as renowned Taoist
Theme: Taoism (understanding "The Way," the natural order of things)
Refrain: Learn to attain by *wu-wei,* "actionless action."
Greatest Hit: *The Complete Works of Chuang–tzu*
Chuang-tzu was an exemplary Taoist who would not have called himself
a Taoist at all. He sought ways to lead a life of benevolence and
righteousness, full of humor, free from strife, unbound by social and civil
conventions.

Confucius (Kung Fu Tzu) (551–479 B.C.E.)
Chinese philosopher, teacher, and government official
Theme: Confucianism
Refrain: Follow the Way through ritual, service, and duty.
Greatest Hit: *Analects*
Confucius advocated government by virtue rather than force. Happiness
is achieved by pursuing excellence in personal as well as public life. He
upheld piety, respect, religious ritual, and righteousness as the
components of harmonious living. His influence on Chinese culture is
comparable to if not greater than Aristotle's influence in the West.

Nichiren Daishonen (1222–82)
Japanese Buddhist monk, teacher, and reformer
Theme: Buddhism
Refrain: Buddha's Way is open to everyone, in this very lifetime.
Greatest Hit: "Nam-myoho-renge-kyo" (mantra embodying the Lotus Sutra)
Nichiren was a monk and scholar of Gautama's (Shakyamuni's) teachings,
who successfully challenged the corrupt Buddhist religious establishment of
his day. Nichiren distilled the Lotus Sutra into a powerful mantra, "Nam-
myoho-renge-kyo," which restored the essence of Buddhism to the
common people but also landed Nichiren in deep political trouble –
reminiscent of Socrates, Jesus, Luther, and similar reformers. He narrowly
escaped execution, and endured exile. But Nichiren's Buddhism thrives
world wide today through Soka Gakkai International.

René Descartes (1596–1650)
French philosopher and mathematician
Theme: skepticism, dualism
Refrain: I think, therefore I am.
Greatest Hits: *Meditations, Discourse on Method*
A founder of modern philosophy, Descartes gave us the full-blown
distinction between mind and matter ("Cartesian dualism"). He
emphasized the importance of certainty, achieved through doubt, as the
basis of knowledge. He strove to unify the sciences into one system of
knowing. He tutored Catherine, queen of Sweden.

John Dewey (1859–1952)
American philosopher, educator, and social reformer
Theme: pragmatism
Refrain: Inquiry is self-correcting.
Greatest Hits: *Reconstruction in Philosophy, Experience and Nature, The
Quest for Certainty*
Dewey popularized pragmatic, scientific, and democratic ideals. He
sought to make education value the process of inquiry in contrast to the
rote transmission of knowledge. Tragically, Dewey's philosophy was
taken to an extreme in later-twentieth-century American education,
resulting in the demonization of knowledge and the rote transmission of
barbarism in its place.

Ecclesiastes (circa third century B.C.E.)
A king in Jerusalem (Hebrew "Koheleth"), sometimes identified with
Solomon
Theme: life's purpose and conduct
Refrain: All is futility, and a striving after wind.
Greatest Hit: Ecclesiastes (a book of the Old Testament)
Ecclesiastes was concerned with the egoism and mortality of man. His
writings can be interpreted both optimistically and pessimistically, and
were sometimes banned by rabbis who thought them too hedonistic.
Ecclesiastes has provided titles to novelists, e.g., *Earth Abides* and *The
Sun Also Rises*. He gave the Byrds the lyrics to their hit "Turn, Turn,
Turn." He also provided several great aphorisms, e.g., "There is nothing
new under the sun," and "Cast your bread upon the waters."

Albert Einstein (1879–1955)
Jewish-German-American physicist, humanitarian; 1921 Nobel Prize for
physics
Theme: probing mysteries of reality
Refrain: We must uphold the ideals of kindness, beauty, and truth.
Greatest Hits: Special and General Theories of Relativity, Photoelectric
Effect, $E=mc^2$

Einstein is synonymous with genius, and was named the most brilliant mind of all time in a Y2K survey. Yet he was a humble person who saw deeply into nature's laws, who believed that the universe makes sense, and who advocated peaceful contemplation as man's highest calling. He deplored dictatorship and war, and had a celebrated correspondence with Freud on the essence of human nature.

Ralph Waldo Emerson (1803–82)
American philosopher, poet, essayist, and speaker
Theme: New England transcendentalism
Refrain: Humanity must discover its true potential within.
Greatest Hits: collected essays including "Self-Reliance," "History," "Spiritual Laws"
Emerson was the central figure of American idealism, also known as New England transcendentalism. A proponent of philosophy, arts, individualism, and harmony with nature, and an opponent of slavery and all forms of oppression, Emerson (and his circle, including Thoreau) left a remarkable legacy of enlightened thought, inspiring aphorism, and shining example of civic virtue.

Epictetus (circa 55–135 C.E.)
Roman philosopher and teacher
Theme: Stoicism
Refrain: attachment only to things completely within your own power (such as virtue)
Greatest Hits: *Discourses, Enchiridion*
A freed slave who tutored Marcus Aurelius, Epictetus focused on humility, philanthropy, self-control, and independence of mind. He was said to be more serene than the emperor whom he served.

Epicurus (341–270 B.C.E.)
Greek philosopher and teacher
Theme: practical wisdom
Refrain: superiority of contemplative over hedonistic pleasures
Greatest Hits: *On Nature* (fragments survive), *De Rerum Natura* (poem by Lucretius reflecting Epicurean philosophy)
Although Epicureanism has somehow become misidentified with hedonism ("Eat, drink, and be merry, for tomorrow we die"), Epicurus actually advocated moderate pleasures such as friendship and aesthetic pursuits. He founded one of the first communes ("The Garden"), and regarded philosophy as a practical guide to life. He may have been the original hippie.

Desiderius Erasmus (1466–1536)
Dutch humanist and theologian
Theme: liberalization of medieval Christian institutions

Refrain: Human spirit demands freedom from corruption, superstition, and dogma
Greatest Hits: *Praise of Folly, The Complaint of Peace*
Erasmus criticized and satirized the foibles of his day: chiefly, the stultifying effects of institutionalized religion upon mankind's aspirations. An ordained priest himself, Erasmus never felt at home in the cloisters or the monasticized universities of his day. An influential if rebellious thinker and scholar, his advice was sought by the power brokers of Europe.

Sigmund Freud (1856–1939)

Jewish-German physiologist, physician, psychologist, and inventor of psychoanalysis
Theme: What makes people tick?
Refrain: There is a scientific basis for understanding human thought and behavior.
Greatest Hits: *The Interpretation of Dreams, Civilization and Its Discontents*
Freud was a brilliant original thinker who endeavored to extend scientific laws into psychological domains. His theories remain current and controversial. He invented psychoanalysis, deeply influenced Western psychology, and attracted many talented disciples (e.g., Adler, Jung, Reich) who later broke with him and founded rival schools. Unknown to Freud, much of his philosophy of human nature was articulated by Thomas Hobbes almost three centuries earlier.

Mahatma Gandhi (1869–1948)

Indian philosopher, activist, and statesman
Theme: nonviolent resistance to oppression
Refrain: We can mobilize spiritual and moral force to attain worthy political ends.
Greatest Hit: *An Autobiography: The Story of My Experiments with Truth*
Gandhi adapted and applied key precepts of Indian philosophy (e.g., *ahimsa*, or non-harm) along with Thoreau's principles of civil disobedience to effect India's independence from British rule. His methods profoundly influenced Martin Luther King in America. Gandhi taught moral lessons to his oppressors by purifying his being into a "mirror" that nonviolently reflected their wrongdoing, so as to make them aware of it and mortified by it. Thus they would cease oppression of their own accord.

Khalil Gibran (1883–1931)

Lebanese-American poet and philosopher
Theme: Arab Romanticism

Refrain: imagination, emotion, power of nature
Greatest Hit: *The Prophet*
Gibran's beautiful book of philosophical musings and aphorisms has
become a perennial favorite among young adults.

Kurt Gödel (1906–78)
Czech-German-American mathematician, logician, and philosopher
Theme: incompleteness theorems
Refrain: Not everything can be proved or disproved.
Greatest Hit: *On Formally Undecidable Propositions of Principia
Mathematical and Related Systems I*
Kurt Gödel was able to prove, in 1931, that not every mathematical or
logical question can be answered. This effectively put an end to the
rationalist quest for perfect and complete knowledge. After emigrating to
America, Gödel kept Einstein company at Princeton's Institute for
Advanced Study and proved that time travel is not impossible. On the
eve of becoming a U.S. citizen, Gödel found a logical flaw in the
Constitution that would enable a dictator to take over legally. His friend
Oskar Morgenstern convinced him not to bring this to the judge's
attention at his swearing-in ceremony.

Thomas Green (1836–82)
British philosopher
Theme: idealism
Refrain: Being real means being related to other things.
Greatest Hit: introduction to his edition of Hume's work *Prolegomena to
Ethics*
Opposed to empiricism, Green regarded the mind as more than a
repository of perceptions, emotions, and experiences; rather, it is the seat
of rational consciousness, capable of producing relations, intentions, and
actions. His idea that all our beliefs are interdependent anticipated
Quine's famous "web of belief."

Tenzin Gyatso (fourteenth Dalai Lama) (1935–)
Tibetan Buddhist leader, exiled head of Tibetan state; 1989 Nobel Peace
Prize
Theme: Buddhism
Refrain: enlightenment, compassion, and world peace
Greatest Hit: *The Art of Happiness: A Handbook for Living*
The fourteenth Dalai Lama is the leading exponent of Tibetan Buddhism,
in the service of individual progress, human rights, and world peace.
Although his native land of Tibet has been occupied by China for fifty
years, his philosophical and political mission has been one of patient
reconciliation and compassionate teaching. Tibetans have endured a
terrible plight, and have responded by giving their gift of Buddhism to

the world. This philosophy is the polar opposite of terrorism, and the best hope for human decency and flourishing.

Georg Wilhelm Friedrich Hegel (1770–1831)
German philosopher
Theme: history, politics, logic
Refrain: freedom as self-consciousness in a rationally organized community
Greatest Hits: *The Phenomenology of Spirit, The Logic of Hegel, Encyclopedia of the Philosophical Sciences in Outline, The Philosophy of Right*
Hegel was and remains a very influential philosopher, with wide-ranging ideas about freedom, historical progress, the instability of self-consciousness and its dependence on recognition by others.
Unfortunately, Hegel also influenced Marx and Engels, and became an unwitting apologist for totalitarian doctrines.

Heraclitus of Ephesus (died after 480 B.C.E.)
Greek philosopher
Theme: change
Refrain: All things are in a state of flux; you can't step in the same river twice.
Greatest Hit: *On the Universe* (fragments survive)
Heraclitus advocated the unity of opposites, and was a proponent of *logos* (reason or knowledge) as an organizing force in the world.

Hillel (circa 70 B.C.E.–10 C.E.)
Babylonian-born rabbi, scholar, and legalist
Theme: morality, piety, humility
Refrain: What is hateful to you, do not to your neighbor.
Greatest Hit: *Seven Rules of Hillel* (practical applications of Jewish laws)
Hillel was one of the organizers of the first part of the Talmud, and an advocate of liberal interpretation of scripture. He was revered as a great sage, and his students defined Judaism for many generations.

Thomas Hobbes (1588–1679)
British philosopher
Theme: materialism, authoritarianism
Refrain: Humans are naturally in a war of "all against all," and need a common power "to keep them all in awe."
Greatest Hit: *Leviathan*
Thomas Hobbes founded the fields of political science and empirical psychology. He was the greatest philosopher since Aristotle, and knew it. He wanted for his epitaph "Here lies the true philosopher's stone." His view of humans as supremely egoistic, wildly passionate, easily misguided, constantly power hungry, and therefore highly dangerous

beings was enormously unpopular but apparently sound. He argued that politics must not be a branch of theology, and that only strong government can prevent violence and anarchy. He made much sense and many enemies. His philosophy anticipated Freudian psychology and provoked the Romantic countermovement championed by Rousseau. He tutored Prince Charles II in geometry while in exile during the English Civil War, but was forbidden to impart political instruction.

David Hume (1711–1776)
Scottish philosopher
Theme: empiricism
Refrain: "All our ideas are copied from our impressions."
Greatest Hit: *A Treatise of Human Nature*
The outstanding skeptical empiricist, Hume was nicknamed "the infidel." Opposed to Plato, he believed that no ideas are innate. He also denied the reality of the "self," the necessity of cause and effect, and the derivation of values from facts. All this made him quite unpopular for a time. He also suggested that metaphysical works be burned, and consoled himself with long walks, drinking, and gambling.

Aldous Huxley (1894–1963)
British essayist, novelist, and man of letters
Theme: individualism
Refrain: resistance to psychological conditioning, social engineering, political tyranny
Greatest Hits: *Brave New World, The Doors of Perception, The Perennial Philosophy*
Grandson of biologist T. H. Huxley ("Darwin's bulldog"), Aldous foresaw the dangers of supposing that science and social engineering would bring about utopia. As a warning, he created an enduring and prescient dystopia in *Brave New World*. A great intellectual, he explored consciousness, deplored war, experimented with psychedelia, and appreciated the wisdom of the East.

I Ching (*Book of Changes*), author(s) anonymous (circa twelfth century B.C.E.)
Theme: Tao, practical wisdom
Refrain: how to choose wise over foolish courses of action
The *I Ching* maintains that personal, familial, social, and political situations change according to natural laws which the wise understand and take into account when making decisions. By acting in accordance with Tao, one does the right thing at the right time, and thus makes the best of any situation. I have been consulting the *I Ching* for thirty years, and have never once regretted it.

Daisaku Ikeda (1928–)
Japanese Buddhist, educator, author, poet, and President of Soka Gakkai International
Theme: Buddhism
Refrain: enlightenment, compassion, and world peace
Greatest Hits: *The Human Revolution, The Living Buddha, Choose Life*
Daisaku Ikeda was the third president of Soka Gakkai, the lay organization devoted to practicing and teaching Nichiren's Buddhism. He is founding president of Soka Gakkai International, which carries Nichiren's Buddhism worldwide. He has authored and coauthored dozens of books, built universities in Japan and America, and sponsored many other cultural activities in the service of individual progress and global peace.

William James (1842–1910)
American psychologist and philosopher
Theme: pragmatism
Refrain: "cash-value" (an idea should be judged on how productive it is)
Greatest Hits: *Principles of Psychology, The Varieties of Religious Experience*
James revealed his dual interests in philosophy and psychology by taking a practical approach to philosophy (pragmatism), believing that an idea is "true" if it has useful results. He emphasized both experimental, laboratory approaches to psychology and analytical reflection on experience.

Cyril Joad (1891–1953)
British philosopher and psychologist
Theme: holism, humanism
Refrain: The universe is richer, more mysterious, and yet more orderly than we imagine.
Greatest Hits: *Guide to Modern Thought, Journey Through the War Mind*
Joad is a sadly neglected philosopher who believed in enriching the understanding via multiple and equivalently rewarding modes of inquiry: logical, mathematical, and scientific, but also aesthetic, ethical, and spiritual. A great moralist and humanist, he was also concerned with the philosophy and psychology of human conflict.

Carl Jung (1875–1961)
Swiss psychoanalyst and philosopher
Themes: collective unconscious, synchronicity
Refrain: developmental journey toward a final (spiritual) goal
Greatest Hits: *Psychological Types, Synchronicity*
Jung was originally Freud's leading disciple and heir apparent, but parted company with him over a major philosophical issue. While Freud

postulated a biological basis for every neurosis or psychosis, Jung came to believe that psychological problems are manifestations of unresolved spiritual crises. Jung wrote important introductions to the *I Ching* (Wilhelm-Baynes edition), and the *Tibetan Book of the Dead* (Evans-Wentz edition), making these great works more accessible to the West.

Immanuel Kant (1724–1804)
German philosopher
Theme: critical philosophy, moral theory
Refrain: the categorical imperative: "Act only on that maxim which you can at the same time will to become a universal law."
Greatest Hits: *Critique of Pure Reason, Prolegomena to the Metaphysics of Morals*
Kant was a very influential rationalist, who tried to ascertain the limits of reason. His theory of morality as duty to higher principles, not anticipation of consequences, is compelling to secular idealists.

Søren Kierkegaard (1813–55)
Danish philosopher and theologian
Theme: existentialism
Refrain: free will, individual choice
Greatest Hits: *Either/Or, The Sickness unto Death*
Kierkegaard – the first existentialist – rejected Hegel's systematic philosophy as well as organized religion. In his view, human judgment is incomplete, subjective, and limited. But we are also free to choose and responsible for our choices. Only by exploring and coming to terms with fundamental anxieties can we become liberated within our ignorance.

Martin Luther King Jr. (1929–68)
African-American leader of civil rights movement, peace activist, and essayist, 1964 Nobel Peace Prize
Theme: equal rights for all
Refrain: Political protest and social progress must be nonviolent.
Greatest Hits: *Letter from Birmingham Jail,* "I Have a Dream" (speech)
Dr. Martin Luther King Jr. successfully combined Thoreau's philosophy of civil disobedience with Gandhi's program of nonviolent resistance to oppression, and thus pioneered racial integration in America. King was a noble leader, impassioned writer, and charismatic orator. Sadly, many Americans (of all colors) have still not learned to judge people by "the content of their character," as King insisted they must for there to be racial harmony. Ignoring King, they mistake quota systems for social justice.

Arthur Koestler (1905–83)
Jewish-Hungarian intellectual, author, and social philosopher
Theme: freedom from political oppression

Refrain: Attempts to politicize or scientize humanity are misguided and harmful
Greatest Hits: *Darkness at Noon, The Ghost in the Machine*
Arthur Koestler, like George Orwell and many other Western intellectuals, initially viewed socialism and communism as utopian political movements, and was duped by Marxist-Leninist dialectic and Stalinist propaganda. But once his eyes were opened to the horrors of Soviet-style totalitarianism, Koestler wrote a brilliant and scathing exposé of the Bolshevik revolution – his novel *Darkness at Noon*. He went on to advocate human liberty and creativity in many forms, including freedom from behavioral science.

Alfred Korzybski (1879–1950)
Polish-American philosopher
Theme: general semantics
Refrains: Humans are uniquely aware of time ("time-binding" animals); conventional socialization and language promote unnecessary conflicts.
Greatest Hits: *Science and Sanity, Manhood of Humanity*
Korzybski is another neglected but important philosopher, who viewed the human animal as in its collective childhood, and suggested ways in which we might eventually mature as a species. He explained how structures of language and habits of thought condition and trigger destructive emotions, and sought ways to restructure our thinking.

Gottfried Wilhelm Leibniz (1646–1716)
German mathematician, philosopher, and historian
Theme: rationalism
Refrain: This is the best of all possible worlds.
Greatest Hits: *New Essays on the Human Understanding, Theodicy, Monadology*
While Voltaire lampooned Leibniz's belief that this is the "best of all possible worlds" via the character Dr. Pangloss in *Candide,* Leibniz did believe that everything happens for sufficient reasons, many of which, however, we cannot understand. Leibniz (at the same time as Newton) coinvented the calculus; he also invented binary numbers. He believed in free will.

Emmanuel Levinas (1906–95)
Jewish-French philosopher
Theme: the Other
Refrain: The existence of others compels us to be moral beings.
Greatest Hits: *Entre Nous: On Thinking-of-the-Other, Totality and Infinity*
Levinas was fundamentally concerned about the Western tendency to center philosophy and morality in one's own being, to the neglect of the

Other. Levinas's work on existential phenomenology has influenced Sartre, Merleau-Ponty, and Derrida.

John Locke (1632–1704)
British philosopher and physician
Theme: empiricism, science, politics
Refrain: Experience is the basis of knowledge; the human mind is a tabula rasa (blank slate) at birth.
Greatest Hits: *Essay Concerning Human Understanding, Two Treatises of Government*
Locke is one of the important British empiricists. Originally a physician, he saved the life of the earl of Shaftesbury by innovatively inserting a pipe to drain an abdominal abscess. This led him into favor with powerful people, who sought his philosophical advice. Politically, Locke argued for individual liberties and constitutional rule, which placed him ahead of his time in England and which exerted considerable influence on nascent American political thought.

Niccolò Machiavelli (1469–1527)
Italian *consiglieri*
Theme: political philosophy
Refrain: To be a successful leader you must act in whatever way works, without concern for conventional morality.
Greatest Hit: *The Prince*
With realism that was shocking at the time, Machiavelli declared that the world is not a moral place, and that politics, particularly, is not an ethical enterprise. Bertrand Russell called *The Prince* "a handbook for gangsters," but I'd say it's more like "Despotism for Dummies."

Thomas Mann (1875–1955)
German-American author; 1929 Nobel Prize for literature
Theme: the fate of art and civilization
Refrain: Cultural ebbs and flows constantly challenge our notion of progress.
Greatest Hits: *Buddenbrooks, Death in Venice, The Magic Mountain*
Mann foresaw the rise of fascism in Germany, and fled before it enveloped him. He wrote brilliantly about the struggle between great artistry and bourgeois society, and about the demise of classicism and civilization itself.

John McTaggart (1866–1925)
British philosopher
Theme: idealism
Refrain: Reality is more than material.
Greatest Hit: *The Nature of Existence*

McTaggart believed there was no God, but did believe in individual immortality. His philosophy of time (*b*-series) provides an enduring account of endurance.

John Stuart Mill (1806–73)
Scottish philosopher, economist, and politician
Theme: utilitarianism, libertarianism, egalitarianism
Refrain: individual liberty
Greatest Hits: *On Liberty, Utilitarianism, A System of Logic, On the Subjection of Women*
Mill thought restrictions on individual liberty should be allowed only to prevent harm to others, and was an ardent advocate of free speech, individual responsibility, and social egalitarianism. His brand of utilitarianism differed from Bentham's, in that Mill thought pleasure was not the sole measure of good. "Better Socrates dissatisfied than a pig satisfied," he asserted.

Michel de Montaigne (1533–92)
Jewish-French Renaissance thinker and essayist
Theme: search for truth
Refrain: One discovers truths about mankind by understanding oneself.
Greatest Hits: *Essays*
Montaigne questioned whether man is "superior" to beasts merely because he possesses (or thinks he possesses) true knowledge of the world. His skepticism made him distinguish between knowledge and wisdom.

George Edward Moore (1873–1958)
British philosopher
Theme: analytic philosophy, idealism
Refrain: "The defense of common sense." Goodness cannot be defined, but is intuitively understood.
Greatest Hit: *Principia Ethica*
Moore is most famous for his so-called "naturalistic fallacy," the mistake he claims we make when we try to identify "good" with any naturally existing object or property, or try to measure it in any way. Nonetheless, Moore did assert that actions can be right or wrong, even though "goodness" cannot be defined.

Lewis Mumford (1895–1990)
American humanist and writer
Theme: humanism
Refrain: sustaining and recovering our humanity in the face of technology
Greatest Hits: *Technics and Civilization, The Myth of the Machine*
Mumford has been called "the last great humanist." He had passionate

concern about the dehumanization of man by machine; about art, architecture, and the environment; about civilization and progress.

Iris Murdoch (1919–99)
British philosopher and novelist
Theme: religion and morality
Refrain: the reinstatement of purpose and goodness in a fragmented world
Greatest Hit: *The Sovereignty of Good*
Murdoch revived Platonism as an antidote to the lack of meaning and morality in the twentieth-century world. She conveyed her philosophy primarily and artfully through novels.

Leonard Nelson (1882–1927)
German philosopher
Theme: synthesis of rationalism and empiricism
Refrain: We can reason from our particular experiences to arrive at an understanding of universals.
Greatest Hit: *Socratic Method and Critical Philosophy*
Nelson made an invaluable contribution to philosophical practice by developing the theory and method of Socratic dialogue. When properly applied, Nelsonian Socratic dialogue provides definitive answers to universal questions, such as "What is liberty?," "What is integrity?," "What is love?," and so forth.

John von Neumann (1903–57)
Hungarian-American mathematician and philosopher
Theme: game theory, computing, physics
Refrain: In game theory, decision making in situations of risk, conflict of interest or uncertainty can be analyzed to find the best choice.
Greatest Hit: *Theory of Games and Economic Behavior* (with Oskar Morgenstern)
John von Neumann contributed brilliantly to several fields, including mathematics, computing theory, and quantum mechanics. His invention (with Morgenstern) of the theory of games marks the inception of an entirely new branch of mathematics, which has applications for philosophy, psychology, sociology, biology, economics, and political science – not to mention philosophical counseling.

Friedrich Nietzsche (1844–1900)
German philosopher
Theme: extravagant anticonventionalism
Refrain: the will to power, man versus superman
Greatest Hits: *Thus Spake Zarathustra, Beyond Good and Evil, The Genealogy of Morals*

Philosopher, poet, prophet, and syphilitic, Nietzsche's writings are rarely dull. He despised mainstream society and castigated Christianity as a religion for slaves. He advocated the emergence of an *übermensch* (superman) who would transcend conventional morality – an idea badly abused by the Nazis. Interestingly, he also appeals to postmodernists, whose politics tend toward the other extreme. This is a testament to Nietzsche's genius (or possibly lunacy). He penned pithy aphorisms, and cooked up much provocative food for thought (e.g., "God is dead," "Socrates was rabble.")

Martha Nussbaum (1947–)
American philosopher
Theme: legal, social, and global justice
Refrain: Ongoing educational reform is required to improve the state of the world.
Greatest Hits: *The Therapy of Desire, Sex and Social Justice*
Nussbaum is a distinguished scholar, professor, author, and activist. She has written numerous acclaimed books and works energetically to further women's causes as well as broader interests in legal, educational, and social issues.

José Ortega y Gasset (1883–1955)
Spanish philosopher, essayist, and humanist
Theme: political emancipation
Refrain: We must resist authoritarian regimes or succumb to tyranny.
Greatest Hit: *Revolt of the Masses*
Ortega y Gasset wrote eloquent essays on wide-ranging topics but is best known for his dire political predictions for modern man. He saw clearly that mass movements (like bolshevism and fascism) heralded the tyranny of mindless majorities ("mass-man"), under the sway of ruthless despots, over the thoughtful individual. Mass movements herald the demise of culture and the decay of civilization.

Blaise Pascal (1623–62)
French philosopher and mathematician
Theme: Enlightenment
Refrain: balancing theology and science to redefine man's place in the cosmos
Greatest Hits: *Provinciales, Pensées*
Pascal made many lasting contributions to mathematics (e.g., Pascal's triangle, probability theory) and formulated his famous decision-theoretic "wager": Is it better to believe or disbelieve in God's existence, given that God may or may not exist? (He calculated that it's better to believe.) Pascal viewed man as a self-contradictory being, an "incomprehensible monster," capable of extremes of greatness and misery alike.

Charles Sanders Peirce (1839–1914)
American philosopher and scientist
Theme: pragmatism
Refrain: Truth is an opinion we all ultimately agree on, and represents an objective reality.
Greatest Hits: *Collected Papers*
Peirce is the founding figure of American pragmatism, which was further and differently developed by Dewey and James. To distinguish his version from James's, Peirce coined the term "pragmaticism," which didn't quite catch on. Peirce's philosophy was criticized by Russell for its apparent subjectivity, but in fact Peirce was very scientific in his outlook.

Plato (circa 429–347 B.C.E.)
Greek philosopher and academician
Theme: essentialism
Refrains: The essences of goodness, beauty, and justice can be understood only through a philosophical journey.
Greatest Hits: *The Dialogues of Plato* (including the *Republic*)
Plato founded the Academy (the prototypical university) in Athens. His dialogues involving his teacher Socrates comprise most of what we know about Socrates' philosophy, so the ideas of Plato and Socrates can be difficult to tease apart. Plato is considered to be the founder of philosophical study and discourse as still practiced today.

Protagoras of Abdera (circa 485–420 B.C.E.)
Greek philosopher and teacher
Theme: relativism, sophism
Refrain: Man is the measure of all things.
Protagoras believed moral doctrines can be improved upon, even if their value is relative. He also believed virtue can be taught. He developed dialectical and rhetorical methods later popularized by Plato as the Socratic method. Although "sophistry" has an undeservedly pejorative connotation, the Sophists taught people, for a fee, how to argue persuasively for any given point of view, no matter how patently false or unjust. Thus the Sophists trained the first generation of lawyers.

Pythagoras (born circa 570 B.C.E.)
Greek philosopher and mathematician
Themes: metempsychosis and mathematics
Refrain: All things are based on geometric forms.
Greatest Hits: Pythagorean Theorem, Pythagorean Comma
More is attributed to Pythagoras than is known about him. He apparently taught the doctrine of metempsychosis (the transmigration of souls, or reincarnation), and refrained from eating beans. He is credited with the famous theorem of Euclidean geometry named after him. He is

also credited with the discovery that the twelve-tone (diatonic) musical scale does not permit instruments to be tuned perfectly. This anomaly eventually led to equal-temperament tuning at the time of J. S. Bach (e.g., *The Well-Tempered Clavier*).

Willard Quine (1908–2000)
American philosopher
Theme: analytic philosophy
Refrain: All beliefs depend on other beliefs.
Greatest Hit: *From a Logical Point of View*
Quine was the most important American philosopher of the latter half of the twentieth century. His contributions began in logic and set theory and continued in theories of knowledge and meaning. He is famous for challenging Kant, for shifting away from logical positivism, and for reframing Green's idea that beliefs are always held in conjunction with other beliefs.

Bhagwan Sri Rajneesh (1931–90)
Indian guru and philosopher
Theme: becoming one with the universe
Refrain: All mystical traditions contain valuable teachings and viable practices.
Greatest Hit: *Tao, the Pathless Path*
Rajneesh was among the most charismatic of eclectic gurus, according to the majority of seekers on the path who learned from him (*sannyasins*). He espoused a syncretistic blend of all the world's major religions, esoteric philosophies, therapeutic approaches, and yogic practices. Like many charismatic gurus, he was surrounded by both mystique and scandal.

Ayn Rand (1905–82)
Russian-born American writer and philosopher
Theme: objectivist ethics, Romantic capitalism (libertarianism)
Refrain: the virtues of egoism, the vices of altruism
Greatest Hits: *The Fountainhead, Atlas Shrugged, The Virtue of Selfishness*
Ayn Rand is an important, original thinker, who championed integrity and ability as keys to a productive and prosperous society. In her view, capitalism without exploitation (enlightened self-interest) is the best system; socialism with exploitation (unenlightened collective interest) is the worst. Rand's fictional capitalists are all schooled in philosophy, and they are all virtuous beings.

Sogyal Rinpoche (1946–)
Tibetan Buddhist, meditation master, teacher, and author
Theme: Buddhism

Refrain: enlightenment, compassion, and world peace
Greatest Hit: *The Tibetan Book of Living and Dying*
Sogyal Rinpoche is from the Dzogchen tradition of Tibetan Buddhism,
which teaches some powerful practices. He founded the Rigpa School in
London, which has grown into a network currently operating in eleven
countries. "Rigpa" means "innermost nature of the mind" – and Sogyal
Rinpoche has helped many glimpse it.

William Ross (1877–1971)
British philosopher
Theme: theory of prima facie obligations
Refrain: Some duties must be more stringently followed than others; the
priority depends on each case.
Greatest Hits: *The Right and the Good, Foundations of Ethics*
Ross points out that duties come into conflict, in the sense that we often
have to fulfill one obligation at the expense of another. His theory suggests
that we must prioritize our duties carefully, according to each situation.

Jean-Jacques Rousseau (1712–78)
Swiss philosopher
Theme: romanticism
Refrain: The human being is born a "noble savage" and is corrupted by
civilization.
Greatest Hits: *The Social Contract, A Discourse upon the Origin and
Foundation of the Inequality Among Mankind*
Rousseau focused on the rift between man and nature and the tension
between intellect and emotion, recommending nature and emotion as the
higher way of being. Although his Romanticism provides a
counterbalance to Hobbes's authoritarianism, Rousseau's philosophy of
education is a recipe for disaster.

Jelaluddin Rumi (1207–73)
Persian poet and Sufi master
Theme: union with Godhead
Refrain: Fullness comes through emptiness; understanding through
paradox.
Greatest Hits: *Teachings of Rumi, The Essential Rumi*
Rumi's scholarly life was transformed when he encountered a dervish,
Shams of Tabriz. He became one himself. His poems are a breath of
fresh air; they cajole and sting one into awareness. No subject is taboo
for Rumi: He delights in surprise and candor.

Bertrand Russell (1872–1970)
British philosopher; 1950 Nobel Prize for literature
Theme: realism, empiricism, logic, social and political philosophy

Refrain: Philosophy is an unusually ingenious attempt to think fallaciously.
Greatest Hits: *Principia Mathematica* (co-authored by Whitehead), *History of Western Philosophy, Human Knowledge: Its Scope and Limits, Unpopular Essays*
Russell published more than seventy books in his lifetime; his philosophical analyses ranged over every conceivable subject. He was a great and learned man who did not shy away from political causes and social controversy. He was famously denied a position at the City College of New York, after a New York State court declared him to be an immoral influence on society, mostly because of his then avant-garde (now commonplace) views on open marriage and divorce. While the Athenians killed Socrates for allegedly "corrupting its youth," Americans merely denied Russell employment. Russell might have conceded that this implies social progress.

George Santayana (1863–1952)
Spanish-American philosopher, poet, and literary and cultural critic
Theme: classical American philosophy
Refrain: Philosophy and literature should be guides to what is valuable in life.
Greatest Hits: *The Life of Reason, The Last Puritan*
Santayana was a highly creative and cultured philosopher. Born and raised in Spain, he later taught at Harvard for eight years and became enormously influential in American culture, mostly through popular books. But he spent the balance of his adult life in Europe, as a writer, and refused prestigious appointments in the Ivy League and Oxbridge in order to escape the "thistles of trivial and narrow scholarship" so prevalent in the academy. He prized creativity and intellectual freedom above all else.

Jean-Paul Sartre (1905–80)
French philosopher and novelist; 1964 Nobel Prize for literature
Theme: existentialism, politics, Marxism
Refrain: Free will: "Bad faith" comes from denying responsibility for our actions.
Greatest Hits: *Nausea, Being and Nothingness, Existentialism Is a Humanism*
Sartre was the leading French intellectual of his age. He studied with Husserl (the founder of phenomenology) and Heidegger (the leading German figure in existentialism). A Marxist by conviction, Sartre attempted to found a political party in France. Notwithstanding his Marxist commitments, Sartre staunchly defended his belief in individual responsibility.

Arthur Schopenhauer (1788–1860)
German philosopher
Theme: volition, resignation, pessimism
Refrain: The will stands outside space and time, but following its dictates leads to misery in no time at all.
Greatest Hit: *The World As Will and Idea*
Schopenhauer was well educated, fluent in many European and classical tongues, and had a notoriously difficult relationship with his mother. He is famous for trying and failing to dislodge Hegel, whom he regarded as a sophist and charlatan. He sought refuge from emotional suffering in Indian philosophy. He wrote pungent essays and acerbic aphorisms, and was one of the few philosophers whom Wittgenstein read or admired. Whether this bodes well or ill for Schopenhauer depends on whether you read or admire Wittgenstein.

Lucius Seneca (4 B.C.E.–65 C.E.)
Roman philosopher and statesman
Theme: Stoicism, ethics
Refrain: Philosophy, like life, should be primarily about virtue.
Greatest Hits: *Moral Letters*
Seneca rose from obscurity in provincial Cordoba to become Emperor Nero's tutor, lieutenant, and ultimately victim. Seneca lived and died according to the moral dictates of Stoicism, enduring hardship, triumph, and death with equanimity. He committed suicide in the Roman tradition, by opening his veins in a hot bath, when commanded to do so by the insanely paranoid Nero.

Shantideva (685–763)
Indian Buddhist monk, teacher, and writer
Theme: Madhyamika Buddhism
Refrain: how to help oneself and others escape from suffering
Greatest Hit: *The Way of the Bodhisattva*
Shantideva's teachings about the sources of suffering, and its extinction, are particularly clear and compassionate – and also provocative. The Dalai Lama himself reveals that Shantideva's teachings exerted a profound influence on his understanding and practice.

Socrates (circa 470–399 B.C.E.)
Greek philosopher and teacher
Theme: Socratic method
Refrain: The good life is the examined life, spent pursuing wisdom at all costs.
Greatest Hits: Socrates' ideas are preserved only in Plato's dialogues, so it is sometimes difficult to separate Socrates the man from Socrates the character, and to distinguish between Socrates' thoughts and

Plato's. Nonetheless, the historical Socrates and the historical Plato are easier to separate. Socrates (like the Buddha, Jesus, and Gandhi) was an influential sage who had no official employment or position, but whose wisdom attracted important followers and has grown in stature since his death. Socrates saw himself as a political gadfly, constantly stinging Athenians into awareness of their philosophical shortcomings. He allowed himself to be put to death by the corrupted state, because his reasoned argument compelled him to remain even though his friends had arranged his escape. Thus he prized philosophy above life itself. Plato never forgave the Athenians for executing Socrates. Christians believe that Jesus died to redeem mankind from sin; it may be secularly asserted that Socrates died to redeem philosophers from unemployment.

Baruch Spinoza (1632–77)
Jewish-Dutch philosopher and lens grinder
Theme: rationalism
Refrain: All knowledge can be deduced.
Greatest Hits: *Tractatus Theologico-Politicus, Ethics*
Spinoza's views managed to get him expelled from the Jewish community, while his writings were attacked and banned by Christian theologians. He even attracted hostility in tolerant Holland, where he had taken philosophical refuge. Spinoza believed that self-preservative human passions (i.e., appetites and aversions) lead to predetermined acts, but that we can become free by liberating our reason from the shackles of passion. Like Hobbes, Spinoza thought that we do not like something because it is good; rather, we call something "good" because we like it.

Thomas Szasz (1920–)
American psychiatrist
Theme: abuses of medicine
Refrain: "Mental illness" is not real disease.
Greatest Hit: *The Myth of Mental Illness*
Szasz is an important and controversial figure in American medicine: a psychiatrist who asserts that the notion of "mental illness" is not scientific, but ultimately political. His claim is that psychiatry has been used mostly for the purpose of social control, and therefore that its "diagnostic" literature is largely bogus.

Rabindranath Tagore (1861–1941)
Indian humanist, poet, playwright, and writer; 1914 Nobel Prize for literature
Theme: love of humanity
Refrain: stalwart humanism, transcendent moral sensibility, abundant creativity

Greatest Hits: *The Post Office, The Home and the World*
Tagore was a remarkable human being whose poems, plays, and stories of his native Bengal touched the world with their universality of feeling and compassion. He, like Gandhi (with whom he publicly disagreed at times), was a truly great soul.

Paul Tillich (1886–1965)
German-American philosopher and theologian
Theme: Christian philosophy and theology
Refrain: the inevitability of man's search for God
Greatest Hit: *The Dynamics of Faith*
Tillich is an interesting and important modern Christian philosopher, whose works juxtapose existential problems concerning being and time with solutions offered by Christian theology.

Henry David Thoreau (1817–62)
American writer, poet, and philosopher
Theme: New England transcendentalism (libertarianism)
Refrain: the unquestionable ability of man to elevate his life by conscious endeavor
Greatest Hits: *Walden*, "Civil Disobedience"
Thoreau advocated simplicity, individual responsibility, and communing with the natural environment as keys to the good life. He lived and breathed his philosophy. His theory of civil disobedience exerted seminal influence on both Gandhi and Martin Luther King Jr.

Chogyam Trungpa (1939–87)
Tibetan meditation master, scholar, and artist
Theme: Shambhala
Refrain: The experience of "being" with immediacy, dignity and totality
Greatest Hit: *Shambhala: The Sacred Path of the Warrior*
Trungpa founded Naropa Institute, and developed Shambhala training for aspirants on the path of wholesome existence within themselves and among others. His teachings are fascinating and unique.

Lao-tzu (circa sixth century B.C.E.)
Chinese philosopher
Theme: Taoism
Refrain: complementarity of opposites, attainment without contention, harmonious relations
Greatest Hit: *Tao Te Ching (The Way and Its Power)*
Lao-tzu's identity and the century he lived in are still debated, but regardless, his ideas on living a life in harmony with the Way remain powerful and influential. He appears to have been a senior civil servant who wrote down his philosophy on retirement – apocryphally at the

behest of a border guard, who wouldn't let him leave the province otherwise. He penned a truly great philosophical guide, and thereby founded Taoism.

Sun-tzu (circa fourth century B.C.E.)
Chinese military advisor
Theme: philosophy of warfare
Refrain: Being unconquerable lies with yourself.
Greatest Hit: *The Art of War*
Sun-tzu redefined conflict as a philosophical art form. He taught that the "pinnacle of excellence" is to subjugate your foe without fighting. His philosophy of warfare can be applied analogously to many other kinds of human conflict, from marital strife to office politics.

Voltaire (François Marie Arouet) (1694–1778)
French philosopher, writer, and scathing wit
Theme: French Enlightenment
Refrain: telling it "like it is"
Greatest Hit: *Candide*
Imprisoned for satirizing the government and exiled for insulting a nobleman, Voltaire pulled no verbal punches. His wit has since endeared him to many. He savagely parodied Leibniz's idealism in *Candide*. He is reputed to have said on his deathbed, to priests who gave him one last chance to renounce Satan, "This is no time for making new enemies."

Max Weber (1864–1920)
German philosopher of society
Theme: scientific study of society (sociology)
Refrain: understanding subjective meanings that people attach to social actions
Greatest Hit: *The Protestant Ethic and the Spirit of Capitalism*
Weber was one of the founders of sociology. He endeavored to explicate social phenomena of his day, ranging from bureaucracy to the Protestant work ethic. These among other phenomena still persist, and his explanations remain relevant.

Alfred North Whitehead (1861–1947)
British philosopher
Theme: empiricism
Refrain: Natural science should study the content of our perceptions.
Greatest Hits: *Principia Mathematica* (a collaboration with Russell), *The Concept of Nature, Process and Reality*
Whitehead sought a unified interpretation of everything from physics to psychology.

Elie Wiesel (1928–)
Jewish-Romanian-American humanist, scholar, and author; 1986 Nobel Peace Prize
Theme: exploring life's deepest mysteries
Refrain: We must live as though God exists.
Greatest Hits: *Night, The Forgotten, All Rivers Run to the Sea*
Survivor of Auschwitz, seasoned journalist, professor of humanities, scholar of Judaic lore, interpreter of the Book of Job, and witness for mankind, Wiesel has authored more than forty works. A great soul, he teaches forgiveness alongside remembrance.

Ludwig Wittgenstein (1889–1951)
Austrian philosopher
Theme: philosophy of language
Refrain: the scope and limits of language language as a social instrument
Greatest Hits: *Tractatus Logico-Philosophicus, Philosophical Investigations*
Wittgenstein believed that philosophy has at least one "therapeutic" task: to clarify misunderstandings and imprecisions of language which themselves give rise to philosophical problems. He is one of the most influential philosophers of the twentieth century.

Mary Wollstonecraft (1759–97)
British philosopher and feminist
Theme: egalitarianism
Refrain: Social function should not be based on sex difference.
Greatest Hits: *Vindication of the Rights of Women, Vindication of the Rights of Men*
Wollstonecraft was ahead of her time in asserting women's rights. She wrote articulately and persuasively in favor of egalitarianism. Her correspondence with the great conservative Edmund Burke is illuminating. She was the mother of Mary Shelley, who wrote *Frankenstein*.

Zeno of Elea (490–430 B.C.E.)
Eleatic philosopher
Theme: Parmenidean philosophy
Refrain: denial that change and motion can take place
Greatest Hits: four paradoxes of motion
In defense of his teacher Parmenides and against the doctrines of Pythagoras, Zeno wanted to show that our ordinary sensations of the world, including change and motion, are illusory. To this end he devised four paradoxes produced from common experience of motion, which were not satisfactorily resolved for twenty-three centuries.

Appendix 2

ORGANIZATIONS FOR PHILOSOPHICAL PRACTICE

American Philosophical Practitioners Association (APPA)

The APPA, founded in 1999, is a nonprofit educational corporation that encourages philosophical awareness and advocates leading the examined life. APPA members apply philosophical systems, insights, and methods to the management of human problems and the amelioration of human estates. APPA membership is open to all.

Certified Memberships
Certified memberships are conferred on qualified philosophers who complete APPA training programs and meet other requirements. Certified members are listed in the APPA Directory of Certified Practitioners, and are eligible for referrals and other professional benefits. Certified members are bound by the APPA Code of Ethical Professional Practice, and are committed to regular professional development.

Affiliate Memberships
Affiliate memberships are offered to recognized counseling or consulting professionals in other fields (e.g., medicine, psychiatry, psychology, social work, management, law) who wish to be identified with and become better acquainted with philosophical practice, but who do not necessarily seek APPA certification. Qualified affiliates may become certified.

Adjunct Memberships
Adjunct memberships are offered to holders of an accredited M.A. or Ph.D. in philosophy, or to those with equivalent philosophical backgrounds. Adjunct members are eligible to attend APPA certification training programs, from primary (level I) to advanced (level II), completion of which enables them to become certified members.

Auxiliary Memberships
Auxiliary memberships are offered to friends and supporters of philosophical practice.

The APPA Auxiliary welcomes all who wish to join in this capacity – including students, workers, or retired persons. No special qualifications are necessary, beyond an interest in leading an examined life.

All APPA members receive our newsletter, invitations to events, and other benefits.

The APPA is an inclusive organization. It admits certified, affiliate, and adjunct members solely on the basis of their respective qualifications, and admits auxiliary and organizational members solely on the basis of their interest in and support of philosophical practice. The APPA does not discriminate with respect to either members or clients on the basis of nationality, race, ethnicity, sex, gender, age, religious belief, political persuasion, or other professionally or philosophically irrelevant criteria. For online membership forms and other data, visit the APPA Web site at www.appa.edu, or write to:

APPA
The City College of New York
137th Street at Convent Avenue
New York, NY 10031
tel: 212-650-7827
fax: 212-650-7409
e-mail: admin@appa.edu

Foreign National Organizations

Canada
Canadian Society for Philosophical Practice
1119-942 Yonge Street
Toronto, Ontario M4W 3S8
Canada
tel: 416-935-1694
info@philosophicalpractice.ca
www.philosophicalpractice.ca

President, Michael Picard
Secretary/Treasurer, Sylvia O'Callaghan-Brown

Finland
Finnish Society for Philosophical Counseling
Tykistonkatu 11 B 30
SF-00260 Helsinki
Finland
asmattil@helsinki.fi

President, Antti Mattila
Vice President, Arto Tukiainen

Germany
International Society for Philosophical Practice
Hermann-Loens Strasse 56c
D-51469 Bergisch Gladbach
Germany
tel: 2202-951903 fax: 2202-951907
achenbach@igpp.org
www.igpp.org

President, Gerd Achenbach
www.achenbach-pp.de

Israel
Israel Society for Philosophical Inquiry
Horkania 23, Apt. 2
Jerusalem 93305
Israel
tel: 972-2-679-5090
msshstar@pluto.mscc.huji.ac.il
www.geocities.com/Athens/Forum/5914

Chief Inquirer, Shlomit Schuster

Netherlands
Dutch Society for Philosophical Practice (VFP)
W.vanderVlist@tebenet.nl

President, Yvonne Verweij
Postelstraat 42a, 5211 EB Den Bosch
Netherlands
tel: +31-736138126
yvonne.verweij@wxs.nl

Secretary, Wim van der Vlist
Ed. Schilderinkstraat 80, 7002 JH Doetinchem
Netherlands
tel: +31-31433470.

Treasurer/membership administration, Dick Kleinlugtenbelt
Cattepoelseweg 14, 6821 JW Arnhem
Netherlands
tel: +31-264437250

Norway
Norwegian Society for Philosophical Practice
Cappelens vei 19c
1162 Oslo
Norway
tel: 47-88-00-96-69
contactus@nsfp.no
www.nsfp.no

President, Henning Herrestad

Slovakia
Slovak Society for Philosophical Practice
Department of Social & Biological Communication
Slovak Academy of Sciences
Klemensova 19, 81364 Bratislava
Slovakia
tel: 00421-7-375683
fax: 00421-7-373442
e-mail: ksbkemvi@savba.sk

President, Emil Visnovsky

United Kingdom
Society for Philosophy in Practice
2 Wynnstow Park
Oxted, Surrey, RH8 9DR
United Kingdom
www.society-for-philosophy-in-practice.org

Chair, Nigel Laurie
nigel.laurie@managementphilosophers.com

Vice Chair, Susan Wright
susanewri@aol.com

Editor in Chief of the PPP, Tim LeBon
timlebon@aol.com

Appendix 3

DIRECTORY OF APPA-CERTIFIED
PHILOSOPHICAL PRACTITIONERS

For the most current listings, please visit our Web site at www.appa.edu.

United States

Alabama
James Morrow, Jr.
1055 W. Morrow St.
Elba, AL 36323
tel: 334-897-6522
counselor

Arizona
Richard Dance
6632 East Palm Lane
Scottsdale, AZ 85257
tel: 480-947-4288
fax: 480-429-0737
e-mail:
    rdance@mindfulmedicine.com
counselor

Paul Gatto
3983 N. Paseo de la Canchas
Tucson, AZ 85716
tel: 520-881-9053
e-mail: pgatto@ucsd.edu
counselor

Robert Nagle
8075 E. Morgan Trail
Suite #1
Scottsdale, AZ 85258
tel: 480-649-8430
tel: 480-905-7325
fax: 480-969-5322
counselor

California
Peter Atterton
1566 Missouri Street
San Diego, CA 92109
tel: 858-274-2977
e-mail: atterton@rohan.sdsu.edu
counselor

Wills Borman
22477 Highway 94
Dulzura, CA 91917
tel: 619-468-9693
e-mail: wborman@mindspring.com
counselor

Harriet Chamberlain
1534 Scenic Avenue
Berkeley, CA 94708
tel: 510-548-9284
e-mail: think@flash.net
counselor, facilitator

Kyle Dupen
303 Avenue Cabrillo
Half Moon Bay, CA 94019
tel: 650-726-2522
e-mail: kdupen@coastside.net
counselor

Julie Grabel
Academy of Philosophical
   Midwifery
1011 Brioso Dr. #109
Costa Mesa, CA 92627
tel: 949-722-2206
fax: 949-722-2204
e-mail: julieg@deltanet.com
counselor

Pierre Grimes
Academy of Philosophical
   Midwifery
947 Capital
Costa Mesa, CA 92627
tel: 949-722-2206
fax: 949-722-2204
e-mail: pierreg@concentric.et
counselor, APPA faculty

Sushma Hall
315 W. Radcliffe Drive
Claremont, CA 91711
tel: 909-626-2327
e-mail: sushmahall@hotmail.com
counselor

John Hanley Jr.
34341 Aukland Ct.
Fremont, CA 94555
tel: 510-792-7346
fax: 561-679-7769
e-mail: johnhanleyir@msn.com
counselor, facilitator

James Heffernan
Department of Philosophy
University of the Pacific
Stockton, CA 95211
tel: 209-946-3094
e-mail: jheffernan@uop.edu
counselor

Michael Hermon
1306 Via Del Rio
Corona, CA 92882
tel: 909-898-5962
e-mail: mhermon@msn.com
counselor

Gerald Hewitt
Department of Philosophy
University of the Pacific
Stockton, CA 92511
tel: 209-946-2282
e-mail: ghewitt@uop.edu
counselor

Robert Makus
Department of Philosophy
University of San Francisco
2130 Fulton Street
San Francisco, CA 94117
tel: 415-422-2414
e-mail: makusr@usfca.edu
counselor

Lou Matz
Department of Philosophy
University of the Pacific
Stockton, CA 95211
tel: 209-946-3093
e-mail: lmatz@uop.edu
counselor

Jason Mierek
8831 Hillside St. #C
Oakland, CA 94605
tel: 510-777-0923
e-mail: jmierek@msn.com
counselor

Christopher McCullough
175 Bluxome St., #125
San Francisco, CA 94107
tel: 415-357-1456
e-mail: cmccul1787@aol.com
counselor, facilitator

J. Michael Russell
Philosophy and Human Services
California State University
Fullerton, CA 92834
tel: 714-278-2752
fax: 714-278-1274
e-mail: jmrussell@fullerton.edu
counselor, APPA faculty

Paul Sharkey
819 West Avenue H-5
Los Angeles, CA 93534
tel: 661-726-0102
cell: 661-435-3077
fax: 661-726-0307
e-mail: pwsharkey@email.msn.com
counselor, facilitator, consultant,
    APPA faculty

Regina Uliana
16152 Beach Blvd.
#200 East
Huntington Beach, CA 92647
tel: 714-841-0663
fax: 714-847-8685
e-mail: rlu@deltanet.com
counselor

Lawrence White
1345 Arch Street
Berkeley, CA 94708
tel: 510-845-0654
fax: 510-845-0655
e-mail: LWWHITEMD@aol.com
counselor

Eleanor Wittrup
Department of Philosophy
University of the Pacific
Stockton, CA 95211
tel: 209-946-3095
counselor

Kritika Yegnashankaran
tel: 650-654-5991
e-mail: kritika@stanfordalumni.org
counselor

Martin Young
1102 S. Ross Street
Santa Ana, CA 92707
tel: 714-569-9225
e-mail: mzyoung@uci.edu
counselor

Colorado
Jeanette Crooks
1239 S. Iris Street
Lakewood, CO 80232
tel: 303-980-8346
e-mail: myrtlemaryj@aol.com
counselor

Alberto Hernandez
1112 N. Wahsatch, Apt. A
Colorado Springs, CO 80903
tel: 719-448-0337
e-mail:
    aherandez@coloradocollege.edu
counselor

Ania Rowan
1633 4th Street
Boulder, CO 80302
tel: 303-786-8068
e-mail: ania@qwest.net
counselor

District of Columbia
Alicia Juarrero
4432 Volta Place NW
Washington, D.C. 20007
tel: 202-342-6128
fax: 202-342-5160
e-mail: ja83@umail.umd.edu
counselor

Professor Wilfried ver Eecke
Department of Philosophy
Georgetown University
Washington, DC 20057
tel: 202-687-7613
fax: 202-687-4493
e-mail: Vereeckw@Georgetown.edu
counselor

Florida
Robert Beeson
1225 Osceola Dr.
Fort Myers, FL 33901
tel: 941-332-7788
fax: 941-332-8335
e-mail: rbsun@cyberstreet.com
counselor

Carl Colavito
The Biocultural Research Institute
7131 NW 14th Avenue
Gainesville, FL 32605
tel: 904-461-8804
fax: 352-332-9931
e-mail: encc@aug.com
counselor

Maria Colavito
The Biocultural Research Institute
7131 NW 14th Avenue
Gainesville, FL 32605
tel: 352-332-9930
fax: 352-332-9931
e-mail: diotima245@aol.com
counselor

Antonio T. de Nicolas
The Biocultural Research Institute
7131 NW 14th Avenue
Gainesville, FL 32605
tel: 352-332-9930
fax: 352-332-9931
e-mail: diotima245@aol.com
counselor

Charles Poole
75 SW 75 Street, #C-14
Gainesville, FL 32607
tel: 352-332-3691
e-mail:
    charlespoole@sprintmail.com
counselor

Georgia
Christopher Graves
1721 Kings Down Circle
Altanta, GA 30338
tel: 770-396-5507
e-mail: nous777@compuserve.com
counselor

Mark M. du Mas
2440 Peachtree Road NW
Number 25
Atlanta, GA 30305
tel: 404-949-9113
fax: 404-846-0081
e-mail: mmdumas@msn.com
counselor, consultant

Illinois
Avner Baz
5555 N. Sheridan Road
Chicago, IL 60640
tel: 773-784-4728
e-mail: abaz2@uic.edu
counselor

F. Byron (Ron) Nahser
President & CEO
The Nahser Agency, Inc.
10 South Riverside Plaza
Suite 1830
Chicago, IL 60606
tel: 312-750-9220
fax: 312-845-9075
e-mail: fbnahser@nahser.com
consultant

Tim Weldon
University of St. Francis
500 Wilcox
Joliet, IL 60435
tel: 815-740-3451
e-mail: timweldon20@hotmail.com
counselor

Indiana
Karen Iseminger
19814 Tomlinson Road
Westfield, IN 46074
tel: 317-758-4913
e-mail: kiseminger@uindy.edu
counselor

Maryland
Ruth Kastner
125 Hedgewood Drive
Greenbelt, MD 20770
e-mail: vze445xa@verizon.net
http://www.wam.umd.edu//
    rkastner/counselor

Sidney Rainey
P.O. Box 1451
Bethesda, MD 20827
tel: 505-983-7011
e-mail: sidneyrainey@earthlink.com
consultant

J. Carol Williams
4010 32nd Street
Mt. Rainier, MD 20712
tel: 301-779-4755
e-mail: bar2jcw@yahoo.com
counselor

Minnesota
Todd Wadsworth
2048 Summit Avenue
St. Paul, MN 55105
tel: 651-698-8066
e-mail: trw41@mail.com
counselor

Missouri
David Hilditch
7439 Wayne Avenue
St. Louis, MO 63130
tel: 314-727-1675
e-mail: hilditch@wnr.com
counselor

Montana
Sean O'Brien
Davidson Honors Hall
University of Montana
Missoula, MT 59812
tel: 406-243-6140
counselor

Nevada
Claude Gratton
Philosophy Department
University of Las Vegas at Nevada
4505 Maryland Parkway, Box
  455028
Las Vegas, NV 89154
tel: 702-895-4333
voice mail: 702-897-3727
e-mail: grattonc@nevada.edu
counselor

New Hampshire
James Donelan
35 Blueberry Lane
Peterborough, NH 03458
tel: 603-924-9628
e-mail: donelaj@fpc.edu
counselor

New Jersey
Peter Dlugos
355 Lincoln Ave., Apt. 1C
Cliffside Park, NJ 07010
tel: 201-943-8098
e-mail: pdlugos@bergen.cc.nj.us
e-mail: pdlugos@aol.com
counselor, facilitator

Amy Hannon
2 River Bend Road
Clinton, NJ 08809
tel: 908-735-0728
e-mail: ardea@csnet.net
counselor

Vaughana Feary
37 Parker Drive
Morris Plains, NJ 07950
tel/fax: 973-984-6692
e-mail: VFeary@aol.com
counselor, facilitator, consultant,
  APPA faculty

Jean Mechanic
1365 North Avenue, Apt. 9D
Elizabeth, NJ 07208
tel: 908-351-9605
e-mail: mechanicdr@aol.com
counselor

Charles Ottinger
206 Davis Station Rd., Box 98
Imlaystown, NJ 08526
tel: 609-259-4187
e-mail: cfottinger@earthlink.net
counselor

New Mexico
Jennifer Goldman
619 Don Felix St., Apt.B
Santa Fe, NM 87501
tel: 505-982-9189
counselor

New York
Richard Allen
150 Joralemon St., #10B,
Brooklyn, NY 11201
tel: 718-852-4149
http://client-centered.com
counselor

Barbara Cutney
782 West End Avenue, #81
New York, NY 10025
tel: 212-865-3828
counselor, consultant

Micah Daily
44 Avenue B
New York, NY 10009
tel: 212-477-9641
micah_daily@hotmail.com
counselor

Michael Davidovits
Psychiatry, Mt. Sinai Medical
    Center
Box 1228
New York, NY 10029
tel: 212-241-6881
e-mail: michael.davidovits@
    mountsinai.org
counselor

Andrew Gluck
392 Central Park West, #8C
New York, NY 10025
tel: 212-316-2810
fax: 212-316-4982
e-mail: andy_gluck@msn.com
consultant

Edward Grippe
117 Lakeside Drive
Pawling, NY 12564
tel: 914-855-0992
fax: 914-855-3997
e-mail: ejgphil@aol.com
counselor

Michael Grosso
26 Little Brooklyn Road
Warwick, NY 10990
tel: 845-258-4283
e-mail: mgrosso@warwick.net
counselor

Rony Guldmann
178 W 82 Street, Apt. 1
New York, NY 10024
tel: (917) 596-5723
e-mail:
    ronyguldmann@hotmail.com
counselor

George Hole
291 Beard Avenue
Buffalo, NY 14214
tel: 716-832-6644
e-mail: holegt@buffalostate.edu
counselor, consultant

Craig Irvine
220 Manhattan Ave., Apt. 5V
New York, NY 10025
tel: 212-305-0980
e-mail: irvinec@cpmc3.cpmc.
    columbia.edu
counselor

Chris Johns
Department of Philosophy, 213
    Harriman
SUNY Stony Brook, NY 11794
e-mail: cjohns@ic.sunysb.edu
counselor

Onno de Jong
348 East 9th St. #16
New York, NY 10003
tel: 212-982-3188
fax: 845-236-4416
e-mail: onno@erols.com
counselor

David R. Koepsell, JD/PhD
Adjunct Assistant Professor, Dept.
    of Philosophy
SUNY Buffalo
tel: 716-913-2422
fax: 689-1498 (please notify first)
e-mail: david@drkoepsell.com
http://www.drkoepsell.com
counselor

Lou Marinoff
Philosophy Department
The City College of New York
137th Street at Convent Avenue
New York, NY 10031
tel: 212-650-7647
fax: 212-650-7409
e-mail: marinoff@mindspring.com
counselor, facilitator, consultant,
   APPA faculty

Bruce Matthews
531 West 26th Street, Loft 3R
New York, NY 10001
tel: 212-239-9223
e-mail: philobam@interport.net
counselor

Christopher Michaelson
PricewaterhouseCoopers, LLP
1177 Avenue of the Americas
New York, NY 10036
tel: 212-597-3844
fax: 212-596-8988
e-mail: christopher.michaelson@
   us.pwcglobal.com
consultant

Annselm Morpurgo
6 Union Street
Sag Harbor, NY 11963
tel: 516-725-1414
e-mail: morpurgo@msn.com
counselor

William Murnion
P.O. Box 23, Bellvale NY 10912
tel: 845-986-5406
e-mail: wmurnion@warwick.net
counselor

Elizabeth Randol
17 Mather Street, #2F
Binghamton, NY 13905
tel: 607-771-0475
e-mail: lizard2471@aol.com
consultant

Bernard Roy
396 Third Avenue, #3N
New York, NY 10016
tel: 212-686-3285
fax: 212-387-1728
e-mail:
   bernard_roy@baruch.cuny.edu
counselor, facilitator

Charles Sarnacki
199 Flat Rock Road
Lake George, NY 12845
tel: 518-668-5397
e-mail: csarnacki@hotmail.com
counselor

Mehul Shah
66 Dogwood Lane
Irvington, NY 10533
tel: 914-591-7488
e-mail: mshah1967@aol.com
counselor, facilitator, consultant

Wayne Shelton
P.O. Box 407
North Chatham, NY 12132
tel: 518-262-6423
fax: 518-262-6856
e-mail: sheltow@mail.amc.edu
counselor, consultant

Peter Simpson
College of Staten Island
2800 Victory Blvd. 2N
Staten Island, NY 10314
tel: 718-982-2902
fax: 718-982-2888
e-mail:
    simpson@postbox.csi.cuny.edu
Manhattan address:
425 W. 24th St. #3C
New York, NY 10011
tel: 212-633-9366
counselor

Nicholas Tornatore
585 Bay Ridge PKWY
Brooklyn, NY 11209
tel: 718-745-2911 or 212-535-
    3939
counselor

North Carolina
Andrew Koch
625 Lower Rush Branch Road
Sugar Grove, NC 28679
tel: 828-297-4548
e-mail: kocham@appstate.edu
consultant

Ohio
Lynn Levey
1959 Fulton Place
Cleveland, OH 44113
tel: 216-651-0009
e-mail: lynnlevey@aol.com
counselor

Svetlana Rura
Philosophy Department
College of Mount St. Joseph
Cincinnati, OH
tel: 513-533-3610
e-mail: svetlana_rura@mail.msj.edu
counselor

Pennsylvania
Eric Hoffman
131 Cynwyd Road
Bala Cynwyd, PA 19004
tel: 215-419-6542
e-mail: eeworkshop@comcast.net
counselor, facilitator, consultant

Craig Munns
Central Pennsylvania College
College Hill Rd.
Summerdale, PA 17025
tel: 717-728-2244
e-mail:
    craigmunns@centralpenn.edu
counselor

G. Steven Neeley
900 Powell Ave.
Cresson, PA 16630
tel: 814-472-3393
counselor

David Wolf
P.O. Box 162
Lake Como, PA 18437
tel: 570-798-2235
e-mail: socratix@epix.net
counselor

Tennessee
Ross Reed
3778 Friar Tuck Road
Memphis, TN 38111
tel: 901-458-8112
e-mail: doctorreed@yahoo.com
counselor

Texas
Amelie Benedikt
3109 Wheeler Street
Austin, TX 78705
tel: 512-695-7900
e-mail: afb@io.com
counselor

Amy McLaughlin
6811 Daugherty Street
Austin, TX 78757
tel: 512-467-8049
e-mail: episteme@swbell.net
counselor

Andrea Messineo
1418 Richmond Avenue
Houston, TX 77006
tel: 713-526-8810
e-mail: panzanella@pdq.net
counselor

Virginia
Bruce Thomas
8 Huntington Drive
Williamsburg, VA 23188
tel: 757-229-9835
e-mail: sthomas@widomaker.com
consultant

Washington
Sandra Dreisbach
6608 A Stanton Ct. SW
Tumwater, WA 98501
tel: 360-357-0842
e-mail: java@mac.com
counselor

Christine Gehrett
1970 Pinecrest Avenue
Coupeville, WA 98239
tel: 360-678-1454
e-mail: cgehrett@whidbey.net
counselor

Britni Weaver
1715 W. Pacific #C
Spokane, WA 99204
tel: 509-838-4886
e-mail: britnijw@yahoo.com
counselor

Other Countries

Canada
Stanley Chan
270 Old Post Road
Waterloo, Ontario
Canada N2L 5B9
tel: 519-884-5384
fax: 519-884-9120
e-mail: stanleyknchan@hotmail.com
counselor

Wanda Dawe
Dawe Counselling Services
163 LeMarchant Rd.
St. John's, NF
Canada A1C 2H5
tel: 709-754-5607
fax: 709-754-8629
e-mail: wanda.dawe@thezone.net
counselor, facilitator

Anthony Falikowski
Sheridan College
1430 Trafalgar Rd.
Oakville, Ontario
Canada L6L 1X7
tel: 905-845-9430 x2508
fax: 905-815-4032
e-mail:
    tony.falikowski@sheridanc.on.ca
consultant

David Jopling
Department of Philosophy
York University
4700 Keele Street
Toronto, Ontario
Canada M3J 1P3
tel: 416-736-2100 ext. 77588
fax: 416-736-5114
e-mail: jopling@yorku.ca
counselor, APPA faculty

Cheryl Nafziger-Leis
16 Meadowlark Road
Elmira, Ontario
Canada N3B 1T6
tel: 519-669-4991
fax: 519-669-5641
e-mail: Leis@sentex.net
consultant

Sean O'Connell
1806, 8920-100 St.
Edmonton, Alberta
Canada T6E 4YB
tel: 780-439-9752
e-mail: phipsibk@netscape.net
counselor

Michael Picard
Pyro Philosophy Shop
565 Fisgard Street, 3rd Floor
Victoria, B.C.
Canada V8W 1R5
tel: 250-385-4646
e-mail: pyro@philosophy-shop.com
www.philosophy-shop.com
counselor

Peter Raabe
46-2560 Whitely Court
North Vancouver, B.C.
Canada V7J 2R5
tel: 604-986-9446
e-mail: raabe@interchange.ubc.ca
counselor

Hugh Williams
P.O. Box 547, 359 Debec Road
Debec, N.B.
Canada E7N 3B2
tel: 506-328-8472
Fax: 506-325-9159
e-mail: hwilliam@nbnet.nb.ca
counselor

France
Anette Prins
Nombre d'Or
Route de Valensole
04800 Gréoux les Bains
France
tel: 33-04-9274-2344 or 33-06-
   8152-1579
e-mail: anette.prins@libertysurf.fr
counselor, APPA faculty

Israel
Lydia Amir
The New School of Media Studies
The College of Management
9 Shoshana Persitz St.
Tel-Aviv, 61480 Israel
tel: 972-3-744-1086
fax: 972-3-699-0458
e-mail: lydamir55@hotmail.com
counselor, APPA faculty

Ora Gruengard
43 Yehuda Hanasi Street
Tel-Aviv, 69391 Israel
tel: 972-3-641-4776
fax: 972-3-642-2439
e-mail: egone@mail.shenkar.ac.il
counselor, APPA faculty

Eli Holzer
33 Halamed Heh Street
Jerusalem, 93661 Israel
tel: 972-02-567-2033
e-mail: esholzer@netvision.net.il
counselor

Italy
Paola Grassi
via Paolo Uccello, 16
Milano, Italy 20148
tel: 39-02-3651-1112
e-mail: e-mail@paola-grassi.it
counselor

Netherlands
Dries Boele
Spaarndammerplantsoen 108
1013 XT Amsterdam
tel: 31-20-686-7330
counselor, facilitator, APPA faculty

Will Heutz
Schelsberg 308
6413 AJ Heerlen
tel: 31-45-572-0323
counselor, consultant, APPA
  faculty

Ida Jongsma
Hotel de Filosoof (Philosopher's
  Hotel)
Anna Vondelstraat 6
1054 GZ Amsterdam
tel: 31-20-683-3013
fax: 31-20-685-3750
e-mail: ijongsma@hotelfilosoof.nl
counselor, facilitator, consultant,
  APPA faculty

Norway
Anders Lindseth
University of Tromso
N-9037 Tromso, Norway
e-mail: andersl@fagmed.uit.no
counselor, APPA faculty

Portugal
Manuel Joao Antunes
Rua Conde de Redondo 59-2° B
Lisbon 1150-102, Portugal
tel: 351-919-115756
e-mail: joao.antunes@netcabo.pt
counselor

Maria Oliveira
Rua Conde de Redondo 59-2° B
Lisbon 1150-102, Portugal
tel: 351-917-090821
e-mail: escreve-me@netcabo.pt
counselor

Turkey
Harun Sungurlu
P.K. 2 Emirgan
Istanbul, Turkey 80850
e-mail:
  sungurludh@superonline.com
counselor

United Kingdom
Alex Howard
8 Winchester Terrace
Newcastle upon Tyne
United Kingdom, NE4 6EH
tel: 44-91-232-5530
e-mail: consult@alexhoward.
  demon.co.uk
counselor

Judy Wall
The CPD Centre
51A Cecil Road
Lancing, West Sussex
United Kingdom, BN15 8HP
tel: 011-44-0193-764301
fax: 011-44-0193-765970
e-mail: lifeplan@cwcom.net
consultant

Appendix 4
FURTHER READING

Achenbach, Gerd, *Philosophische Praxis*, Köln, Germany: Jürgen Dinter, 1984.

Borman, William, *Gandhi and Non-Violence*, Albany: State University of New York, 1986.

Bucke, Richard Maurice, *Cosmic Consciousness*, New York: The Citadel Press, 1970.

Causton, Richard, *The Buddha in Daily Life: An Introduction to the Buddhism of Nichiren Daishonin*, London: Rider, 1995.

Cohen, Elliot, *Philosophers at Work*, New York: Holt, Rinehart and Winston, 1989.

Cooper, Rabbi David A. *God Is a Verb: Kabbalah and the Practice of Mystical Judaism*, New York: Riverhead Books, 1997.

De Waelens, Alphonse, and Wilfried Ver Eecke, *Phenomenology and Lacan on Schizophrenia: After the Decade of the Brain*, Leuven: Leuven University Press, 2001.

Deurzen, Emmy van, *Paradox and Passion in Psychotherapy*, New York: John Wiley and Sons, 1998.

Ehrenwald, Jan, ed, *The History of Psychotherapy*, Northvale, NJ: Jason Aronson Inc., 1997.

Erwin, Edward, *Philosophy and Psychotherapy*, London: Sage Publications, 1997.

Grimes, Pierre, *Philosophical Midwifery*, Costa Mesa: Hyparxis Press, 1998.

Hadot, Pierre, *Philosophy As a Way of Life*, London: Blackwell, 1995.

Held, Barbara, *Back to Reality: A Critique of Postmodern Theory in Psychotherapy*, New York: W.W. Norton & Co., 1995.

Herrestad, Henning, Anders Holt, and Helge Svare, eds. *Philosophy in Society*, Oslo: Unipub Forlag, 2002.

Howard, Alex, *Philosophy for Counseling and Psychotherapy*, London: Macmillan Press Ltd., 2000.

Kapleau, Philip, *The Three Pillars of Zen*, New York: Doubleday, 1969.

Kennedy, Robert, *Zen Spirit, Christian Spirit*, New York: The Continuum Publishing Company, 1997.

Kessels, Jos, *Socrates op de Markt, Filosofie in Bedrijf*, Amsterdam: Boom, 1997.

Lahav, Ran, and Maria Tillmanns, eds. *Essays on Philosophical Counseling*, Lanham: University Press of America, Inc., 1995.

LeBon, Tim, *Wise Therapy*, London: Continuum, 2001.

Marinoff, Lou, *Plato, Not Prozac!: Applying Philosophy to Everyday Problems*, New York: HarperCollins, 1999.

Mattila, Antti, *Seeing Things in a New Light: Reframing in Therapeutic Conversation*, Helsinki: Helsinki University Press, 2001.

McCullough, Chris, *Nobody's Victim: Freedom from Therapy and Recovery*, New York: Clarkson Potter, 1995.

Morris, Tom, *If Aristotle Ran General Motors*, New York: Henry Holt & Co., 1997.

Nahser, F. Byron, *Learning to Read the Signs: Reclaiming Pragmatism in Business*, Woburn: Butterworth-Heinemann, 1997.

Nelson, Leonard, *Socratic Method and Critical Philosophy*, Translated by Thomas Brown III. New York: Dover Publications, 1965.

Nicolas, Antonio de, *The Biology of Religion: The Neural Connection between Science and Mysticism*, Tokyo Honganji: International Buddhist Study Center, 1990.

Russell, Bertrand, *The Conquest of Happiness*, New York: Garden City Publishing Co., 1930.

Schramme, Thomas, and Johannes Thome, eds. *Philosophy and Psychiatry*, Berlin: De Gruyter, 2003.

Sharkey, Paul, ed. *Philosophy, Religion and Psychotherapy: Essays in the Philosophical Foundations of Psychotherapy*, Washington: University Press of America, 1982.

Spinelli, Ernesto, *The Interpreted World*, London: Sage Publications, 1989.

Szasz, Thomas, *The Myth of Mental Illness*, New York: Harper & Row, 1961.

Woolfolk, Robert, *The Cure of Souls: Science, Values and Psychotherapy*, San Francisco: Jossey-Bass Publishers, 1998.

A NOTE ON THE AUTHOR

Lou Marinoff is the author of the international hit *Plato, Not Prozac!*, published in twenty languages and sold in seventy-five countries. A professor of philosophy at the City College of New York, Marinoff is also the founding president of the American Philosophical Practitioners Association.

A NOTE ON THE TYPE

The text of this book is set in Linotype Sabon, named after the type founder, Jacques Sabon. It was designed by Jan Tschichold and jointly developed by Linotype, Monotype and Stempel, in response to a need for a typeface to be available in identical form for mechanical hot metal composition and hand composition using foundry type. Tschichold based his design for Sabon roman on a fount engraved by Garamond, and Sabon italic on a fount by Granjon. It was first used in 1966 and has proved an enduring modern classic.